PENGUIN REFERENCE

The Penguin Dictionary of Islam

Professor Azim Nanji was born in Nairobi, Kenya, and was educated at Makerere University in Uganda and McGill University, Canada. He has taught and lectured widely and was Professor and Chair of the Department of Religion at the University of Florida from 1988 to 1998. Since then he has been the Director of the Institute of Ismaili Studies in London. He has authored, co-authored and edited several works including *The Historical Atlas of Islam* (with Malise Ruthven) (2004), *The Muslim Almanac* (1996) and *Mapping Islamic Studies* (1997). In 2008 he will take up an appointment in the Abbasi Program in Islamic Studies at Stanford University.

Razia Nanji was born in Kampala, Uganda and educated at Makere, McGill and the University of Western Ontario. A librarian, she has served as a specialist in Reference and Public Services at the University of Florida.

The Penguin Dictionary of
ISLAM

Azim Nanji
with Razia Nanji

For our parents

PENGUIN BOOKS

Published by the Penguin Group
Penguin Books Ltd, 80 Strand, London WC2R 0RL, England
Penguin Group (USA) Inc., 375 Hudson Street, New York, New York 10014, USA
Penguin Group (Canada), 90 Eglinton Avenue East, Suite 700, Toronto, Ontario, Canada M4P 2Y3
(a division of Pearson Penguin Canada Inc.)
Penguin Ireland, 25 St Stephen's Green, Dublin 2, Ireland (a division of Penguin Books Ltd)
Penguin Group (Australia), 250 Camberwell Road, Camberwell, Victoria 3124, Australia
(a division of Pearson Australia Group Pty Ltd)
Penguin Books India Pvt Ltd, 11 Community Centre, Panchsheel Park, New Delhi – 110 017, India
Penguin Group (NZ), 67 Apollo Drive, Rosedale, North Shore 0632, New Zealand
(a division of Pearson New Zealand Ltd)
Penguin Books (South Africa) (Pty) Ltd, 24 Sturdee Avenue, Rosebank, Johannesburg 2196, South Africa

Penguin Books Ltd, Registered Offices: 80 Strand, London WC2R 0RL, England

www.penguin.com

First published 2008
005

Copyright © Azim Nanji, 2008
All rights reserved

The moral right of the author has been asserted

Set in ITC Stone Sans and ITC Stone Serif
Typeset by Data Standards Ltd, Frome, Somerset
Printed and bound in Great Britain by Clays Ltd, Elcograf S.p.A.

ISBN 978-0-141-01399-2

www.greenpenguin.co.uk

MIX
Paper | Supporting
responsible forestry
FSC
www.fsc.org   **FSC® C018179**

Penguin Books is committed to a sustainable
future for our business, our readers and our planet.
This book is made from Forest Stewardship
Council™ certified paper.

Contents

Introduction

The village of Likoni, where I grew up, sits by the sea looking out at the Indian Ocean channel that forms the entrance to the modern Kenyan port of Mombasa, on the eastern coast of Africa.

Like hundreds of such settlements dotted along trade routes that crossed oceans and lands, Likoni was both rooted in the culture of the soil where it grew and at the same time open to influences and peoples that plied their trade along the coast. The people of the Swahili coast, of which Likoni and Mombasa are a part, came into contact with Muslims from the Arabian coast as early as the eighth century. Architectural remains of places of prayer and of small settlements reveal this early contact and its growing influence upon the indigenous people of the region. When Ibn Battuta, the famous fourteenth-century traveller, arrived in the region he found small but thriving Muslim communities that had emerged following contact with peoples of African, Arab and Asian origin.

It is this cosmopolitanism that defined my experience of growing up as a Muslim. We spoke Swahili, the common language that linked the population, as well as our own respective mother tongues, and were becoming increasingly acquainted through English with the heritage of the West and its modern forms of knowledge and education. Mosques, *jamat khanas*, temples, churches as well as traditional African places of gathering shared this cosmopolitan space.

It is, of course, easy to idealize childhood, but this strong memory of a triple heritage, and the relationships and friendships it offered, remain for me the central elements of a Muslim upbringing: acceptance of diversity, tolerance for pluralism and a strong respect for the autonomy of each religious community but with enough permeability to enable us to find commonalities within this shared space.

These memories jostle now with a retrospective sense of differences between religious groups and lurking racial divides, but rather than retreat into separatism and unthinking parochialism, our Muslim education fostered mutual acceptance and openness. The daily assembly held in our schools included readings from the scriptures of many faiths, and in the classroom Muslims sat alongside Hindus, Sikhs, Zoroastrians and Christians.

In historical terms, this was not an exceptional experience. Muslims in the past often lived and interacted in cosmopolitan worlds, whether in Andalusia, Central Asia, India or the Mediterranean. It is often forgotten that the heritage of classical antiquity, of Aristotle, Galen, Plato and Socrates, is also the heritage of Muslims, who translated, interpreted and further developed their writings, which in their Latin form became the inheritance of pre-Renaissance Europe. During the Convivencia of Andalusia, which began in the eighth century, Muslims, Jews and Christians lived in peaceful coexistence for almost 800 years before wars and the Spanish Inquisition put an end to such cultural tolerance and understanding for centuries.

The academic career I have chosen has led me to explore how major religious and cultural traditions travel across time and space. Over the centuries the followers of many religions have engaged in conflict, seeking often to dominate if not to erase others. However, in its finer moments, religion has transcended difference and forged creativity through art, architecture, literature and philosophy – a shared language that enhances the greater human landscape. In our time, it can be argued that to rekindle such a spirit has become a matter of urgent necessity. Muslims, and those among whom they live, find themselves awkwardly placed within a world that perceives Muslims and others to be caught up in a 'clash of civilizations', and so has formed a generalized and homogenized theological image of both the religion and the diverse histories of those who practise it. Militant groups, often led by equally militant leaders, have gained prominence and visibility beyond that warranted by their numbers or influence. In many cases they are simply bent on conflict and deluded by 'nostalgia' for a non-existent past. The threats and alienations they perceive may be partially rooted in the conditions of our time, as well as the accelerated pace of change and globalization, but by promoting violence and wilful self-destruction they have alienated most of the world, including the majority of their fellow Muslims who are increasingly distancing themselves from this minority. In part this stems from the realization that, historically, Muslim society thrives when it is committed and open to knowledge and able to maintain a balance between different communities of interpretation and struggles when it becomes narrow and rigid, such as when one particularly assertive faction has sought to impose its views and practices to the exclusion of all others.

Most Muslims live in what is called the developing world, many in some of its poorest countries. The inheritance of the nation-state, following a long and turbulent period of European rule and the subsequent Cold War, seriously disrupted the development of many of these societies and dramatically affected their quality of life. The search for state boundaries, workable forms of governance and sustainable economic development presents major challenges, particularly when the colonial legacy includes bitter territorial divisions and recriminations, as in the Middle East, Kashmir and parts of the former Soviet Union and former Yugoslavia. Poverty, war and lack of security have also led to the displacement of populations. Refugees as well as migrants have sought to leave their ancestral homelands for new homes in the West. Their unfamiliarity with societies informed by secular traditions has often compounded the difficulties of adaptation and integration into new and starkly different cultural and social environments. Such issues cannot be viewed simply through a theological lens that erroneously focuses on some congenital deficiency among Muslims which prevents them from taking their place in the modern world.

History contains many examples of Muslims both building and contributing to societies, with and among others. The crises affecting parts of the Muslim world today have specific origins and facets which will have to be addressed individually rather than exacerbating old tensions through clumsy and ill-conceived interventions. The removal of ignorance about each other's histories is a necessary first step and can act as a cultural bridge to remind us of achievements as well as mistakes.

This historical dictionary thus sets out to provide through its entries a perspective on the historical, intellectual, spiritual and institutional pluralism that has developed among Muslims over fourteen centuries while examining regional and national developments. It also illustrates the evolution of Muslim thought and societies in local as well as contemporary global contexts to reveal the diversity that exists among individual Muslims, their traditions and various historical periods. It includes theology, law, philosophy and science, the arts and literature, education and learning, and architecture and the environment. It also seeks to touch upon the dramatic changes that have affected and continue to be reflected in all aspects of Muslim life and society.

In summary, being 'Muslim' has, in historical terms, reflected a broad engagement with the material as well as the spiritual dimensions of life, and a commitment to achieving a balance between dimensions of belief and faith and the contexts and conditions of daily life. This ongoing process evolved differently as historical and geographical conditions changed and Muslim communities arose in different regions of the world. This accounts for both the diversity one finds within the faith and also the plurality of thought and institutions that has developed over time.

The legacy and presence of Muslims is today everywhere. As questions continue to arise about the relevance and significance of this historical heritage and the intensification of theological forces that are often the cause of conflict, it may be worth reminding ourselves that, while the Quran addresses personal as well as collective goals, it does not reduce the idea of a faith community simply to prescriptions and attributes. Rather, in connecting human values and social integration, it points to a larger, more cosmopolitan ethic:

> The good does not lie in turning your faces to the East or the West. It consists in belief in God, the Final Day, Angels, Books, and the Prophets. It is to give out of love for Him, from your cherished possessions, to your family, to orphans and those in need, and the refugee, those who ask for help and for those living in slavery. It is those who pray and are giving, honour their word and are steadfast and patient in the midst of adversity, hardship and peril. They are the people of moral excellence. (Quran 2:177)

Azim Nanji
October 2007

Guide to the Dictionary and Acknowledgements

A dictionary of this kind is essentially a work of synthesis, accessible to the general reader but resting on scholarship that draws on primary as well as secondary sources. Our debt to this long standing and still developing tradition is reflected partially in the Bibliography, which identifies and recommends those works available in the English language.

The Penguin Dictionary of Islam reflects the generally accepted forms of transliteration of the terms but without diacriticals. Cross references are used to guide readers where there are English terms and equivalents from the Muslim traditions. A chronology enables the reader to see selected major events and turning points in Muslim history.

The synthesis is also the outcome of many years of teaching and lecturing in different parts of the world and my first debt of gratitude is to the different audiences, primarily enthusiastic but patient university students, for whom Islam had to be often summarized and synthesized in weeks if not days and hours. Then there are academic colleagues, teachers and friends from across the world who, in our interaction, have offered their insights and helped to sharpen my own understanding, awareness and expressions. Over the last ten years the Institute of Ismaili Studies has been my academic home and I am very grateful to all those who during that time made it a richly rewarding and stimulating environment for scholarship and learning.

Some individuals gave specific help during the preparation of this work: Susan Lewis and Fayaz Alibhai in Florida; Helga Haack, Alnoor Merchant, Khadija Lalani and Dinah Manisty of the Institute's Library and Gurdofarid Miskinzoda, who provided very helpful research assistance and also assisted with the Bibliography. Many thanks to the various editors at Penguin who took a major interest in this work, starting with Nigel Wilcockson during its early stages, to Kristen Harrison, who has helped to bring it through its final stages, and to Trevor Horwood for his careful copy-editing.

I am particularly grateful to the Aga Khan Trust for Culture for permission to reproduce artefacts and images from their very significant and rich collection, many of which will be part of the new Aga Khan Museum in Toronto.

We have dedicated this work to our parents. While their experiences had exposed them to only a part of the global Muslim heritage, they inspired a passion and respect for what they could not know, and taught us how we might grow in knowledge and awareness and more significantly to respect the heritage of all those amongst whom we lived and those who had lived before us. We hope the *Dictionary* captures that spirit.

Azim Nanji
Razia Nanji
January 2008

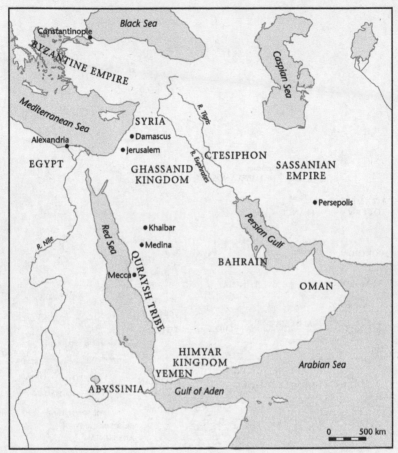

The Near East on the Eve of Islam

The Muslim World under Colonial Rule after World War I

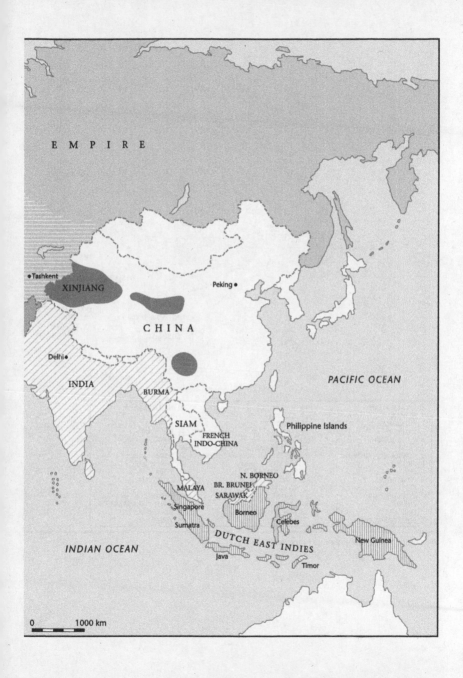

E M P I R E

• Tashkent

XINJIANG

Peking •

C H I N A

Delhi •

INDIA

BURMA

SIAM

FRENCH
INDO-CHINA

PACIFIC OCEAN

Philippine Islands

N. BORNEO
BR. BRUNEI
SARAWAK

MALAYA

Singapore

Borneo

Celebes

Sumatra

DUTCH EAST INDIES

New Guinea

INDIAN OCEAN

Java

Timor

0   1000 km

1 AFGHANISTAN	16 ERITREA	30 NETHERLANDS
2 ALBANIA	17 GAMBIA	31 NIGER
3 AZERBAIJAN	18 GEORGIA	32 NIGERIA
4 BAHRAIN	19 GHANA	33 PAKISTAN
5 BANGLADESH	20 GUINEA	34 QATAR
6 BENIN	21 GUINEA BISSAU	35 SENEGAL
7 BOSNIA-HERZEGOVINA	22 ISRAEL (Including GAZA STRIP	36 SIERRA LEONE
8 BRUNEI	and WEST BANK)	37 SINGAPORE
9 BURKINA-FASO	23 JORDAN	38 SYRIA
10 CAMEROON	24 KUWAIT	39 TAJIKSTAN
11 CENTRAL AFRICAN REPUBLIC	25 KYRGYSTAN	40 TOGO
12 COTE D'IVOIRE	26 LEBANON	41 TURKMENISTAN
13 CYPRUS	27 LIBERIA	42 UNITED ARAB EMIRATES
14 DJIBOUTI	28 MACEDONIA	43 UZBEKISTAN
15 EQUATORIAL GUINEA	29 MALAWI	44 YUGOSLAVA

Significant Muslim Communities in the World Today

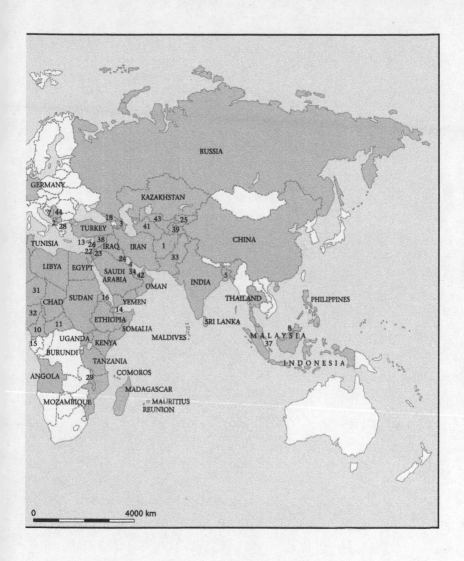

RUSSIA

GERMANY

KAZAKHSTAN

7 44
2 18 43 25
28 TURKEY 3 41 39
TUNISIA 13 38 CHINA
26 IRAQ IRAN 1
22 23 24 33
LIBYA EGYPT 4
SAUDI 34 42
ARABIA OMAN INDIA 5
31 YEMEN THAILAND PHILIPPINES
CHAD SUDAN 16 14
32 ETHIOPIA SRI LANKA
10 11 SOMALIA 8
15 UGANDA KENYA MALDIVES MALAYSIA
BURUNDI 37
TANZANIA INDONESIA
ANGOLA 29 COMOROS
MOZAMBIQUE MADAGASCAR
MAURITIUS
REUNION

0   4000 km

Abbasids Muslim dynasty whose period of rule, in varying degrees of dominance, lasted from 750 to 1258. They came to power claiming descent through an uncle of the Prophet Muhammad, al-Abbas. After claiming that the then ruling dynasty, the UMAYYADS, had become unjust and decadent, the leaders of the movement seized power through a series of battles in Persia and Syria, promising a return to justice and legitimate rule. One of the caliphs, al-Mansur (754–775), built the city of Baghdad, which became the capital of the dynasty. The reign of HARUN AL-RASHID (789–809) is generally regarded as ushering in a period of significant cultural development marked by a flowering in the arts, literature, architecture and science. Over time the dynasty dissolved into a number of petty principalities, as other more powerful dynasties came to be established in Egypt and Spain. In 1258 the MONGOL invasion led to the sacking of Baghdad. One of the relatives of the last Abbasid caliph of Baghdad was installed by the then MAMLUK Sultan al-Zahir Baybars (reigned 1260–1277) as caliph in Egypt with the title of al-Mustansir in 1261. However, the caliph and his successors had little influence in the affairs of the state and remained powerless, ceremonial houses. The decline in power and fortune led to the eventual disestablishment of the dynasty.

Abd Allah ibn Abd al-Qadir (1796–1854) Noted Malay scholar and writer. He is regarded as a pioneer of Malay literature dealing with Muslim themes. His most famous work, *Hayat Abdullah* (his memoirs), is useful for the historical references and his personal opinion on historical developments. His fame also rests on his work on Malay prose, which ultimately catapulted Malay into the official language of the peninsula.

Abd Allah ibn Abd al-Muttalib (545–570) Father of the Prophet Muhammad. He died shortly before his son's birth. The very few details that we have on Abd Allah are connected with his aborted sacrifice by his father (the grandfather of Muhammad). Literature on the biography of the Prophet includes what little is known about his father and his marriage to AMINA BINT WAHB (the mother of Muhammad).

Abd Allah al-Mahdi (873–934) First of the FATIMID imams and caliphs, who laid the foundations of a new state in North Africa in 909, and founded as his capital the city of Mahdiya in present-day Tunisia.

Abd al-Aziz ibn Saud (1880–1953) Founder and first ruler of the modern kingdom of SAUDI ARABIA. After capturing Riyadh in 1902, he was able through a series of alliances and battles to establish Saudi rule in the region of Najd. Subsequently his supporters, inspired by the teachings of Muhammad ABD AL-WAHHAB, were able to expel the OTTOMANS and conquer the HIJAZ. A unified kingdom, with Abd al-Aziz as king, was established in 1932. With the discovery of oil in 1937–8 and the granting of oil concessions, the new kingdom became an important factor in international affairs as its economy flourished and influence spread. Members of the family continue to play a key role as the ruling elite of the Kingdom.

Abd al-Majid I See TANZIMAT.

Abd al-Majid II (1868–1944) Known as Abdülmecit II in Turkish. Last of the line of OTTOMAN caliphs. He was elected by the Great National Assembly as caliph on 1 November 1922. The same Assembly deprived him of the title by abolishing the Caliphate on 3 March 1924. He died in exile in Paris.

Abd Manaf See ABU TALIB.

Abd al-Qadir al-Jilani (1077–1166) Muslim scholar and preacher. He is credited with founding the Sufi QADIRIYYA order. After his death, Abd al-Qadir's followers ascribed miracles to him and began the practice of tracing his spiritual genealogy back to the Prophet. His most famous work is the *Revelations of the Unseen* (*Futuh al-ghayb*) and his mausoleum in Baghdad is a major devotional centre and site of visitation.

Abd al-Rahman III (891–961) The most famous of the UMAYYAD rulers of Spain (*see* AL-ANDALUS), Abd al-Rahman III established his rule in CÓRDOBA and declared himself to be a caliph in 912. His reign, spanning more than fifty years, is generally regarded as a time of political and cultural attainment and among the most successful periods of Umayyad rule in the country. By the time he died he had managed to extend and consolidate his authority in Andalusia and to create a wealthy and powerful state with considerable prestige. As a result of his efforts Córdoba became an important metropolis rivalling the great cities of the time.

Abd al-Wahhab, Muhammad ibn (1703–1792) Muslim reformer and founder of WAHHABISM. He was born in Najd to a family of religious scholars. Following a preparation consisting of traditional education in Quranic and legal sciences according to the Hanbali School of Sunnism (*see* SCHOOLS OF ISLAMIC LAW), he travelled to Medina where he was introduced to a stricter interpretation of the Hanbali doctrine and the teachings of IBN TAYMIYYA (d. 1328). Influenced by this teaching and some of the scholars of Medina, Abd al-Wahhab began preaching against many Sufi and Shia practices and doctrines. The conversion of a tribal chief to his views and his marriage to one of the chief's daughters allowed him to create an alliance through which his teachings were spread more widely. Political support of Muhammad ibn Saud (d. 1765) enabled Abd al-Wahhab to promote and even enforce his views more widely across the Arabian peninsula, and a significant number of followers had been drawn to the cause by the time of his death. His work *Kitab al-Tawhid* outlines his main teaching and argues for a more literal reading of Quranic verses and prophetic traditions to the exclusion of other historical exegesis and schools of interpretation. It also calls for the forcible elimination of practices not in conformity with this understanding of Islam.

Abdülmecit I *See* TANZIMAT.

Abdülmecit II *See* ABD AL-MAJID II.

Abdur Rauf al-Singkili or **Teungku Kuala** (c. 1615–1693) He is regarded as the first scholar of the Malay/Indonesian archipelago to provide a major commentary of the Quran in Malay. He was a member of a Sufi order and was a leading Muslim scholar in the court of ACEH.

Abim A Muslim youth movement. Founded in Malaysia in the early 1970s, its programme of youth involvement focused on reinforcing Muslim identity to mobilize efforts in various fields such as education, culture, science and economic life for men and women. Among its most active members and leaders have been prominent political figures, such as Anwar IBRAHIM, whose leadership enabled this movement to remain a strong force in the political life of modern Malaysia.

Abkhaz A people living in western Caucasia on the Black Sea. They came under Muslim influence during the time of the OTTOMAN EMPIRE. A small population of Muslims has survived in the region under successive Russian and then Soviet regimes until the present time. It is currently regarded as a part of Georgia, a former republic within the Soviet Union.

abortion The Quran expressly forbade the pre-Islamic practice of burying unwanted female children alive. In general, most Muslims, in accordance with the Quranic principle that human life is sacred, consider abortion as unethical, except where a mother's life or the family's welfare may be endangered. Moreover, even though scholars have differed over the nature of the fetus, they agree that God has endowed it with the right to both life and inheritance. There continues to be discussion and debate over the question of therapeutic abortion, which is accepted by most Muslim scholars and supported by the policies of most Muslim states.

Abraha Sixth-century Christian king from southern Arabia. According to Muslim tradition he led an abortive expedition against MECCA in the 'Year of the Elephant' (c. 570), so called because of the use of elephants in the invasion. He is said to have built a magnificent church in Sana, Yemen.

Abraham Called Ibrahim in the Quran, he is considered in Islam to be a major prophet. He preached belief in One God and combated the idolatry of his father and the people. He founded a sanctuary for the worship of God at the site of the KA'BA. Abraham's commitment to sacrifice his son is commemorated by Muslims at the end of the period of the HAJJ, the annual pilgrimage, with the celebration of ID AL-ADHA.

Abu Bakr (c. 570–634) First of the four RIGHTLY GUIDED CALIPHS. According to Sunni Muslim tradition, he assumed stewardship of the Muslim community after the death of the Prophet Muhammad. One of the early converts to the teachings of the

Prophet, Abu Bakr is regarded as a very close companion of the Prophet, accompanying him on the HIJRA to Medina in 622 and leading the pilgrimage in 631. When the Prophet became ill, Abu Bakr led the congregational prayers on his behalf. His daughter, Aisha, was married to the Prophet. Abu Bakr died only two years after becoming caliph. Because of his loyalty to the Prophet and his devotion to Islam, he is known as 'the sincere and trusted one' (al-Siddiq).

Abu Bishr Amr ibn Uthman See SIBAWAYHI.

Abu Dharr al-Ghaffari (d. 652) Companion of the Prophet and early convert. Most commonly known by the name of Jundub ibn Junada. He is believed to have been among the first converts to Islam. He is highly regarded for his piety and his asceticism and as a transmitter of traditions from the Prophet. Traditions on his authority are included in the Sunni collections of MUSLIM and AL-BUKHARI.

Abu al-Faraj al-Isfahani (897–967) Author and historian who is acknowledged for his famous collection the *Kitab al-Aghani* (*Books of Songs*), a history of poets and their lives which was subsequently put to music. The work is widely regarded as having had a significant influence on the further development of Arabic literature and culture.

Abu Hanifa al-Numan (699–767) Founder of the Sunni Hanafi SCHOOL OF ISLAMIC LAW. He studied in Medina with JAFAR AL-SADIQ, a Shia imam, and is credited with developing the use of *qiyas* (analogical reasoning) in legal writings. His teachings constituted the basis of what would eventually become the Hanafi tradition of legal thought. He also played an important role as theologian and teacher.

Abu Hurayra (d. 678) A Yemeni who, after accepting Islam, became a companion and devoted follower of the Prophet. He is remembered largely as a major transmitter of traditions from the Prophet and his name occurs repeatedly in the chain of such transmissions, recounting from direct experience the actions and sayings of the Prophet.

Abu Muslim (d. 754) Military leader who spearheaded the ABBASID revolution against the UMAYYAD dynasty. He organized an army under a black flag to symbolize the restoration of legitimate rule by the Prophet's descendants. Though rewarded for his efforts by being made governor of a province, he came to be perceived as a threat to the new rulers. One of the subsequent Abbasid rulers executed him for alleged treasonable activities.

Abu Nuwas (c. 747–813) Arab poet who achieved fame during the reign of the Abbasid caliph HARUN AL-RASHID. He composed much of his poetry in Baghdad. Both his contemporaries and later poets saw him as setting a new trend in the development of Arabic poetic tradition.

Abu Said ibn Abi Khayr (967–1049) Sufi preacher. Abu Said was particularly noted for his commitment to an ascetic lifestyle and service to the poor. He was a very popular preacher and is believed to have participated with his audience in the practice of SAMA, devotional ritual involving the performance of music.

Abu Sufyan (d. c. 653) A prominent leader and merchant in Mecca who belonged to the clan of QURAYSH. Abu Sufyan opposed the Prophet Muhammad and also commanded the army that fought the Muslims during the battle of Uhud in 625. He subsequently negotiated peace and became a Muslim. His daughter was later married to the Prophet. His son MUAWIYYA is prominent in Muslim history as the first UMAYYAD caliph.

Abu Talib (d. 619) Uncle and guardian of the Prophet Muhammad and father of Ali, the first Shia imam. He is also called Abd Manaf and is said to have held the office of provider of food and water for pilgrims to MECCA. He was protective of Muhammad at a time when the rest of the Meccans were intent on persecuting him and his death constituted a great loss of support for the Prophet.

Abu Yazid al-Bistami (d. 874) Also known as Bayazid al-Bistami, he is among the major Sufi figures of the ninth century. His preserved statements about the nature of religious experience represent a celebrated genre of ecstatic sayings in Muslim mystical literature. His teachings were preserved by oral transmission.

Abu Yusuf al-Kufi (d. 807) Early Muslim jurist. Abu Yusuf was born in Baghdad. He became a pupil of ABU HANIFA AL-NUMAN and played an important role in the establishment of the Hanafi School of Sunni law. He worked closely with the Abbasid ruler HARUN AL-RASHID to develop solutions to legal and administrative issues facing the growing Muslim state and society.

Abubacer *See* IBN TUFAYL.

Abul Wafa al-Buzajani (940–998) Major figure in the development of mathematics and astronomy. Abul Wafa al-Buzajani lived in Baghdad. His work on trigonometry and his geometrical constructions have been preserved as part of his contribution to the field of medieval mathematical sciences.

Abunaser *See* AL-FARABI, ABU NASR.

Abyssinia *See* ETHIOPIA.

Aceh Northern part of Sumatra, one of the islands of the Indonesian archipelago, Aceh was one of the first areas in Indonesia to accept Islam and became the seat of a flourishing sultanate.

Islam spread to the region as early as the thirteenth century and a series of Muslim rulers developed a prosperous state until the beginning of the twentieth century. It is noteworthy that four princesses ruled over Aceh in the seventeenth century. By 1910 the Dutch, after a lengthy conflict known as the Aceh War, had defeated the kingdom and established colonial rule. In 1942 Aceh was occupied by the Japanese. A series of rebellions to counter the brutal occupation took place until the Japanese surrender in 1945. Internal rivalries caused a major conflict over authority and with the formation of the Republic of Indonesia in 1949 Aceh was integrated into the new state. While Aceh has remained part of Indonesia since, there has been constant opposition to central authority and a continuing effort to maintain its inherited Muslim traditional identity and institutions. This has from time to time resulted in contention over the acceptability of such traditionalist, SHARIA-based practices in the context of Indonesia's broadly defined and pluralistic social and legal framework.

adab An Arabic term employed in Muslim thought and literature that has many connotations associated with intellectual, literary, moral and ethical discourse and the value of norms of human conduct. In its practical aspect, it can refer to appropriate qualities necessary for proper personal behaviour, upbringing and mode of conduct in daily life and social interaction. It also stands for the cultivation of knowledge and literary learning that signifies humanistic values of individual achievement. In its literary aspect, *adab* signifies the material and spiritual culture generated in writing and other artistic accomplishments. *See also* ETHICS.

Adam Name of the first created human who, according to the Quran, symbolizes the unity of humanity and the ideal of stewardship on earth (Quran 39:6). In the Quranic narrative of creation, after being taught knowledge by God, Adam and his mate are settled in the garden to live in conformity to divine will. After disobeying the command not to approach the Tree of Knowledge (*ilm*, also known as the Tree of Eternity, *khuld*, or often simply 'the tree') they are relegated to life on earth, promised guidance and eventually redeem themselves and are forgiven. Adam is also chosen by God to be a messenger. The Quranic account became, in due course, the basis of an enlarged Muslim tradition about Adam, drawn from a variety of biblical and folk sources, but it remains an important reference point for the ultimate goals of human life and its destiny.

adat Particularly in its Indonesian, Malaysian and South Asian contexts, this concept refers to the practices and customs of the region. Such custom and local tradition often complemented the SHARIA as a source of practice, establishing mutually enabling frames of reference for personal, social and community law. In modern times, as in the past, there have been areas of contention, but on the whole *adat* remains a powerful resource for local identity and regional practice and tradition in Muslim societies living in these regions.

adhan The Muslim call to the daily ritual prayer, which has been traditionally recited by a MUEZZIN. It is in Arabic and consists of the following elements in recitation:

> God is most great (*Allahu Akbar*; recited four times).
> I affirm/witness that there is no divinity other than Allah (recited twice).
> I affirm/witness that Muhammad is the messenger of God (recited twice).
> Come to prayer (recited twice).
> Come to salvation. (The Shia and the Zaydis add, 'Come to the best of deeds.') (Recited twice.)
> God is most great (recited twice).
> There is no divinity other than Allah.

Adil-Shahi The Muslim dynasty that ruled the kingdom of Bijapur in India from 1489 to 1686, when it was integrated into the MOGHUL empire. One of the rulers,

Yusuf Adil Shah, introduced the SHIA tradition to the kingdom. Bijapur is well known for its historic monuments. SIKANDAR SHAH, the last ruler of the dynasty, died in 1700 in captivity.

adl The Arabic term in the Quran that connotes the idea of justice. For the MUTAZILA and the SHIA, the idea of the justice of God represented one of the basic concepts in the divine dispensation for the values of humankind and underlined accountability and choice as aspects of human agency.

al-Afghani, Jamal al-Din *See* JAMAL AL-DIN AL-AFGHANI.

Afghanistan A Muslim country in South Asia. Afghanistan has an estimated total population of 16 million, made up of diverse groups that include Pushto, Tajik and Turkic peoples. Most Afghans are Sunni and follow the Hanafi SCHOOL OF ISLAMIC LAW but there is a significant SHIA minority.

Muslim Arab armies entered the area at the beginning of the eighth century and a succession of Muslim empires ruled into the eighteenth century. British and Russian intrusion and the ensuing Anglo-Afghan Wars resulted in a truncated territory. Previously a monarchy, Afghanistan has in recent times gone through a turbulent period including occupation by the former Soviet Union, whose armies retreated following a prolonged war of liberation by Afghani guerrillas known as *mujahidin*. Following this, various dissident groups, in many instances receiving external support, have engaged in a bitter civil war. After the end of Soviet occupation, the country descended into chaotic conflict until the rise of the TALIBAN, who after overcoming various rivals imposed a harsh regime and a strict code of behaviour.

An American-led invasion after the events of 11 September 2001 led to the overthrow of the Taliban. In 2004 Hamid Karzai was elected President of Afghanistan. Since then the country has gone through a period of reconciliation and reconstruction, with wide international support. Its stability remains fragile in the face of continuing violence and conflict, particularly where remnants of the Taliban continue to create division.

Aflatun *see* PLATO.

Aga Khan Title of the spiritual leader or imam of the Nizari Ismaili Muslims (*see* ISMAILIYYA) since the nineteenth century. Aga Khan I (d. 1881) and Aga Khan II (d. 1885) represent the period of transition in the emergence of the community in modern times.

Much of the institution-building and direction for the community in the twentieth century was initiated by Sir Sultan Muhammad Shah, Aga Khan III (d. 1957), an international statesman, who was imam for over seventy years. He was succeeded by Karim Shah, Aga Khan IV (b. 1936), who has further developed these institutions, adapting them to the needs of the worldwide community since 1957, when he became imam. He has also created the AGA KHAN DEVELOPMENT NETWORK and institutions that have increased the reputation of an outstanding and effective global network promoting cultural, economic and educational development in many parts of the world.

In 2007 the community celebrated the fiftieth year of his accession.

Aga Khan Award for Architecture Launched in 1977 by the present Aga Khan, Karim Shah, its purpose is to stimulate a concern for the built environment in the Muslim world and to help develop resources and skills to meet building demands as well as to preserve the historically significant architectural heritage of Muslims in the face of increasing degradation.

Aga Khan Development Network The Aga Khan Development Network (AKDN) is a contemporary endeavour of the Ismaili imamat to realize the social conscience of Islam through institutional action, bringing together a number of institutions built up over the last four decades. Its mandate is to improve living conditions and opportunities for all and to encourage through education, health care and economic and social development the building of local capacity and institutions to meet the challenges of poverty as well as growth in a globalized environment. The network operates predominantly in Asia and Africa but also in Europe and North America. Among its significant initiatives is the establishment of private universities in Pakistan, Central Asia and East Africa.

Agha Hashar Kashmiri (1879–1935) Urdu dramatist regarded as one of the foremost writers of drama in that language. His writings draw upon Muslim as well as Western influences, particularly from the plays of Shakespeare. Agha Hashar is buried in Lahore, Pakistan.

Aghlabids A dynasty that ruled in northern Africa in the ninth century, from 800 to 909. The Aghlabid capital was Qayrawan in modern-day Tunisia. It was founded by Ibrahim ibn al-Aghlab, an ABBASID governor, and the region experienced significant development in urban and cultural life under the rule of his successors, while maintaining considerable independence and military power. Although the dynasty ruled in the name of the Abbasid caliph, they exercised great autonomy, which allowed them to maintain their control over the region through the appointment of family members as heirs.

Agra This city, currently in the state of Uttar Pradesh in India, was a residential centre for the MOGHUL emperors. The history of Agra began long before the Muslim conquest. It was famous for its textile industry, stone, marble and gold work which was exported overseas, including to the courts of Europe. Its most famous monument is the TAJ MAHAL.

ahd A Quranic term signifying covenant or pact as between God and human beings whereby the latter accepted stewardship of the earth. By extension it could also mean a pact between various parties. The term has also been used in a variety of other contexts, including political agreements and civil contracts.

ahkam The plural of the Quranic term *hukm*, meaning 'command' or 'authority'. In an extended sense, the term is applied to judicial decisions or the application of rules in SHARIA courts.

Ahl al-Bayt (lit., 'People of the House') A term used to describe the family of the Prophet. Among the Shia it is applied to the Prophet, his daughter FATIMA, her husband ALI IBN ABI TALIB and their children HASAN and HUSAYN IBN ALI. By extension, however, it includes all those claiming descent from the latter, such as the royal families of Jordan and Morocco.

Ahl al-Dhimma or **Dhimmi** (lit., 'People of the Pact of Protection') Non-Muslims living under Muslim rule or within a Muslim territory whose lives, religion and sacred places were protected. Their autonomy and freedom of religious life and institutions were assured by Quranic prescription. Dhimmi paid a tax known as *jizya*. Though primarily referring to Jews and Christians in the earlier period, the term also came to be applied to other religious communities throughout Muslim history, who lived under various degrees of autonomy in different periods and places.

Ahl al-Fatra *Fatra* (lit., 'an interval of time') commonly refers to the interval between Jesus and Muhammad. While no messenger is believed to have been sent by God during this period, true belief lived among various people who are known as the Ahl al-Fatra. Among them is considered to have been Waraqa ibn Nawfal who lived in Prophet Muhammad's time and affirmed him as a messenger from God.

Ahl al-Kitab (lit., 'People of the Book' (Quran 5:58)) A term referring to Jews, Christians and SABIANS who believe in God and the Last Day, and act righteously. The application of the term has been extended to include other religions believed to possess sacred scriptures, thereby establishing a commonality among faith communities to whom divine revelation had been granted. They were protected within Muslim territories and were treated as AHL AL-DHIMMA.

Ahmad Badawi (1199–1276) One of the most venerated figures of Sunni Muslim piety in Egypt. His mausoleum in Tanta, Egypt, is a major centre for visitation and devotional activity. One of his most famous admirers is said to have been the MAMLUK Sultan al-Zahir Baybars.

Ahmad ibn Tulun (835–884) Governor of Egypt during the ABBASID period, he went on to establish an autonomous dynasty, the Tulunids, in 872. He was known for his commitment to scholarship as well as his military talents. He also initiated economic and agrarian reforms that enabled the dynasty to establish its independence despite formally acknowledging the rule of the Abbasid caliph. He is associated with the building of the well-known mosque in Cairo, named after him.

Ahmad Gran (1506–1543) Muslim of Somali origin. Ahmad Gran led a military campaign in the sixteenth century to conquer Ethiopia. His initial successes won him control of many regions in the country, but he was eventually defeated by a joint Ethiopian/Portuguese army.

Ahmad ibn Hanbal (780–855) He is regarded as the founder of what eventually became the Hanbali SCHOOL OF ISLAMIC LAW. From an early age he devoted himself to the study of traditions, travelling extensively for the purpose. He studied under the well-known jurist al-Shafii in Baghdad. His compilation is known as the *Musnad*, one of the most extensive and authoritative Sunni collections of HADITH. In contrast with the other well-known collections, the *hadiths* in this work are arranged according to the first transmitter rather than subject matter. Ibn Hanbal's opposition to the enforced acceptance of the MUTAZILA doctrine under the Caliph AL-MAMUN led to his imprisonment, in particular because he opposed the doctrine of the createdness of the Quran, an important aspect of the Mutazili teaching, which al-Mamun sought to impose. After al-Mamun's death, he was pardoned by Caliph al-Mutawakkil, who ended the inquisition of scholars who disagreed with al-Mamun's position. Hanbal continued his work as a scholar and his reputation was such that his funeral is believed to have been attended by several hundred thousand people. In Muslim history he is admired as a scholar and a model of pious and non-violent resistance to the imposition of doctrine by ruling authorities.

Ahmad Khan, Sir Sayyid (1817–1898) Reformer and educator. He was a major figure in the Muslim modernist reform movement in India and the founder of Aligarh College. His writings and efforts reflect the belief that progress by Muslims can best be achieved by incorporating rather than condemning positive aspects of modernization. He supported the establishment of Western models of education and encouraged Muslim cooperation with the British. Sayyid Ahmad Khan was knighted by the British government for his efforts. In some circles, his attempts to reconcile the thought of the Quran with modern science and his questioning of such institutions as polygamy were condemned. ALIGARH MUSLIM UNIVERSITY, as the institution he founded is now called, offers Islamic studies alongside a modern Western curriculum, believing that an integration of the two affords the best form of education to prepare Muslims for the modern world.

Ahmad Sayyid Barelwi (1786–1831) Indian Muslim reformer. During the period of British colonial rule in India several Muslim reform movements emerged. One of them was led by Ahmad Sayyid Barelwi, who combined a commitment to the Sunni Hanafi SCHOOL OF ISLAMIC LAW and adherence to the Sufi QADIRIYYA. His teachings focused on strict adherence to the observances of the SHARIA, a strong belief in the intercessory role of the Prophet and participation in Sufi practices, including the visiting of shrines and the traditions and practices associated with them.

His followers, known as Barelwis, continue to play an influential role in Pakistan and India and among immigrants from South Asia who have settled in Britain, continental Europe and North America.

Ahmad Shah Durrani (c. 1722–1773) Afghan military commander who established a new dynasty in Afghanistan in 1747 and sought to extend influence in the region through a series of invasions of India and for a while succeeded in capturing Delhi, the capital of the MOGHUL empire. At the time of his death in 1773 he exercised control over Afghanistan and parts of the Indian subcontinent, but under his successors both the territories and the dynasty soon fell apart.

Ahmad Sirhindi, Shaykh (1564–1624) Sufi NAQSHBANDIYYA leader in India and noted Indian Muslim thinker of the MOGHUL period. He attempted to restore a balance between traditionalist Muslim thought based on the Quran and the SHARIA and what was then perceived to be the unorthodox expression of Sufi thought and practices. His ideas have been influential in stimulating reform among subsequent generations of scholars in the Indian subcontinent.

Ahmadiya Movement that developed under British rule in India, led by Mirza Gulam Ahmed (c. 1835–1908). The movement claimed messianic and prophetic status for its founder (its members differed over his exact status). It became active as a missionary movement and propagated its faith in Africa and more recently in the West. Because of its religious claims, the movement or its promotion is proscribed in Pakistan and various other Muslim countries and it is regarded as being outside the pale of Islam.

Ahrar, Nasir al-Din (1404–1490) Sufi NAQSHBANDIYYA leader best known for his preaching and influence in Central Asia. His political influence resulted in the Timurid conquest of Samarkand in 1451 (*see* TAMERLANE). He continued to be influential in political and religious affairs, believing that his mission should encompass a role as mediator between rulers and the people.

Aisha bint Abu Bakr (613–678) Daughter of Caliph ABU BAKR. Aisha was married to the Prophet after the death of KHADIJA, his first wife. She is regarded as an important conduit of tradition from the Prophet. After the death of Caliph UTHMAN IBN AFFAN she joined in an unsuccessful rebellion against the new caliph, ALI IBN ABI TALIB, and was forced to retire to private life in Medina. Accounts of the life of the Prophet contain numerous references emphasizing her close relationship to the Prophet.

Aisha al-Mannubiya Muslim woman of Tunisian origin, active during the thirteenth century. Aisha al-Mannubiya, by virtue of her piety and commitment to a Sufi way of life, became a figure of veneration, particularly for women. Her mausoleum near Tunis attracts many visitors who seek to benefit from her example.

Akbar (1542–1605) Emperor of the MOGHUL dynasty who extended the empire and implemented a stable administrative and fiscal system. He is particularly well known for his ecumenical outlook in matters of faith and religious practice. The majority of the peoples he ruled were non-Muslim. In 1581 he founded an eclectic belief system called Divine Faith (Din-i-Ilahi). To consolidate alliances he married Hindu princesses without asking them to give up their faith and encouraged tolerance towards all religions. His attempt to create a new ceremonial capital at Fathepur Sikri failed, though the palace structures that were built still survive. By 1576, the whole of northern India had been annexed to the empire and it was further enlarged during the next twenty-five years under his rule.

Akhbari Refers to the group among the Twelver Imami Shia (*see* ITHNA ASHARIYYA) who consider the tradition of their imams as providing a foundational resource for understanding Muslim faith and practice. Their views came to represent a minority tendency, since they wished to make the traditions of the twelve imams an exclusive source of legal regulation.

akhlaq *See* ETHICS.

Akhund A title given to religious scholars of high rank in Iran and in Turkey.

al- *Al-* is the definite article in Arabic and is retained in many personal names and phrases. It is commonly ignored during alphabetic ordering, as in this volume.

Alamut *See* NIZAM AL-MULK; RASHID AL-DIN SINAN; TUSI, NASIR AL-DIN MUHAMMAD IBN MUHAMMAD.

Alawi The term refers to a group of Muslims with very specific beliefs about ALI IBN ABI TALIB, the fourth caliph and the first Shia imam. The group has also been referred to as Nusayri, since many of its views were developed by Ibn Nusayr, a ninth-century scholar. Because the group focuses its central doctrine almost exclusively around Ali and his veneration, it has been regarded by other Muslims as extreme in its outlook. A small and very secretive group, the Alawis have attained significance in modern times because of their presence in Syria in particular, where Hafez Assad (1930–2000), an Alawi, became president and was also able to gain official recognition of the then leader of the Shia community in Lebanon, Musa Sadr. In Syria as well as in Lebanon and Turkey, the Alawis have tried to build ties of mutual recognition and tolerance with Sunni and Shia groups. *See also* ALEVI.

Alawi dynasty A family name applied to the Moroccan royal family because of its claim of descent from ALI IBN ABI TALIB through his son Hasan. The dynasty gained control of Morocco under various sultans between 1664 and 1727. Following the imposition of a Franco-Spanish protectorate in 1912, there was a struggle for independence which was achieved in 1956. The present king is Muhammad VI. *See also* ALAWI.

Albania European country whose Muslim majority of over 3 million represents approximately 65 per cent of its population. Muslim influence spread and grew in the area after the extension of the OTTOMAN EMPIRE during the fourteenth century and its oldest mosque dates back to 1380. The Ottoman Turkish name for Albania was Arnawutlug. Under communism, there was a ban on religious activity and hundreds of mosques and religious centres were destroyed by the government. Since the end of communist rule in 1991 Muslims have resumed religious activities within an emerging more democratic framework, creating organizations and developing ties with other Muslim societies as Albania strives to achieve durable stability and economic development as a post-Soviet European nation.

Alevi A Shia religious community which constitutes a significant minority in Turkey. They are also found in Bosnia-Herzegovina and in other parts of Europe. The community's roots lie in Shia doctrine and history and a strong association with the role of Imam ALI IBN ABI TALIB. They do not recognize either a framework of designated continuing central authority or a structure of representative religious leadership.

As with the ALAWI in Syria, the centrality of Ali to the Alevi and the devotion and veneration they accord to him are considered extreme by other Muslims. In modern times, because of their particular association with the province of Anatolia as well as with the Bektashi order, they have gained a more autonomous status and recognition in secular Turkey, where some contemporary Alevis see their heritage as a type of wisdom tradition rather than a religiously defined doctrine.

Alexander the Great (356–323 BC) Greek general and conqueror. In the Quran and subsequent Muslim tradition, Iskandar, as he is called, became seen as a leader and protector of his community from the forces of evil represented by Gog and Magog. The Quran refers to him as the 'one with two horns', an epithet widely interpreted among Muslims to suggest his world conquests and universal influence.

Alf Layla wa Layla A collection of stories in Arabic whose popularity in both the Muslim world and the West, where it is known as *A Thousand and One Nights*, has resulted in many of the tales becoming very widely known. Its origins probably go back to the ninth century and represent an amalgamation and integration of stories from the cultural traditions of Egypt, Iran and India. Some are built around historical figures, a well-known example being the Abbasid caliph HARUN AL-RASHID.

Alfarablus *See* AL-FARABI, ABU NASR.

Algazel *See* AL-GHAZALI, ABU HAMID MUHAMMAD.

algebra The Latinized form of the Arabic term *al-jabr*, which signified work related to the solution of equations in mathematical treatises composed by Muslim scholars. The major exponent of this science was al-Khwarizmi, a ninth-century Muslim mathematician. *See* MATHEMATICS.

Algeria Country in the central part of North Africa known as the Maghreb. Algeria has a population of 25 million, virtually all Sunni Muslim. The major indigenous languages are Arabic and Berber, the latter used mainly by Berber groups of the Sahara, such as the Tuareg. Islam spread to the region in the seventh century and the area became an integral part of the larger Muslim world ruled by various dynasties. French colonial rule was established in 1834.

Algeria became independent in 1962 after a long period of resistance. Two decades of socialist rule were followed by the active involvement in political life of different Muslim organizations and political parties. Fearing a victory by the Islamic Salvation Front (*see* FIS), a legal political party, the ruling government cancelled the general elections in 1991. This resulted in a state of emergency and political and social turmoil accompanied by a brutal conflict that led to the deaths of thousands. The unrest continued for more than a decade. More recently there has been greater stability and efforts at reconciliation and development utilizing the natural resources of the country.

Alhambra (lit., 'The Red') The most famous example of later Andalusian Muslim architecture, the Alhambra was constructed as a fortress and palace in Granada, Spain, by the NASRID ruler al-Ghalib in the thirteenth century and subsequently enlarged by his successors.

Alhazan *See* IBN AL-HAYTHAM, ABU ALI AL-HASAN.

Ali-Ahmad, Sayyid Jalal (1923–1969) Iranian writer. His novels, essays and other writings constituted a critique of what he perceived to be the rampant Westernization of Iran. He was also a school teacher who integrated perspectives on education and culture in his writings that touch upon religious as well as political issues.

Ali ibn Abi Talib (598–661) Cousin and son-in-law of the Prophet. Ali was among the earliest converts to Islam, the first imam of the Shia and the fourth caliph. He was married to the Prophet's daughter Fatima and was one of his staunchest supporters, renowned for his skills as a warrior and for his knowledge and piety.

While he did not always agree on policy with the caliphs who succeeded the Prophet, he continued to work with them and played an important role in early Muslim life and society, eventually becoming the fourth caliph in 656 after the assassination of UTHMAN IBN AFFAN. By that time political and group differences were beginning to put a strain on Muslim unity. He faced a rebellion led by two companions and one of the wives of the Prophet, AISHA BINT ABU BAKR. A more significant threat to his authority and Muslim unity came from Muawiyya, the governor of Syria. While an attempt was being made to arbitrate differences, Ali was murdered while at prayer, in 661.

According to Shia belief, the Prophet had already formally designated Ali to succeed as head of the community, and in their view he is regarded as the legitimate leader of the Muslims and the first imam in a line descended from him through Fatima. He provided guidance and interpretation in understanding the Quran and his role is regarded as complementing the mission of the Prophet. The affirmation of this role of succession and authority, known as *walaya*, is included in the Shia declaration of faith.

Ali is also revered by Sufis as a teacher of the esoteric and spiritual understanding of Islam, by virtue of both his special relationship to the Prophet and his own example of piety and devotion. Most Sufi teachers trace their spiritual genealogy back to the Prophet through Ali. Both the day of his proclamation as imam at GHADIR KHUMM and his birthday are commemorated by the Shia as festivals. While the Sunni perspective on his role differs from that of the Shia, Ali is clearly one of the most revered figures among Muslims after the Prophet. His teachings have been preserved in a work entitled *Nahj al-Balagha* (*Peak of Eloquence*). He is buried in Najaf, where his tomb is a major centre of pilgrimage for Shia Muslims.

Ali al-Rida (765–818) Eighth in the line of Ithna Ashari imams (*see* ITHNA ASHAR-IYYA). Respected for his knowledge and scholarship, he was designated in 817 as his successor by the ABBASID Caliph al-Mamun, who was seeking a rapprochement with the Shia. Imam al-Rida died suddenly under suspicious circumstances in 818, his followers believing that he was poisoned. His tomb grew into a pilgrimage site, eventually known as Mashhad (Place of Martyrdom), and today is a major centre of learning as well as one of the most visited pilgrimage sites in Iran.

Aligarh Muslim University Previously Aligarh College. Aligarh is a city in Uttar Pradesh, India. Its college was originally founded as the Muhammadan Anglo-Indian Oriental College, a school of higher education, in 1875 by Sir Sayyid

AHMAD KHAN. The curriculum was intended to balance European models and traditional Islamic studies. All subjects were, however, taught in English. The school became a symbol of the modernist reform movement and was turned into a university in 1920. Incorporated as a comprehensive, modern seat of learning, Aligarh Muslim University continues to be an influential Muslim educational institution in the subcontinent.

All-India Muslim League *See* MUSLIM LEAGUE.

Allah The Quranic, Arabic term for God in Islam. Central to Islam is the belief in the unity of God, affirmed in the statement of witness of the faith: 'There is no god but Allah'. Allah is described in the Quran as both transcendent and all-powerful, the creator of all and yet close to human beings, compassionate, merciful, forgiving, just and Lord of the DAY OF JUDGEMENT. He is remembered also through his attributes, the 'most beautiful names', which are involved in prayer and contemplation. He reveals messages and scriptures to humanity, in particular through a line of prophetic figures and messengers, of which the message of the Quran, revealed through Muhammad, is the final one. The formula used to express God's greatness – *Allahu akbar* – is called *takbir* in Arabic.

Almohads Dynasty which ruled Morocco and Spain from 1130 to 1269. The name derives from the Arabic *al-muwahhidun* meaning 'the unitarians' and reflecting their uncompromising reformist zeal regarding the unity of God. Their leader IBN TUMART was of Berber origin. His successor Abd al-Mumin was able to consolidate a considerable portion of North Africa under his control through a series of military campaigns. Taking the title caliph, he established a dynasty and propagated IBN TUMART's teachings.

Almoravids Dynasty which ruled in Spain and North Africa from 1056 to 1147. It grew out of a revivalist movement among the Berbers under the leadership of Abd Allah ibn Yasin. His successor, Yusuf ibn Tashfin, founded Marrakesh as a capital in 1062, assuming the title Amir al-Muslimin (Commander of the Muslims), a title still used in North Africa today. The dynasty's rule expanded after Andalusian Muslims sought military aid against Christian offensives and Yusuf responded by conquering the country. The name derives from the Spanish pronunciation of *al-murabitun* ('the bound ones'), referring to the religious impetus behind the dynasty's beginnings, led by those who were 'bound' to perform their religious duty. The Almoravids were defeated after a century by the ALMOHADS.

almsgiving *See* SADAQA; ZAKAT.

Amadu Bamba (1857–1927) Founder of the MURIDIYYA order in West Africa. Amadu Bamba's attempts to organize his followers led to his imprisonment and exile by the then French colonial government. The Muridiyya, following his emphasis on the value of faith and the ethic of work, organized themselves economically and have been successful in the peanut trade. Their centre is in Touba, in Senegal, where the shaykh is buried and which has become a major centre of pilgrimage for his followers and scholarship associated with his teachings.

amal In the Quran the term refers to morally worthy acts. The concept of *amal* was developed further in Muslim law, theology and philosophy. In the Muslim tradition *amal* was also connected with the Hellenistic idea of the link between action (especially good action) and knowledge about the nature of things, which the Muslim tradition also connected with belief in God.

The title Amal was also used by a Muslim organization representing a political party of the Imami Shia in Lebanon.

Amat al-Wahid (d. 987) Jurist. The daughter of a judge in Baghdad, she studied jurisprudence, issued legal decisions and was also acknowledged for her piety and religious devotion.

Amina bint Wahb (d. 576) Mother of the Prophet Muhammad who, after the early loss of her husband, brought up Muhammad in Mecca. She died when he was only six years old and is celebrated in Muslim tradition by a number of stories about her pregnancy and the birth of the Prophet.

Amir Ali, Sayyid (1849–1928) Writer and lawyer. Sayyid Amir Ali established a national association for Indian Muslims to promote better awareness of political and intellectual issues. His *Spirit of Islam*, written in 1891, is an attempt to cast Muslim history and thought in the spirit of a progressive, modern faith.

Amir Khusraw Dihlawi (1253–1325) Poet and musician in India, Dihlawi was also a disciple of the noted Sufi leader NIZAM AL-DIN AWLIYA. In addition to his contributions to music, particularly the development of the GHAZAL and poetry in several languages, he wrote on the culture and history of the time.

Amir al-Muminin (lit., 'Commander/Prince of the Faithful or Believers') Title of the caliph, the first use of which is commonly attributed to Caliph UMAR IBN AL-KHATTAB. Though it was intended to be used exclusively for the single office that was recognized for its authority in the then Muslim world, leaders of several dynasties in Islam claimed the title in vying for recognition. Among the Shia it is used exclusively for ALI IBN ABI TALIB and his designated descendants. In the Quran (4:59) it refers to those who are to be obeyed in addition to God and the Prophet Muhammad. In more recent times the title has come to be used to refer to local rulers or claimants to authority ostensibly undertaking JIHAD in the name of Islam.

amira *See* HIJAB.

Amman Declaration In 2006 Jordan hosted a major gathering of leading Muslim scholars, who unanimously agreed to accept all the major Sunni and Shia SCHOOLS OF ISLAMIC LAW as representing the pluralism within Islam and further acknowledged that those who foster violence and extremism against other Muslims and non-Muslims through their views are acting illegitimately and are an affront to all that Islam stands for.

Ammar Ibn Yasir Companion of the Prophet and supporter of ALI IBN ABI TALIB. He is regarded as a knowledgeable transmitter of traditions and respected for his piety and his struggle on behalf of Islam during its period of infancy.

Ampel, Sunan Raden Rashmet One of the Wali Songo, a group of wise scholars and devotees who preached Islam and led its initial spread in Java and subsequent growth in the fifteenth century in Java and Surabaya in Indonesia.

Amr ibn al-As (d. 663) Soldier and politician. He accepted Islam during the time of the Prophet and became one of the most important commanders in the subsequent conquests and expansion of Muslim rule. His campaigns included those that led to the conquest of Syria and Egypt. He was made Governor of Egypt and joined MUA-WIYYA in his rebellion against ALI IBN ABI TALIB.

Amra bint Abd al-Rahman (d. 717) Prominent among the second generation of Muslims, Amra bint Abd al-Rahman was well known for her role in transmitting prophetic tradition and recognized for her great learning. In several instances her transmission of tradition has been regarded as legal precedent.

al-Andalus The Muslim name for the Iberian Peninsula which was part of the world of Islam for almost seven centuries, beginning in 711 with the initial campaigns under the command of TARIQ IBN ZIYAD and then Musa ibn Nusayr. An independent state came to be established there by a branch of the UMAYYAD dynasty, which ended with the reign of ABD AL-RAHMAN III, who ruled for fifty years and proclaimed himself a caliph. During this period Córdoba became a major cultural, intellectual and political centre. The kingdom became divided after 1009 and Andalusia came to be ruled by several factions. Under the ALMORAVIDS and the ALMOHADS, it experienced great prosperity and prestige.

From the thirteenth century onwards, Muslim rulers began to lose control of territory to various coalitions of Christian kings. The NASRID dynasty based in Granada was the last to fall, leading to the completion of RECONQUISTA in 1492.

Muslim society in Andalusia was pluralistic, consisting of peoples of Arab, Berber and Spanish origin, and the presence of Muslims, Christians and Jews gave it a cosmopolitan culture, much in evidence in the arts and architecture of major cities such as Córdoba, Granada, Seville and Toledo. It produced its own distinctive artistic and musical tradition and architectural monuments such as the mosques of Córdoba and Seville, the palaces of the Madinat al-Zahra and the famous ALHAMBRA in Granada. Among the legacies of the people was a form of Hispanic Arabic, which eventually died out with the departure of the MORISCOS in the seventeenth century. It also exercised a strong influence which still survives today in the Spanish language and culture. At its height, Andalusia's cultural values and achievements are believed to reflect a convivencia, a mutually enriching concord among its various peoples and faiths.

angels Belief in angels is taught in the Quran. They are a separate category of creation from human beings, whose creation they witnessed. The archangel Gabriel is regarded in Muslim tradition as the intermediary of the message of the Quran to the Prophet. The only other angel mentioned in the Quran is Michael (Mikhail), who assisted God with the creation of the world. Muslim tradition recognizes two other archangels: Israfil, who will sound the trumpet on the Last Day, and Azrail, the angel of death. Two angels are said to record the good and bad deeds in each life, an account which will be presented on the DAY OF JUDGEMENT. There is some difference of opinion in Muslim sources regarding Satan, some believing that he was originally an angel who was corrupted by pride and disobedience.

Anis, Mir Babar Ali (1802–1874) Urdu poet. He came from a family of poets and devoted his life to writing verse. Anis is noted for his *marthiya*, a form of devotional poetry that has as its central theme the martyrdom of Imam HUSAYN IBN ALI.

apostasy Wilful rejection or abandonment of one's faith is condemned by the Quran, though it is clear about not compelling faith (Quran 2:256: 'There is no compulsion in religion') and urging an attitude of forgiveness (Quran 2:109).

Muslim scholars and jurists subsequently integrated into their writings discussion of and presumptions about apostasy and disbelief, primarily as a deliberate act of renunciation, although retaining the broader concept of rejection of faith as all-encompassing.

After the death of the Prophet in 632, several converted tribes reverted to tribal authority and reversed the commitment they had made in adopting Islam. Caliph ABU BAKR undertook campaigns against them and put down the rebellions, which in some cases were led by those who claimed to be new prophets.

In more recent times the question of apostasy has taken on a more contentious as well as political aspect and for a small minority has become a basis for justifying violence against the authority or presence of other Muslims whose views they regard as constituting heresy.

aqida Often translated as 'creed', 'dogma' or 'article of faith'. Among the various schools of Muslim thought, these generally include the unity of God and the status of the Quran, prophets and prophecy, the responsibilities of human beings, belief in heaven and hell, and issues related to faith and unbelief.

aql The rational or reflective capacity of human beings. In the Muslim intellectual tradition *aql* became associated with the 'intellect'. In the Quran, Adam is taught the 'names of all things' by God, implying that the composite status of humanity as created beings was accompanied by a capacity to have access through reason to all resources of knowledge. For most Muslim philosophers and thinkers the intellect complemented and interacted with knowledge based on revelation.

Arab League *See* LEAGUE OF ARAB STATES.

Arabic One of the Semitic languages, Arabic, the language of the Quran, is the primary language today of more than 150 million people. It developed throughout the history of Islam as one of the world's major languages.

As Islam spread to other parts of the world, Arabic as the primary language of formal prayer, religious writings, law, theology and philosophy was adapted and further enriched local languages such as Hausa, Persian, Swahili, Turkish, Urdu and others. All these languages adopted the Arabic script, and in several instances continue to use it.

architecture Muslim architecture is represented in a diversity of forms across the world. Yet this diversity in its many expressions exhibits a shared sense of engagement, purposes in the use of space and a common set of values that cut across regional, climatic and cultural differences.

Muslim architecture encompasses many built forms, places of devotion and worship, memorials, domestic spaces, military buildings, palaces, institutions of learning, commercial buildings and marketplaces, places of rest and leisure and examples of monumental structures celebrating power and achievement.

There are a number of common themes and elements that can be identified in Muslim architecture. The most important is based on the appreciation of the principle of unity that characterizes the built environment. Other concerns include continuity with the past, recognition of regional and vernacular practice and the use of natural elements as materials to reflect the architectural use of water, vegetation, mud etc. Modern Muslim architecture is facing the challenge of interpreting this diverse historical heritage with sensitivity and of meeting the demands of growing populations and fast-expanding cities. Several architects of Muslim origin continue to play an influential role in the architectural community of the world, often contributing to new ideas and developments in their work.

Aristotle (d. 322 BC) Greek philosopher whose works came to the attention of Muslims from the ninth century onwards. His available works were translated into Arabic and were read widely by Muslim philosophers and intellectuals. Among the major Muslim figures who interpreted and further developed Aristotelian ideas were AL-KINDI, Abu Bakr Muhammad ibn Zakariyya AL-RAZI, AL-FARABI, IBN SINA and IBN RUSHD.

They appropriated his conceptual framework for analysis, interpreting, adapting and revising his ideas to define their own philosophical positions in the realm of logic, physics and metaphysics. In adapting the Aristotelian system they also sought to reconcile their views with what they regarded as foundational Muslim beliefs in the Quran, maintaining in general a belief in the transcendental unity of God.

The Aristotelian tradition was transmitted to medieval Europe, particularly in the forms expounded by Ibn Sina and Ibn Rushd. This tradition, as reflected in the works of subsequent Muslim scholars, still constitutes part of the curriculum of traditional centres of Muslim learning, particularly in Iran.

art The different cultural and historical contexts within which artistic expression emerged among Muslims suggest a character that is both diverse and multidimensional.

Like all artistic traditions, Muslim art is built from the elements that existed in different cultures, but it was also inspired by values and an impetus for creativity engendered by the new faith. The Quran evokes striking symbols of light and illumination and their association with spaces of worship. The early development of art among Muslims was attached to architecture and found in the designs within mosques and other public spaces, as well as in textiles and ceramics. Another form that developed was calligraphy, particularly in enhancing replications of the Quran or Quranic verses in mosques and other buildings. Though there are early examples of artistic representation in palaces and other places attached to the court, the more significant work has survived elsewhere. In the artistic tradition that was evolving there are representations of humans and animals, though later representation of the human form and likeness was discouraged and even condemned by some Muslim scholars.

Many of the dynasties and rulers of the Muslim world were patrons of art and encouraged artists to contribute to the buildings associated with their rule such as palaces and gardens and also mosques and other religious buildings. The FATIMIDS, for example, mark a new impetus in creativity reflected in representational art, the mausoleum and the MUQARNAS, as well as in the design of mosques and textiles known as *tiraz*. The developments in Andalusia and much later in MOGHUL India and SAFAWID Iran represent more examples of the flourishing and development of art in Muslim societies. Miniature painting, for instance, developed into the finest reproduction of masterpieces associated with the cultural and artistic heritage preserved among Muslims. While this artistic heritage has continued to inspire the work of modern Muslim artists, there has been a remarkable assimilation of modern motifs in the work of some architects and artists, reflecting a growing concern that art should not be frozen in its past forms but should continue to be inspired by the need to address contemporary concerns and conditions.

Vase carrying the inscription 'Blessing to its owner', tenth century.

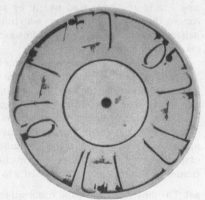

Bowl carrying the inscription 'Be aware of the fool ...'

asabiyya A central concept in the philosophy of history of IBN KHALDUN. It signified for him the quality of bonding and solidarity that bound society in its various formative stages. As rural and tribal solidarity led to growth and expansion, this quality became diluted and alternative and very often coercive forms of allegiance came to be developed by kingdoms, states and empires.

al-Ashari, Abul-Hasan (873–936) Recognized as the founder of Sunni KALAM of the Ashari SCHOOL OF ISLAMIC LAW. Originally a follower of the Mutazili school and among the best regarded exponents of MUTAZILA views in Basra, he became convinced at some point in his intellectual development that rationalism could not entirely and satisfactorily explain questions of faith. His sudden conversion from the Mutazila to Sunnism is a subject of much speculation. He continued, however, to employ the Mutazili methodology of reasoning to support Sunni precepts in what is now regarded as the Ashari school of thought, arguing at the same time against major aspects of Mutazila doctrine. His view of God as a transcendent entity whose actions could not be circumscribed by human logic led to the formulation of a theological view that used the tools of rationalism without being entirely bound or limited by them. These and other aspects of the teaching he was to develop were principally based on a particular interpretation of the Quran and prophetic traditions which a group of scholars and followers identified as belonging to the Ashari school of Sunni theology.

Ashura The tenth day of Muharram, the first month in the Muslim CALENDAR, generally regarded as a recommended day of fasting, according to the tradition of the Prophet. For the Shia, however, it has the significance of being the day when Imam HUSAYN IBN ALI was martyred at KARBALA. *See also* TAZIYA.

Askia Mohammad (c. 1442–1538) Muslim ruler of the African kingdom of Songhay in the late fifteenth century. His life is recounted in the epic oral and written traditions of West African Muslims. He is praised for his devotion to the cause of spreading Islam in the region, and for his piety, scholarship and benevolent rule.

Asma bint Umais al-Khatamiyya (d. 660) Contemporary of the Prophet and one of those who immigrated to Abyssinia. She is regarded as a source for traditions of the Prophet.

Assalamu alaykum *See* SALAM ALAYKUM.

astrology While developing simultaneously as an area of inquiry linked to the study of ASTRONOMY, the field of astrology came to be studied separately in the Muslim world.

Generally referred to as *ilm al-nujum* ('the science of the stars'), astrology focused on the determination of auspicious timings for major events such as battles as well as significant projects at a more human level, such as horoscopes for individuals, families and rulers to chart birth, marriage and other events. The most well-known of the earlier works on astrology is that of Abu Mashar al-Balkhi called the *Kitab al-Madkhal al-Kabir*, generally translated as *The Book of Introduction*.

astronomy Although the Greek astronomer and geographer Ptolemy provided the model of an earth-centred universe on which Arab and Muslim astronomers built their study of the heavens, several Muslim astronomers, drawing also from Indian sources, made observations and calculations which were considered much more accurate than Ptolemy's. The complementary development of mathematical sciences allowed Muslim astronomers to rethink the field and seek applications to practical issues such as determining the calendar and the times and direction of prayer. By blending and expanding ideas often based on original Greek concepts, their theories led to an enhanced field of astronomical studies which later profoundly influenced Western scientific exploration, beginning with Copernicus.

atabat (lit., 'thresholds') The term is applied to the shrines in the Iraqi cities of Najaf, Karbala, Kazimayn and Samarra containing the tombs of six of the imams of the Twelver Imami Shia (see ITHNA ASHARIYYA).

Atatürk See MUSTAFA KEMAL.

Attar, Farid al-Din Muhammad ibn Ibrahim (d. c. 1229) Sufi mystic and the author of a classic Sufi allegory, *Mantiq al-Tayr* (*The Conference of the Birds*). He is well known for many other works, including a biographical account of the lives and activities of many important Sufi figures. *See also* SUFISM.

authority All authority in Islam is referred back to God, who is the ultimate 'Sovereign of the Worlds'. However, God grants authority, particularly to Prophets and messengers, and in the case of Islam to the Prophet Muhammad. As a paradigm of authority, his roles encompassed the communication of revelation from God, the interpretation and implementation of divine guidance, the leadership of his followers, the headship of the Muslim community and its territories and the institutionalization of practices and structures that supported the daily life of Muslims of his time, including their security and welfare.

Averroes See IBN RUSHD.

Avicenna See IBN SINA.

Awami League Major political party in Bangladesh. It originated in what was previously East Pakistan and took on a greater secular and nationalistic tendency under the leadership of Shaykh Mujibur Rahman (d. 1975), which led to the war of secession that preceded the establishment of Bangladesh in 1971.

awliya The friends of God, those deemed by their piety, devotion and spirituality to have attained nearness to and understanding of God. In Sufi tradition they play an important role as reference points and intermediaries for those seeking the spiritual path. The tombs and burial sites of many *awliya* are considered to possess BARAKA (blessing), which may be accessed by visiting and praying at their tombs.

aya (pl., *ayat*) A verse of the QURAN. *Ayat* is also the term used to refer to signs of God's creative power and meaning in the universe.

ayatollah (lit., 'sign of God') Title used for the most outstanding religious authorities among Imami Shia in Iran and Iraq. The rank is based on leadership qualities, knowledge, charisma and scholarship. The title is generally attributed by a consensus among scholars and often an individual has passed through various other ranks based on training and scholarly reputation.

Ayesha Variant spelling of AISHA.

Ayyub Quranic Arabic name for the biblical Job. He is regarded in Muslim tradition as a prophet who endured patiently and whose distress was eventually removed by God, with whom he sought refuge.

Ayyubids Dynasty consolidated by SALAH AL-DIN AL-AYYUB (Saladin). The Ayyubids ruled Egypt, Syria, Yemen and other centres in the Middle East from 1171 until the MAMLUK conquest in 1250. The dynasty established connections with Italian port cities and engaged in negotiations with European rulers over territorial disputes and during the various crusading ventures into the Holy Land.

Azad, Abu al-Kalam (1888–1958) Writer and poet of Muslim India. Azad published a journal, *al-Hilal*, wrote a commentary on the Quran and urged a renewal of Muslim thought to meet contemporary needs. After the partition of the subcontinent he chose to remain in India, serving as Minister of National Education. He is also considered a pioneer of Urdu poetry.

Azari Turkish dialect spoken by the Muslim peoples of Azerbaijan and various parts of Iran. Among the great poets of early Azari literature are Shaykh Asfarayini and Nesimi. Its most well-known folk work is the classical *Kitab-e Dede Korkutta*.

Azerbaijan One of the Muslim republics of Caucasus formed after the collapse of the Soviet Union in 1991. The population of the country consists mainly of Azeris, Armenians and Russians. Azerbaijan is also the name of the neighbouring province in Iran. The republic has a population of 7 million Muslims who make up approximately 87 per cent of the population, the majority of whom belong to the ITHNA ASHARIYYA school of Shiism. Religious minorities include Russian and Armenian Orthodox Christians and a small number of Zoroastrians. Historical conversion to Islam took place through Sufi orders and the mystical influence is reflected in Azeri poetry and music. Shia Islam was introduced as the official doctrine during the SAFAWID period. Upon its emergence from communist rule in 1991, Azerbaijan declared itself to be a secular state. It has been a member of the Council of Europe since 2001 and a member of NATO since 1994. Like several other former Soviet republics, Azerbaijan is also a member of the Commonwealth of Independent States (CIS), linked to Russia. Most religious institutions and buildings in the country, including a Muslim seminary established in 1991, have been built since independence under the patronage of other Muslim countries, such as Iran, Oman and Saudi Arabia. Azerbaijan has close ethnic ties with Turkey, but in terms of religious adherence it is much closer to the predominantly Shia Iran. Rich in oil and natural gas, it has attracted investment from major international oil companies and its resources and location are considered to be of strategic interest.

al-Azhar University University in Cairo generally regarded as one of the foremost institutions of Sunni Muslim learning, al-Azhar was founded as a place of learning and a mosque by the Shia FATIMID caliph al-Muizz al-Din Allah MAADD in the tenth century. It is at present an important centre of learning and teaching of law and theology which attracts students from all over the Muslim world. In its modern formation and role as a university in Egypt, it took on the features of other universities, but has managed to sustain its style and reputation as a seat of traditional learning and training of Sunni Muslim religious scholars.

Bâ, Amadou Hampâté (also **Amadou Hampateba**) (1900–1991) Contemporary African writer who played an important role in collecting Muslim oral traditions of FULBE and Bambara origin. Hampateba is famous as a historian, theologian, ethnographer, linguist and writer. He also wrote extensively on the religious life of Muslim societies in West Africa and recorded the lives of important scholars and Sufis in the region.

Bâ, Mariama (1929–1981) Senegalese writer whose work reflected an engagement with the issues of women's emancipation from traditional roles and status as represented in her society. Her 1964 novel *Une si longue lettre* (*So Long a Letter*), for which Bâ won the Noma Award for Publishing in Africa, explores the dilemma of an educated woman whose husband takes a second wife. Like AMINATA SOW-FALL, she explores issues of womanhood and modernity with sensitivity and concern, as well as respect for the values of the past.

Babad Tanah Jawa The Java Chronicles. These chronicles provide a traditional account of the history of the various rulers of Java and the spread of Islam at the time of the Mataraur dynasty in the fifteenth and sixteenth centuries.

Babur (1483–1530) Common name of Zahir al-Din Muhammad, founder of the MOGHUL dynasty in India in 1526. Of Central Asian origin, a descendant of Timur (TAMERLANE), Babur left behind his memoirs and poetry, which reflect a highly cultured and cosmopolitan ruler. He invaded India in 1526, heralding the beginning of several centuries of Moghul rule in the subcontinent.

Badr, battle of A crucial battle in 624, the first and most memorable battle of the early period, in which the emerging Muslim community fought a much larger and better equipped Meccan force and defeated it. According to historians, the Muslims under the leadership of the Prophet, numbering about 300, lay in wait near Badr, a small town on the route from Mecca to Syria. One of the major opponents of the Prophet, the feared Abu Jahl, led the Meccan army at this battle. Abu Jahl himself was killed at the battle and the Muslims managed to take numerous prisoners and much booty. As a result, Muhammad managed to secure his first major victory which also became a turning point in his career. Various Quranic verses are associated with Badr, including 8:9–12, in which God promises help for those who fight in his cause. The battle itself is portrayed as a sign of God's support and the eventual triumph of the Prophet's mission.

badw (sing., *badawi*) Arabic word for Bedouin. The term reflects the style of pastoral nomadism of Arab peoples from ancient times to the present.

Baghdad Capital of modern Iraq. It was created as a new capital by the second ABBASID caliph, al-Mansur, in the eighth century. It subsequently grew into one of the major centres of Muslim political and cultural life. It remained the seat of the Abbasid caliphs until 1258, when the city was captured and raided by the MONGOL army.

Bahais The followers of Mirza Husayn Ali Nuri (1817–1892). Nuri was the leader of a religious movement in Iran and he came to be known as Baha Allah ('Splendour of God'). The Bahais regard their faith as a new religion separate from Islam, based on their recognition of Baha Allah as the prophet whose coming was foretold by the Bab, a religious figure in Iran, who declared himself to be the gateway (*bab*) linking followers to the hidden imam of the Twelver Imami Shia (see ITHNA ASHARIYYA). He was executed for attempting to spread his beliefs in 1850.

The Bahai religion has since spread all over the world. Its principles include belief in the oneness of God, humanity and all religions.

Balkans Traditionally, the geographic region in the south-east of Europe including the contemporary states of Greece, Macedonia, Serbia, Montenegro, Croatia, Bulgaria, Bosnia and Herzegovina, Albania and parts of Turkey. Islam spread to this region around 1264. It eventually came under OTTOMAN control and remained so at least until the seventeenth century. During Ottoman rule there was significant migration and settlement of peoples from other parts of the empire to the Balkans. With the conquest of Constantinople in 1453 by the Ottoman Sultan MEHMED II the policy of unification of the Ottoman Empire brought the Balkans within its fold and made it an integral part of the Muslim world. The Ottoman infrastructure and institutions also benefited from trade and commerce, and the region came to enjoy a period of relative peace and prosperity. The decline of the Ottoman Empire from the late eighteenth century onwards made the Balkans a point of conflict in the military struggle between the European powers and the Ottomans. By the end of the nineteenth century the Ottomans had lost control over much of the area and with the end of the empire in the 1920s the region and its peoples entered a new phase in their history. The influence of Muslim values, institutions and cultural patterns, however, continued in much of the Balkans and in the daily lives of its population.

Bambara *See* SEGU.

Bangladesh South Asian republic. Formerly East Pakistan, Bangladesh is the third largest country in South Asia and was established in 1971 after a lengthy and bitter civil war. It is estimated that over 80 per cent of the population (est. 140 million) is Muslim. A majority of the Muslim population is Sunni, so follows the Hanafi SCHOOL OF ISLAMIC LAW. Islam was brought to Bengal at the beginning of the thirteenth century by Muslim Turkish soldiers. After the establishment of Muslim power,

National Assembly Building, Sher-e-Bangla Nagar, Dhaka, Bangladesh.

the frontier of Muslim influence was extended over the next two centuries, until it was incorporated into the MOGHUL empire in 1576. The evolution of Muslim society took place within a primarily agrarian culture, incorporating much of local, indigenous tradition. After the decline of the Moghuls Bengal was subsequently incorporated into the expanding British Empire. In 1947, when British India was divided, the region became part of the new nation of Pakistan and was called East Pakistan, until its separation in 1971.

Its history since independence has been marked by a struggle to fight the problems of poor economic development constantly under threat from seasonal floods and internal divisions, exacerbated by its leaders' inability to reconcile party differences and forge national unity. In spite of the many challenges, Bangladesh provides examples of innovative efforts at development for its rural population and the vitality of its literary and cultural traditions. *See also* GRAMEEN BANK.

al-Banna, Hassan (1906–1949) A reformer who founded the MUSLIM BROTHERHOOD in Egypt in 1929. The reform organization broadened its goals to include a change in the political order in Egypt and established branches in various other neighbouring countries. The Brotherhood also developed an armed wing that was responsible for attacks against various state institutions. Al-Banna himself was killed in 1949. In recent times the Muslim Brotherhood, which has been prosecuted in Egypt for decades, has been allowed to participate in national politics and elections. His younger brother, Gamal al-Banna (b. 1920), was at first also a member of the Muslim Brotherhood. Subsequently his approach to Islamic sources and traditions as well as the role of Islam in public life has undergone significant change. He now argues for a view in which Muslim scholars would seek to interpret the Quran and Sunna unhindered by the views of scholars of the past, and would seek to apply the message of Islam in accordance with the conditions and requirements of life as it is lived in the present.

al-Baqillani, Abu Bakr (d. 1013) A Sunni Ashari theologian who contributed significantly to the development and systematization of Ashari KALAM. He was also a noted jurist and polemicist.

baraka A Quranic term for blessing or beneficent favour from God. Particularly in Shia and Sufi tradition, the quality has come to be associated with the Prophet and his descendants who possess the capacity to mediate such blessing to others. In the Quran it is also associated with the LAYLAT AL-QADR (Night of Power) during Ramadan (Quran 97) and with the symbolic olive tree referred to in the *ayat an-nur* ('verse of light') (Quran 24:35).

In popular and folk tradition in the Muslim world, *baraka* may be associated with burial places of venerated and pious individuals and also objects such as amulets (containing Quranic verses) which ward off evil and provide protection and security.

Barelwi, Ahmad Sayyid *See* AHMAD SAYYID BARELWI.

Barzani, Mustafa Mulla *See* MUSTAFA BARZANI, MULLA.

basmachi A term used by the Soviets to describe Muslims who resisted communist efforts to control Central Asia in the early 1920s and 1930s. After the imposition of Bolshevik control and authority, many Muslim groups joined to constitute this broad-based movement to oppose communist rule and to call for unity under Islam. The movement was eventually suppressed and died out.

basmala The formula 'In the name of God, Most Beneficent, Most Merciful' with which each of the Quranic chapters or *suras* begin (except for *sura* 9). In Muslim practice, it is invoked at the beginning of most events and important actions. *See also* QURAN.

Bay Fall *See* MURIDIYYA.

bay'a In Muslim tradition *bay'a* was used for the formal allegiance accorded by an individual to the caliph or imam of the time. When Muhammad's authority was accepted, new Muslims gave him their formal allegiance.

Bayazid Ansari (1525–1573) A Sufi teacher, Ansari is credited as the founder of a religious and national movement in Afghanistan. He undertook extensive preaching and organized his followers into a community His activities generated hostility from the ruling authorities, leading eventually to his murder. He was the author of several literary works in Pashto dialects. He is also known for his contribution to the development of indigenous poetry and music.

Bayazid al-Bistami *See* ABU YAZID AL-BISTAMI.

al-Baydawi, Abd Allah Ibn Umar (d. 1291) Muslim scholar and compiler of the *Anwar al-Tanzil wa-Asrar al-Tawil* (*Lights of Revelation and the Secrets of Interpretation*), one of the standard Sunni commentaries on the Quran. He edited the work of a previous scholar, ZAMAKHSHARI, and eliminated what he regarded as controversial elements. By thus condensing and synthesizing the work of previous commentaries, al-Baydawi created what has become one of the most respected and widely used commentaries on the Quran.

Bayt al-Hikma (lit., 'House of Wisdom') The institution established in Baghdad by the ABBASID Caliph al-Mamun (d. 833) to translate philosophical and scientific works of antiquity into Arabic. There was also an observatory attached to the institution.

Bayt al-Mal The traditional 'treasury' of the Muslim community. The wealth flowing into the expanding Muslim state in early history was deposited for appropriate distribution to serve for the welfare of Muslims.

bazaar Word of Persian origin meaning 'market' or 'place of commerce'. Over time, bazaars were organized as a central feature of most Muslim cities, towns and business centres, including elaborate covered areas similar to those still found in cities such as Damascus, Istanbul, Fez and Tehran.

Begums of Bhopal Women rulers of Bhopal, a state in central India, between 1819 and 1926, the last of whom, Begum Sultan Johan, abdicated in 1926. They were all well known for their scholarship and their patronage of MOGHUL architecture and gardens, which survive to our day.

Bektashiyya A Sufi order originating in Turkey. Its founding is attributed to Haji Bektash Wali, a Sufi of the thirteenth century from Anatolia. In time the order became organized and institutionalized, reflecting a specific ritual activity, form of dress and the establishment of the *tekke*, centres of residence and devotional activity. From Turkey, the Bektashi order spread to the Balkans. It remains active in both regions as well as in many other parts of the world.

Bengal *See* BANGLADESH.

Bengali An Indo-European language spoken by over 200 million Muslims in BANGLADESH and the state of Bengal in India and by migrants in Britain, North America and elsewhere. From its formative period in the tenth century, Bengali Muslim literature has developed a number of genres to express the historical, religious, cultural and literary traditions of Islam among Bengali-speaking Muslims.

Benin West African country whose capital is Porto Novo. Benin has an estimated Muslim population of about 2 million, about 15 per cent of the total population. The spread and growth of Islam, mostly in the last two centuries, has been accomplished by Muslim merchants or Sufi teachers from neighbouring Muslim areas and is concentrated in the north-western part of the country.

Berbers Group of non-Arab peoples in North Africa who make up the base populations of Morocco and Algeria. They became Islamized following the spread of Islam to North Africa after the seventh century. There are numerous Berber dialects and a well-developed tradition of folklore and literature. *See also* TUAREG.

Bhutto, Benazir Prime minister of Pakistan twice from 1988 to 1990 and 1993 to 1996, the first woman to be so elected. She was the daughter of the former Pakistani prime minister Zulfikar Ali Bhutto, whose Pakistan People's Party was in power until 1977, when he was imprisoned and subsequently executed.

Benazir Bhutto returned from exile to Pakistan in 2007 to contest the premiership but was assassinated following an election rally.

Bible The Quran affirms the scriptures of the Jews and Christians, referring to the Hebrew Bible as 'Tawrat' and the Christian scriptures as 'Injil'. It also makes reference to the Psalms of David, called 'Zabur'. These are believed to have been revealed by God in their original form, but to have subsequently undergone revision.

bida Some Muslim scholars regard *bida* as innovation, signifying the introduction of something new into practice for which there is no precedent. The concept was developed primarily by Sunni jurists to argue whether an innovation might be considered good or bad, but for more conservative scholars all *bida* held a wholly negative connotation.

Bihishti Zewar (lit., 'Heavenly Ornaments') A book of instruction, religious teaching and appropriate conduct for Muslim women. It was written in Urdu by an Indian Muslim scholar, Mawlana Ashraf Ali Thanawi, in the early 1900s and reflects an attempt to represent a traditional view of Muslim behaviour appropriate to the changing environment of Muslim Indian life under British influence.

Bihzad Fifteenth/sixteenth-century miniaturist. Bihzad is associated with the SAFAWID dynasty in Iran. His miniatures and calligraphic works are considered to be among the finest artistic achievements of the age. He influenced many pupils and his output was copied extensively.

Bilal (*fl.* c. 650–700) One of the earliest converts of African origin to Islam, and the first MUEZZIN of Islam. According to Muslim tradition, Bilal was a slave whose owner tortured him and forced him to remain in the hot sun all day with a rock on his chest in an attempt to make him renounce Islam. Instead of denying his faith, he affirmed God's unity by repeating 'One, One!' Bilal was purchased by ABU BAKR, who deplored the treatment he had received and freed him. Muhammad chose Bilal to call the faithful to prayer and he served Abu Bakr in that capacity as well. Because of his role in defending Islam and as a companion of the Prophet, he is accorded great respect and honoured in Muslim tradition.

Bilqis *See* SHEBA, QUEEN OF.

bimaristan A word of Persian origin denoting a hospital in Muslim medical tradition. Virtually every major dynasty and ruler in Islamic history founded or established institutions for the care of the sick. *Bimaristans* were well endowed, often by individuals, staffed by attendant physicians and included pharmacies and other facilities for patients.

bint Component of many Arabic names which signifies 'daughter of'. The masculine form is *ibn*.

birth control Since the Prophet is known to have permitted birth control, most Muslims regard contraception in its various forms as acceptable. There have, however, in modern times been differences of opinion about the various methods available. In general, though, except for the use of abortion, Muslim scholars have been supportive of family planning initiatives.

al-Biruni, Muhammad ibn Ahmad Abu Rayhan (973–1050) Scholar of encyclopedic knowledge. While at the court of MAHMUD OF GHAZNA in Central Asia he produced works on mathematics, history, astronomy, botany, zoology and science. He also translated classics of Sanskrit literature into Arabic during his trips to India, writing a major work on the region which included a description of Indian religions. He wrote extensively and the total number of his works is estimated to be almost 200. Called *al-ustadh*, the teacher, by his biographers, he was in contact with IBN SINA, with whom he shares the distinction of being one of the great Muslim scientists of the medieval period.

Black Stone A stone set within the outside wall of the KA'BA and touched or kissed by pilgrims during the HAJJ.

Bohoras Community of ISMAILIYYA, most of whom live in the Indian subcontinent. The Bohoras were converted to Islam by Muslim preachers from about the eleventh century onwards. They belong to the line of Ismailism that gave allegiance to al-Mustali after 1094 and are also known as Mustali Tayyibi Ismailis (*see also* MUSTA-LIYYA). In 1539 their head, who is designated as Dai al-Mutlaq or Sayyidina Saheb, moved from Yemen to India The present leader is Dr Mohammed Burhanuddin, who lives in Mumbai and provides leadership to an international community, encouraging its social development and solidarity as well as a strong tradition of learning.

Bornu Region in West Africa. In the sixteenth and seventeenth centuries it constituted a Muslim kingdom whose ruler had the title 'Mai'. Today it is a province in north-east Nigeria.

Borujerdi, Muhammad Husayn (1875–1962) Imami Shia theologian in Iran. At the time of his death, Borujerdi was regarded as the most outstanding scholar and identified as the MARJA AL-TAQLID, the source of emulation and a reference point of scholarly authority.

Bosnia-Herzegovina Newly established state, formerly part of Yugosla-

Sherefudin's white mosque, Visoko, Bosnia-Herzegovina.

via. The Muslim population (representing approximately 40 per cent of the total) has always coexisted with Orthodox and Roman Catholic Christians in the region. Most of the people share a common Serbo-Croatian ethnic and linguistic heritage. Islam spread to the region during the fifteenth to the nineteenth centuries. Muslim influence is reflected in the arts, culture and architecture of the area. In 1992 Bosnia declared independence from Yugoslavia and the various groups in the region became engulfed in a brutal civil war across many sectarian lines. Bosnian Serbs aided by fellow Serbs from Yugoslavia embarked on a brutal policy against Muslims. The persecution and suffering of Bosnian Muslims aroused worldwide indignation which eventually led to international intervention. Some of the major perpetrators of massacres against Muslims have since been brought to justice before an International Court of Law in The Hague.

Bourguiba, Habib (1903–2000) Leader of Tunisia's independence movement and the country's first president from 1957 to 1987.

Brunei A sultanate located on the north-west coast of Borneo. Islam is considered the national religion and approximately 63 per cent of the population (a majority of which is Malay) is Muslim of the Shafii SCHOOL OF ISLAMIC LAW. Islam's influence was first felt as early as the fourteenth century by the Brunei Malays when the Sultan of Johore installed one of their leaders as sultan. Full political sovereignty was achieved in 1984. In 1990 Brunei, at the urging of the sultan, adopted the concept of Malay Islamic Monarchy (*Melayu Islam Beraja*), which emphasizes three elements: strict observance of Islam, the distinctive nature of Brunei culture and the sovereignty of the monarchy. There continues to be, however, discussion concerning the role Islam should play in the affairs and governance of the state and an equitable use of its oil wealth.

Bukhara Muslim city in present-day Uzbekistan. Famous in the past as a hub of culture and trade, it came under Muslim rule in the eighth century and, in time, acquired a reputation as a centre of learning. It became the capital of an Uzbek sultanate after 1500 and remained in their control until Russia attempted to seize it in the Bolshevik Revolution of 1917. Bukhara eventually became part of the Uzbek Socialist Soviet Republic and, following the disintegration of the Soviet Union, the Republic of Uzbekistan. More recently some of its major historical monuments have undergone extensive restoration.

al-Bukhari, Muhammad Ibn Ismail (810–870) One of the foremost Sunni collectors of traditions concerning the Prophet. Already during his lifetime he was considered a great authority on the subject. He travelled throughout Arabia, Egypt, Iraq and Syria in order to record sayings of the Prophet, reportedly collecting 600,000, of which he only considered a small percentage worthy of inclusion in his work, the *Sahih*. This work is regarded as one of the major sources of HADITH in the Sunni tradition and is among the six canonical collections. According to the author, he included only traditions of the highest reliability in his *Sahih*. The traditions are arranged according to subject.

Bulgaria Eastern European nation with a Christian majority representing 80 per cent of the population but with an important Sunni minority who follow the Hanafi SCHOOL OF ISLAMIC LAW. Ethnically and religiously diverse, Islamic influence in the region dates back to the OTTOMAN EMPIRE, during which period many converted to Islam. Islam has experienced a dramatic increase in both membership and activity in Bulgaria since the end of communism there in 1991 and the subsequent freedom granted to religious minorities.

burial *See* CEMETERY; FUNERAL PRACTICES.

burka, burkha or **burqa** *See* HIJAB.

Burkina Faso African nation formerly known as Upper Volta, Burkina Faso became independent from France in 1960. It has a Muslim population representing approximately 25 per cent of the total and is a member of the ORGANIZATION OF THE ISLAMIC CONFERENCE (OIC). A recent Muslim resurgence has had more social than political impact and the growing influence of Arabicization seems to indicate the presence of reformist tendencies.

Burma *See* MYANMAR.

Buyids or **Buwayhids** A dynasty which ruled Iraq and Iran from 934 until about 1055. The Buyids controlled lands still nominally under ABBASID sovereignty. However, while recognizing the Abbasid caliphs, they styled themselves sultans, taking on extravagant titles to indicate their power. Generally regarded as Shia in orientation, the Buyids created a major alternative sphere of political and intellectual influence.

Byzantium 'Byzantine Empire' is the term conventionally used since the nineteenth century to describe the Greek-speaking part of the Roman Empire during the Middle Ages. Its capital was Constantinople. Its history was influenced by its contacts, as well as conflicts, with Muslim dynasties and the expansion of Islam in regions formerly under Byzantine rule. The Arabic word used to refer to Byzantine and Byzantines is 'Rum', which appears in the Quran (30:1–5) as well as in many traditions attributed to the Prophet Muhammad. Rum also often features in the vast Muslim historical literature where the splendours of the Byzantine court and its ceremonies and the administrative and military organization of the empire are often described in great detail. Constantinople in particular was the subject of much admiration because of its architecture. There were important influences and artistic exchanges between Byzantium and the Muslim world. In 1453, the OTTOMAN Sultan MEHMED II captured Constantinople and made it his new capital, henceforth called Istanbul. The Orthodox Patriarchate continued to be based there, though the main Orthodox church, Hagia Sophia, came to be a mosque and its Christian illustrations were covered over. Its architectural and monumental style would be echoed in later Ottoman architecture. Today the Christian illustrations are once again visible to the public, recalling its past heritage and present status as a crossroads of many civilizational influences.

C

Cairo Traditional and present-day capital of Egypt. Since the thirteenth century Cairo has retained its status as an important centre of the Muslim world. The Arab invasion in 643 led to the first permanent settlement of Muslims at Fustat. The site was transformed into a capital city under the name of al-Qahira by the FATIMID dynasty in 970, since when Cairo has always functioned as a significant reference point for its traditions of culture, education, political power and influence. Cairo acquired particular prominence after the advance of the MONGOLS and the fall of Baghdad in the thirteenth century, taking over as the centre of Muslim learning and giving refuge to those escaping the invasion in the East. It contains some of the best-known mosques and centres of learning in Muslim history, among which those of the Fatimid and MAMLUK periods are particularly prominent.

calendar The Muslim calendar is a lunar calendar and is based on the cycle of the phases of the moon. It is independent of seasons. The names of the Muslim months are:

1. Muharram
2. Safar
3. Rabi al-Awwal
4. Rabi al-Thani
5. Jumad al-Ula
6. Jumad al-Thani
7. Rajab
8. Sha'ban
9. Ramadan
10. Shawwal
11. Dhu al-Qa'da
12. Dhu al-Hijja

It is believed that every month starts with the actual local sighting of the new crescent. That is why the Muslim months fall on different Gregorian months each year.

The Muslim *hijri* calendar (usually indicated as AH) dates from the year 622, the year marking the migration of the Prophet from Mecca to Medina. *See also* HIJRA.

caliph (Arabic, *khalifa*) Used in the Quran in reference to Adam in his custodial capacity on earth (2:28) and also to David (38:25). In the sense of deputy or successor to the Prophet it was first applied to ABU BAKR, who led the Muslim community after the Prophet's death. Abu Bakr and his successors Umar, Uthman and Ali are known as the RIGHTLY GUIDED CALIPHS because they had known the Prophet and patterned their lives after him. In 1924, following the disintegration of the OTTOMAN EMPIRE and the creation of the Republic of Turkey, the new assembly abolished the title, which is no longer in use in the Muslim world for any political leader. In recent times some Muslim groups have made the restoration of a true CALIPHATE one of their goals.

Caliphate (Arabic, *Khilafat*) The office of leadership that emerged in the Muslim community upon the death of the Prophet Muhammad in 632. The holder of the position came to be known as a CALIPH.

The definition and role of the Caliphate underwent many changes as different forms of leadership evolved, as did the type of authority assumed or in some cases assigned to the caliph. The primary functions of a good caliph, as articulated in Sunni sources, were to ensure the security and welfare of those he ruled, ensure the proper application of the SHARIA, and supervise the administration and governance of the territory under his rule.

The last of the great Sunni Caliphates, the OTTOMAN sultans, held this office for several centuries before the formal aboliton of the Caliphate by the new Turkish National Assembly in 1924. *See also* IMAM/IMAMA.

calligraphy The aesthetic, artistic rendering of the Arabic script is one of the foremost of the fine arts among Muslims. A number of classic styles of calligraphy evolved in different parts of the Muslim world, but the tradition has continued to be inspired by artistic creativity which has generated a multitude of ways and techniques for representing the Arabic script.

The tradition of Quranic calligraphy has developed over a thousand years and is represented in thousands of manuscripts preserved both in the Muslim world and in museums worldwide. *See also* QURAN.

Cameroon West African country. Muslims, representing the Sunni Maliki SCHOOL OF ISLAMIC LAW, constitute approximately 25 per cent of the population. Since independence in 1980 the incorporation of religious education into the Cameroon education system has grown significantly and programmes featuring Muslim culture and teaching are now broadcast on national radio.

caravanserai Places along the caravan routes which served as rest stations and places for commercial transactions on the ancient trading routes of the Muslim world. The most common form has a central courtyard surrounded by guest rooms on its four sides and other areas of common use for prayer, bathing, storage and commercial activities.

cemetery Muslim burial practices have led to the creation of cemeteries on the outskirts of most towns, cities and villages in the Muslim world. The cemetery is a place of respect, where prayers may be said for those who have died and as a reminder of the inevitability of death and judgement. *See also* FUNERAL PRACTICES.

Rüstem Pasha Caravanserai, Edirne, Turkey.

Chad West African state. More than half the estimated population of 6 million is Muslim. A significant percentage of the country's Muslims speak Arabic, influenced by the spread of Islam by Arabic-speaking immigrants from the twelfth century onwards. Chad became independent from France in 1960. More recently, because of political tensions, large numbers of refugees from neighbouring SUDAN have sought shelter in Chad.

chador *See* HIJAB.

charity *See* SADAQA; WAQF; ZAKAT.

Chechnya Region in the central Caucasus, now part of Russia. It is inhabited by Chechen Muslims, who were first converted in the seventeenth and eighteenth centuries. They resisted Russian advances fiercely but were finally overcome in 1859. More recently the Chechen people have sought greater autonomy, which has resulted in military conflict with the Russian government. In 1994 the Russian military attacked and bombed Grozny, the capital of Chechnya, in order to put down the rebellion. While the intensity of the conflict has lessened to a certain extent, efforts by groups of Chechens to seek independence from the RUSSIAN FEDERATION continue.

China There are approximately 40 million Muslims in China, representing 5 per cent of the population. The two major groups are the Hui (who are Chinese and dispersed throughout China) and the Xingjian (ethnic groups outside the Hui who are also separate in language and culture and are found, for the most part, in the north-west frontier region). Islam was initially introduced to China along the south-

A Donxian Muslim descends the stairs to the front gate of Mufti Gonbe in Gansu Province, China.

eastern coast by Arab and Persian traders sometime during the Tang dynasty (618–907). Since 1979 20,000 mosques have been opened and over a million copies of the Quran have been distributed. As a result of pressure from various countries and human-rights advocates, the Chinese government began establishing relationships with Muslim states in 1989. The implications of this process for Chinese Muslims and whether they will benefit from greater liberalization and economic development in China remain to be seen.

Chiragh Ali (1844–1895) Indian Muslim intellectual who advocated reform in the development and adaptation of Muslim jurisprudence to meet contemporary needs. He also tended to dismiss most of the conclusions of traditional Muslim jurists, believing that the stipulations of medieval legal systems could not be applicable to the conditions of modern Indian Muslim life under the British.

Chishtiyya Sufi order. Chishtiyya was believed to have been founded in Ajmer, in the north-west of India, by Muin al-Din Chishti (1141–1236). The eponym, however, is the Chisht village near Herat in western Afghanistan, which is said to be where the founder of the order, the Syrian Khwaja Abu Ishaq, settled. It is one of the most widely organized groups, and is found in various parts of India. Its teachings and institutions were spread by Chishti disciples and devotees led in particular by Farid al-Din Ganj-i-Shakar (d. 1265) and Nizam al-Din Awliya (d. 1325). Among the devotional practices common to the Chishtiyya are the recitation of divine names, in concert or silently, retreats, and the use of chanting and music. There is an extensive literature attributed to the various figures in the tradition.

Christianity Christians are acknowledged in the Quran as 'People of the Book' (AHL AL-KITAB), to whom revelation was granted through Jesus. Christianity lost its position as the majority religion in various areas that eventually came to be dominated by the Muslim presence. A number of Christian communities, however, continued to live and thrive under Muslim rule in the Middle East and Europe.

circumcision The practice of circumcision of male children, while not mentioned in the Quran, is generally accepted as being in accord with Prophetic practice. Most modern Muslims oppose female circumcision, which they argue represents historically an indigenous custom in some parts of the world to which Islam has spread, but one which has no sanction at all in Islam.

clothing See HIJAB.

commerce See TRADE.

Comoros Island nation off the east coast of Africa. The four largest islands declared themselves independent from France in 1975 and after a brief period as a secular nation became a federal Islamic republic in 1978. Islam was a dominant cultural force even before the Comoros became a French colony. The French were careful not to interfere with existing Muslim tradition and encouraged adherence to the SHARIA. Most of its 500,000 population are Muslim, a majority of whom are Sunni and follow SHAFIIYYA rituals in respect to marriage and divorce. Iranian-trained Sunni Muslim cleric Ahmed Abdallah Mohamed Sambi, popularly known as 'the Ayatollah', became the Comoran leader in the first peaceful change of power in the country's post-independence history. In May 2006 he was elected president with 58 per cent of the vote.

Companions of the Prophet (Arabic, *sahaba*) A description generally applied to those who were closest to the Prophet in his lifetime. By extension, the title then referred to the Muslims with him and, in time, anyone who had seen him. Their closeness to the Prophet and their important role in supporting him and in the events of the early history of Islam render them historically significant. They are believed to have played a key role in the transmission of the prophetic tradition. Interest in the companions and their role in Muslim history and learning prompted the writing of biographical literature in which a pattern of relative rankings was developed. The four RIGHTLY GUIDED CALIPHS (Abu Bakr, Umar, Uthman and Ali), other prominent figures who fought alongside the Prophet and those who supported him during the difficult times are considered to be among the *sahaba*. After the time of Caliph Umar, *sahaba* or their descendants received prominence because of the economic and social privileges accorded to some of them by the developing state structure, such as entitlement to and ownership of newly conquered lands and properties.

Constantinople Capital of BYZANTIUM. Although the growing Muslim Caliphate was taking over the majority of former Byzantine territories, the capital itself fell under Muslim rule only in 1453 when it was conquered by the Ottoman Sultan MEHMED II. He is thus known as Mehmed the Conqueror. Upon the conquest it became the new capital of the thriving OTTOMAN EMPIRE, and came to be known as Istanbul.

Constitution of Medina *See* TOLERANCE.

conversion In its Quranic context, conversion takes place when God's guidance is accepted freely and the convert is committed to act in accordance with this guidance. At another level, conversion can also be an act of inner transformation, which can be a result of a personal, inner search complemented by divine favour. In its formal aspect, conversion takes place through the affirmation of the SHAHADA, attesting belief in one God and acceptance of the Prophet Muhammad as God's messenger.

Muslim emigration and conquest was accompanied by a process of conversion of people in newly settled territories. It was a relatively gradual process in most areas and was undertaken primarily by traders, mystics and scholars, very often from among those native to these regions who had initially converted. Conversion to Islam remains ongoing, particularly in parts of Africa, Asia, North America and Europe.

Córdoba Spanish city. During Muslim rule in Andalusia, it became a flourishing cultural centre and capital of the UMAYYAD Caliphate. It is renowned for its architectural monuments, such as the Great Mosque (La Mezquita) begun in 787, and the Madinat al-Zahra, the administrative city. Noted scholars of all faiths, such as IBN HAZM, IBN RUSHD and the Jewish philosopher Moses MAIMONIDES, studied in the city and contributed to its importance as an intellectual and cultural centre.

Côte d'Ivoire West African state. Côte d'Ivoire gained independence from France in 1960. It is estimated that 30 per cent of the population is Muslim, a majority of whom are Sunni of the Maliki SCHOOL OF ISLAMIC LAW. Members of this community belong to one of three Sufi brotherhoods: QADIRIYYA, TIJANIYYA, and SANUSIYYA (in order of dominance). Most of the Muslim population is found in the north-west of the country.

Crusades European Christian military expeditions undertaken from 1096 onwards with the aim of the capturing the 'Holy Land' under Muslim rule. While Palestine was recaptured by SALAH AL-DIN AL-AYYUB (Saladin) after an initial loss, the Crusaders had gained Sicily and the majority of the Iberian Peninsula by the thirteenth century. The Crusades, though they essentially failed in their military objectives, did in effect have some positive results in terms of the exchange of knowledge and increase in trade and commerce between Europe and the Muslim world. The first Crusade (1096–1099) was the most effective among them, for the Crusaders managed to establish four states in the Holy Land and territories around it. The rest were insignificant military campaigns which had little impact on the Muslim world of the time.

Cyprus Mediterranean island state. Cyprus was first conquered by the Muslims in 647, but oscillated between Muslim and BYZANTINE control. Cyprus remained under Byzantine auspices for the most part until the CRUSADES, when it was captured by a coalition of princes led by the English King Richard the Lionheart. It came under OTTOMAN rule in 1573. Great Britain occupied and administered Cyprus from 1879 to 1959. It became independent in 1960. Various differences between the Greek and Turkish Cypriot communities led to military conflict and in 1964 the United Nations sent in a peacekeeping force. Eventually, in 1974, following a military coup by Greek officers, Turkish troops intervened, creating a division of the island into Turkish and Greek zones that remains today.

Daghistan Multinational republic in the Caucasus region. Daghistan is bordered on one side by the mountains and on the other by the Caspian Sea. Though initial contact with Muslims dates back to the eighth century, more significant developments in Islamization took place under Timurid (*see* TAMERLANE) and OTTOMAN rule. In 1920 it was absorbed into the Soviet Union but is now an autonomous republic of the RUSSIAN FEDERATION.

Dahlan, Kiyai Haji Ahmad *See* MUHAMMADIYYA.

dai (pl., *duat*) One who summons or calls for a particular cause. The word commonly refers to the propagandists and missionaries of the Shia, in particular the Ismailis. *See also* ISMAILIYYA; DA'WA; FATIMIDS.

Damascus Also called 'al-Sham' in Arabic, it is the present-day capital of Syria. It was earlier a BYZANTINE city when conquered by the Muslim general KHALID IBN AL-WALID in 635. Upon assuming the Caliphate, MUAWIYYA IBN ABI SUFYAN, the rebel governor of Syria, established Damascus as the capital of the UMAYYAD dynasty (661–750). Damascus became one of the most important cities of the Muslim world, producing many influential scholars and thinkers. The city is still a place of pilgrimage for Shia Muslims in particular because it is the site of the tomb of Zaynab, sister of HASAN and HUSAYN IBN ALI. Also among its most significant monuments are the Great Mosque, the mausoleum of SALAH AL-DIN (Saladin) and several historical mosques and *madrasas*. The great mosque contains the shrine of JOHN THE BAPTIST.

Dan Fodio, Uthman *See* UTHMAN DAN FODIO.

Dar al-Hikma (lit., 'House of Wisdom') An academy of learning. Concentrating on the sciences and philosophy, it was created by the FATIMIDS in Cairo in 1005. In addition to an extensive library, it provided a place of meeting and discussion for scholars representing many specialties including religion, law, philosophy, mathematics and the sciences. When the Fatimid dynasty was ended by SALAH AL-DIN (Saladin), he closed the institution.

Dar al-Islam (lit., 'House of Islam') Traditionally the territory and regions in which Muslims predominated or over which they exercised political rule.

Dara Shikoh (1615–1659) Eldest son of the MOGHUL Emperor SHAH JAHAN and a practising Sufi and noted scholar. Dara Shikoh wrote extensively on spiritual themes and subjects and was also committed to synthesizing aspects of Hindu and Muslim spirituality. His best-known work in that regard is *Majma al-Bahrayn* (*The Merging of Two Streams*). His younger brothers, who opposed both his religious views and his candidacy as emperor, mounted a military campaign against him and, after his capture, had Dara Shikoh executed on a charge of heresy.

Darfur Region in the western part of SUDAN that has in recent history become the centre of a major humanitarian disaster, afflicting the several million Muslims who live in the midst of conflict and severe economic deprivation. The region, like most of the country, has suffered from the devastating consequences of a long civil war. Militias from outside the province have been largely responsible for displacing the population and creating the conditions that have intensified internecine conflict and the ensuing crises of hunger and disease. International efforts to end the insecurity and violence have been generally unsuccessful.

darwish A term used in Persian and Turkish to connote a Sufi. More particularly it has also been used to refer to the adherents of the MEVLEVI order.

al-Darzi, Muhammad ibn Ismail *See* DRUZE.

Darziyya *See* DRUZE.

da'wa (lit., 'invitation' or 'call') In the Quran and among certain Muslim groups *da'wa* came to signify the summoning of people to the practice of true Islam as well as to a particular political cause, as in the case of the ABBASIDS in the eighth century. Among the FATIMIDS, the *da'wa* was the formal institution responsible for preaching and for education. Its use has continued to modern times among Muslims to indicate the continuing goal of preaching and inviting to Islam. The agent of the *da'wa* is called DAI.

Day of Judgement Referred to in the Quran as the event that will mark a final reckoning for individuals as well as peoples.

death The universality and inevitability of death is acknowledged and taught in the Quran, but as part of a greater divine design where death is a critical event in human life as a passage to an afterlife. Human life is therefore a preparation for the reality and eventuality of death, which is also seen as a return to the place of ultimate origin, that is, in spiritual terms, to the source which is God. At the time of death, Muslims invoke the Quranic affirmation 'from God we are and to Him is our return'.

Death is to be accompanied by appropriate prayers, ritual purification and burial, for it is envisaged that those who die having lived a good life will be rewarded.

Death and the afterlife constitute important subjects for discussion and debate in Muslim thought, from law and theology to philosophy and mysticism, and, although there are significant differences regarding issues related to death among Muslim scholars, there runs through Muslim tradition the common conviction that death does not represent a diminishing of human life but rather an enhancement of

the ethical purpose for which human beings were created. *See also* FUNERAL PRAC-
TICES.

Delhi City in northern India. For a long time from the thirteenth century onwards
it served as the capital of Muslim rulers in India. Among the architectural monuments for which it has become well known are the QUTB MINAR, the Jami Mosque, the
Red Fort, the buildings associated with the burial site of the great Sufi NIZAM AL-DIN
AWLIYA and the tomb of the MOGHUL Emperor Humayun. 'Old Delhi', as this traditional quarter has come to be known, has now been surpassed as the political and
commercial centre by New Delhi, the present capital of India. However, many of the
monuments and spaces are undergoing restoration and revitalization.

Demak Capital city of the first Muslim state in Java in the fifteenth century. It is the
site of an historically important mosque built in the Javanese architectural tradition.

Deoband A city in the state of Uttar Pradesh, India. The origin of its name is often
associated with the ancient temple of Devi situated in the city. Deoband boasts
numerous mosques and other buildings of religious and historical importance,
but today it is predominantly famous for its centre of Muslim religious learning,
the Dar al-Ulum. Established in 1867, this provides education and training in Quranic, legal and intellectual sciences for Sunni scholars. It has continued to produce
eminent scholars and leading members of an important organization of Muslims in
India known as the Jamiat Ulama-i-Hind, and its conservative influence extends to
many Muslims who have migrated from the subcontinent.

Dervish Pasha (d. 1603) Soldier, author and an OTTOMAN Grand Vizier. A Muslim
of Bosnian origin, Dervish Pasha served as commander of the Ottoman army on the
Hungarian front in the war in Europe against the Austrian Habsburgs. He was also a
noted poet and writer in Turkish.

dhikr ('lit., 'remembrance' or 'reminder') This practice of remembering God is mentioned often in the Quran as a form of personal and private PRAYER of devotion to
God: 'You who believe, remember God very often' (Quran 33:41).
   Among Sufis and other Muslims who practise contemplation and personal meditation, the use of *dhikr* has come to be a means of attaining spiritual experience and
closeness to God.

Dhimmi *See* AHL AL-DHIMMA.

Dhu Nun al-Misri (d. 861) Early Sufi teacher. Dhu Nun al-Misri was noted for his
efforts to provide practical guidance as well as for developing a systematic teaching
on how to attain spiritual progress. He was regarded as the head of the Sufis in his
time.

dietary rules *See* HALAL.

din Arabic term used in the Quran which has come to signify an encompassing
notion of 'religion' as the combination of a divinely ordained direction and obli-

gations fulfilled by human beings, as part of shared commitments expressed through a faith community.

divine inspiration *See* WAHY.

divorce Islam permits divorce in certain circumstances. The intention to divorce has to take into account a period of waiting known as *idda* consisting of three menstrual cycles to avoid pregnancy. Should the wife be pregnant, the divorce has to be postponed until the child is born. During this period the husband covers all her expenses. Divorce by mutual consent is also allowed and a petition of divorce by the wife may include grounds such as cruelty, impotence, apostasy, etc. It must be noted that each of the SCHOOLS OF ISLAMIC LAW has developed varying rules governing how divorce is to be effected and, in modern times, such aspects of personal law have been integrated and revised differently in different parts of the Muslim world.

diwan A system created by Caliph UMAR IBN AL-KHATTAB to organize and regulate the growing Muslim treasury and to disburse funds appropriately. *Diwan* also denotes a collection of poetry or prose.

Djibouti A small state in the Horn of Africa. The Republic of Djibouti, which won independence from France in 1977, is predominantly Muslim (94 per cent of the population), a majority of whom are Sunni.

Dome of the Rock *See* JERUSALEM.

Druze Religious community found primarily in present-day Lebanon, Syria and Israel. It arose in the eleventh century in Syria as an offshoot of the ISMAILIYYA but perceiving itself as a new religion. It emphasized the idea of the total and exclusive messianic role of Imam al-Hakim, one of the FATIMID Ismaili imams, after his death. The Druze regard themselves as monotheists and possess their own writings, spiritual leaders and scholars and distinctive practices.

The name Druze is commonly associated with one of the early leaders of the community and most vigorous missionaries of the new doctrine in Cairo, al-Darzi ('the tailor'). The doctrine, which was developed by a scholar named Hamza and developed further by al-Darzi, is transmitted within the community from generation to generation through initiated scholars. This teaching is mainly built on the letters of Hamza written between 1017 and 1020.

dua Form of devotional prayer generally distinguished from ritual PRAYER. Such prayers for blessings or appeals against calamity, including supplication and invocation, play an important part in the religious life of Muslim individuals as well as communities.

Durrani Afghan people and dynasty that ruled Afghanistan from 1747 to 1819. Ahmad Shah Durrani was their most important ruler.

durud A formulaic blessing of the Prophet in Arabic. It is recited as an act of devotion and piety.

education The Quran invoked knowledge as a key tool of human development and for understanding the divine purpose and a guided ethical life. There are also many traditions attributed to the Prophet encouraging the education of boys and girls and emphasizing the pursuit of learning as an important goal in life. Throughout history Muslims have established a variety of institutions of learning, ranging from traditional schools for Quranic instruction to major *madrasas* for training and teaching in law and theology to higher institutions of learning where a variety of other sciences were taught. Many rulers became patrons of learning, establishing educational institutions and observatories and providing support and patronage for individual scholars and scientists.

Many of these institutional patterns continue to provide education to Muslims in their religious formation and their respective heritages, but in the last 150 years or so new institutions patterned on schools and universities in the West have also been created. Perhaps no other area of social development among Muslims has received so much attention as education, but sadly these efforts have often proved inadequate and in many parts of the Muslim world levels of literacy continue to be relatively low, especially among females. Conversely, institutions devoted to religious training and learning have multiplied, in some cases supported by the state and propagating particular points of view. As a result of globalization many Muslims continue to seek education in different parts of the world and major Western universities and systems of education continue to be influential at all levels. *See also* AL-AZHAR UNIVERSITY; BAYT AL-HIKMA; DAR AL-HIKMA; MADRASA; UNIVERSITIES.

Egypt Middle Eastern state. Egypt is predominantly Muslim (90 per cent of the population), a majority of whom are Sunni. The Maliki SCHOOL OF ISLAMIC LAW is dominant in northern Egypt and the Shafii School in the south. Among other religious communities with a long history are the Coptic Christian (the largest), Greek Orthodox, Eastern and Latin Rite Catholic and Protestant. The majority of the former Jewish population has emigrated to Israel and North America.

Islam has been both a presence and a continuing influence in Egypt since 634, when it was conquered by Muslim armies and incorporated into the growing empire. Several dynasties have ruled the region, which attained major prominence in the medieval Muslim world under the FATIMIDS, who established Cairo as its capital. Following the downfall of the Fatimids, it was ruled by successive Muslim

A family visits and pays their respects at the tomb of Fatima al-Nabawiyya in Cairo, Egypt.

dynasties, the AYYUBIDS, the MAMLUKS and the OTTOMANS. The French army under Napoleon invaded Egypt in 1798, establishing a period of European involvement and occupation leading to British colonization in 1882, which finally ended in 1954, preparing the way for an independent Egyptian nation. (*See also* MUHAMMAD ALI.)

Modern Egyptian nationalism has been expressed through a linking of identity founded on the Arab heritage and language as well as a legacy combining Pharaonic, Christian and Muslim elements. The current political form of the state includes a multiparty elected parliament and an Islamic Advisory Council. The legal framework combines English common law, the Napoleonic Code and Muslim legal tradition. Islam is affirmed strongly by the state, but discontent continues to be expressed by groups with ISLAMIST tendencies, who are permitted some degree of political participation.

Eid or **Id** *See* ID AL-ADHA; ID AL-FITR.

Elijah (Arabic, Ilyas) He is referred to in the Quran as a messenger from God (37:123–132; 6:85) who preached to his people against the worship of Baal.

Elijah Muhammad *See* MUHAMMAD, ELIJAH.

Erbakan, Necmettin (b. 1926) Turkish politician who served as prime minister from 1996 to 1997. Erbakan served as head of the Refah Partisi (Welfare Party) and its subsequent off-shoots, which seek to legitimize Muslim politics and programmes, as envisaged by the original party platform.

Eritrea State in the Horn of Africa. Eritrea became fully independent in 1993 following a lengthy struggle while it was a province of Ethiopia. The region was the first outside the Arab peninsula to come into contact with Islam when it extended hospitality to early Muslims seeking refuge from persecution in the time of the Prophet. After Italian and British rule it was incorporated as an autonomous unit in Ethiopia in 1952. Today its population, estimated to be 4 million, is predominantly Muslim. The major languages are Tigre and Tigrinya. Most Muslims follow the Maliki or Hanafi SCHOOL OF ISLAMIC LAW, and among the Sufi orders in the region the largest is that of the Mirghaniyya.

eschatology Quranic teachings on the afterlife have been the subject of detailed elaboration in Muslim theological and philosophical writings. These include such topics as the DAY OF JUDGEMENT, DEATH, resurrection, HEAVEN, HELL and the intercession of God. This life is believed to be a preparation and a passage for the next. In relation to eschatology, Muslim thinkers have also discussed and debated issues around justice and accountability.

esotericism *See* ISMAILIYYA; SUFISM; TARIQA.

ethics In identifying core ethical perspectives, the Quran emphasizes the virtues of charity, compassion, sincerity, fulfilment of one's commitments, trust, patience and fortitude (as an example there is the oft-cited verse on righteousness, 2:177). As taught in the Quran and embodied in the Prophet's own behaviour and example, these and other virtues provide a foundation for proper ethical behaviour.

Such ethical values came to be articulated in several ways throughout Muslim history. First there was a process of elaboration and a determination of how such prescriptions and obligations could be formalized as part of the SHARIA, the code of conduct, articulated within the framework of law, through jurisprudence. Law and ethics thus became linked in Muslim thought and were translated into social and inter-personal obligations and prescriptions.

The second form of expression was more philosophical and was based on the application of rational, theological and philosophical analysis. The integration of the philosophical heritage of antiquity (including ancient Greek and classical philosophy, medicine and sciences, as well as the heritage of the ancient Mediterranean and the Near East) into Muslim culture gave rise to an intellectual science of ethical thought as part of Muslim philosophy. This tradition interpreted and enhanced the ancient tradition but also developed a synthesis appropriate for its own culture and civilization. Philosophical treatment of ethics is also considered under the rubric of *akhlaq* (lit., 'innate disposition', although in practice the scope is wider than this would imply), but ethical thought in general embraces political and social as well as legal aspects.

A third aspect of ethics in Islam has to do with the emergence of ADAB, which has many connotations, implicit in proper moral, ethical and social behaviour. *Adab* was characterized by values that had become the hallmark of a cosmopolitan Muslim civilization and not only embodied aspects of human behaviour and action but also implied proper learning, artistic understanding and cultural and aesthetic appreciation.

In modern times as Muslims have begun to address a wide range of emerging ethical issues, this pluralistic heritage provides a means to address the diversity of contexts and peoples that comprise the world of Islam and its changing conditions. *See also* SHARIA.

Ethiopia State in the Horn of Africa. Of the 60 million population in Ethiopia, approximately 50 per cent are Sunni Muslims who follow the Shafii SCHOOL OF ISLAMIC LAW. Muslims first entered Ethiopia in 615 when the Prophet Muhammad, to spare some of his followers from persecution, sent them across the Red Sea to the country then known as Abyssinia and the court of the Christian king, the Negus, who protected them even when the Meccans sent an envoy demanding their extradition. Islam has continued to be an integral part of Ethiopia throughout its history, coexisting with the earlier dominant Christian tradition, sometimes in conflict and struggle for political power. Ethiopia's civil and social life has been greatly influenced by Islamic law and culture. Islam also spread in the region through trade and the work of Sufi teachers and orders.

During the twentieth century Ethiopia experienced periods of rule by emperors, colonization by Italy, military coups and civil war as well as war with neighbouring Somalia. Central authority was challenged and eventually conceded the establishment of an independent ERITREA.

ethnicity *See* TOLERANCE.

Europe The Muslim presence in Europe dates back to the earliest period and is marked by contacts across Gibraltar that in time gave rise to the establishment of Muslim rule in Andalusia (*see* AL-ANDALUS) in the eighth century. Historical relations between Muslims and Europeans involve war and conflict such as the CRUSADES but also reflect cultural, scientific and artistic exchanges which proved mutually enriching. Many of these influences persist to our day in European languages, literature and art.

The battle of Poitiers in 732 represented Muslim attempts to extend their influence further into Europe. Over time, this influence would stretch across the Iberian Peninsula and parts of Italy but was ended by the SPANISH INQUISITION, as Muslims were forced either to leave or be assimilated. During the fourteenth and fifteenth centuries Muslim influence spread to the BALKANS under the OTTOMANS. Also, with the rise of MONGOL influence in Russia many Tatars and others among the populations in the Crimea and beyond had adopted Islam. With the fall of the Ottoman Empire and the rise of European colonialism and influence, control of these territories was lost, but Muslim populations remained in the region.

In the twentieth and twenty-first centuries there has been a marked flow of immigrants from Muslim regions in Africa and Asia to Western Europe. Their presence in most European countries complements that of other Muslims who have much longer and locally integral presence in Europe. This today includes the Muslims of Russia, Eastern Europe, France, Germany, Great Britain and various other countries. The total population of Muslims in Europe is estimated to be well over 30 million, of diverse background, historical as well as theological. Across Europe, as questions raised by the larger issues of migration, cultural integration, pluralism, citizenship and more recently EXTREMISM have become the focus of public attention, the Muslim population finds itself more affected by these than other immigrants to Europe.

extremism The phenomenon of extremism has in general affected most if not all societies and has had its basis in history, in politics and in social life as well as in religion.

In Muslim contexts the idea occurs in the writings of heresiographers, where the concept of exaggeration in belief or action was often used to stigmatize groups that did not meet a particular standard of orthodoxy. Such groups were then accused of being *ghulat* (exaggerators), a pejorative term meant to designate the extremism of their belief. Some Sunni writers used the term for Muslim groups, Shia or Sufi, with whose views they disagreed.

In more recent times extremism has come to be associated with Muslim groups whose ideological position, particularly on political matters, has led them to violent actions against those they disagree with, those in authority who are regarded as unlawful rulers and countries from the West, whose policies and actions are judged to be against Islam. Such extremist formulations and activities are limited to a very small minority, and their actions and views are generally condemned by the majority of Muslims as being outside the pale of Islam. Such extremist groups tend to spread their teachings and seek adherents primarily through websites or covert activity, particularly among younger Muslims.

F

Fakhr al-Din al-Razi *See* AL-RAZI, FAKHR AL-DIN.

falsafa *See* PHILOSOPHY.

faqih *See* ULAMA.

faqir Quranic term for a needy or very poor person. By extension the term was developed in the Muslim mystical tradition to connote persons so devoted to God that they had rejected material possessions.

al-Farabi, Abu Nasr (870–950) Eminent Muslim philosopher born in the region known as Turkestan, and known to the medieval West as Alfarabius or Abunaser. Al-Farabi was regarded among Muslim philosophers as 'the second teacher' because of the esteem in which he is held after Aristotle. His many works encompass commentaries on Aristotelian and Platonic thought, logic, metaphysics, ethics, political philosophy and other philosophical subjects. He saw his scholarly goal as framing the fundamental elements of Muslim thought within the context of philosophical and rational inquiry and developing a capacity within Islamic culture for the integration of philosophy as a method of analysis and an intellectual discipline. His works in political philosophy attempt to provide the means to establish an intellectual and rational framework for examining the relationship in state and society between virtue, ethics and the role of political leadership.

faraid The term for the defined and required portions of an estate, as enjoined by the Quran. *See also* INHERITANCE.

Farazdaq (640–c. 728) Poet of the early Muslim period. He was known for his satirical and panegyric verse and identified with support for the family of the Prophet.

fard An incumbent religious duty, applied in Muslim law to those acts regarded as obligatory.

Farewell Pilgrimage The Prophet Muhammad's last pilgrimage to Mecca in 632, in which he is said to have delivered his last sermon at Mount Arafat. The Muslim pilgrimage ceremony is designed on the basis of the rites performed during this pilgrimage, which include circumambulation of the KA'BA. The Prophet died soon after completing the pilgrimage.

Farrad Mohammed *See* NATION OF ISLAM.

Farrakhan, Minister Louis (b. 1933) Present leader of the NATION OF ISLAM, whose members claim to be following the true teachings of the founder, Elijah MUHAMMAD.

fasting The practice of fasting during the month of RAMADAN is enjoined by the Quran and is regarded in Muslim tradition as a major pillar of the faith. In addition to the month-long fast from dawn to sunset, Muslims optionally fast on other days, following the practice of the Prophet. *See* SAWM.

Fathy, Hassan (1899–1999) Egyptian architect. His work has influenced a revival of the basic principles of Muslim architectural practice that can be adapted to the everyday needs of communities. He encouraged a better understanding of vernacular styles, indigenous practices and the use of materials that were better suited to local conditions. His book *Architecture for the Poor* documents his effort to give concrete form to his ideas in designing the town of New Gourna and his frustrations with government bureaucracy and local politics. His legacy as an architect, planner and teacher has been continued by his many students.

al-Fatiha The opening chapter of the Quran. It is recited during the daily ritual and on many other occasions, particularly at the graveside. Its meaning may be rendered as follows:

> In the Name of God, most Gracious, most Merciful. Praise is for God, the Lord of all the Worlds, the Gracious, the Merciful, Sovereign of the Day of Judgement.

> We worship and ask only you for help. Guide us to the right path, the path of those you have graced, not of those with whom you are displeased nor of those who have gone astray.

Fatima (b. c. 614) Daughter of the Prophet and his first wife Khadija. Fatima is often referred to as Fatima al-Zahra (the radiant). She became the wife of ALI IBN ABI TALIB, the fourth caliph and the first imam of the Shia. Their sons HASAN and HUSAYN IBN ALI are held in high esteem by all Muslims and their descendants are considered as *sharifs*, an honorific for those who trace their ancestry back to the Prophet through his two grandsons. Among the Shia she is venerated as a figure of great piety and as one of the Five Pure Ones (*see* PANJ TAN-I PAK).

Fatimids Shia Ismaili dynasty which ruled in Egypt and North Africa from 908 to 1171. The name derives from the connection of its rulers to FATIMA, the daughter of the Prophet. In this way, the Fatimids claimed to be the rightful heirs to Muslim rule. At its height, Fatimid sovereignty extended to many parts of the Middle East, the Mediterranean and parts of India. The period of Fatimid rule is particularly noteworthy for its cultural, scientific and economic achievements.

fatwa Legal opinion rendered by a Muslim scholar regarded as having appropriate status and training. Such opinions may be sought from scholars who are known as MUFTI in the Sunni tradition and as *mujtahid* (*see* IJTIHAD) among the Shia, but are not necessarily binding.

While the idea originated in the need to provide religiously credible and well-established responses to questions of practice of the faith and daily behaviour, the concept developed throughout Muslim history into a more formal, legal notion. The *mufti* acted in a consultative capacity in Muslim courts as well as interpreting Islamic law as an appointed official of the state. The practice of issuing a *fatwa* has continued in modern times as a mechanism for dealing with personal, social, legal and religious issues.

festivals *See* ASHURA; ID AL-ADHA; ID AL-FITR; MAWLID AL-NABI; NAVRUZ.

Fez Moroccan city, capital of the Merinid (or Marinid) dynasty of Morocco from the mid-thirteenth to mid-fifteenth century. It is a city of significance because of the historical preservation of its traditional urban character. It is said to have been established by Idris II, the founder of the IDRISID dynasty. Among its best-known religious monuments is the QARAWIYYIN mosque, one of the oldest in the region, which also developed into a major centre of learning of law and theology, particularly under the Sunni Maliki SCHOOL OF ISLAMIC LAW.

Fihr *See* QURAYSH.

al-Fihri, Fatima bint Muhammad *See* QARAWIYYIN.

finance *See* GRAMEEN BANK; INTEREST; ISLAMIC BANKING; RIBA.

fiqh The Muslim science of jurisprudence, including its logic, methodology and applicability. Four major Sunni schools of Muslim law emerged, varying to some extent with regard to the details of interpretation and application of *fiqh*. Shia schools of jurisprudence emphasize the role of IJTIHAD and rely on Prophetic traditions as well as the teachings of their imams.

The composite body of law produced by the science is referred to as the SHARIA. An expert in jurisprudence is called a *faqih*. *See also* USUL AL-FIQH.

Firdawsi (940–1020) Persian poet who is credited with being the founder of the Persian epic poem. His best known work is the SHAHNAMA (*Epic of the Kings*), which narrates the stories and legends associated with the pre-Islamic rulers of Iran. It is regarded as one of the great epics of Persian literature.

FIS The Front Islamique du Salut, an ALGERIAN Muslim political party known in English as the Islamic Salvation Front. Initially it was an organization that rallied Muslims who were seeking an alternative in Algeria to the failed economic, social and political policies of the socialist regime. The organization became an officially registered political party in 1989 and constituted one of the main opposition groups to the existing government. After a successful campaign in local elections in 1990, the FIS was expected to win overwhelming support in the national elections the following year. Anticipating this eventuality, members of the army staged a coup, bringing about a military regime and disbanding the FIS. This was followed by recurring deadly violence between factions which represent 'Islamist' views and the government, which in many ways paralysed civil institutions and society in

Algeria. More recently there has been some restoration of order in the country and attempts at reconciliation.

fitna A calamity or period of divisive anarchy. This refers in particular, in Muslim history, to the discord and conflict that occurred among early Muslims following the death of the third caliph, UTHMAN IBN AFFAN, and which led to civil war.

food See HALAL.

France Since French censuses do not record religious affiliation it is difficult to estimate the number of Muslims who live in France. The estimate varies from 5 to 7 per cent of the population, thus ranging from 3 to 4 million. Muslims settled and created communities in a region in southern France over a forty-year period during the eighth century and during the tenth century tried, unsuccessfully, to gain dominion. Many Muslim traders and merchants entered France during the Middle Ages and Spanish Muslims, deported at the beginning of the seventeenth century, moved beyond the Pyrenees. Migration and military excursions, trade and France's colonizing activities in Africa have made Islam an integral part of French history. The most recent population of Muslims consists of migrants and workers from the Maghreb, West Africa and other parts of the Muslim world influenced by French presence.

Fulbe or **Fulani** (sing., Fula) Muslim peoples of West Africa, particularly in the region of the Gambia and neighbouring area. In the nineteenth century they constituted an important part of the state created by UTHMAN DAN FODIO.

fundamentalism The general notion is derived from the reaction of some American Protestants in the nineteenth century to what they perceived as an erosion of core Christian beliefs and values in the face of changes brought about by scientific and other forms of knowledge that were having a strong influence on patterns of thought in the societies of the time. In response, they developed a core set of fundamentals that they believed to be unchanging and unchangeable.

This idea has come to be applied to tendencies in other religious traditions, including Islam, when the response to changes in modern times echoes this emphasis on fundamentals as expressing clear and well-defined constants in matters of belief and practice. Such fundamentalism has also come to be identified with current movements labelled 'ISLAMIST'. Among some Muslims such fundamentalism, which can be separated from conservative interpretations, focuses on what is believed to be core doctrines and practices set out in the Quran and SUNNA, to the exclusion of historical developments and diverse interpretations which are regarded as 'departures' and even heretical.

By extension these fundamentals ought to permeate the whole of Muslim life and society, including the political, and define its features in their totality. Thus Muslim fundamentalists attempt to establish such a mode of Muslim life through activism and in some cases even by the use of force.

Like other forms of fundamentalism, the appeal of such reactive views lies in a variety of factors. The most salient among them are the fragmentation created by the conditions of modernity; the perceived alienation generated by influences from other cultures, primarily Western; the failure of nationalism; policies of modernization; the failure of ideals such as democracy, human rights, and economic and social justice; and the continuing and long-standing post-colonial conflicts that continue to fester and provoke further disillusionment and even radicalization.

funeral practices In Muslim tradition, death and burial involve a number of established rituals and practices.

Although they may differ slightly from one Muslim region to another, there is a common underlying set of funeral practices. The SHAHADA is whispered in the ear of the dying person. Sometimes verses of the Quran and small prayers are also recited. The dead body is given a ritual ablution (*ghusl*) and wrapped in a clean and simple shroud in preparation for burial. In most Muslim societies the body is placed on a bier and carried to a CEMETERY, generally accompanied by male members of the family and others. As a rule, no coffin is used except in special circumstances, for example to transport the body to the burial place, whereupon it is returned to the bier to make the last part of the journey. Prayers are recited at the side of the grave facing the *qibla*, the direction for prayer.

Generally, members of the family and other mourners gather to share food and offer consolation. Among other traditions is a ceremony, sometimes held on the fortieth day after the person died, to offer prayers for the salvation of the deceased. Many funeral practices are modelled on the funeral of the Prophet Muhammad, which is described in detail in the accounts of his life. Among these is the way in which the dead body should be ritually washed and placed in the grave.

The main stages involve the preparation of the body for burial, transportation to a cemetery, a mourning period and, where possible, erection of tombstones or a funerary structure above the grave. The body is washed and shrouded in a white cotton cloth and a funeral prayer is recited which includes verses of the Quran. Within Muslim tradition a body should be buried immediately or as soon as possible after death. When placing the body in the grave the face is positioned in the direction of the KA'BA. In most Muslim societies women are generally not allowed at the graveside during the burial ceremony.

Death is believed by Muslims to mark a transition from this life to the next and while accompanied by an experience of grief and mourning, is also seen in the light of Quranic teaching that promises an eternal life of peace and joy to the righteous.

Gabriel (Arabic, Jibril) The angel who according to Muslim tradition acted as an intermediary for the message of revelation to the Prophet.

Galen (d. c. 199) Ancient Greek physician known in Muslim scholarship as Jalinus. His works in the field of medicine were translated into Arabic and integrated into the study and practice of medicine by Muslim physicians of the medieval period.

Galiev, Sultan (1880–1936) Communist official. He was a Muslim of Central Asian origin, a compatriot of Stalin and the highest-ranking Muslim in the communist hierarchy at the time. His differences with Stalin over policies in Central Asia led to his arrest and subsequent disappearance.

Gambia West African state. Islam was first introduced into the region in the tenth century by merchants who used the trade routes to teach about the Prophet. Many of Gambia's developments reflect those of its surrounding neighbour SENEGAL. Approximately 85 per cent of Gambia's population is Muslim, although there is a great deal of ethnic diversity.

garden The image of the garden as paradise occurs over a hundred times in the Quran. It symbolizes the joy, tranquillity and companionship of the righteous and the concept of perpetual peace, harmony and happiness associated with God's reward in the hereafter. The linking of the garden imagery of the afterlife to create an analogous environment combining water, vegetation, flowers and landscape represents an important aspect of creativity in Muslim civilization, giving a visual form to and acting as a reminder of the idea that life in all its forms embodies a connection between matter and spirit.

Gasprinski, Ismail Bey (1851–1914) Muslim scholar, reformer and journalist. Of Chechen origin, Gasprinski advocated the building of common religious, cultural and linguistic bonds among the Muslims of Central Asia.

geography The exploration and representation of the world as it was known to them was of major interest to Muslim geographers and travellers. The depiction of the world was inspired by the spread of Muslim influence and rule over different regions of Africa, Asia and the Mediterranean but also by a growing familiarity with the traditions of cartography and geography acquired from ancient Greek and other traditions of mapping the world.

Shalimar Gardens, Lahore, Pakistan.

Muslim geographers and navigators played an important role in influencing European mapmakers. In particular Roger II of Sicily (1097–1154) is known to have commissioned the Muslim geographer al-Idrisi (d. 1165) to create a map of the world. Abdul-Majid, the Indian Ocean navigator, is said to have influenced the journeys of Portuguese discoverers and the Ottoman naval figure and mapmaker Piri Reis (d. 1554) produced well-known maps to facilitate sea voyages during his time.

Ghadir Khumm (The Pool of Khumm) It is located in an oasis between Mecca and Medina where the Prophet stopped on his return from the FAREWELL PILGRIMAGE and, according to Shia tradition, designated ALI IBN ABI TALIB as his successor. The day and event are commemorated by the Shia with an important festival.

Ghalib, Mirza Asad Allah Khan (1797–1869) Poet. Ghalib is regarded as one of the foremost poets of Urdu in the Indian subcontinent. Early periods of his life were spent in Abar, but he then moved to DELHI and lived most of his life there. His poetry in both Persian and Urdu is held in high regard.

Ghana Country in West Africa. It has an estimated Muslim population of 3 million, about 14 per cent of the total. The name Ghana is also associated with the ancient African kingdom referred to by Muslim geographers and travellers whose king, though a non-Muslim, treated his many Muslim subjects with respect and tolerance. Among Sufi groups in Ghana, the largest are those of the TIJANIYYA and QADIRIYYA.

ghayba The state of being hidden or in occult concealment, a belief of the Ithna Ashari Shia (*see* ITHNA ASHARIYYA) regarding their twelfth imam, Muhammad ibn Hasan al-Askari, also known as AL-MAHDI. It is believed that after an initial disappearance in 874, during which he communicated through intermediaries, the imam finally vanished. The community awaits his return and the restoration of true justice. *See also* MUSTALIYYA.

ghazal Form of love poem in Muslim literature modelled on the pre-Islamic Arabic ode. The form is used extensively in Sufi mystical poetry in several languages as a way of expressing devotion.

al-Ghazali, Abu Hamid Muhammad (1058–1111) Jurist, theologian and mystic. Al-Ghazali's writings and thought had a major influence on the development of Sunni Islam. In his autobiography he describes his quest for truth and his successful pursuit of a Sufi life. His major works of theology synthesize various mystical, intellectual and religious aspects of Muslim tradition and offer a strong rebuttal of many philosophical and esoteric orientations within Islam. Al-Ghazali's most important work is the *Ihya ulum al-din* (*Revival of the Religious Sciences*), in which he formulated his understanding of the relationship between the exoteric and esoteric aspects of life, blending Sufi spirituality with Sunni religious law and practices. His experience of Sufi life strengthened his conviction that human beings were capable of developing nearness to God and of knowing Him. Al-Ghazali has served as a model of educational and rational commitment in the articulation of Islam and is recognized in modern times as one of the foremost medieval authorities among major Sunni schools of thought.

al-Ghazali, Zaynab (b. 1917) Modern Egyptian educator and writer. Al-Ghazali was an important member of the MUSLIM BROTHERHOOD. Her activities to inspire greater Muslim self-understanding and activism led to her imprisonment in the 1960s. She continues to be an activist through her role as educator and writer.

Ghaznawids Dynasty originating in Turkey that ruled in parts of Central Asia, eastern Iran and today's Afghanistan from 977 to 1186.

MAHMUD OF GHAZNA, son of the founder of the dynasty, Sebuktegin, invaded India and extended his rule there, but it was his successors who established Lahore in northern India (now Pakistan) as their capital, making it a major political and cultural centre of Muslim life.

Ghurids Successor dynasty to the GHAZNAWIDS. It ruled parts of the same territory but extended its influence to neighbouring regions until the early thirteenth century.

ghusl Ablution of the whole body prior to the performance of prayer. *Ghusl* is stipulated in Muslim tradition under certain conditions, such as during menstruation or illness and after sex. It is also performed for the dead before burial.

Gisu Daraz, Sayyid Muhammad (1321–1422) Sufi scholar in medieval India. Gisu Daraz is particularly well regarded for his knowledge of Hinduism and Indian thought. His many works reflect an attempt to present Sufi teachings in local contexts. He belonged to the CHISHTIYYA order.

God *See* ALLAH.

Gokalp, Ziya (1876–1924) Pen name of Mehmed Ziya. He was a leading intellectual of the period of transition in Turkey from the OTTOMAN EMPIRE to the emergence of the modern Turkish nation-state. In his capacity as a writer, poet and political thinker he promoted rethinking of the political role of Islam and advocated a secular nationalist state modelled on ideas developed in Europe.

Gospels *See* INJIL.

Grameen Bank A network of community and financial institutions based on the principle known as micro-credit. The Grameen Bank originated in Bangladesh and was founded by the economist Muhammad Yunus. It has now been replicated in many developing countries. The goal was to enable urban and rural dwellers and workers, particularly women, to have ready access to credit and financial resources to improve the daily conditions and working environment of their lives.

Muhammad Yunus and the Grameen Bank were awarded the Nobel Peace Prize in 2006.

Granada Spanish city. Granada's architectural heritage from Muslim times has made it a major centre of tourism as well as for scholarly study of the history of Islam in Andalusia in southern Spain. It was also the capital of the last Muslim dynasty in Spain, the NASRIDS. Among some of its distinctive monuments are the ALHAMBRA, the Generalife and the remains of some of the city's ancient fortifications. Recently the city has made an extensive effort to preserve and restore further the various elements of this architectural heritage. *See also* AL-ANDALUS.

Great Britain *See* UNITED KINGDOM.

Guinea West African state. Guinea won full independence from France in 1958. Of the 7.5 million inhabitants, between 90 and 95 per cent are estimated to be Muslim. Most are Sunni who follow the Maliki SCHOOL OF ISLAMIC LAW. Islam was introduced to the region when Muslim merchants first entered Guinea from Ghana during the eleventh century.

Guinea-Bissau West African state. Guinea-Bissau became a republic in 1974 when it secured independence from Portugal. Approximately 38 per cent of the population, a majority of whom live in the interior, are Sunni Muslims. Islam was first introduced in the early nineteenth century after the FULBE *jihad* led by UTHMAN DAN FODIO.

Gulbadan Daughter of the first MOGHUL Emperor BABUR. She lived in the sixteenth century and is said to have recorded events of the early period of Moghul rule and the role of learning and culture among the women of the court.

Gulf States *See* KUWAIT; OMAN; QATAR.

Gulhane Decree *See* TANZIMAT.

Guyana Country in South America. It achieved independence from Great Britain in 1966. The first Muslims in Guyana arrived as slaves in the eighteenth and nineteenth centuries. Between 1834 and 1917 over 300,000 Muslim labourers came to Guyana from the Indian subcontinent. Of that total one-third returned home. Approximately 9 to 13 per cent of the population is Muslim and a majority of these are Sunni.

H

Habba Khatun Poet and musician. Habba Khatun lived in the sixteenth century and is said to have devoted much of her time to the education of women. She has attained legendary status in Kashmiri Muslim tradition. She is also credited with introducing love lyrics into Kashmiri poetry.

hadith The term applied to the sayings and actions of the Prophet Muhammad. These accounts were collected and systematized after his death by Muslim scholars specifically devoted to the task. The mode of recording these narratives, which in their earliest settings were oral accounts from living memory, was to precede the narration of the substance by reference to the person or persons through whom it was transmitted.

Subsequently, *hadith* were put into collections for the purpose of teaching transmission and application to the daily lives and activities of Muslims and their communities.

The most significant collections for the Sunni community are those traditions compiled during the ninth century by AL-BUKHARI, MUSLIM IBN AL-HAJJAJ, Abu Daud (d. 888), IBN MAJA (d. 887) and AL-TIRMIDHI. These authors gathered the entire corpus of traditions that had been in circulation during the two first centuries of Islam. The Shia added to their corpus of *hadith* the sayings of their imams and those sayings (which they also refer to as *akhbar*) of the Prophet authenticated by their imams. Important compilations in the Shia Islam are those of al-Kulayni (d. 939), IBN BABA-WAYH and Muhammad AL-TUSI.

The *hadith* constitute a major source in the development of Muslim law through the concept of Sunna and complement the Quran in interpreting, understanding and applying aspects of Muslim belief and practice.

Some modern Western scholarship on Islam has regarded the majority of *hadith* as being unreliable and invented after the death of the Prophet. Others argue that *hadith* reflect more the theological and legal debates of the second and third centuries of Islam rather than historical reality. Muslim scholars in general assert that, while the element of invention was always present, the scrupulous attention paid by Muslim collectors of *hadith* to authenticating the content and validating the role of transmitters has enabled the established part of the tradition to be separated from that which can be regarded as unreliable.

The term *hadith qudsi* refers to those traditions that transmit the words of God as part of a narrative attributed to the Prophet, and thus have a special distinction, but are not part of the Quran.

Hafiz (1325–1390) Poet and mystic. Hafiz (given name Khwaja Shams al-Din Muhammad), who lived and wrote in Shiraz in Iran, is regarded as one of the great masters of the *ghazal* form of Persian poetry. His lyric poems are about human and divine love, and the subtle imagery evokes the full range of love poetry in Muslim literature and mysticism.

Hafsa Wife of the Prophet Muhammad and daughter of the second caliph UMAR IBN AL-KHATTAB. According to tradition, one of the earliest written collections of Quranic verses was entrusted to her for safe keeping.

Hafsa bint al-Hajj al-Rukuniyya (d. c. 1190) Poetess. Hafsa was active in the then Muslim city of GRANADA, in AL-ANDALUS. Only a small portion of her work has been preserved. In her own time, she was noted for her skills as a poet as well as her participation in the cultural life of the city.

Hafsid North African and Mediterranean dynasty. The Hafsid ruled from 1229 to 1574. Their capital, Tunis, was an important participant in international trade and commerce with Europe and a notable seat of learning which attracted many scholars from AL-ANDALUS after the loss of Muslim power in Spain.

Hagar Wife of ABRAHAM. *See* HAJJ; PILGRIMAGE.

Ha'iri, Shaykh Abd al-Karim Yazdi (1859–1937) Ha'iri Yazdi was one of the best-known Shia scholars of his time. He was the founder of an educational institution which is noted for its contribution to religious learning, based in Qom, Iran.

Hajj The annual pilgrimage to the KA'BA in Mecca. It takes place during the month of Dhu al-Hijja, the last month of the Muslim CALENDAR. The Quran enjoins the pilgrimage on all able Muslims who possess the necessary financial means and can undertake the journey without causing any hardship to their families.

The rites performed during the pilgrimage are based on the example and practice of the Prophet and consist of:

1. The expression of one's state of personal purity and commitment to the pilgrimage by wearing two white pieces of clothing that cover the body (known as *ihram*), and abstinence from acts of violence, etc. that are inappropriate for the performance of this duty.

2. The performance of the *tawaf* or circumambulation of the Ka'ba seven times, during which pilgrims approach, acknowledge and may kiss the Black Stone, set in one corner of the Ka'ba.

3. The running (or walking quickly) between two hills, Safa and Marwa, seven times. This ritual recalls the desperate search for water by Hagar, Abraham's wife and mother of his son Ismail. Water miraculously sprang from the ground at a spot called the Well of ZAM-ZAM. Pilgrims purify themselves at this spot and carry the water from the spring home to share with others.

Hajj Terminal, King Abdul Aziz International Airport, Jeddah, Saudi Arabia.

4. Marking the ninth day of the month by gathering on a plain known as Arafat and spending it in contemplation and reading of the Quran.
5. Departing at sunset on that day and spending the night under the open sky at Muzdalifa.
6. Congregating at Mina, an adjacent site, on the tenth day, and participating in a ritual of stone throwing at three pillars, symbolizing the rejection of forces of evil that sought to tempt Abraham from fulfilling the divine command to sacrifice his son. Following that the pilgrims offer an animal sacrifice to commemorate the triumphant, transforming miracle that accompanied Abraham's sacrifice. The day is celebrated worldwide by Muslims as the ID AL-ADHA.

Pilgrims may now stay on for further voluntary performance of rituals or return home. In either case, they change into normal clothing, marking their return to daily life, reinvigorated in faith and spirit by the performance of the pilgrimage.

al-Hajj Umar Tal *See* SEGU.

halal Quranic term for that which is lawful or allowed. In general, it connotes that which is appropriate for use or practice and in particular refers to the permitted categories of food and drink. *Halal* food includes the meat of permitted animals that have been ritually slaughtered, hunted game over which the divine name has been invoked and praised, fish and seafood.

The overall goal of the concept is to provide rules and perspectives for choices regarding that which is permissible, clean and pure, and a moral code displaying reverence for life in all its forms.

Hali Khwaja Altaf Husayn (1837–1914) Urdu writer and founder of modern Urdu literary criticism. Some of Hali's compositions became important expressions of a call to revival and reform, among them his epic poem *Mussadas*. His work also focused on the plight of women in his time.

Halima Foster-mother of the Prophet Muhammad. He is believed to have spent some of his early years with her.

al-Hallaj, Husayn Ibn Mansur (857–922) Sufi poet, writer and mystic. His controversial statements – in particular an allegation that 'I am the Truth' – resulted in a trial for heresy and subsequent execution. Though contentious, his life constitutes an example of mystical living and attainment for most Sufis, who, while not condoning his excesses, regard his ecstatic utterances as flowing from his absolute love for and attachment to God. After his death his disciples organized themselves into an order known as the Hallajiyya.

Hamas Palestinian Muslim organization. It was established in 1987 in the occupied West Bank and Gaza. Hamas has a large following among Muslims living there and has argued for the establishment of an Islamic state of Palestine following a JIHAD to free the Palestinians from Israeli occupation. More recently the organization won a majority in the parliamentary elections to represent the Palestinian Authority and found itself entangled in intensive conflict with Israel, which regards it as a terrorist organization, as well as with other existing political parties in Palestine.

hammam A steam bath. The *hammam* is often referred to in popular parlance as a 'Turkish' bath. It was found in all traditional Muslim cities and towns to provide for major ablutions and was an important architectural feature in the Muslim urban setting.

Hampateba, Amadou *See* BÂ, AMADOU HAMPÂTÉ.

Hamdard Foundation Charitable organization established in Pakistan and India to provide health services in the tradition of *yunani*, or Greco-Arab medicine, but including Indian and Chinese practices. It is also concerned with education and has established universities in India and Pakistan.

Hamza Fansuri (d. c. 1600) Noted Indonesian scholar and Sufi. He is one of the earliest known authors of Muslim works of devotion and teaching in the Malay language.

Hamzanama An artistic rendering of a well-known heroic account in Muslim literature of the tales of Hamza, an uncle of the Prophet. Undertaken during the reign of the MOGHUL Emperor AKBAR in the latter part of the sixteenth century and combining text and painting, the original Hamzanama, consisting of some 1,400 folios, is regarded as a masterpiece. Sadly, it has survived only in part.

Hanafi School of Islamic Law *See* SCHOOLS OF ISLAMIC LAW.

Hanbali School of Islamic Law *See* SCHOOLS OF ISLAMIC LAW.

hanif Quranic term for individuals devoted to the worship of one God and who are seen as models of piety. An example is Ibrahim (ABRAHAM), who is said to be neither Christian nor Jew, but a *hanif.*

Haram al-Sharif Arabic term for 'the noble sanctuary' whose root meaning connotes 'sacredness'. It is applied specifically to the area in the Old City of Jerusalem that includes the Dome of the Rock and the al-Aqsa Mosque. The cities of Mecca and Medina are referred to as the 'Haramayn', or the two sacred centres, because of the presence of the KA'BA and the tomb of the Prophet, respectively.

harim Widely known in its popularized form, 'harem', *harim* refers to the private interior spaces of traditional Muslim homes designated as women's living quarters.

al-Hariri, Abu Muhammad (1054–1122) Muslim poet. Al-Hariri wrote in Arabic and is famous for developing the genre of poetry known as the *maqama* ('sessions' or 'assemblies'), which told stories associated with the adventures of a roguish figure in rhyming prose.

Harun al-Rashid (766–809) Fifth ABBASID caliph. He was popularized in the *Thousand and One Nights* (ALF LAYLA WA LAYLA) and associated with the Golden Age of Abbasid achievement and conquest, as well as the cultural life and brilliance of the capital city, Baghdad.

Hasan al-Askari (d. 873) Eleventh imam of the Ithna Ashari Shia (see ITHNA ASHAR-IYYA). He was succeeded by his son Muhammad (AL-MAHDI), the twelfth and last imam.

Hasan al-Basri (642–728) Early Muslim intellectual of Iraqi origin and an important religious figure of the UMAYYAD period. He was born in Medina, but spent most of his life in Basra, where he died. Hasan al-Basri was well known as a preacher and teacher and also for his theological views regarding freedom and predestination. His sermons are examples of the earliest Muslim writings as well as Arabic prose. Hasan witnessed many important events of the early history of Islam including the battle of SIFFIN and the conquest of eastern Iran. Although he vehemently criticized abuse of authority, he expressed dislike of armed rebellion against rulers. A devout intellectual, his teachings had enormous influence on later religious and intellectual groups and schools. He is also highly regarded for his pious and ascetic lifestyle.

Hasan ibn Ali (624–670) Grandson of the Prophet and son of ALI IBN ABI TALIB and FATIMA. He and his brother HUSAYN are regarded among the Shia as the rightful claimants to succession to the caliphate after the death of Ali. Eventually forced to renounce his political claims by MUAWIYYA, he is believed to have been poisoned.

Hashim, Banu The family to which the ancestors of the Prophet belonged. Linkage to the family has been claimed by rulers of many past and present dynasties. *See also* SHARIF.

Hausa Muslim peoples who live in the northern part of modern Nigeria and surrounding regions. There are an estimated 25 million Hausa. The Hausa language is widely spoken in the region. Influenced by Arabic and using the Arabic script, it is an important vehicle for the expression of Muslim thought and practice.

Haydar al-Amuli (1320–1385) Shia writer whose works reflect a synthesis of Sufism and Shiism. His thought has influenced subsequent thinkers within the Twelver Shia tradition (*see* ITHNA ASHARIYYA).

Hayy ibn Yaqzan The name of the main figure in the philosophical tale attributed to IBN SINA and IBN TUFAYL. In it a spontaneously generated human being applies the tools of the intellect to the process of self-discovery and attaining knowledge of God.

Hazrat-Masuma *See* QOM.

health Among the sayings of the Prophet that have been preserved in Muslim tradition is one that states: 'Seek treatment, for God has not created a disease for which He has not also created a cure.'

Together with the practice of traditional medicine in different Muslim societies, there also evolved a scientific tradition of medical study and treatment, drawing from the classical heritage of Greek medicine but going beyond it and constituting one of the most significant to Muslim contributions to civilization. The science was accompanied by the creation of institutions to treat the sick, and many examples of endowed hospitals and healthcare facilities can be found from the early periods of Muslim history onwards. This heritage has also inspired the rise of medical research, education, treatment and healthcare in more modern contexts: the policy of many Muslim nation-states reflects established Muslim values in providing care for the sick and indigent. Generally, however, in many of the poorer parts of the Muslim world, access to healthcare for most of the population lags considerably behind accepted international standards.

heaven The imagery of heaven in the Quran is in sharp contrast to that of HELL, reflecting reward, nearness to God, peace and joy. Other analogies of heaven include the GARDEN and the ideal of companionship of the pure.

hell The Quran uses a number of terms to describe the place of punishment in the afterlife. It is signified by symbols of fire, deprivation, pain and suffering as well as feelings of eternal guilt and remorse.

heresy (Arabic, *ilhad*) Actions that are construed to be opposed to an established belief or that subvert religion are deemed heretical and subject to sanction within the framework of traditional Muslim law and practice. *See* APOSTASY.

hijab The most widespread current use of this Quranic term applies to a covering as a means of separating and distinguishing women. The requirements according to traditional Muslim legal practice indicate forms of covering as an act of modesty, so as not to exhibit one's body for public display or as a way of being sexually suggestive. Among some Muslims it has come to define an assertion of Muslim identity and a way of separating 'believing' Muslim women from others. In some European countries the *hijab* has come to be considered as a form of exclusion and separation by Muslims and a perceived denigration of a woman's position in society. Muslim women committed to the *hijab* argue for it, in such circumstances, as an expression of freedom and of their right to religious expression.

There are various forms of veiling that differ almost in every country and region where Muslims live, such as: *burqa, chador, amira, purdah* or *pardah, jilbab, khimar* and *niqab*. Essentially, they all refer to a piece of cloth of various designs that women wear to cover some or all parts of their body.

Hijaz The part of the Arab peninsula where the central events of early Muslim history took place. It includes the cities of Mecca and Medina.

hijra The migration of the Prophet and his followers from MECCA to MEDINA in 622. Muslim history came to be dated from this event, which inaugurated a new CALENDAR.

hikma The notion of wisdom but also by extension applied in Muslim thought to philosophy and science. Among Muslim philosophers such as IBN SINA (Avicenna), wisdom involved the study of specific sciences and the acquisition of knowledge which in turn informs ethical action guided by a fuller understanding of the good.

The idea of *hikma* received particular emphasis in the thought and works of Ismaili writers as well as in the philosophical tradition of Imami Shiism as it developed more fully in Iran after the sixteenth century.

al-Hilli, Allama Jamal al-Din Hasan Ibn Yusuf (1250–1325) Leading Shia Imami scholar of his time. Al-Hilli came from a prominent family of Twelver theologians (*see* ITHNA ASHARIYYA). His early education started under the guidance of his family. He was also a student of the famous philosopher and astrologer Nasir al-Din TUSI (d. 1274). A prolific writer, al-Hilli is the author of several hundred works to be found in many private libraries of Iraq and Iran. His writings encompass various branches of theology, law and grammar. His scholarship is held in high esteem and he is called by his title 'Allama-i Hilli' (the Sage of Hilla). His works are considered to be the foremost exposition of the beliefs and practices of the Imami Shia.

Hindustani *See* URDU.

Hisham Ibn al-Hakam (d. 796) An Imami Shia scholar active during the eighth to ninth centuries. His exposition of doctrine and theology contributed to the further definition and evolution of Shia thought.

Hizb al-Tahrir Also known as Hizb al-Tahrir al-Islami (the Islamic Liberation Party), Hizb al-Tahrir was founded in Jerusalem during the early 1950s by Taqi al-Din al-Nabhani (1909–1972) as a political party with the aim of establishing a universal Islamic state. The party has a large number of followers in several Arab states, Central Asia, and some Western countries such as Germany, Denmark and the United Kingdom. The party is banned in Russia and Uzbekistan as well as several Middle Eastern states. Although Hizb al-Tahrir has openly denounced violence and terrorism, its proscription in the UK has been debated since 2005, so far without resolution.

Hizbullah Group of Shia Muslims in Iran who constituted themselves into a political party during the time of the Iranian Revolution from 1978 to 1979. It is believed to have inspired a party of the same name in Lebanon, with whom it is linked in terms of organization and tactics of militant opposition. The Hizbullah of Lebanon constitute a major political and religious force in the region they control in the south of the country, where the majority of the population are Twelver Shia (*see* ITHNA ASHARIYYA). From there they have been engaged in constant conflict with Israel, which has accused the group of terrorist activity.

hospital *See* BIMARISTAN; HEALTH.

Huda Sharawi (1882–1947) Egyptian writer, activist and philanthropist. She organized women's associations to give her countrywomen a voice in modern Egyptian life and was an active participant in many women's rights conferences around the world.

al-Hudaybiyya The site of a village where, during the Prophet's time, early negotiations resulted in agreements that allowed Muslims to reduce tension between themselves and their enemies in Mecca, preparing the way for eventual Muslim control of the city.

hudud (lit., 'limits') In Muslim legal practice, punishments laid down for crimes and prohibited acts. In general, such punishments have been superseded by modern penalties in many Muslim countries, though they have been periodically restored to demonstrate affinity with the SHARIA.

al-Hujwiri, Abu al-Hasan Ali Ibn Uthman Sufi writer active during the eleventh century. His best-known work, *Kashf al-Mahjub* (*The Unveiling of That Which Is Hidden*) systematized Sufi teachings and practice. His tomb, Turbat-e Jam, is a place of pilgrimage.

Hulagu Khan *See* MONGOLS.

human beings Human beings are amongst God's most noble creation and have a special place within the created order. As part of a pluralistic world community, this common origin and innate human dignity offers the possibility that no matter what the material conditions, ethical life is to be governed by moral reasoning, choice and accountability. Being Muslim, in the past or present, is therefore based on moral and spiritual perspectives that transcend particular geographical or historical conditions.

While God's will is revealed in the Quran and complemented by the SUNNA, Muslims are also urged to exercise reason in understanding revelations and reflecting on human choice. In the account of the creation of humanity, as narrated in the Quran, Adam is shaped from clay, enlivened by spirit and endowed with the capacity to 'name things' (Quran 2:31). This suggests a layered and multidimensional being, in whom material, spiritual and intellectual orientations are combined. Adam is referred to as a *khalifa* (caliph) or vicegerent, granted custody of the earth and guided by God to create conditions that enabled life to be lived in dignity and according to an ethical and moral purpose. Being human, in this broad sense, thus has a special, even privileged, status in creation according to the Quran (95:4) and brings with it accountability for the choices that are made, as illustrated in the story of creation. The concept of accountability also relates to belief in life hereafter, and the notion of a DAY OF JUDGEMENT.

Hunayn Ibn Ishaq (808–873) Physician and Syrian Christian scholar. His role as a translator and mediator of ancient Greek works into Arabic was a critical resource for the emergence of the intellectual sciences in the Muslim world during the ninth century.

Husayn Ibn Ali (626–680) Grandson of the Prophet and Shia imam. Husayn's death, in a massacre in 680, along with his followers and several members of his family, has become the focus of a major commemorative event celebrating his martyrdom and his role in seeking justice against tyrannical rule. He was the younger brother of HASAN, born to ALI IBN ABI TALIB and FATIMA. During the imposed reign of the UMAYYAD ruler YAZID IBN MUAWIYYA he became a focal point of opposition for Muslims who wished to see him restored as the leader of the Muslim community. In addition to his status as an imam among the Shia, he is revered by all Muslims and is the subject of a vast literature that developed to memorialize his life and example. *See also* MUHARRAM; TAZIYA.

Husayn, Taha (1889–1973) Egyptian writer and reformer. His various writings prompted a review of the heritage of Arabic literature and provided a critical perspective on cultural, educational and social issues facing early twentieth-century Arab society. He is best known for his autobiography and his controversial work *On Pre-Islamic Poetry*.

Husaynids Dynasty that ruled Tunisia from 1705 to 1957, when the last ruler was deposed and a new nationalist movement led by Habib BOURGUIBA took over.

husayniyye or *hussayniyya* A religious space dedicated in Shia practice for the commemoration of Imam HUSAYN IBN ALI's life and martyrdom. *See also* RAWZAH-KHVANI; TAZIYA.

Hussein, Saddam (1937–2006) President of Iraq from 1979 until his regime was overthrown by an invasion led by US troops on 9 April 2003, although he managed to evade capture for eight months. In 2006 he was publicly tried for murdering Iraqi citizens, sentenced to death in November and hanged on 30 December.

Hyderabad The name of two major cities. One is in Pakistan in the province of Sind, the other is in South India and was the capital of a former state ruled by a Nizam which became part of India after the partition of British India in 1947.

ibadat Category of actions in Muslim law related to practices of the faith.

Ibadiyya One of the surviving communities of the KHAWARIJ tradition. Its influence today can be found in Oman, East Africa, especially in Zanzibar (off the East African coast) and parts of North Africa. In Oman, the Ibadi framework of jurisprudence and political authority has held sway for centuries. The present ruling family in Oman is believed to be ruled by an imam elected according to tradition, after consultation among leading scholars. The eponym of the group is said to be Abd Allah ibn Ibad, who parted with other Khawarij in order to adopt practices that were considered to be more in accord with those of other Muslims with whom they wished to coexist in peace. The Ibadiyya have continued to build on their traditions of scholarship and to cultivate religious learning.

Iblis or **Satan** (Arabic, Shaytan) The devil. According to some Muslim scholars, he was one of the beings created from fire, who refused God's command to prostrate himself before Adam because he believed him to be inferior, having been created from clay. For this disobedience Iblis was expelled from heaven but granted power to tempt humankind away from the divinely prescribed religion. Muslims seek protection from such temptation before recitation of the Quran and before any ritual action. The greatest act of seduction by Iblis according to the Quran, following parts of the Biblical story, was to tempt Adam and his companion to trespass against God's command.

ibn Component of many Arabic names which signifies 'son of'. The feminine form is *bint*.

Ibn al-Allaf Abu Bakr al-Hasan Ibn Ali (833–930) Poet and compiler of traditions who served in the ABBASID court, where he became a confidant of Caliph al-Mutazz. His fame rests on a poem describing his anguish at the death of his cat, probably an allusion to the violent death of the caliph.

Ibn Aqil, Abu al-Wafa (1040–1119) Noted jurist and theologian. His scholarship is regarded as an important contribution to the consolidation of medieval Sunnism.

Ibn al-Arabi, Abu Bakr Muhammad Muhyi-al-Din (1165–1240) Sufi scholar and mystic philosopher. Ibn al-Arabi's considerable erudition and his influence as a Sufi thinker and intellectual earned him the epithet 'The Greatest Shaykh'. His home was in Murcia, Spain, but he travelled widely and lived in several Muslim cities. He finally settled in Damascus, where he died. His contribution extended to fields other than Sufism and included the application of a philosophical framework to the understanding of Muslim thought and its mystical dimensions. Among the many concepts he developed in his voluminous writings, he is particularly noted for the doctrine of *wujud*, a consciousness that permeates one's sense of existence, and his views on the 'Perfect Human', in whom this consciousness is fully actualized.

Ibn Babawayh or **Babuya, Abu Jafar Muhammad** (923–991) Also known as al-Suduq. Theologian and jurist. Ibn Babawayh is an authoritative figure in Imami Shia theology and jurisprudence. He lived in Baghdad.

Ibn Badis, Abd al-Hamid ibn al-Mustafa (1889–1940) Muslim reformer and one of the leaders of the nationalist struggle in ALGERIA. Ibn Badis provided leadership to the Muslim ULAMA of the time against French occupation.

Ibn Battuta, Shams al-Din Muhammad ibn Abd Allah (1304–1377) One of the greatest travellers and explorers of his time. His travels covered the Middle East, Africa, Asia Minor, Western Asia, India and China. Ibn Battuta's travelogues constituted a major source of information on various regions in this period and have been translated into many languages.

Ibn al-Farid, Umar ibn Ali (1181–1235) Poet. His corpus of writings, preserved in his *Diwan* (a collection of writings, prose and poetry), is a classic of Sufi poetry in Arabic. He earned great respect in Cairo during his lifetime.

Ibn Hawqal, Abu al-Qasim ibn Ali (*fl.* mid to late 10th century) Muslim geographer. Circa 977 he wrote *Kitab Surat al-Ard*, a description of the contemporary Muslim world, including details of the economic and administrative organization of various regions.

Ibn al-Haytham, Abu Ali al-Hasan (Latin, Alhazan) (965–1039) Well-known Muslim physicist and mathematician who worked under the patronage of the FATI-MIDS. The author of over one hundred works, his greatest achievements were in the field of optics and mathematics.

Ibn Hazm, Abu Muhammad Ali ibn Ahmad (994–1064) Intellectual of Andalusian origin. Ibn Hazm's writings encompass history, law, theology, philosophy and poetry. His interests reflect the cosmopolitan environment of cities such as CÓRDOBA and the developed state of knowledge and culture of the time.

Ibn al-Husayn, Abu al-Tayyib Ahmad *See* AL-MUTANABBI.

Ibn Idris, Ahmad (1750–1837) Founder of the Idrisid Sufi tradition in Morocco. His influence was felt in many places and his descendants are to be found in Egypt and the Sudan.

Ibn Ishaq, Muhammad (704–767) Historian. Perhaps best known for his role as a source of information and transmission on the Prophet's life which was later edited and compiled to produce a biography.

Ibn Khaldun, Abd al-Rahman ibn Muhammad (1332–1406) Historian and sociologist. Born in Tunis, he is regarded as one of the most influential social historians of the medieval period. His most famous work is the *Muqaddimah* (preface to his *Kitab al-Ibar*), in which he developed a theory of history to account for the recurrent rise and fall of empires and dynasties. His historical and social analysis was based on observation of current political, economic and social forces. Ibn Khaldun developed the concept of *asabiyya* (social bonding and solidarity) to explain the emergence, development, unification and decline and fall of societies and states. He has been called by some scholars the 'Father of Sociology'.

Ibn Maja, Abu Abd Allah Muhammad ibn Yazid (824–887) Compiler of the *Kitab al-Sunan*, regarded as one of the six authoritative collections of Sunni HADITH.

Ibn Majid, Shihab al-Din Ahmad (b. c. 1432) Geographer and navigator. Ibn Majid's works provided detailed descriptions of and data on the Indian Ocean and other coastal regions of Africa and Asia. He is perhaps best known for guiding the Portuguese explorer Vasco da Gama across the Indian Ocean, from Malindi (in present-day Kenya) to the coast of India.

Ibn Masud, Abd Allah ibn Ghafil (d. c. 652) One of the COMPANIONS OF THE PROPHET. Ibn Masud is said to have received the Quran directly from the Prophet and was noted for his ability to recite it. In his later life he acted as a teacher and missionary for the newly established faith of Islam.

Ibn Maymun, Musa *See* MAIMONIDES, MOSES.

Ibn al-Muqaffa, Abd Allah (720–756) Writer. He lived in Iran and converted to Islam as an adult. Ibn al-Muqaffa is best known for his translation into Arabic of Persian and Indian narratives and folk tales. His compilation *Kalila wa Dimna* is an example of a work of Indian origin, available in the Pahlavi language of pre-Islamic Iran, which he then translated into Arabic.

Ibn al-Nadim (d. 995) The author of the *Fihrist*, a well-known reference work on all books written in Arabic that were known to him. It is an extensive resource on various subjects, such as comparative religion and the sciences.

Ibn al-Nafis, Ala al-Din Ali ibn Abi al-Haram (c. 1210–1288) Physician and intellectual. He was born in Damascus, but later moved to Egypt and settled there. Although he continued to focus on medicine, he was also well versed in grammar, logic and the traditional religious sciences. In Egypt he became the personal physician of the MAMLUK Sultan al-Zahir Baybars while continuing to teach Shafii law and logic.

Ibn Rushd, Abu al-Walid Muhammad ibn Ahmad ibn Muhammad (1126–1198) Philosopher and legal theorist, known in the West as Averroes and also called by Dante the Great Commentator because of his translation and knowledge of Aristotle. He served as *qadi* (judge) in Seville and is famous for his theory of the 'unity of the intellect' and his attempt to reconcile divine revelation and rational philosophy. He also undertook a defence against the criticism of philosophical thought in Islam, generated by Abu Hamid Muhammad AL-GHAZALI's attack on philosophy.

Ibn Saud, Abd al-Aziz *See* ABD AL-AZIZ IBN SAUD.

Ibn Sina, Abu Ali al-Husayn (980–1037) Philosopher and physician, known in the West as Avicenna. He is renowned as the 'Hakim', exemplifying his role as both a wise thinker and a physician. A prodigy from childhood, he mastered the traditional Muslim sciences as well as most of the classical works of antiquity known to Muslims, and earned his living as a physician, developing his professional reputation in several courts. His work gave him access to the great library collections of his time and he wrote voluminously on all subjects. His corpus contains over 250 works. His *Qanun* (*Canon*), a work on medicine, served as an authoritative text in the Muslim world and the West until the seventeenth century. His philosophical works established his reputation as one of the greatest Muslim philosophers and

Ibn Sina manuscript on medicine.

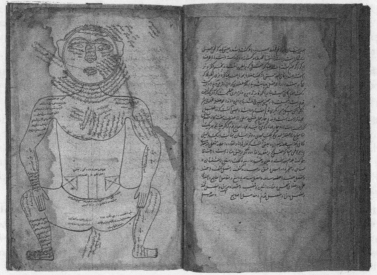

Tashrih manuscript of Mansur on anatomy.

one of the leading exponents and interpreters of Greek philosophy. His works were translated into Latin and his philosophical legacy continues to be influential in some parts of the Muslim world, particularly Iran, to this day.

Ibn Taymiyya, Taqi al-Din Ahmad (1263–1328) Scholar and jurist of the Hanbali SCHOOL OF ISLAMIC LAW. Ibn Taymiyya's conservative stance on the religious and political issues of the time brought him frequent censure and imprisonment. He argued for an interpretation of the Quran and SUNNA based on the tradition of the *salaf* (early Muslims). He was a strong opponent of innovation (BIDA) and attacked Sufi thought and practice in his prolific writings, including even such established scholars as Abu Hamid Muhammad AL-GHAZALI and IBN AL-ARABI. According to tradition, his death in prison was caused by deprivation of writing materials and his funeral was attended by thousands of mourners who revered him as a saint. Later his tomb was often visited by people seeking intercession (SHAFAA). His thought has influenced various Muslim thinkers and movements including the followers of WAHHABISM, who have perceived in his work support and arguments for their traditional or conservative stance on Muslim practices and beliefs.

Ibn Tufayl, Abu Bakr Muhammad (c. 1109–1186) Known in the West as Abubacer. He was the author of *Hayy ibn Yaqzan*, a philosophical narrative that explores the divide between philosophical understanding and the literalist approaches to religion. *See* PHILOSOPHY.

Ibn Tumart (1080–1130) Religious reformist. He preached an uncompromising doctrine of divine unity in North Africa. His followers were called *al-Muwahhidun* ('the unitarians'), the term from which ALMOHADS is derived. Ibn Tumart attacked the laxity of belief and practice he found among the Berbers of his day, translating the Quran into Berber in an effort to convert them to what he believed was the genuine faith. The Almohads ruled parts of North Africa and the Iberian Peninsula for many decades.

Ibrahim *See* ABRAHAM.

Ibrahim, Anwar (b. 1947) Malaysian Muslim thinker and politician. He played an important role in founding a Muslim movement known as ABIM urging educational, social and political reform in addressing the contemporary needs of Muslims in Malaysia. He was imprisoned after being accused of sodomy and related crimes and became opposed to the ruling party of which he had been a member. Since his release from prison, he has once again sought to play an active role in the affairs of the country.

Ibrahim ibn Adham (d. c. 777) Early Sufi. His life is remembered as exemplifying asceticism following rejection of the kingdom of which he was a ruler.

Id al-Adha or **Eid al-Adha** 'The Feast of Sacrifice' which is celebrated on the tenth day of Dhu-al-Hijja, the last month of the Muslim CALENDAR, to commemorate the sacrifice by ABRAHAM of his son, for whom God miraculously substituted a ram. The sacrifice is believed by Muslims to have taken place on Mount Mina and pillars symbolizing the devil (who tempted Abraham to abandon the sacrifice) are stoned by pilgrims at this site. The pilgrimage's concluding ritual is the sacrifice of an animal, usually a goat, sheep, cow or camel, and the distribution and sharing of the sacrifice with the poor and needy. The festival also marks the end of the pilgrimage and is an event for worldwide celebration by Muslims and the occasion for large-scale community prayer.

Id al-Fitr or **Eid al-Fitr** The festival which marks the end of the fast performed during the month of Ramadan. The celebration includes gathering for communal prayers, the preparation and sharing of traditional dishes and the giving of gifts and distribution of alms to the poor and needy.

al-Idrisi, Abu Abd Allah Muhammad (1100–1165) Geographer famous for his description and map of the known world compiled at the behest of Roger II, the Norman king of Sicily.

Idrisids Muslim dynasty of Alid origin, founded by Idris I (d. 791), which ruled over Berber areas from 789 to 926. It was succeeded by the ALMORAVID dynasty.

Idrisiyya Sufi tradition in Morocco founded by Ahmad IBN IDRIS in the thirteenth century.

ihram The state of ritual purity of a pilgrim during the performance of the HAJJ. It also refers to the seamless white garment worn by those participating in the Hajj and UMRA. There are a number of activities forbidden to pilgrims while in *ihram*. These include wearing perfume, cutting of the nails or hair, warfare, the killing of plants or animals and any kind of sexual activity.

ihsan A term that has come to signify among Muslims the idea of virtue, the performance of good deeds as well as the quality of moral excellence.

ijaz al-Quran The concept in Muslim thought of the inimitability of the Quran, proof of its divine origin. It is explained through the uniqueness and transcendental nature of the revelation as well as the uniqueness of Muhammad receiving and communicating it.

ijma Consensus of the learned community of religious scholars and jurists at any given time. It is one of the foundations of SUNNI legal theory and a source of law. *See also* AL-SHAFII; SHARIA; USUL AL-FIQH.

ijtihad The concept of exercising independent judgement concerning a legal or theological question. Traditionally it came to be understood as the application of rational thought to interpret matters of religious practice and law. While it became confined among certain Muslim groups to legal matters, the concept has been interpreted by many modern Muslim thinkers as an intellectual tool for dealing with modern and contemporary issues in the light of Muslim sources. One who practises *ijtihad* is called a *mujtahid* and is expected to be knowledgeable in the sources, methods and principles of Muslim law and theology. Among the Shia, *ijtihad* is regarded as an ongoing process, because legal reasoning and intellectual effort is used to supplement other sources.

Ikhwan al-Safa A group of Muslim intellectuals, living in Basra in the tenth century, who authored a series of works collectively known as *Rasail Ikhwan al-Safa* (*Epistles of the Brethren of Purity*). Drawing on multiple sources, the series provides an integrated view of knowledge aimed at producing a widely educated person whose life would be governed by philosophical and moral principles.

Ilhad See HERESY; MULHID.

Ilm Quranic term signifying knowledge. In Muslim scholarship this was also used to preface the various fields of knowledge and disciplines that developed in the medieval age. For example, arithmetic was referred to as *ilm al-hisab*: the science of numbers.

Ilyas See ELIJAH.

Imam Ali See ALI IBN ABI TALIB.

Imam/Imama The concept of authority in Islam led to a variety of definitions and was the primary cause for the distinction between the Sunni, the Shia and other communities of interpretation among Muslims.

According to the Shia, the Imama emerged as an institution after the death of the Prophet, when, according to their interpretation and tradition, ALI IBN ABI TALIB was designated by the Prophet as the person in authority whose role was to assure adherence to Islam, consolidate the growth of the newly established community and state and act as interpreter and guide in matters of religious faith and practice revealed in the Quran. (*See* SHIA ISLAM.) Over time this belief came to include the idea of a continuing line of imams from among the immediate male descendants to fulfil the goals of the institution, each having been specifically designated for the role by his predecessor. They could, however, be only those in direct descent from the Prophet's daughter FATIMA and her husband, Ali.

The Sunni definition, elaborated over time, specified that the first four caliphs, including Ali, were all legitimate authorities who fulfilled the conditions of a rightful Imama. However, after this period, a ruler could be considered the rightful imam if he fulfilled certain conditions of character and genealogy not restricted to the descendants of Fatima and Ali. Other schools of thought including the KHAWARIJ and MUTAZILA developed differing positions.

The ideal of how authority should be exercised is shared by most Muslim groups, encompassing both the continuity of the faith and the welfare of the community and others under their purview. *See also* ISMAILIYYA; ITHNA ASHARIYYA; NASS; SHIA; ZAYDIYYA.

Imam-bara The spaces of and devotion among the Imami Ithna Ashari Shia (*see* ITHNA ASHARIYYA) used to commemorate the martyrdom of Imam HUSAYN IBN ALI.

Imamzada The term refers to the descendant of an imam, but more specifically to the tombs and shrines of Twelver Shia imams (*see* ITHNA ASHARIYYA) which are visited by devotees and have become major centres of pilgrimage and devotional acts.

insan HUMAN BEING. The Quran teaches the creation of humanity out of one soul, out of which emerges human diversity (Quran 38:72, 15:26). It speaks of man as a layered being – physical, spiritual and intellectual – while also addressing human weaknesses and propensity for conflict. It is therefore necessary that God sends guidance, in order that human life can be lived in an ethical way. *See also* ADAM.

India The largest, most populous South Asian country, India became a democratic and secular state in 1947 after it won its independence from Britain. Although Muslims compose only 12 per cent of India's estimated 1 billion population, that still translates into 120 million people, giving India one of the largest Muslim populations in the world after Indonesia, Bangladesh and Pakistan. A majority of the population is Sunni, of the Hanafi SCHOOL OF ISLAMIC LAW, and the rest are Shia, Ithna Ashari or Ismaili. The Muslim community is extremely diverse ethnically, politically, economically and socially. Muslim entry into India began in 712, with further expansion continuing with the GHAZNAWID invasions. Muslim rule was eventually established in Punjab and Kashmir and, following further peaceful extension as well as incursions and conquests, reached its greatest influence under the MOGHULS (1526–1856).

Britain, whose influence in India had begun to increase since the establishment of the East India Company in 1599, and which in time superseded Portuguese and French interests in the area, completed the task of establishing control after putting down a mutiny in 1857 and integrating India into its empire. The pattern of creating political structures and electorates with group affiliation based on a sense of community reinforced divisions along religious lines (as in the British division of Bengal into two states), and in time led to a political network that promoted the idea of creating a Muslim state out of some of the provinces of British India. The ALL-INDIA MUSLIM LEAGUE became the most important voice for an independent state for the Muslims of British India and in 1947, in an atmosphere of violence, two new independent states, India and Pakistan, were created. The status of several regions, including Kashmir, was not fully resolved and this led to conflict between the two countries.

Since partition the Muslim minority in India has tried to maintain its identity while attempting to integrate within the larger framework of a secular state. The recent rise of Hindu nationalist parties, with their call to give primacy to the Hindu tradition in India, has on occasion resulted in violence against Muslims and their places of worship. The most notable incident was the destruction of the Babri Masjid in Ayodhya in 1992. Kashmir continues to be a volatile region, where Indian troops continuously face resistance from groups seeking independence or autonomy.

As India undergoes dramatic economic growth, its Muslim population tends to lag behind in the fields of education and economic development. However, as India and Pakistan are now actively seeking to resolve their long-standing differences over Kashmir, the future bodes well for greater cooperation in areas of shared concern.

Muslim women recite devotions at the shrine of Shaykh Muin al-Din Chishti in Ajmer, India

Indonesia The largest, most populous Southeast Asian state. A former Dutch colony, Indonesia has the largest population of Muslims (90 per cent of its 180 million people) of any country in the world. The population of Indonesia represents over 300 different ethnic groups who speak a total of over 250 languages and dialects. Almost all Muslims are Sunni of the Shafii SCHOOL OF ISLAMIC LAW. Islam is believed to have been introduced to the region in the thirteenth century with dramatic expansion in the fifteenth and sixteenth centuries. The growth and extension of Islam was not by conquest but rather through trade and the work of Sufi teachers. Java and Sumatra had become Muslim by the eighteenth century and Indonesia was to become more significantly involved with the rest of the Islamic world during the nineteenth and twentieth centuries.

The official constitution of Indonesia is embodied in the Pancasila, a framework of five principles which emphasize belief in God and a just and civilized humanism. These principles reflect Indonesia's goals of balancing and mediating the ideals of pluralism and its religious diversity. Since 1965, when President Sukarno was overthrown after a military coup, the country came to be ruled by another military leader, General Suharto, who himself had to resign in 1998 after public protests. The current president is Susilo Bambang Yudhoyono, who won the presidential elections in 2004.

A number of cultural modes of expression in Indonesia provide a synthesis between indigenous traditions and the influence of Muslim culture. The *wayang*, a theatre performance used to narrate the stories of Muslim heroes, is an example. Sufism has always been important in the life of Indonesian Muslims and is reflected in the contributions of writers on Muslim themes in the local languages. Following opposition and eventually the overthrow of military rule in 1998, Indonesia has adopted a broader, more democratic form of governance. A small minority of Muslims has persisted in expressing its opposition through violent means, but on the whole Indonesia continues to reflect its long tradition of moderation and pluralism.

Ingush Muslim people of the Caucasus region. The Republic of Ingushetia, where the majority of the Ingush people live, is part of the RUSSIAN FEDERATION. The Ingush converted to Islam from the late seventeenth century. During Soviet rule Ingushetia was part of an autonomous region that included CHECHNYA. As part of an attempt to 'rehabilitate' them, numerous Ingush were deported to other parts of the Soviet Union. More recently the Russian intervention in Chechnya has resulted in political difficulties for people in this region.

Inheritance The Quran prescribes a series of guidelines by which inheritance is to be governed. It introduced a system that included women and specified a framework for intestate succession. Sunni and Shia SCHOOLS OF ISLAMIC LAW have differed over the interpretation and implementation of the Quranic rules of inheritance (the Shia system giving a more favourable portion to women). The key, however, to Quranic prescriptions was the revision of pre-Islamic rules by extending rights to more family members, protecting the rights of spouses and daughters and permitting inheritance to pass through the female line.

In most Muslim countries the Muslim tradition of inheritance continues to be prevalent as part of the system of personal law, but is also undergoing revision and review in line with the developments of different national policies and constitutions.

Injil Arabic term applied in the Quran to the Gospels, believed to be derived from the Greek word *evangelion*. The Quran describes the Injil as part of the divine message given to Jesus. Most Quranic citations of Injil appear in relation to the Torah (*see* TAWRAT), the book revealed to Moses. Muslim scholarship built on these materials and embraced biblical accounts and stories as preserved in traditional Muslim historical, literary and mystical works.

Inshallah (from Arabic: *in sha'a allah*) A very common Muslim expression, meaning 'if God wills'.

Institut Agama Islam Negara (IAIN) The National Institutes of Islamic Studies throughout Indonesia are part of a programme of higher-education institutions which for the past century have concentrated on teaching various aspects of Islam and preparing teachers for their important role in educating students within the state system of education. Some of these institutions are now evolving into fully fledged universities.

Intercession *See* SHAFAA.

Interest The Quran opposes strongly the practice of RIBA, generally understood to refer to the unfair and usurious practices of pre-Islamic times, which worked to the disadvantage of the borrower and allowed the lender unlimited opportunity to charge and extort.

In modern times, this has led several Muslim scholars, institutions and governments to ban the charging of interest, believing that it is a source of exploitation and an obstacle to a just economic system, in line with their aspirations to accord with past Muslim practice. A number of alternative models of economic activity have developed in contemporary practice under the umbrella of ISLAMIC BANKING.

inter-faith development The Quran teaches religious diversity, affirming that God has communicated to humanity from the beginning by way of messengers and revelations. This broad spirit of inclusiveness and mutual acceptance reflects ideals by which Muslims have been guided in their relations with other religions. Historically, Muslims, even when in power, have coexisted particularly with the 'People of the Book' (AHL AL-KITAB), i.e. Christians and Jews, but also with Buddhists, Hindus and Zoroastrians. This is not to deny that there has been conflict or to suggest that Muslim rulers in particular were always guided by ideals, but there is general agreement among most scholars that Muslims were usually tolerant of other religions in their midst. There have been periods during which intellectual exchange and dialogue were particularly evident, such as in Muslim Spain, Fatimid Egypt and the reign of the Moghul Akbar in India.

In modern times, with the rise of new forms of inter-faith dialogue, several Muslim leaders and organizations have taken initiatives to cultivate better inter-faith relations, both to enhance mutual understanding and also to foster, on the basis of shared values, common approaches to problems of poverty, war and environmental concerns.

Internet The spread of information technology and the world wide web has increased contact among Muslims in different parts of the world and also enabled a vast amount of information to be made available.

The spectrum of information, as with all matters on the internet, is extremely wide and often unmediated and unreliable. Often the internet is used to promote views of those hostile to Islam on the one hand and of groups seeking to advance radical or extremist agendas on the other.

Intifada The term used to describe the specific Palestinian uprising in Gaza and the West Bank that began in 1987 to protest against Israeli occupation. What appeared to begin as a spontaneous uprising soon developed into a more organized movement with a significant impact over the next decade. However, in more recent times, internal divisions within various Palestinian factions have undermined the authority and credibility of the movement.

Iqbal, Sir Muhammad (1876–1938) Writer, poet, mystic, philosopher, social critic and political thinker. Sir Muhammad Iqbal was born in British-ruled India, in the city of Lahore. Educated in the classical sciences and poetry, he also studied at a government college and went on to pursue higher education in Britain and Germany. He obtained a law degree as well as a doctorate in philosophy. On his return to India he became involved in politics but he continued to teach and write. His intellectual contribution is best reflected in his poetry and other works written in Urdu, Persian and English. His ideas encompass Muslim as well as European philosophy.

Iqbal's view of the centrality of personal and spiritual growth is based on an integration of the Quranic concepts of God, the universe and human life and potential. The mystical traditions of Islam inspired his vision of an 'eternal becoming', embodying true human fulfilment at the intellectual and spiritual levels. His social and political message was aimed at condemning excessive imitation of alien values and, over time, he came to accept the need for developing a separate Muslim nation-state in the subcontinent. His 1930 address to the ALL-INDIA MUSLIM LEAGUE is regarded as the intellectual manifesto for the creation of Pakistan. Iqbal died in Lahore in 1938.

Iran Ancient Middle Eastern land, also known formerly as Persia and, since 1979, the Islamic Republic of Iran.

The majority of the Muslim population is ITHNA ASHARIYYA, i.e. Imami Shia. There is a Sunni minority as well as some Ismaili Shia and a small Jewish community. BAHAIS, who are regarded with disfavour, are diminishing in number.

In the early part of the seventh century Iran was ruled by the SASSANID dynasty, whose empire also extended into neighbouring areas such as IRAQ. Muslim armies conquered Iraq in 637 and five years later defeated the Sassanid army again to complete the conquest of Iran and its territory. The diffusion of Muslim belief and practice took place gradually over succeeding centuries and previously dominant traditions such as ZOROASTRIANISM were reduced to small minorities. During the period of ABBASID rule Iran flourished as one of the centres of Muslim culture and learning and many of the traditions of Iranian court life and institutions were adopted by the Abbasids.

The MONGOL invasion in the thirteenth century dealt a devastating blow to the region's economic and cultural life, but after the conversion of some of the Mongol princes to Islam there began a period of recovery that re-established the pre-eminence of Iran and Central Asia. This continued under succeeding rulers, in particular the SAFAWID dynasty that ruled from 1501 to 1722. Under the Safawids, Shia tradition and practice became more established, blending Sufi and Shia traditions to reorient the structure and practice of religious life in Iran.

After the break-up of Safawid rule, other regimes continued the same pattern of relationship between the state, the religious scholars and the landowners, based on various ethnic and regional groups. European incursions in the nineteenth century – particularly from Russia, which wished to increase its control over neighbouring territory, and Britain, which eventually controlled Afghanistan – forced Iran to modernize its army and adapt to a changing economic climate, dictated by the European presence.

Among the reforms was a demand for a constitution and broader representation. This culminated in a constitutional revolution in 1905–6 and involved many important religious scholars. Eventually, centralized rule under a monarch, the shah, was established. In 1925 an army officer named REZA KHAN came to power, instituted a dynasty (the Pahlavi) and imposed a series of wide-ranging reforms and changes aimed at modernizing Iran along European lines, but retaining a strong, authoritative monarchy. Iran's importance in international affairs due to its emergence as a source of oil, particularly during World War II, led to efforts by Western powers to control policy. A short-lived attempt at nationalization was suppressed and the monarch, Reza Khan's son, Muhammad Reza, was reinstated and constitutional rule re-established. While increasing oil revenues during his reign created the appearance of a growing economy and international stature, the policy of autocratic rule and perceived 'Westernization' and foreign influence provoked widespread opposition culminating in a revolution in 1979, led by Ayatollah KHOMEINI.

The new Islamic republic has adopted a formal constitutional and legal framework to reflect its version of an Islamic state which consists of elected and non-elected bodies, including a president, a parliament, a Council of Guardians and an Assembly of Experts, at the head of which is the *rahbar* or guide and leader. Iran has also supported movements elsewhere to promote its synthesis of religious ideology and politics, and engaged in the 1980s in a long drawn-out, bitter and damaging war with Iraq following an invasion by the Iraqi military. Since the death of Ayatollah Khomeini in 1989 Iran has continued to function as an Islamic republic. As a result of its staunch opposition to Israel and American policies in the region and its support of various groups such as HAMAS and HIZBULLAH as well as the antipathy of some Muslim states which oppose its policies and status as a Shia polity, Iran has often been perceived as a threat to stability in the region. Its progress in developing a nuclear capability has further exacerbated already strained relations with the international community.

Iran is home to a rich heritage of Muslim monuments and architecture, as exemplified in cities such as Isfahan. Mashhad in northern Iran is a major pilgrimage centre, organized around the shrine of Imam Ali Reza, as is Qom, where his sister Masuma's shrine is located. Qom is also a major centre of learning and education. A significant demographic feature of contemporary Iran is that more than half of its population of 70 million is believed to be under thirty years old.

Iraq Middle Eastern republic and former kingdom. Iraq has been Muslim since the BYZANTINE-controlled territory of which it formed part was conquered by Muslim armies during the seventh century. It attained pre-eminence under ABBASID rule, after Baghdad was created as the Abbasid capital. The majority of the current population is Muslim, of which more than half are Imami Shia. The other Muslims are Sunnis of the Hanafi School and Christian and Sabaean minorities make up the remainder. Following an extensive period as part of the OTTOMAN EMPIRE, Iraq became part of the British Mandate after World War I. In 1932 Iraq gained independence as a constitutional monarchy allied to Britain.

Following a number of military coups, Iraq sought federation with Egypt and

Jordan. The short-lived attempt was aborted and a series of military and civilian groups struggled for power until the emergence of Saddam HUSSEIN as the head of a socialist party called the Ba'ath, who then consolidated his power and centralized all aspects of the government. From 1980 until 1988 Iraq was involved in a long drawn-out war with its neighbour IRAN. It also invaded Kuwait in 1990 and was expelled by an alliance of international forces led by the United States. It was ordered to meet conditions for disarmament and to cease its repression of the Kurdish minority and those religious groups opposed to the government. However, Saddam Hussein's constant evasion of these demands led to another invasion in which American and other international troops overthrew his regime and sought to install a new democratic order in Iraq. In spite of the continuing presence of troops from various nations and the holding of general elections, the country continues to be plagued by sectarian and political conflict, bordering on a condition of civil war.

Iraq contains many important Shia religious centres, such as Kufa, Samarra, Najaf and Karbala, which are among the most visited places of pilgrimage by Shia Muslims, the last two being burial places of Imam ALI IBN ABI TALIB and Imam HUSAYN IBN ALI respectively.

Isa The Quranic name for JESUS.

Isaac (Arabic, Ishaq) The son of ABRAHAM. He is mentioned several times in the Quran as a prophetic figure in a line of other prophets often referred to as representing a lineage of continuing guidance from God. His birth fulfilled a divine promise to Abraham. Muslim tradition generally holds that it was ISMAIL (Ishmael) and not Isaac who was to be the intended sacrifice in the narrative of God's commandment to Abraham to offer his son.

Isfahan See SAFAWIDS.

Ishmael (Arabic, Ismail) The son of ABRAHAM by Hagar, Ismail is believed by Muslims to be the son God commanded Abraham to sacrifice and for whom He substituted a ram. According to Muslim tradition, Abraham and Ismail rebuilt the KA'BA as a place of worship of God.

Iskandar See ALEXANDER THE GREAT.

Islam (lit., 'submission') The word comes from the Arabic root s-l-m, which also connotes peace. Thus Islam signifies for Muslims the ideal of conforming to the divine will and thereby engendering peace and equilibrium.

One often-quoted verse of the Quran (5:3) refers to the establishment of Islam as a religion (din): 'Today, I have perfected your religion, completed My favour and approved for you Islam as your religion.' The Quran thus locates Islam within the larger tradition of human religion as signifying the continuous interaction of communities of faith with human history and divine revelation. Islam is the culmination of this process, linked to but encompassing and superseding previous religions.

Over the period of its diffusion since the seventh century, Islam has become the faith of people from all parts of the world, reflecting a great deal of diversity in its expressions and in regional patterns of daily life. It is also marked by intellectual, theological, spiritual and institutional pluralism. As Muslim communities emerged around the world, they gave multiple expressions to belief in Islam as an all-encompassing dimension in their personal, social and communal lives. The many terms included in this Dictionary illustrate the vastness and variety of this heritage, its many contributions and continuing influence in Muslim societies worldwide, and more recently tensions resulting from activities by extremist groups seeking to impose their view of Islam on others through violence and intimidation.

Islamic banking In seeking to respond to the need for INTEREST-free banking, some Muslim countries and institutions in recent times have created Islamic banks. These financial institutions lend money to borrowers to invest in projects and thereby become partners, sharing risk in the event of a loss, and the profit in the case of success. Depositors are not, of course, guaranteed a fixed return, but become partners of the bank, to whom they entrust their money to invest in beneficial ventures. Such institutions now compete in many parts of the world with established banks and financial institutions. An Islamic Development Bank has also been organized jointly by Muslim countries to conform to such practices. *See also* INTEREST; MUSHARAKA; RIBA.

Islamic Salvation Front (Front Islamique Du Salut) *See* FIS.

Islamist The term that has increasingly come to be used for those Muslim groups seeking to enforce an ideological view of Islam in the political and social life of Muslim societies. It has also more broadly been applied to those who seek to establish norms of Muslim conduct in the affairs of society without necessarily seeking to challenge those in authority or encouraging extremism, including the use of violent means.

Islamization By the end of the ninth century Muslims had settled over a large territory. The Muslim CALIPHATE replaced the earlier empires of the Sassanids and Byzantines. The Arabs of the peninsula became the rulers of Alexandria, Antioch, Damascus, Jerusalem and other centres of the old orders and civilizations. The traditional narratives of early Islamic conquests tell us that the population of these territories, however, did not become Muslims immediately and exclusively. The religion was accepted at a much slower pace than the political rule itself. Islamization of the peoples was a gradual and complex process. At first the Arab Muslims did not endeavour to Islamize the population of the conquered territories. The system of *mawla* (clienthood) was introduced to Arabize those who wanted to accept Islam. Various religions existed side by side, and Jews, Christians and Zoroastrians often outnumbered Muslims. The process of Islamization went beyond accepting Islam as a religion only and included acceptance of the authority of the Muslim state, way of life and cultural forms that over time created very cosmopolitan societies.

Islamophobia A term used to describe hatred of Islam and Muslims.
Like other forms of hatred and hostility, the basis of Islamophobia rests on

perceived historical enmity between Muslims and the cultures of the West and in wilful misrepresentation of the teachings of Islam as 'foreign', 'alien' and 'barbaric' relative to modern notions of a civilized society. Particularly in very recent times, Islamophobia has been fuelled by migration from the Muslim world, especially to Europe, and by conflicts in and with countries in the Middle East that are deemed to threaten the world order.

Ismail *See* ISHMAEL.

Ismailiyya Branch of Shia Islam. It emerged as a group following the death of Imam JAFAR AL-SADIQ in 765, when a dispute arose regarding his successor. Those who gave allegiance to the line of imams descended from Imam Jafar's son, Ismail, are known as Ismailis. They achieved prominence during the tenth century with the establishment of the FATIMID Ismaili dynasty, based in North Africa and Egypt, which ruled for two centuries. During this period Ismaili influence was felt in the intellectual and cultural life of Muslim society with the establishment of their capital in Cairo and the founding of AL-AZHAR UNIVERSITY in 969–972. Cairo attracted many scholars, contributing to a vibrant intellectual environment under the patronage of the Fatimids.

Ismailism also became established in Iran, Central and South Asia and Yemen, enabling a federation of communities and regions to be directed from Cairo, linked by religious ties within a wider pluralistic state where the economy and trade flourished and which included Sunni Muslim, Jewish and Christian communities.

Following the break-up of the Fatimid dynasty, the Ismailis became divided again over succession. This led to two further branches, the Nizari and Mustali Ismailis (MUSTALIYYA). The former established a state in Iran and Syria which lasted until it was destroyed at the time of the MONGOL invasion in the late thirteenth century. For several centuries, the Ismailis survived periods of persecution and marginalization, often representing themselves as Sufi groups. The Nizari Ismailis at present give allegiance to Karim AGA KHAN as their spiritual leader and imam. They live in more than twenty countries, where they constitute active communities engaged in economic and social development. The Mustali Ismailis were based in Yemen for a time and eventually moved their centre to India, where their present head, Dr Sydena Mohammed Burhanuddin, provides religious leadership to a worldwide community, in the absence of the imam, who is believed to be in a state of concealment (SATR).

Ismailism has developed over time a tradition of intellectual and esoteric interpretation of faith and its role in personal and public life. Often because of this emphasis, its views have been regarded as unorthodox and have been criticized by more traditionally minded scholars. *See also* SHIA.

Isnad The chain of transmitters through whom HADITH have been reported, constituting a means of authenticating the accounts.

Israel Modern Jewish state created in 1948. Most of its minority Arab population (est. around 7 million), some 20 per cent of the total population, is Muslim, the rest being Christian. The conflict between Israel and its Arab neighbours since its founding has adversely affected the former pattern of Muslim life and control over religious, social and political affairs through the steady disestablishment of much of the Palestinian Muslim population, and in particular the dispute over control of Jerusalem has generated antipathy and opposition to Israel among Muslims in general.

The conflict has also resulted in the resurgence of political activism among certain Muslim groups, such as HAMAS. With the start of peace talks some divisive issues are the subject of negotiation but overall resolution often appears remote and difficult, thereby causing instability in the region as a whole.

Israiliyyat Narratives about biblical personages and ancient Israel preserved in Muslim literary and historical works. They also constituted an important resource for story tellers. With the establishment of the written Muslim tradition, the use of *israiliyyat* lost much of its importance. Later, heavy reliance on *israiliyyat* was condemned by strict scholars, who replaced *israiliyyat* in their works with HADITH endorsed by the established *hadith* collections.

Istanbul Major city in present-day Turkey. Formerly Constantinople, it was captured by the OTTOMANS from BYZANTINE rule in 1453 and renamed Istanbul. The new capital was completely reorganized, and became the centre of Ottoman architectural and cultural development. It contains some of the most important historical monuments of the dynasty, including the church of Hagia Sophia which was remodelled as a mosque, the Topkapi Palace, the Sultan Ahmet 'Blue' Mosque and some of the best examples of religious and public architecture designed by the famous sixteenth-century architect SINAN, particularly the Sulaymaniye Mosque. Istanbul continued as the administrative centre of the new Turkish republic until 1923, when Ankara became the capital, and has evolved into a modern metropolis that still reflects the legacy of the past.

Ithna Ashariyya The branch of Shiism that follows the line of twelve imams, regarding them as the rightful successors of the Prophet and the first imam, ALI IBN ABI TALIB. It is also known as Twelver Imami Shiism.

Following the death of Imam JAFAR AL-SADIQ in 765, some of the Shia gave allegiance to his son, Musa al-Kazim, whose descendants continued to be recognized as the rightful imams by the followers. In 874, the Ithna Asharis believe, the twelfth imam Muhammad AL-MAHDI disappeared, and will return at the end of time as the divinely guided leader (*mahdi*).

After this event, known as GHAYBA ('occultation'), the community continued to be guided by representative scholars, who acted as deputies. These scholars, in their custodial role, continued the teachings of the imams and led the organization of the community, providing it with a documented and codified legal and theological grounding.

In the course of Muslim history a number of ruling dynasties espoused the cause of Twelver Shiism. The best known was the SAFAWID, which controlled IRAN from 1501. During its rule Twelver Shiism became the established state SCHOOL OF ISLAMIC LAW and the role of scholars and jurists came to be further elaborated and institutionalized as part of the framework of the state.

The Twelver Shia interpretation of Islam emphasizes foundational beliefs known as *usul al-din*, the fundamentals of faith, and *furu al-din*, religious practices. The role of the intellect becomes significant in the interpretation of the faith and enables the scholars and jurists of the tradition to provide guidance for individuals in matters of practice.

The devotional spirit of Ithna Ashari Shiism towards the imams and their families is expressed by visiting their shrines, which are found in cities in Iraq and Iran such as Karbala, Najaf, Mashhad, Samarra and Kazimayn. Another important tradition is the commemoration of the martyrdom of Imam HUSAYN IBN ALI during the first ten days of the month of Muharram.

The most numerous branch of the Shia, the Ithna Asharis predominate in Iran and Iraq and are also found in significant numbers in Azerbaijan, Lebanon, the Gulf States, Saudi Arabia, India, Pakistan, East Africa, Europe and North America. Since the 1979 revolution in Iran, the Ithna Ashari school of thought has become further integrated into Iranian political, social and institutional life through the direct creation of structures that allow religious scholars to play an active and significant role in the government of the country.

Under the leadership of Ayatollah Ruhollah KHOMEINI, the concept of WILAYAT AL-FAQIH was formally institutionalized within the context of the constitution of a modern nation-state in Iran, empowering scholars and jurists to play such a role.

Iwan Architectural term. A vaulted hall, opening directly on to a courtyard. It evolved into a characteristic feature of Muslim buildings such as *madrasas* and mosques.

Iznik A town in Turkey noted for its distinctive style of tilework which flourished during the OTTOMAN EMPIRE.

Jabir Ibn Hayyan An early Muslim thinker of the eighth century, noted for his contribution to alchemy and its development in relation to a philosophical and gnostic understanding of Islam. While it is not clear how much of the corpus attributed to Jabir consists of his own writings, he exercised a major influence on the subsequent development of alchemy. He is also reputed to have contributed commentaries on important works of astronomy, astrology, medicine, music, mathematics and magic.

Jacob (Arabic, Yaqub) Jacob is referred to in the Quran as following in the tradition of Abraham.

Jadidism Intellectual movement of the nineteenth and early twentieth century which emerged among Muslims of Central Asia and the regions that had come under Russian control. It sought to reform and revive Muslim learning and institutions to respond to the challenges of change at that time.

Jafar al-Sadiq (699–765) Sixth imam of the Shia. Together with his father, MUHAM-MAD AL-BAQIR, Jafar al-Sadiq is regarded as one who consolidated the foundations of Shia legal thought and the systematization of its doctrinal basis. During a time of political and religious conflict and turmoil he sought to maintain spiritual leadership of the majority of the Shia, attracting scholars of all persuasions to his teachings.

Jahanara Begum (1614–1681) Daughter of the MOGHUL Emperor SHAH JAHAN and his wife MUMTAZ MAHAL. She was an established scholar and exponent of Sufi teachings. Jahanara Begum endowed the building of the Friday mosque in Agra.

Jahangir (1569–1627) MOGHUL emperor, generally known for his patronage of the arts. However, his reign led to worsening relations with the Sikh population of the Empire.

jahiliyya The period of ignorance before the coming of Islam. It indicates the absence of faith in God and a society deprived of divine revelation and guidance, bound by its tribal worldview.

Jalal al-Din Rumi (1207–1273) Among the greatest mystical poets of Islam. The Persian writings and poetry of Rumi, or Mawlana as he is often called, constitute a vast treasury of stories, interpretations, expositions and verses that illustrate Sufism and its central themes and concepts. He was born in Balkh, now part of Afghanistan, and died in Konya in Turkey, where his tomb and the surrounding complex attract many visitors.

A significant influence on his spiritual development was a mysterious figure, a wandering mystic by the name of Shams al-din Tabrizi. The *Mathnawi*, his most famous work, often refers to this influence and intimacy which sparked his quest for spirituality. In his other writings, including his *Diwan*, Rumi creates a framework for expressing his vision of love, unity and an awareness transcending human and social difference, which the true mystic can attain. More recently, the universal appeal of his work has brought him to the attention of other societies, particularly in the West. His writings have been translated into many different languages. His disciples formed themselves into an order called the MEVLEVI, which is active in many parts of the world. For an example of his verse, see SUFISM.

Jali An ornamented and perforated screen, made of stone and found largely in Muslim monuments on the Indian subcontinent.

Jalinus *See* GALEN.

Jamaat-i-Islami Pakistani political party and movement. It was founded in Lahore in 1941 by Mawlana Sayyid Abu al-Ala MAWDUDI, who led the organization until 1972 and died in 1979. The Jamaat was established initially to provide a platform to address the needs of Muslims in British India. Mawdudi and many of its leaders moved to Pakistan during the period of upheaval and transition after partition in 1947. There it emerged as a political movement with a strong agenda based on reviving traditional Muslim institutions and patterns in Pakistani society. The Jamaat's main platform was the creation of a Muslim society and it challenged the early government of Pakistan to implement a fully Islamic constitution.

Though it participated in several national elections, the Jamaat never won enough seats to take power and it therefore continued to play the role of opposition party. Since 1972 its leaders have sought to develop alliances with like-minded parties and leaders, continuing to put forward its policy of 'Islamicization' of the state at all levels. It has had a strong missionary orientation and been influential in rallying support among Muslim settlers and students in Britain, continental Europe and North America, through the creation of organizations and educational institutions.

Jamal al-Din al-Afghani (1838–1897) Modern Muslim reformer, activist, and writer. He claimed to be from Afghanistan but other sources suggest that he was born in Iran. He is, however, known to have been educated in Afghanistan and India. Subsequently he undertook a series of extensive travels in the Muslim world. He passionately supported pan-Islamic ideas while embracing the modernism of the age and promoting a revival of philosophical Muslim thinking. Al-Afghani urged Muslims to unite against European rule and despotic rulers. He also criticized certain scholars for their traditionalist mentality or, at the other extreme, an acceptance of Western institutions. He gathered followers during his travels and worked closely with MUHAMMAD ABDUH, founding a periodical called *al-Urwa al-wuthqa*, which was addressed to concerned Muslims everywhere.

Al-Afghani spent the last years of his life under the watchful eye of the OTTOMAN Sultan Mehmed VI, who had invited him to his court in Istanbul, where his presence was resented by some religious scholars. Since he did not leave behind any significant written works, al-Afghani's life and thought have generated controversy but his role as an activist and reformer have continued to influence Muslims in various parts of the world.

jamat khana Space for devotional and congregational activity. It is associated primarily with Sufi groups. The term is also used for the congregational centres of the Nizari Ismailis. *See also* SPACES OF GATHERING.

jami The Friday mosque, the main congregational centre for the Friday noon prayer in a traditional Muslim city.

Jami, Abd al-Rahman (1414–1492) Sufi poet who wrote in Persian. He is best known for recounting in one of his poems the story of JOSEPH and Zulaykha.

Jamiat Ulama-i-Hind *See* DEOBAND.

Java Chronicles *See* BABAD TANAH JAWA.

Jerusalem (Arabic, al-Quds) Ancient city with central historical significance in Jewish, Christian and Muslim history. Jerusalem is believed by Muslims to be the home of the 'distant mosque' (al-Masjid al-Aqsa) referred to in the Quran (17:1). It is thus associated with the Prophet's *isra* or *miraj* (ascension), a night journey where the Prophet was taken up through the seven heavens to the divine throne. Jerusalem was conquered by the Muslim armies in 635. Eventually, on the site of the ancient Temple Mount, a mosque called al-Aqsa and a sanctuary, the Dome of the Rock (al-Qubbat al-Sakhra), were built to commemorate the prophet's journey and the presence of Islam. This area is known as the HARAM AL-SHARIF, the Noble Sanctuary. It is revered by Muslims also because of its association with prophetic figures mentioned in the Quran such as JESUS, David and SOLOMON and is a major centre for pilgrimage.

Jerusalem remained under mostly Muslim control until the beginning of the twentieth century. Since Israel gained control of all of Jerusalem following the 1967 war against Arab states, its status has remained a contested issue between Israel and the Palestinians in the context of the pursuit of lasting peace in the region.

Jesus The Quranic name for Jesus is Isa. He appears extensively in the Quran, which describes events such as his miraculous birth, his preaching, his miracles and his death. The Quran regards him as one of the great prophets and messengers to whom God granted revelation; a spirit from God and also as the word of God. The Quran denies the doctrine of the Trinity as it compromises the unity of God and associates another with God. Jesus is a highly venerated figure, particularly among Sufi Muslims, who see him as a model of the true devotee consumed by his love for God.

Jibril *See* GABRIEL.

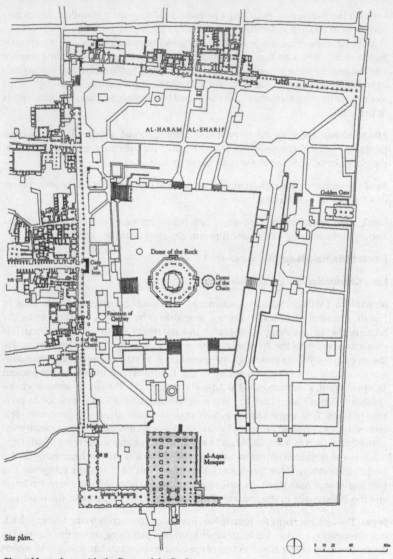

AL-HARAM AL-SHARIF

Golden Gate

○ Dome of the Rock

Dome of the Chain

Gate of Iron

Fountain of Qaitbay

Gate of the Chain

Maghrabi Gate

al-Aqsa Mosque

Islamic Museum

Site plan.

0 10 20 40 80m

Plan of Jerusalem, with the Dome of the Rock.

jihad As a general term, the struggle to create a just and divinely ordered society. The Quran refers to armed defence and justly executed warfare, for which Islam specifies the conditions of war and peace, the treatment of captives and the negotiation and resolution of conflict.

In juristic writings Muslim scholars developed further the idea of *jihad* both as concerned with the defence of Muslim society and also as an extension of its borders. Such writings include extensive discussions of all aspects of warfare, including the notions of justifiable aggression, the authority for and conduct of war, the appropriate treatment of captives, including women, children and the elderly, and the role of arbitration and negotiation in bringing hostilities to an end.

Among Sufi Muslims and others, the idea of *jihad* as warfare represented an incomplete understanding of the concept and interpretation of Prophetic tradition. They emphasized the distinction between the lesser *jihad*, for war and defence, and the greater *jihad*, the struggle for mastery of one's own self to gain deeper spiritual understanding of the inner meaning of the faith.

In contemporary times Muslims have defined *jihad* in broader terms to encompass ideas of resistance to colonial rule, the struggle for emancipation and the fight against injustice and tyranny as well as ignorance. The term JIHADIST is now sometimes used in the media, to describe those who argue for and undertake war against the state or those they believe to be against the restoration of a true Muslim society and state. To such groups, Muslims and non-Muslims are equally culpable and therefore legitimate targets against whom violence and killing is justifiable.

jihadist Literally, one who undertakes JIHAD. However, in recent times the term has come to refer to those groups in the Muslim world who believe in remaking Muslim societies and fighting against Western influence through acts of violence, including suicide missions.

Their imagined ideal of the Muslim world includes a unified society under a single authority which would impose Islam on all, by force if necessary. While such groups appear to be increasing in influence by exploiting regional and global conflicts and are very active in propagating their views through the internet and other means, they generally represent only a small minority and their policies are rejected by most Muslim authorities as utterly unrepresentative of and opposed to the ideals of Islam.

jilbab See HIJAB.

jinn This term in the Quran refers to beings who are invisible and yet possess great powers, good and evil.

Jinnah, Muhammad Ali (1876–1948) Muslim political leader and founder of the modern state of Pakistan, for which he is known as the Great Leader (Qaid-i-Azam). A lawyer by training, he founded the India Muslim Congress on his return to India from England, which pressed for independence from Britain. He later realized that the goals of independence would disadvantage Muslims and so created a separate party, the MUSLIM LEAGUE, to rally Muslims to the cause of a separate state.

In 1947 the British Empire in India was dismantled and the territory partitioned into two countries, India and the predominantly Muslim Pakistan. Jinnah's writings and speeches indicate that he was an advocate of a modern and democratic state in which Muslims and non-Muslims would have equal rights under the law. He died in 1948.

Job *See* AYYUB.

John the Baptist Referred to in the Quran as Yahya and called a prophet, he is a gift from God to the elderly Zachariah and his barren wife, in response to their prayers. In Muslim tradition his role is further developed as a precursor to Jesus. He is believed to be buried within the precincts of the Great Mosque in Damascus, which is as a result also a site of Christian pilgrimage.

John of Damascus Well-known theologian of the Eastern Orthodox Christian tradition, whose contacts with Muslims enabled him to write about Islam and to debate key issues on which Christian and Muslim views differed, particularly on the unity of God and the Trinitarian doctrine as well as the acceptability of images of the Divine in the form of icons.

Jordan Middle Eastern monarchy which evolved in 1946 out of the former British-ruled emirate of Transjordan. Following the first Arab–Israeli war in 1948–9, parts of Palestine that contained a growing refugee population were incorporated and the state was renamed the Hashemite Kingdom of Jordan. Following the assassination of King Abdullah his son Hussein ibn Tallal assumed the throne formally in 1952 and ruled until his death in 1999, a long period marked by important political, economic and religious changes and challenges.

The population is predominantly Sunni and is represented through a variety of institutions and organizations. The MUSLIM BROTHERHOOD is organized as a political party in alliance with other groups and has been active in promoting its religious policies but without actively seeking to oppose the monarchy. There are a number of other organizations including the HIZB AL-TAHRIR whose agendas are more confrontational but they do not have recognized political status. The impact of these and other Muslim groups within Jordan cannot be underestimated, given the ongoing instability and disruption in the region created by the Palestinian conflict with Israel and the presence of many Muslims of Palestinian origin who have found refuge and a home in Jordan. The present monarch, King Abdullah, has spoken out strongly against radicalizing influences in the region and encouraged Muslims to come together to build a common platform to address their challenges in a peaceful and negotiated manner. *See also* AMMAN DECLARATION.

Joseph (Arabic, Yusuf) Chapter 12 of the Quran narrates the story of Joseph as the 'most beautiful of narratives'. It tells the story of his life and particularly his efforts in overcoming obstacles and his triumph as a prophetic figure endowed with the capacity to decipher dreams and provide leadership to Egypt in times of crisis.

Judaism At the time of the birth of Islam there were several Jewish settlements in Arabia. The Quran regarded the revelation to the Prophet Muhammad as part of a continuous tradition, which included the Hebrew Prophets and recognized the Torah (*see* TAWRAT) as revelation. Jews were regarded as 'People of the Book' (AHL AL-KITAB) and, like other protected religious communities, were granted freedom to associate, practise their faith and retain their community structures. The rapid expansion of Islam in neighbouring regions brought Muslims into contact with other Jewish communities, who over time came under Muslim rule, contributing to the extension of trade and commerce in various regions. In certain areas such as Egypt, North Africa and Andalusia, Jews contributed to the larger intellectual community, often producing works on Jewish theology in Arabic. In 1492, when Jews and Muslims were expelled from Spain, the former migrated to North Africa and other Muslim lands. Under OTTOMAN rule Jews maintained their contribution to various aspects of economic and commercial life, while retaining their religious autonomy. In a minority of instances they were subjected to persecution, but in general it is fair to say that Jews under Muslim rule were able to contribute to the larger civil society, were permitted religious freedom and frequently adopted the language and often the cultural practices of the various regions in which they lived.

Jundub ibn Junada See ABU DHARR AL-GHAFFARI.

Juwayni, Abd al-Malik (1028–1085) Sunni scholar. Juwayni was one of the foremost scholars of Sunni theology and teacher of the noted theologian Abu Hamid Muhammad AL-GHAZALI. He was also known as the Imam of the Two Holy Cities (Imam al-Haramayn) for having taught in Mecca and Medina.

K

Ka'ba (lit., 'cube') Referred to in the Quran as the house of God, the Ka'ba is the most important sanctuary in Islam.

The structure, now located in the centre of the mosque at Mecca, is the site of the annual pilgrimage, the HAJJ. Encased in the wall on the outside of the Ka'ba is the Black Stone which is ritually touched or kissed by pilgrims. Muslims believe that the first Ka'ba was constructed by the Prophet ADAM and subsequently rededicated to the worship of God by ABRAHAM and his son ISHMAEL. By restoring it as the centre of Islamic ritual, the Prophet Muhammad abolished its use as a pre-Islamic shrine, which housed images of deities. It also constitutes the *qibla*, the direction to be faced during prayer.

kafir *See* KUFR.

kalam Theological reflection, leading to the study and discussion of faith, aimed at expressing the content matter of the faith in a coherent and rational manner. Over time *kalam* became a discipline taught at institutions of learning.

kalima *See* SHAHADA.

Kanem Ancient Muslim kingdom in the central Sudan region. Kanem developed as an important trading state in the twelfth and thirteenth centuries. It was also known as a centre of Muslim scholarship. The name is used for a region in present-day Chad.

Kano City in northern Nigeria. Kano has been a major centre of Muslim learning since the fifteenth century. The Kano Chronicles, a record of its history, traces the early presence of Muslims in the area and the subsequent emergence of Kano. One of the foremost scholars of Muslim law and theology, Muhammad AL-MAGHILI, lived there during the fifteenth century, making it an important centre for legal scholarship and practice. The city developed as a political centre and became a major link in a trading network. In the nineteenth century it became part of the SOKOTO CALIPHATE created by UTHMAN DAN FODIO and his successors, and remains to this day an important centre for Muslim culture and life in northern Nigeria.

Karbala Site of the martyrdom of the Shia imam and grandson of the Prophet, HUSAYN IBN ALI, in the year 680. Today it is a place of pilgrimage and a major town in Iraq. The sanctuary, housing the tomb of Imam Husayn, is visited by thousands of pilgrims, particularly during the month of Muharram. *See also* ASHURA.

Kashani, Ayatollah (d. 1962) Major Imami Shia religious scholar. Ayatollah Kashani played an important public role in Iran in the twentieth century. He is remembered for his engagement in the issues facing Iran and as an advocate of the integration of religious views in political affairs and decisions. He was also a renowned teacher and scholar.

Kashmir Region in the Himalaya. Kashmir is currently divided between India (the province of Kashmir) and Pakistan, where the portion under its control is called Azad Kashmir. The region first came into contact with Muslims in the eighth century, but Muslim rule was not established until the eleventh century, when a Hindu king converted to Islam and declared himself a sultan. Several dynasties ruled in the region until the time of MOGHUL ascendancy in the sixteenth century. Moghul rule was followed by a brief period of Sikh rule, until British intervention in 1846 and the transfer of Kashmir to the ruler of neighbouring Jammu, Raja Gulab Singh. During the movement for Indian independence from Britain the Muslim population of Kashmir sought a constitutional government. At the time of partition, and following war between India and Pakistan, a ceasefire line was established in Kashmir. The part under Indian control has since experienced periods of turbulent opposition in the quest for autonomy while India and Pakistan have engaged in two wars and a series of ongoing conflicts over Kashmir's status. Prolonged negotiations between the two countries to resolve the dispute continue at the time of writing.

The majority of the region's population is Muslim, with the Sunnis predominating. A significant Shia minority is also found in Kashmir.

Kasrawi Tabrizi, Sayyid Ahmad (1890–1946) Iranian scholar and activist. He served as a civil judge and university professor and published pamphlets that attacked existing political, cultural and religious policies which, he said, caused the country to be backward and divided. Kasrawi was assassinated in 1946 by a member of a religious organization for his attacks on religion.

Katib Çelebi, Mustafa ibn Abd Allah (1609–1657) Turkish scholar. One of the most noted scholars of the OTTOMAN period, he is considered outstanding for his historical scholarship and his extensive studies of the geography of the empire.

Kazakhstan Central Asian republic, formerly part of the Soviet Union. Out of a population of around 15 million, approximately 40 per cent are ethnic Kazakh who identify with Islam and follow the Hanafi SCHOOL OF ISLAMIC LAW. The spread of Islam in the area in the late eighteenth century was encouraged by Catherine the Great, who saw it as a way of controlling the nomads of the region. The recent establishment of a *muftiyat* (an Islamic high council, whose members are MUFTIS) located in Alma Ata signalled Kazakhstan's desire to separate politics and religion, and the state continues to function as a secular entity which has so far prohibited the establishment of any ideologically based political party, including any based on religion. The constitution guarantees religious freedom and Muslim scholars from Turkey and other neighbouring regions have participated in educating people in Islam. Because of its petroleum resources, Kazakhstan has attracted investment from the RUSSIAN FEDERATION, Europe and America and is considered an important Western ally in the region.

Kazan Khanate Muslim state founded in the fifteenth century. It ruled over what is present-day Tatarstan in Russia. It was in constant conflict with the ruling Russian dynasty and was defeated in 1552. There then followed a period of forced assimilation into Russian culture and conversion to the Orthodox Church.

Kenya East African state. A former British colony, Kenya gained its independence in 1963. About 15 to 20 per cent of its population of around 28 million follow Islam, a majority of whom are Sunni who follow the Shafii SCHOOL OF ISLAMIC LAW. There are, however, followers of other Sunni and Shia schools in the country. The history of Islam in the coastal region of Kenya goes back to ancient times and archaeological remains suggest Muslim presence as early as the eighth century. Following the Islamization of the coast in the next several centuries, a distinctive Swahili Muslim culture emerged as a result of contacts between African, Indian Ocean and Arab Muslims. The northern region of Kenya, bordering on Somalia, is largely Muslim with a nomadic population. Recent conflict in Somalia has made Kenya home to many refugees who have fled the war-torn region.

Khadija (d. 619) First wife of the Prophet and one of the first converts to Islam. Khadija, a widow, was engaged in business when she first met Muhammad and hired him to operate her caravan trade. She then married him and gave birth to two sons and four daughters during their twenty-five years of marriage. Only one of her daughters outlived the Prophet and both sons died in infancy. Khadija's support, companionship and understanding were critical for the Prophet in his time of trial and doubt during this early part of his mission. She remains an important role model of active public life and family support for many Muslim women.

Khalid ibn al-Walid (d. 642) Military leader. In the early period of Muslim history, he fought against the Prophet. However, after his conversion Khalid ibn al-Walid became one of the great military commanders of the period of early Muslim conquest, particularly in Iraq.

Khalide, Edib Adivar (1884–1964) Renowned Turkish writer, novelist and teacher. She served in the Turkish war of independence and as a deputy in parliament and is regarded as one of the dominant figures of modern Turkish literature.

khalifa See CALIPH.

khanqa or *zawiya* Place for devotional gathering and meditation among the Sufis. *See also* SPACES OF GATHERING.

kharaj Muslim legal term for a land tax. The earliest practice emerged with reference to conquered territory, when Muslim authorities guaranteed land to its owners, who were required to pay a tax on such land.

khatib (pl., *khutaba*) Official preacher who delivers Friday sermons. In time the task of delivering a sermon became the prerogative of the religious scholars and leaders at the Friday prayer in mosques. The *khatib* has a special pulpit (*minbar*) in the mosque from where he delivers his KHUTBA.

Khawarij or **Kharijis** Early Muslim group that chose to leave the Muslim community (*khawarij* means 'those who left'). This was done because they disagreed on doctrinal grounds with the new caliph, ALI IBN ABI TALIB, over how to resolve the crisis generated by MUAWIYYA's attempt to seize authority over the Muslim community. They expressed their opposition through militant means while developing their own framework of theological and political interpretation. Though the major group passed out of existence, a small sub-group called the Ibadi still survives, found mainly in Oman, Zanzibar and parts of Algeria (*see* IBADIYYA).

Khayyam, Umar or **Omar** *See* UMAR KHAYYAM.

Khidr Legendary figure in Muslim mystical tradition, based on a reference in the Quran (48) to a servant of God, who accompanies MOSES and leaves him after a series of enigmatic episodes whose significance he explains to a sceptical Moses. In mystical tradition, he is referred to as the 'spiritual guide' and friend of God.

khimar See HIJAB.

al-Khoei, Sayyed (1899–1992) Grand Ayatollah who lived primarily in Najaf in Iraq and was the most respected scholar and leader of the Imami Shia community. His followers considered him as a *marja*, one whose knowledge and piety made his life an exemplary point of reference and emulation. After his death, the al-Khoei Foundation was set up to direct a network of charitable and educational activities in different parts of the world. His son Sayyid Abdul Majid al-Khoei was also a prominent scholar and continued the work of the al-Khoei Foundation after he found refuge in London following the death of his father. He was assassinated in Najaf in 2003.

Khomeini, Ayatollah Ruhollah (1902–1989) Acknowledged leader of the Islamic revolution in Iran in 1979 who led a popular uprising against the Shah of Iran, Muhammad Reza Pahlavi, causing him to be dethroned and thereby ending a long period of monarchy in the country.

He received his religious training in Qom and like most scholars there travelled frequently to the Iraqi cities of Najaf and Karbala, where he kept in touch with other Shia scholars.

In 1963 he led various protests against the policies of the Shah and was exiled eventually to Najaf. He continued to write against the regime and criticized the pattern of Westernization and undue American and European influence on Muslim values and traditions, defending the role and the place of the SHARIA.

In 1978, he was expelled from Iraq and spent a year in exile in Paris, from where he continued his opposition. Following the expulsion of the Shah in 1979, Ayatollah Khomeini became Iran's spiritual leader at the head of a group of jurists who formed the guardianship of the jurisconsult (*wilayat-i-faqih*), exercising authority and ensuring that political and governance processes in Iran (primarily in the hands of the MAJLIS) were in accordance with what they regarded as the teachings of Islam.

In 1980 Iran was invaded by Iraq and Ayatollah Khomeini pursued an active military strategy to resist the invasion. Eventually, after much loss of life, a ceasefire was agreed in 1988. During this period Iran had become isolated from most Western countries, though it remained active in promoting its revolution in the region. In 1989, shortly before his death, Ayatollah Khomeini drew further world-wide attention by declaring a FATWA against the British author Salman Rushdie, accusing him of heresy for writing his novel *The Satanic Verses*. Khomeini's mausoleum is a major site of pilgrimage in Iran today.

Khumm, Pool of *See* GHADIR KHUMM.

khutba Sermon or address. The *khutba* is formally associated with the Friday prayer, when it is delivered by the imam of the mosque prior to the congregational worship. *See also* KHATIB.

Khwaja Abu Ishaq *See* CHISHTIYYA.

al-Kindi, Abd al-Masih ibn Ishaq (d. c. 866) Philosopher and scientist. He is regarded as the first major polymath scientist and intellectual whose knowledge and writings encompassed the study and exploration of the classical heritage in diverse fields. Often called the Philosopher of the Arabs, al-Kindi has had great influence on later Muslim philosophers and scientists. Al-Kindi's approach to the classical heritage of rational sciences was to reconcile belief in God and supremacy of the Muslim scripture with the content and methods of philosophy. In addition to works of philosophy, al-Kindi also wrote on logic, arithmetic, geometry and astronomy.

knowledge The concepts of knowledge and learning are at the heart of Muslim thought and are believed to be incumbent on believers both by virtue of the teachings of the Quran, where the intellect is granted as a gift from God to human beings, and also because of the overriding importance attached to the pursuit of knowledge and learning in the tradition of the Prophet Muhammad.

The importance of knowledge in Muslim history is attested to by the significance of education, from the religious to the philosophical, the preponderance of institutions and libraries to promote study and learning and the general openness of Muslims in pre-modern times to learning from and further developing knowledge traditions from several cultures including Greek, Persian and Indian sources.

The challenges represented by the development of new forms of knowledge in modern times, emanating particularly from the West, has provided an impetus for most Muslims to reconsider their own standards of attainment in various fields of education and science and their ability to give access to this knowledge to all segments of Muslim society.

Koran *See* QURAN.

Kubrawiyya *See* NAJM AL-DIN KUBRA.

kufr In its original meaning signifies one who is 'ungrateful to God'. Later it came to be used to denote 'infidel, non-believer, atheist'. The person accused of *kufr* or unbelief is referred to as *kafir* (pl., *kafirun*).

Kurds Muslim peoples who are found in several Middle Eastern countries, including Iran, Iraq, Syria and Turkey. They came into contact with Muslims during the early period of the expansion of Islam into their regions and over time converted and became integrated into the framework of Muslim political life and society. The majority of the Kurds are Sunni and Sufism has played an important role in the transmission and practice of their religious life.

After the division of the Middle East into various colonial and national entities, following World War I, Kurdish nationalists sought a region of their own called Kurdistan and fought for their nationalist aspirations, particularly in Iraq and Turkey. Hostilities have continued intermittently until today, and in some instances the repression has been particularly brutal against Kurdish guerrilla activity in Iraq and Turkey. Since the fall of Saddam HUSSEIN, the Kurdish region of Iraq has gained significant autonomy and representation in the new structure of government.

Kuwait Gulf state. An oil-rich kingdom, Kuwait became independent from British rule in 1961. The population is estimated at 2 million, of which 85 per cent are Muslim. Approximately 45 per cent are Sunni who follow the Maliki SCHOOL OF

Water Towers, Kuwait City, Kuwait.

ISLAMIC LAW, 35 per cent are Imami Shias while the remainder follow the Shafii School. The Shia have a significant influence in the economic and social life of the country. Kuwait was invaded by Iraq in 1990, but a joint force of Western and Arab troops drove out the Iraqi army, restoring the rule of the emir. More recently the election process has been more widely employed in Kuwait to appoint local officials and representatives.

Kyrgyzstan Central Asian republic, formerly part of the Soviet Union. Approximately 55 per cent of the population of around 5 million are Sunni Muslims of the Hanafi SCHOOL OF ISLAMIC LAW. Islam was introduced to the region in the eighteenth century by Muslim traders. *The Epic of Manas* contains the inherited accounts of the history of the Kyrgyz people.

Lahore City in Punjab in Pakistan. Lahore developed as a major centre of culture, particularly during the MOGHUL period. Its most important monuments are its fort, known locally as the Shahi Qila, the Shalimar Gardens and various mosques and tombs. It continues to be an influential cultural centre and is home to many writers, poets and musicians.

Lamu Town in modern Kenya. Lamu was an important Muslim island community, and the urban features of Swahili Muslim culture have been retained there virtually intact. It continues to be an important centre for Swahili literature and has a distinctive tradition of honouring the Prophet's birthday in a week-long celebration.

Latin Originally the language of the Roman Republic and the Roman Empire, it also became one of the languages of the Western Church and scholarship after Christianity became the dominant tradition of the empire. Although by the time of the rise of Islam, Greek and Arabic were widely used within the Roman Empire, Latin retained its official role as the language of government and eventually of the practice and the liturgy of Roman Catholicism. The emergence of the Muslim world as the centre of political power and scholarship, and the establishment of Arabic as the lingua franca of the Near East, supplanted the dominant role of Latin in the region, particularly in scholarship after the ABBASID Caliph al-Mamun established the BAYT AL-HIKMA (House of Wisdom), where books were translated from Greek and Syriac into Arabic. Once all the existing knowledge was translated into Arabic and the language developed its own scientific vocabulary, it rapidly took over from Latin as a language of science and culture.

law See SHARIA.

Layla and Majnun Beloved and lover who feature in one of the best-loved romantic tales in Muslim literature. Their love for each other became a model for literary and poetic expression of devotion to God in Muslim mystical literature.

Laylat al-Qadr The Night of Power. This is the night referred to in *sura* 97 (*Surat al-Qadr*), during the month of Ramadan, in which according to Muslim tradition the revelation of the Quran first came to the Prophet. The devout gather to spend the night in acts of devotion, contemplation and recitation of the Quran.

League of Arab States An international organization, also known as the Arab League, created in 1945 and composed of twenty-two independent Arab nations.

Although originally formed to facilitate coordination among its members and to discuss political and strategic challenges and issues faced by the region, it has since developed its scope further by extending cooperation in non-political areas, including culture, economy, law, etc.

Lebanon Middle Eastern state. A multi-religious and culturally diverse country, Lebanon was constituted as a state under French control in 1920 and became formally independent in 1941. In 1943 Bishara al-Khuri was elected as the first President. Its population of around 5 million consists of Christian groups who make up about 40 per cent of the population with Muslims and the DRUZE representing the remainder. The Shia are in a slight majority among the Muslim population.

Various groups were involved in a brutal civil war that started in 1975 and reduced what had been perceived to be a relatively peaceful and prosperous cosmopolitan society into one devastated by religious and civil strife and violence. In addition, the establishment of a buffer zone by Israel in the south of Lebanon exacerbated the conflict by drawing Lebanon into the wider political confrontations in the region.

In 1989 the various religious and military groups agreed to an accord that was meant to initiate a period of relative stability and reconstruction of civil society. Within its framework, the president was to be a Maronite Christian, the prime minister a Sunni Muslim and the parliamentary speaker a Shia Muslim. Interfaith organizations were created to promote better relations and cooperation among different faith groups.

The withdrawal of Syrian troops from the south of the country was intended to promote a more peaceful state of affairs but the growth of HIZBULLAH in the south and its continuing confrontation with Israel have more recently plunged Lebanon into war, causing increased tension and widespread disruption to civil life and political institutions.

Leo Africanus (b. 1489 and died sometime after 1550) Early chronicler. A Muslim of Spanish origin, whose name was Hasan al-Zayyati, he left an account of his life and travels in the Muslim world and in Europe. He was converted to Christianity in 1520 and is believed to have returned to Tunis before his death.

Liberia West African nation with a population of around 4 million. Islam first came to the region after the sixteenth century, and its spread was intensified in the nineteenth as the area opened up with the settlement of slaves freed from the United States. There is presently a significant Muslim minority. Muslims have continued to receive increasing recognition in public life and schools and institutions have been set up to promote development in social and economic life.

After decades of political instability and internal conflicts, Ellen Johnson-Sirleaf, a Harvard-trained economist, became the first woman president of Liberia in 2005.

Libya North African state. This Arab Muslim country has a population of around 6 million which is predominantly Sunni, following the Maliki SCHOOL OF ISLAMIC LAW. Islam was first introduced in 647, and its history has been part of the overall development of the region traditionally referred to as the Maghreb or Ifriqiyya. During the OTTOMAN period the areas which eventually constituted Libya were administered by governors and military heads.

A Sufi order called the SANUSIYYA, founded by Muhammad al-Sanusi (1787–1859), helped to unite various Sufi groups in the region, and these various groups organized trade and agricultural activities and revitalized religious life. Italian designs on the region eventually led to an invasion in 1911 and Italy subsequently colonized much of the territory, forcing the Sanusi leaders into exile. In 1932 the Italians consolidated their territorial gains to create the colony of Libya.

After Italy's defeat in World War II, Libya came under first British control and then a United Nations mandate, gaining independence in 1951 when the Sanusi leader, Ahmed Idris, was declared king. The Idrisid line was challenged by other nationalist groups and eventually, in 1969, a military coup brought Muammar al-Qaddafi to power. His political, foreign and religious policies have in the last three decades generated opposition both inside and outside the country. Qaddafi's own definition of Muslim practice and his attempts to interpret the Quran have been disputed, though they continue to be enforced within the country. In 2003, Qaddafi agreed to destroy the country's chemical, nuclear and biological weapons and opened Libya up to trade and diplomatic relations after a long period of international isolation.

Lot (Arabic, Lut) The Quran recounts the biblical story of Lot in which in his role as God's messenger he was sent to Sodom to warn the people about the consequences of their excesses and their impending doom. His calls to return to the true path and obey God were ignored. God subsequently sent angels to warn Lot and his family to leave the city before it was destroyed. Lot's wife perished as punishment for disobeying her husband. The account, like others in the Quran, explains and highlights the consequences of disobedience and rejection of God's messenger.

Loya Jirga (lit., 'Great Assembly') In Afghanistan, the traditional assembly of tribal or regional leaders and figures of any importance (religious, military, royal) summoned by the ruler. It can be called on an irregular basis and can last until consensus is reached. More recently the Loya Jirga has been summoned to arrive at a consensus on building administrative stability following Afghanistan's recent crisis, to discuss the draft of the Afghan Constitution in 2003 and again to arrive at agreement to resolve long-standing disputes within groups in Afghanistan and to discuss conflicts on the border with Pakistan.

Luristan Luristan ('Land of the Lurs'), so named in the sixteenth century, is a region in south-western Iran. It was a centre for bronze-working from the fourth millennium BCE and continued as such until the seventh century BCE. In contemporary times the Lur are a nomadic people, a majority of whom are Shia. It is thought that as many as 500,000 currently live in Iran.

Lut *See* LOT.

M

Ma Hua-Lung (d. 1871) A pivotal Chinese Muslim leader who led a movement to establish Muslim autonomy in the north-west region of China, integrating Chinese and Muslim elements in his activities and basing his teachings on a reaffirmation of Islam against attempts to dominate and bring Muslims under the total control of Chinese imperial rule and influence. After a successful imperial campaign to put down the movement, Ma Hua-Lung surrendered to prevent further destruction and starvation of his supporters and was executed in 1871.

Ma Ming-Hsin (d. 1781) Sufi saint of the NAQSHBANDIYYA order in China who attempted to bring about reforms in Sufi practices. Local Chinese authorities sought to interdict his movement, believing that it would give rise to sedition and instability. He was captured and eventually executed, but left behind a strong following of what came to be known as the New Teaching.

ma sha'a Allah (lit., 'that which is what God wills') This Quranic expression is widely used to express approbation and affirmation of that which is believed to be in accord with the will of God.

Maadd, al-Muizz al-Din Allah (931–975) FATIMID imam and caliph. He extended the Fatimid Empire from North Africa to Egypt, founding the city of Cairo and AL-AZHAR UNIVERSITY.

Madani, Abbas (b. 1931) Abbas Madani founded the Islamic Salvation Front (*see* FIS) in Algeria, a political movement that sought to promote the role of traditional Muslim institutions in the state. His activism and opposition to government policies led to his arrest and imprisonment. His writings and political activities represented an attempt to promote legal and political change based on an agenda of Islamic reform. Throughout the dramatic disintegration of civil life in Algeria since the aborted elections of 1992, Madani has remained in prison, reluctant to engage in a dialogue with the military rulers of the present government that might bring about an end to the violence and conflict.

madhhab See SCHOOLS OF ISLAMIC LAW.

al-Madina *See* MEDINA.

madrasa A Muslim institution of learning and study that evolved into a centre for training in religious and legal sciences, particularly among Sunnis. The establishment of such centres was initiated by Nizam al-Mulk in the eleventh century through the Nizamiya *madrasa* in Baghdad. It was specifically created and endowed for the training of Sunni scholars and teachers. Over time *madrasas* became major legal and theological institutions throughout the Muslim world. Occasionally, the term is also used to designate, in general, schools or centres of learning that provide religious instruction. In contemporary Muslim societies the *madrasa* has also served as a starting point for developing an integrated wide-ranging curriculum for early childhood education. In certain parts of the Muslim world such institutions have also been exploited in order to indoctrinate students through a narrow, ideologically driven agenda to instigate opposition to ruling governments and perceived alien influences in society. *See also* PESANTREN, TALIBAN.

Magat Diop, Sokhna *See* MURIDIYYA.

al-Maghili, Muhammad (c. 1440–1503) Jurist and scholar. During the fifteenth century al-Maghili travelled to and settled in West Africa, where his writings and judgements on legal matters became influential in the application and practice of Maliki law (*see* SCHOOLS OF ISLAMIC LAW).

al-Maghrib (lit., 'the West') More specifically in the context of Muslim history and geography, the term refers to North Africa, the countries of Algeria, Libya, Morocco and Tunisia.

al-Mahdi (lit., 'the Guided One') The Mahdi is an eschatological figure, whose appearance is expected at the end of time and prior to the DAY OF JUDGEMENT. In Imami Shiism he is believed to be the twelfth imam who has existed in a state of occultation (*see* GHAYBA) since his disappearance in the ninth century. This figure, known in Shia tradition as Muhammad al-Mahdi or the Imam al-Zaman, is believed to have gone into a state of *ghayba* in SAMARRA, a city in modern Iraq which has become a major centre of pilgrimage. Sunni tradition accepts the idea of the appearance of the Mahdi but does not associate his identity with the Shia imam. Throughout Muslim history there have been a number of figures claiming to be the Mahdi, in different regions of the Muslim world.

al-Mahdi, Abd Allah *See* ABD ALLAH AL-MAHDI.

Mahfouz, Nagib (1911–2006) Egyptian writer. Several among Mahfouz's many works of fiction explore issues of tradition and change and their impact and role in the lives of individuals and societies. A minority have regarded some of his works as blasphemous, resulting in an unsuccessful attack on his life. In 1988 Mahfouz was awarded the Nobel Prize for Literature.

Mahmud of Ghazna (971–1030) A ruler of the GHAZNAWID dynasty founded by his father, Sebuktegin, in the tenth century. In order to take control of the province of Ghazna given to his brother Ismail by Sebuktegin, Mahmud defeated his brother in 998 and imprisoned him for life. Mahmud consolidated his power in Afghanistan and then carried out a number of military forays into India and nearby regions. He turned Ghazna into a wealthy capital city, using the booty he acquired from plundering Hindu and Buddhist temples to enlarge and consolidate Ghaznawid control of the region. He also sought the support of scholars and poets by offering them his patronage.

mahr The gift paid to the bride by the groom as part of the marriage contract which remains her property even in the event of divorce. *See* MARRIAGE.

Maimonides, Moses (1135–1204) Jewish scholar, physician and Rabbi. Maimonides lived in Córdoba under Muslim rule, eventually moving to Fez and then Egypt. His writings concentrated on theology, law, logic and medicine. He wrote in Hebrew as well as in Arabic including his great commentary on the Jewish Mishnah. In addition to their very significant contribution to medieval Jewish thought, many of his works reflect the cosmopolitanism of the intellectual milieu of the time. His famous work *Dalalat al-Hairin* (*Guide of the Perplexed*) reflects a selective acceptance and application of the tools of philosophy. Many of his works were translated into Latin and acquired popularity in Europe. He is also known by his Arabized name Musa ibn Maymun.

majlis In pre-Islamic times, this Arabic word referred to a council of tribal leaders. In Muslim usage it signified generally a session or gathering for religious, scholarly or literary purposes. In modern times it refers to representative political or civil institutions in many Muslim countries, as in the instance of the LOYA JIRGA in Afghanistan, a consultative body of elders. In other countries it is used to designate parliament, as in the case of Majlis-i Oli of Tajikistan and Majlis al-Sha'b of Syria.

Majlis-i-Shura A representative body specifically entrusted with the task of ensuring the integration of Muslim traditions of law and practice in national life and affairs. Such bodies exist in Pakistan and several other Muslim countries and reflect a growing trend in these countries to respond to a variety of public expectations regarding the role of their Muslim heritage in issues of governance and policy.

al-Majlisi, Mulla Muhammad Baqir (1627–1698) Imami Shia teacher, jurist and prolific writer. Al-Majlisi was active as a leader in SAFAWID times and noted for his extensive work on HADITH and as an influential figure in public life. His writings continue to be regarded as authoritative in the Imami Shia tradition today.

Majnun *See* LAYLA AND MAJNUN.

Majus The term originally designated an ancient Iranian caste of priests and was used in Arabic to refer to followers of ZOROASTRIANISM.

Makhfi (1638–1702) Pen name of Begum Ziba al-Nisa, the learned poet and calligrapher and daughter of the MOGHUL Emperor Aurangzeb. A patron of learning, she became known for her extensive library. After being accused of intriguing against the emperor, she was imprisoned and died while incarcerated.

Makkah *See* MECCA.

Malamatiyya A group of Sufis originating in the ninth century whose adherents rejected all outward shows of piety. They were motivated by the conviction that actions should not be undertaken to seek approval and therefore all displays of feeling were also to be shunned. While some aspects of their tradition were adopted within certain Sufi circles, their attitudes and practices never received general acceptance.

Malay The language shared and spoken mainly by the peoples of Indonesia, Malaysia and Brunei but also used in southern Thailand and Singapore. While one among many languages and dialects in this ethnically and linguistically very diverse region, Malay has emerged as the lingua franca of a region with strong historical roots and an ancient literary heritage. It is also the language which gave local expression to the area's Muslim tradition and is reflected in historical works, poems and narratives preserved in writing from at least the sixteenth century.

Malaysia Malaysia is a federation of thirteen states located in Southeast Asia, with a population of approximately 20 million, more than half of whom are Muslim. The rest are Buddhists or followers of Chinese religions, primarily of Chinese origin, Hindus from India or members of smaller groups who adhere to indigenous religious traditions or to Christianity. Islam was introduced to the region from the twelfth to fourteenth centuries and a number of Muslim states developed, assisted by trade with other parts of the Muslim world. Islam was spread by missionaries and traders, and Sufi practices and traditions became integrated into Malay devotional and spiritual life. The presence of Islam in the region extended to neighbouring Thailand and also to Mindanao in the PHILIPPINES. Malay literature preserves accounts of the conversion of various kings and the activities of early Muslim preachers, regarded as saint-like figures who brought and taught Islam to the people of the region.

European influence in the region began with Portuguese incursions in the sixteenth century in an attempt to seize control of international trade. This was followed by Dutch expansion in the region. The Dutch expelled the Portuguese, seizing several important islands and ports and suppressing local opposition. While the Dutch subsequently sought to control and dominate what became INDONESIA, their influence over the Malay region diminished with the rise of the British Empire in the East Indies. British colonial rule lasted until independence was achieved in 1957. In 1965 Singapore, which had been part of the federation, withdrew to become a sovereign nation. Malaysia today consists of a number of states that were formerly sultanates and also includes the Bornean states of Sabah and Sarawak.

After independence, Islam was officially recognized in the Constitution, which acknowledged the multi-religious and multicultural character of the country's population. There has, particularly in the last twenty-five years, been a major effort on the part of the central government to promote education, encourage the greater integration of Muslim law in the judicial system and identify its Muslim heritage as an integral part of the national identity. Islamic banks and educational institutions, including universities, have been created with government support and funding.

Malaysia has moreover emerged as a growing economic power in the region and as an effective partner in regional and Muslim affairs, and has continued to maintain a democratic framework within which to balance its need to identify with its Muslim heritage with other regional and global factors. It seeks to play a leading role in promoting Islam as a religion of tolerance and peaceful coexistence.

Malcolm X (1925–1965) American Muslim leader. Born Malcolm Little, he converted to the teachings of Elijah MUHAMMAD and became a leading figure in the NATION OF ISLAM movement. Following a pilgrimage to Mecca, he changed his name from Malcolm X to El-Haj Malik el-Shabazz and resigned from the Nation of Islam. He was assassinated in 1965, allegedly as a consequence of his opposition to the Nation. His speeches, activities and example of seeking civil rights for African-Americans have made him a representative minority symbol in the United States.

Maldives Island nation in the Indian Ocean with a population of 250,000 that is almost entirely Sunni Muslim of the Shafii SCHOOL OF ISLAMIC LAW. Islam spread to the islands in the ninth century. The Maldives was declared an Islamic republic in its constitution in 1968 (and by amendment in 1970 and 1975). Islam is the state religion and the judicial system integrates local traditions of Muslim law in its practices. The Maldives have also attracted significant tourism in recent times.

Mali Formerly the French Sudan, Mali, a West African state, became a republic in 1960. About 90 per cent of its population of 9 million is Muslim, a majority of whom follow the Maliki SCHOOL OF ISLAMIC LAW.

Like its neighbours, the initial Muslim influence came by way of trade along the Saharan routes. By the thirteenth century Islam was sufficiently well established for a small kingdom, known as Mali, to come into existence. The Malian epic SUNDIATA records the heroic conquests and deeds of the king, Keita Sundiata, and evokes the traditions of an illustrious kingdom. Over the next two centuries Mali came to be a dominant political and religious force in the region. Among its well-known rulers, called *mansa*, was MANSA MUSA, who in the fourteenth century established contact with Egypt and Morocco and enhanced learning and culture in his kingdom. Among its major centres of learning and trade was Timbuktu.

Sufi practices and traditions became integrated into devotional life in Mali during the period of the great nineteenth-century JIHADS, with the TIJANIYYA and QADIRIYYA orders being the most important. French colonial influence arrived towards the end of the nineteenth century, when the French created a colony called the French Sudan. Political autonomy was not won until 1956. Various civil and military regimes have alternated in government and created institutions to maintain control over Muslim affairs and activities.

Malik ibn Anas (c. 715–796) Muslim jurist and one of the most respected scholars of FIQH in Sunni Islam. He is also acknowledged as one of the founders of a Sunni SCHOOL OF ISLAMIC LAW. At a time of increasing need for systematizing the different practices and modes of legal reasoning in early Muslim society, Malik argued for standards based on the consensus and practice of MEDINA. Malik's work and systematization of materials and issues created an important early framework for the development of legal practice and reasoning in Islam. He is also known as Imam Malik.

Malik Shah (1055–1092) One of the sultans of the SALJUQ dynasty. While nominally subject to the ABBASID caliph in Baghdad, Malik Shah used his military power and influence to exercise control over a significant part of the Middle East including nearby regions of Central Asia. With the help of his vizier and chief minister, NIZAM AL-MULK, he played an important part in consolidating relations with the weakened Abbasid caliph and championed the cause of Sunni Islam in the region.

Maliki School of Islamic law *See* SCHOOLS OF ISLAMIC LAW.

Malta Mediterranean island state. Malta came under Muslim rule between 870 and the Norman conquest in 1090. The memory of a Muslim presence on the island survives in names, coins and inscriptions.

Mamluks Dynasty in Egypt and Syria which was founded by an army of Turkish slaves who revolted in 1250 and overthrew the existing rulers, the AYYUBIDS. (*Mamluk* means 'something or someone possessed or owned' and was used to refer to military 'slaves'.) The Mamluks were instrumental in preventing the MONGOL advance toward Syria and Egypt and remained in power until the OTTOMAN conquest of 1517. After that they maintained a major role as a military force until the nineteenth century.

During the period of their ascendancy, the Mamluks were the strongest Sunni dynasty in the Middle East and controlled important religious centres such as Mecca, Medina and Jerusalem. The major cities in Egypt and Syria such as Cairo, Damascus and Aleppo flourished as centres of trade, culture and architecture and the Mamluks encouraged the further development of already established centres of Sunni learning within their dominion.

al-Mamun The seventh ABBASID caliph who ruled from 813 to 833 with his capital in Baghdad. His reign was marked by an unsuccessful attempt to enforce the MUTAZILA interpretation of Muslim theology as the doctrine of the state. A form of inquisition called the *mihna* was undertaken against scholars who were opposed to Mutazila doctrine, but the word applies to any attempt by the state to impose a particular interpretation of Islam on scholars. Al-Mamun founded the DAR AL-HIKMA, a centre for translation into Arabic and study of the scientific and philosophical works of antiquity including the heritage of Greece, Persia and India. One of his abortive initiatives was to reconcile divisions between Sunni and Shia by appointing as his successor ALI AL-RIDA, who subsequently became an Ithna Ashari imam. The attempt failed because Ali died in 818, and his followers accused al-Mamun of having had him poisoned. One of al-Mamun's brothers, al-Mutawwakil, reversed his policies.

manaqib A genre of praise and hagiographic poetry and prose. More specifically, a genre used to celebrate the virtues of the COMPANIONS OF THE PROPHET, important scholars and Sufi leaders, and Shia imams.

al-Manar An Arabic journal founded by RASHID RIDA in 1898 to express a reformist view of Muslim thought and promote religious and social action to revive Muslim values and identity in societies under European rule and influence.

Mandé or **Mandingo** A West African people linked by a common ethnic and linguistic heritage who converted to Islam from the eleventh century onwards. Their tradition of oral narratives recounts the reigns of important Muslim rulers in the region, such as the epic SUNDIATA, which recounts the story of the Mali ruler Keita Sundiata. The narrators of oral tradition are known as *griot*.

mankind *See* HUMAN BEINGS.

Mansa Musa (d. 1337) Muslim ruler of the kingdom of Mali. During Mansa Musa's reign from 1312 to 1327 Mali and its capital, Timbuktu, became known for a tradition of Muslim scholarship and also for trade and commerce.

Mansur (d. c. 1624) A painter of miniatures, active during the MOGHUL period, known as the 'wonder of the age'. His artistic interpretation of landscape, animals, flora and birds and his representation of nature were widely imitated after his death.

mantiq Arabic term denoting the science of logic in Muslim philosophy, where it has been regarded variously as the 'servant of the sciences' and as an essential tool and discipline in the pursuit of organized knowledge.

Mappila Muslim community in south-west India. It is considered to be among the first Muslim communities to have been established in South Asia. Muslim and Hindu communities lived in relative harmony until 1498, when the Portuguese arrived. Between then and independence in 1947 Mappila territory was also ruled by the Dutch, British, French and British again. A revolt in 1921 was unsuccessful. The Mappilas have maintained their tradition of Muslim expression in literature and devotional writings in their own language. In Kerala, south India, numerous examples can be found of Mappila mosque architecture and a thriving coastal Muslim community of fishermen and traders.

Maqam Ibrahim (lit., 'Place of Abraham') Traditionally believed to be the footprint of Abraham, marked in a stone 60cm wide by 90cm high located near the KA'BA. During the circumambulation of the Ka'ba the Prophet is said to have prayed behind the stone.

Marja al-Taqlid or **Marja-i Taqlid** A title given to a *mujtahid* (*see* IJTIHAD) in the Shia Imami tradition who is recognized for his model scholarship, knowledge and personal piety and as the leading religious authority of his time.

al-Maraghi, Mustafa (1881–1945) Rector of AL-AZHAR UNIVERSITY. His reforms in the curriculum and his educational efforts were based on his view of Islam as a religion compatible with the needs of the time and a spirit of ecumenism.

marriage The Quran and the teachings of the Prophet emphasized the centrality of the institution of marriage and addressed in a systematic way the rules and regulations governing it. With the development of organized legal traditions among Muslims, the codification of such rules and regulations was further elaborated and expressed in great detail in the body of law known as the SHARIA.

Quranic teaching on marriage represented a rejection of some of the assumptions and traditions surrounding the practice in pre-Islamic Arabia and a major reform in both the status of marriage and particularly the rights of married women. It affirmed the universality of marriage, relating it to other natural phenomena – 'and of everything, there is a pair' – and provided a context for viewing it in its biological and social contexts and as an expression of the personal need for companionship, affection and status.

The Quran restricted the system of unlimited polygamy of pre-Islamic times, permitting only up to four concurrent wives and urging equality of treatment at all times. This emphasis is interpreted by many modern Muslims as favouring a monogamous approach to marriage. Various Muslim countries have considered and implemented a series of reforms governing marriage to bring its regulations in line with other social and personal legislation.

See also NIKAH.

marthiya Elegiac poems honouring the memory of important figures, in particular Imam HUSAYN IBN ALI. They are found in virtually every important language of Muslim literary expression.

martyrdom As in other Abrahamic religious traditions, the concept of martyrdom is common in Islam. The Quran refers to those who 'die in the way of God' as martyrs who would be rewarded for their struggle and sacrifice. This struggle, as in early Christianity, was undertaken against those who wished to suppress or kill the religion's leader and his followers, and martyrs acted in defence of faith, family or co-religionists.

Among the Shia, the self-sacrifice of some of the imams for the sake of Islam, and particularly the example of HUSAYN IBN ALI, are held up as exemplary acts of martyrdom. By extension, the concept came to be extended to those who sought to defend the faith by intellectual means through writing or preaching at a time of great importance or persecution.

The notion of seeking martyrdom through suicide is rejected by Muslim scholars, though some have argued that military acts leading to death are justified. In more recent times such acts that cause indiscriminate destruction and death have been severely condemned by the majority of Muslim leaders and scholars as being opposed to the ethical values of Islam, shared with all major faiths and other traditions.

Marwa One of two small hills (the other is Safa) which are an integral part of the pattern of rituals in the annual *Hajj. See* HAJJ; PILGRIMAGE.

Mary (Arabic, Maryam) The mother of Jesus, to whom is devoted a chapter of the Quran. Jesus is referred to in the Quran as 'the son of Mary', to whom he was miraculously born. She is highly venerated in the Muslim tradition and seen as an example of a committed believer.

Mashhad A shrine city located in north-eastern Iran. It is associated with the martyrdom and grave of one of the Twelve imams (*see* ITHNA ASHARIYYA), ALI AL-RIDA. Because of the growing fame and importance of the shrine, Mashhad has become a major centre of visitation, devotional practice and learning for the Imami Shia all over the world. *See also* SAFAWIDS.

mashrabiyya A feature of Muslim architectural design, represented in particular by lattice-like wooden window panels.

masjid *See* MOSQUE.

al-Masjid al-Haram (lit., 'the Sacred Mosque') The mosque complex in Mecca containing the KA'BA.

Masjumi An Indonesian political party created by a coalition of Indonesian Muslims during the period of Japanese occupation of the country in 1943. The party's goal was to create an alliance and represent in a coordinated and consultative manner the views of different Muslim organizations. Masjumi was eventually disbanded and its views are now represented through alternative organizations, particularly the Partai Muslimin Indonesia.

maslaha Concept of the public welfare or common good in Muslim juridical thought. It has been interpreted to reflect a broader concern for public interest through a more flexible approach to the application of the principle of QIYAS. In general, it afforded legal scholars and the state a degree of flexibility in meeting exigencies or situations where the welfare of the community as a whole might be compromised.

In recent times advocates of reform have argued that the principle permits the addressing of social and legal issues that had not arisen previously, so that every new generation is able to interpret Muslim tradition and legal practice in the context of the needs of the time. Some of these issues relate to economic aspects, such as modern forms of banking and finance, others to ethical issues, such as family planning and modern medicine, and issues of governance such as political representation and human rights.

Masudi, Abu al-Hasan Ali ibn al-Husayn (893–956) Early Muslim historian. His work was encyclopedic in scope, encompassing history, geography, philosophy, science and law. His fame rests on his *Kitab Muruj al-Dhahab* (*Meadows of Gold*), a work devoted to history containing a global account of nations and prophets until the time of the Prophet Muhammad and the history of Muslims since then.

mathematics Muslim mathematicians played an important role during the medieval period in developing this science, which encompassed algebra, arithmetic and geometry and was linked to other subjects such as astronomy and optics. The work of these mathematicians was vital in the transmission of these sciences to medieval Europe.

Building on the work of the ancient Greek, Persian and Hindu mathematicians, Muslim mathematicians worked on numbers and algebraic equations and developed elaborate tables for calculations affecting the Muslim CALENDAR as well as the direction and times of prayer. In particular, considerable efforts were put into advancing Euclidean geometry, and while much of the work established a solid theoretical base for the study of forms and shapes it also had a strong applied dimension, as in the work on optics by IBN AL-HAYTHAM (Alhazan) and Nasir al-din TUSI. One aspect of these applications can be seen in the highly elaborate geometric designs and shapes that decorate Muslim buildings and monuments.

al-Maturidi, Abu Mansur Muhammad (873–944) Founder of a school of Sunni theology, al-Maturidi was born near Samarkand. He was also a jurist and commentator on the Quran. He was opposed to the various approaches to theology of such groups as the MUTAZILA and the SHIA, and is also said to have engaged in polemics against Christians, Jews, Zoroastrians and Manichaeans. Building on the interpretation of the Hanafi doctrine popular in Balkh and Central Asia at the time, al-Maturidi did not entirely reject rationalism, as some Ashari theologians had, but helped in devising a distinctive approach in the context of the debate then current.

Mauritania West African state. It has a population of nearly 2 million people, half of whom are of Arab or Berber background and half of Fulbe and Wolof heritage. Almost the entire population is Muslim. The history of Muslim diffusion in Mauritania dates back to the early medieval period. It became a French territory in 1817 and a colony in 1920, gaining independence in 1958. In more recent times it has been severely afflicted by climate change, which has caused both drought and desertification.

Mawdudi, Mawlana Sayyid Abu al-Ala (1903–1979) The founder of a modern Muslim movement and political organization known as JAMAAT-I-ISLAMI. His ideas and writings have exercised considerable influence on a wide circle of Muslim thinkers and their followers, who believed in a revivalist vision of Islam, grounded in a view of tradition reflecting idealized norms. In his view, Islam was capable of providing, through its traditional but reorganized institutions, a framework for organizing all facets of contemporary life and society, including political, economic and social institutions. His writings and views as a journalist and, subsequently, as the main architect of the Jamaat's political platform led him into conflict with the various military and elected regimes in Pakistan.

As a result, Mawdudi spent a considerable time in prison. Under his leadership the Jamaat failed to win any of the major elections held in Pakistan and was unsuccessful in averting the division of Pakistan in 1971 that led to the establishment of Bangladesh. Aspects of his thought, as well as his activities, received widespread support among similar Muslim movements in other parts of the world where Muslims of South Asian origin settled following migration to Europe, the United Kingdom and North America. He died in the United States, following an illness, in 1979.

Mawlana *See* JALAL AL-DIN RUMI.

Mawlawiyya *See* MEVLEVI.

Mawlay Idris Moroccan town where Idris I and Idris II, the founder and the successor of the IDRISID dynasty of the ninth century, are buried. The mausoleum built to commemorate their memory attracts many visitors.

Mawlid al-Nabi Also known as Milad al-Nabi, it marks the birthday of the Prophet celebrated on the twelfth day of Rabi al-Awwal, the third month of the Muslim CALENDAR. It is among the most celebrated festivals across the Muslim world.

Mecca (Arabic, Makkah) The birthplace of the Prophet, site of the KA'BA, AL-MASJID AL-HARAM and the annual HAJJ. It is located in the Hijaz, now part of the Kingdom of Saudi Arabia. While the Prophet migrated to MEDINA following persecution in Mecca, the latter remained as the holy city and the site of the annual pilgrimage, which in Islamic tradition was performed under the direction of the Prophet a few years later. The structure and environment of Mecca have undergone a steady erosion by rampant and often thoughtless attempts at modernization as the city seeks to accommodate the more than 2 million pilgrims that visit during the *Hajj* and at other times of the year.

mecelle The original word in Arabic, *majalla*, meant a book which contained wisdom. It was later extended to refer to any type of writing. *Mecelle*, the Turkish derivative, was a uniform system of the laws of contract and obligation. It was in effect in the OTTOMAN EMPIRE from 1869 until the institution in Turkey of the Swiss Civil Code and other national laws in 1927.

Medina (Arabic, al-Madina) City in present day Saudi Arabia known as Yathrib in pre-Islamic times. The Prophet Muhammad migrated to Medina in 622 (an event known as the *hijra*) and it became the centre of the early Muslim community. The Prophet died and was buried in Medina, where his tomb and that of some of his immediate family are found. After the death of the Prophet Medina lost its place as the centre of Muslim polity, which moved further north to Iraq and Syria. However, as the second city in Muslim history, Medina attracts a vast number of Muslim pilgrims.

Mehmed II (1432–1481) Also known as the Conqueror, Mehmed II conquered BYZANTINE Constantinople in 1453, declaring it his capital. He is thus regarded as the first sultan of the new OTTOMAN EMPIRE. In time, he added the BALKAN territories to his growing empire. An innovative military leader, Mehmed II is said to have designed cannons for use in taking Constantinople. His policies towards the local population extended protection to Christian churches and monasteries in all the conquered territories. Besides Persian, Arabic and Turkish, Mehmed II knew some Latin and Greek and was a major patron of the arts. He is also said to have composed poetry.

Memon Sunni Muslim trading community in Gujarat, India, whose members have also migrated in recent times to other parts of the world, primarily to Africa, North America and the United Kingdom.

Mevlevi Also known as Mawlawiyya and Mewlewiyye. Sufi order inspired by JALAL AL-DIN RUMI and often referred to as WHIRLING DERVISHES because of the dance performed by devotees to the accompaniment of music and the remembrance of God, which acts as a means of devotion and provides a higher level of spiritual awareness. The Mevlevi order is distinguished from other Sufi orders by the importance given to *sama*, a devotional practice of various degrees of ritualization accompanied by music, song and dance performed in a purpose-built structure. The ritual dance depicts the varying stages of the awakening of the soul. The Mevlevi, like other Sufi orders in Turkey, were banned in 1925 with the decision by MUSTAFA KEMAL (Atatürk) to close down the meeting houses of all Sufi orders and suppress their activity. The most prominent centre of gathering and the order's famous library in Konya were closed down. The Mevlevi order now has unrestricted activity in Turkey and also in other parts of the Muslim world and in the West.

Mewlewiyye *See* MEVLEVI.

Midhat Pasha (1822–1884) Grand vizier who is considered the 'father' of the 1876 Constitution which curtailed the absolute power of the OTTOMAN sultans and allowed for a limited initial form of representative participation.

mihrab Niche in the wall of a mosque showing the direction in which worshippers turn their face while praying (*qibla*). Almost invariably decorated, they display a variety of regional artistic inspiration including examples of calligraphy. In Quranic usage, an elevated or honorific position.

Milad al-Nabi *See* MAWLID AL-NABI.

millet A term encompassing the idea of a faith community and a nation as well as a religion. It came to be applied within the OTTOMAN EMPIRE (1300–1918) to non-Muslim communities. The *millet* system gave non-Muslim subjects autonomy to conduct their internal religious, social and communal affairs while retaining their protected status. The major non-Muslim communities of the time were Jews, Greeks, and Armenians, representing various religious groups, each with its own ecclesial head.

Mina A small town east of Mecca where the concluding rites of the annual pilgrimage are conducted and where pilgrims stay overnight. A key ceremony involves the collection of pebbles and the stoning of three pillars representing Satan. According to tradition, when Abraham was leading Ishmael to the sacrifice, the devil tempted him and Abraham rejected Satan by throwing stones. *See also* HAJJ.

minaret Vertical architectural feature of a mosque. It has traditionally served as the place from where the MUEZZIN calls the faithful to prayer. Its style varies considerably in different parts of the Muslim world, but in all cases it is a distinctive landmark in any landscape where Muslim settlement is found.

minbar A pulpit in the mosque, ordinarily located next to the MIHRAB, from where the preacher, called the KHATIB, delivers the sermon. The Prophet is believed to have given his addresses to the community from such a raised place in Medina. Over time the tradition of giving a sermon, generally on Friday, became a regular and often very elaborate feature within the mosque.

Ahmad ibn Tulun Mosque, Cairo, *minbar* and *mihrab*.

Mindanao An island in the south of the PHILIPPINES where the majority of Muslims found in the region live. These Muslims, known as *Moros* in Spanish, were converted by traders and Muslim preachers active in Southeast Asia during the fifteenth century and were linked to Muslim communities in Malaysia and Indonesia.

During Spanish rule in the sixteenth century, they resisted attempts at conversion to Catholicism. When Spain ceded the Philippines to the United States in 1898 the Muslims were forced to accept the new rulers, though they tried to maintain their distinctive practices and institutions, resisting integration into the new colonial framework. They tended to be excluded from civil and political structures, a process that continued after the Philippines gained independence in 1946.

Since then the Muslim population has been campaigning to define itself as a separate entity and demanding independence. This has resulted in major conflict and ongoing violence. Recent attempts by the government to restore peace and grant a degree of autonomy to the region have been resisted by groups such as the Maro National Liberation Front and its offshoots, who remain engaged in what they call guerrilla warfare. Some local leaders in more recent times have sought to ally themselves with movements such as AL-QAEDA.

Mir Damad (d. 1631) In full, Mir Muhammad Baqir ibn Shams al-Din Damad, a renowned ITHNA ASHARI scholar of the SAFAWID period. His theological works were used in both Shia and Sunni institutions of learning. In view of the extent of his vast corpus of writings he has often been called the Third Teacher, i.e., after ARISTOTLE and AL-FARABI.

Mir Muhammad Taki (1713–1810) Urdu poet regarded as among the foremost of the subcontinent. While retaining the power and invention of the GHAZAL, he is also known for the simplicity of his style and language.

miraj An event referred to in the Quran (17:1) as marking the Prophet Muhammad's ascent to heaven and developed in Muslim exegetical tradition to include a detailed description of his night journey to paradise. It is described as a journey from the place of sacred prayer (*masjid al-haram*) to the furthest place of prayer (*masjid al-aqsa*). Interpreted variously and linked to other Quranic verses and Prophetic traditions, the event has come to symbolize the connections between revelatory experience, the Prophet's own spirituality and the mystical idea of the encounter with the Divine. In Sufi and other esoteric traditions of Islam, the *miraj* became a model for seeking spiritual union as the fulfilment of an inner journey and has given rise to a vast literature in many languages. The event has also spawned a tradition of art, including both pictorial and symbolic representation.

Miskawayh (932–1039) Historian and intellectual whose major contribution was in the area of ethics, combining philosophical analysis with the practical issues to be addressed by moral reasoning. His thought reflects the strong emphasis on humanistic aspects of Muslim intellectual life that flourished in the late tenth and eleventh centuries.

modernist Muslim thought As with other major religious traditions, there continues across the Muslim world a vibrant tradition of thought that seeks to respond to challenges and issues arising from change and modernization. Among these responses there is a specifically modernist tendency that contrasts with a more traditionally orientated and conservative reformulation of the place of Islam in the modern world.

Broadly, modernist Muslim thought reflects three major trends. The first is a particular emphasis on rethinking the role of the main sources of Muslim tradition and authority in the light of developments of modern thought and practice. While affirming the primacy of the Quran, some Muslim thinkers have advocated a reinterpretation of the relevance of its message, by affirming the historical plurality of the traditions of Quranic interpretation and arguing that, in every period, Muslims have sought to relate Quranic teaching to the reality of their lived environments. They also emphasize the application of historical, anthropological and literary methods of analysis as an additional way of gaining greater insight.

A second area of emphasis is that a normative understanding of Islam must take account of the pluralism of Muslim thought, past and present. By historicizing Muslim thought and practice, it is argued, one is not limited by past tradition; rather, faith can be seen in more dynamic terms as capable of retaining its pluralistic forms while adapting to changing circumstances.

The third area of emphasis relates to specific reformulations of traditional notions of authority, governance, order and human rights. In arguing for a more radical reassessment of institutional practice and norms, these thinkers call for greater democratization, affirmation of universally shared values, particularly as they affect the rights of men and women, and a focus on addressing social injustice through more equitable economic policies. They are also strong advocates of legal reform and peace and dialogue in situations of conflict.

There is, of course, no universal consensus on any of these issues, even among Muslim modernists, but they represent a growing trend across the spectrum of Muslim societies, a trend that is sometimes not fully acknowledged and recognized.

Moghul dynasty Founded in 1526 by BABUR, the Moghul dynasty ruled from India for over two centuries. At its height, the Moghuls exercised control over an empire that covered a large part of South Asia (present-day India, Pakistan and Bangladesh) and adjoining territory to the north. The empire included peoples of many faiths and ethnic backgrounds, and was distinguished by its cultural achievements, architectural monuments and cities. In the time of emperors such as AKBAR there was a broad degree of tolerance extended to all segments of the population. Some of the most important Moghul monuments have survived, the best known being the TAJ MAHAL, the tomb of Emperor HUMAYUN and the Red Fort in DELHI, the Shalimar Gardens in LAHORE and Babur's tomb in Kabul.

money *See* GRAMEEN BANK; INTEREST; ISLAMIC BANKING; RIBA.

Mongols Under Genghis Khan (1167–1227) and his successors, the Mongol people embarked from their native Mongolia during the thirteenth and fourteenth centuries on one of the most extensive conquests in history, including that of China and parts of Europe and Asia. In the process they united with several Turkic-speaking peoples, including the Tatars.

Their invasions brought them to the Muslim world, where Mongol armies caused great devastation. Under one of Genghis Khan's sons, Hulagu Khan, the Mongol army attacked and devastated Baghdad and brought a significant amount of territory within Mongol control. Various dynasties led by Mongol rulers who converted to Islam emerged in the empire. As they settled they contributed to the unification of the region and became patrons of institutions of learning and culture.

months of the year *See* CALENDAR.

Moors European term for the Muslim conquerors of Spain and the Muslim peoples of North Africa.

Moriscos Name applied to those Muslims who became nominal Christians and remained in Spain after the RECONQUISTA until their final expulsion in the early part of the seventeenth century. They had been ordered to convert as part of a major effort on the part of the Catholic Church and the state to delegitimize the use of Arabic and traditions associated with the Andalusian Muslims. The repression often resulted in violence and retaliation. Morisco influence is reflected in the continuity of architecture, music and literature inspired by the world of Muslim AL-ANDALUS.

Morocco North African state with a population of about 30 million, nearly all Muslim. The former Jewish community in Morocco has dwindled considerably as most emigrated to Israel after 1948. Islam was introduced to the Berber (non-Arab) population during the ninth century. The region has a history of exposure to strong reform movements beginning in the eleventh and twelfth centuries, and an important role in linking North and West Africa through trade and conversion. It is also notable for its institutions of learning and a tradition of Sufi teachers, who are remembered for their poetry, devotion and scholarship. Morocco became independent from France in 1956 and is currently ruled by King Muhammed VI, whose family claims direct lineage from the Prophet Muhammad. Islam was declared the state religion in 1962 and the constitution has confirmed the legitimacy of the monarch. The judicial system is based on the SHARIA and the French Civil Code but is undergoing reform, particularly in aspects of personal law.

The form of Islam most dominant in Morocco is influenced by the Maliki SCHOOL OF ISLAMIC LAW and by a long association with Sufism.

Moses (Arabic, Musa) The Quran and Muslim tradition present Moses as one of the major prophetic figures of history. He is given the title 'one who had discourse with God' (Kalim Allah). As a messenger of God and a prophetic leader, his life is seen as exemplary, because he overcame great odds to deliver his people from tyranny and was the recipient of a revelation, a book called the TAWRAT (Torah).

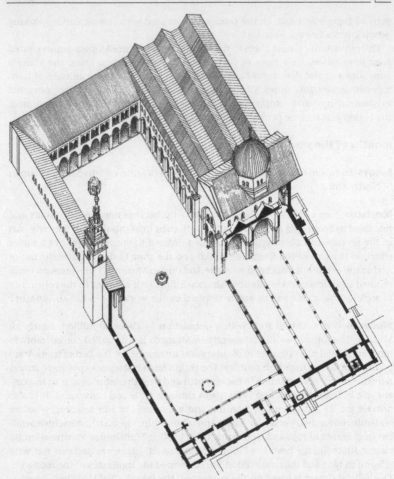

Plan of the Umayyad Mosque (the Great Mosque) in Damascus.

mosque Space for prayer in Islam. The word is derived from the Arabic *masjid*, meaning 'place of prostration'. According to the Quran, the first space dedicated to worship in human history is believed to be that surrounding the KA'BA in Mecca. The first organized mosque in the Prophet's time was part of his house in Medina.

The mosque design that eventually emerged in the expanding Muslim world was based on components which were believed to reflect the Prophet's mosque. They were located in areas deemed central and convenient to the community and consisted of an open space, often enclosed, a MIHRAB, a MINBAR, an elevated location for calling people to prayer and a place for ablutions. The location served as a space for both public communal prayer and public gathering. The systematic development of these components, as evidenced by some early mosque architecture, was conditioned by local environmental factors, available building materials and the role the rulers wished the mosque to play in relation to places of worship belonging to Christians or Jews, the monotheistic communities with whom Muslims came into greater contact as they expanded.

Every new region that became part of the Muslim world eventually had a mosque built to signify the presence and primacy of the new faith. Thus the mosque also became symbolically attached to political power. While following no rigorous design, most mosque builders tried to reflect tradition and yet be innovative within the architectural standards of the region. Thus there exists a great deal of diversity in the size, style and function of mosques, ranging from very large Friday mosques (also attached to institutions of learning) to small rural structures that meet the needs of smaller populations.

Development in both architecture and construction continues in contemporary Muslim society, which, while drawing inspiration from the past, still seeks to use modern idioms when creating spaces for prayer, contemplation and gathering.

Among emerging Muslim societies in the Western world, mosques have also come to serve as centres for a variety of community-related activities. In rare cases, mosques have been used to propagate ideologically charged political views by radicalized individuals and to recruit younger people to such causes.

Mostar City in present-day Bosnia. It has a multi-religious and ethnic population while retaining the strong influence of OTTOMAN urban life. Several of its mosques, *madrasas* and other architectural treasures were badly damaged during the civil war in the region, but many, including its famous bridge, have since been rebuilt or restored.

Muawiyya ibn Abi Sufyan (c. 605–680) Founder of the UMAYYAD dynasty. A COMPANION OF THE PROPHET, he used the occasion of the conflict following the death of the third caliph, UTHMAN IBN AFFAN, to oppose his successor, ALI IBN ABI TALIB. After Ali's assassination, he seized control of the young Muslim state and initiated a period of both autocratic rule and territorial expansion.

mudaraba A traditional Muslim legal concept of contract incorporated into some contemporary financial systems, reflecting an equity-sharing agreement whereby one party provides capital and the other the labour and enterprise. It is recognized as a tool of investment by those who regard interest of any kind in the modern economy of Muslim states to be unacceptable. *See also* INTEREST; ISLAMIC BANKING.

muezzin The individual who makes the call to prayer from a mosque, from either its minaret or a raised spot adjacent to the building. The first *muezzin* according to tradition was BILAL.

Mufid, al-Shaykh (950–1022) Leading Shia scholar and jurist of his time. He studied with other important scholars in Baghdad under the BUYID rulers who supported Shia scholarship. He wrote extensively on a variety of religious subjects and transmitted many traditions from past Shia imams. The title of shaykh ('elder') reflected his status as the teacher of many of the leading Shia scholars.

mufti A recognized authority on matters of law and practice. An opinion rendered by a *mufti* is known as a FATWA. *See also* ULAMA.

muhajir This term was first applied to those Muslims who migrated with the Prophet Muhammad from Mecca to Medina. By extension it is also applied to migrants throughout Muslim history as they moved in search of more enabling conditions or trade or to escape persecution, war and famine.

Muhammad (c. 570–632) Messenger of God to whom the Quran was revealed. He was born in MECCA around 570 according to Muslim tradition, which has preserved biographical accounts of his life, known as SIRA. Orphaned at an early age, he was raised by his uncle, ABU TALIB. As a young man, he was entrusted with managing trade on caravan routes and earned the reputation of being a reliable and trustworthy merchant. He married KHADIJA, a businesswoman, and their marriage lasted twenty-five years until her death.

Muhammad also sought a life of contemplation and often spent time in solitude in the hills around Mecca. In the year 610 these spiritual retreats culminated in a revelatory experience both similar to and continuous with those of past prophetic figures and scriptures. Henceforth, he began the task of preaching and conveying the divine message being revealed to him. In spite of opposition from Mecca, and the persecution of his family and followers, Muhammad continued his mission. After some time he chose to migrate to Medina. This migration, or HIJRA, marked a new turn in the life and fortunes of the nascent community of Muslims, as his followers came to be called. The community was able to organize itself, develop the institutional framework necessary to articulate its social ideals and establish the regular practice of major rituals. However, it continued to be threatened by hostile forces from Mecca and a number of battles were fought in which the Muslims eventually prevailed. Other minority groups, including certain Jewish communities who had allied themselves with Meccan forces, were punished and expelled, but a framework of respect and tolerance for Jews and Christians as 'People of the Book' (AHL AL-KITAB) was established to regulate relations between Muslims and other faith communities.

The military success led to negotiations and an eventual truce, and Muhammad and the Muslims were allowed to return to Mecca in triumph to perform the pilgrimage and to restore the sacred precinct of the KA'BA to the worship of God. Many Meccans and other Arabs converted to Islam and by 632 Islam had become an important presence as an institutionalized faith in the Arabian Peninsula. Muhammad was recognized as the Messenger of God and leader of this new entity. In the same year, following a short illness, Muhammad died on the 12th day of the month of Rabi al-Awwal, during year 10 of the new Muslim era.

His practice of prayer and devotion; his spirituality; his example of humility, compassion, and justice; his role as husband and parent; his acts of kindness to children, orphans, the disadvantaged, and animals and birds; and his commitment to the use of reason and the pursuit of knowledge, all serve for Muslims as a model of ideal conduct. It is this picture of Muhammad as a teacher, exemplar and friend of God that has given him a special place in the hearts of Muslims through the ages. In their daily prayers and whenever his name is mentioned, they invoke God's blessings on him and his descendants, as a continuing mark of remembrance and gratitude. Praise of Muhammad, his prophetic qualities and his position as the chosen messenger of God has been recorded in all Muslim languages and folk traditions, celebrated in poetry, and commemorated on his birthday. Above all, for Muslims he is the recipient of God's final revelation preserved in the Quran.

Muhammad, Elijah (1897–1975) Black American nationalist and religious activist; second leader of the NATION OF ISLAM. Following his conversion to Islam, he sought to organize his followers into a community with a strong moral code and preached a doctrine of black people's superiority and messianic role. Many of his policies and writings were criticized, but he succeeded in creating a well-organized and self-reliant community that would continue under new leadership after him, revising and adapting many of his original doctrines and policies.

Muhammad Abduh (1849–1905) Muslim reformer, professor of theology, Grand Mufti of Egypt and member of the Supreme Council of AL-AZHAR UNIVERSITY. In his writings and teaching he sought to reconcile foundational Muslim principles and beliefs with the emerging ideas of nineteenth-century technology and Western influence that were affecting the Muslim world. His views led to his exile, part of which he spent in France. There he and JAMAL AL-DIN AL-AFGHANI published a newspaper which promulgated ideas of reform.

In his writings he argued strongly that Muslim society was in need of urgent reform on the basis of Quranic values and principles. He shared with al-Afghani the view that Muslims should be inspired by the early followers of the Prophet to reflect a congruence between revelation and the judicious use of applied reason. He also addressed himself to political issues but was more concerned to reform the legal system based on the idea of public welfare and the common good. He faced considerable opposition during his lifetime but his work did attract some support and his ideas constituted an early source of inspiration for reformist groups of the twentieth century.

Muhammad Ali (1769–1849) Following the expulsion of Napoleon's forces from Egypt, Muhammad Ali became Governor of Egypt in 1805 under an OTTOMAN mandate, but moved quickly to declare himself *khedive* ('lord'), a role in which he acted as the virtual ruler of Egypt.

After consolidating his power, Muhammad Ali built Egypt into an autonomous state, reorganizing the military, adopting European models of administration and introducing agricultural reforms while modernizing the infrastructure of roads, adding railways and bringing about economic reforms. He also gained control over parts of Arabia and the SUDAN. The military dictatorship that he created was continued by his descendants, who embarked on new projects such as the Suez Canal between 1859 and 1869. His rule also marked the era of emerging Egyptian nationalism.

Muhammad al-Badr Hamid al-Din (1926–1996) The last ruling Yemeni Zaydi Imam (*see* ZAYDIYYA). He died on 6 August 1996 in London and is buried in Brookwood cemetery, Surrey.

Muhammad al-Baqir (676–743) Shia imam who in his role as teacher and scholar helped develop the distinctive foundations of Shia theology and jurisprudence among an active intellectual circle of followers.

Muhammad ibn al-Qasim al-Thaqafi (d. 715) Military commander. He headed the first Muslim army to conquer the Sind in India in 711. He is believed to have been the youngest commander to lead a Muslim army at the time.

Muhammad Husayn Haykal (1888–1956) Egyptian writer prominent for his promotion of legal training and also his attempt to portray the life of the Prophet and Muslim traditions in a more contemporary light. He received an Egyptian and Western education, graduating from the Sorbonne in Paris. He is the author of the first well-known modern Arab novel, *Zaynab* (1914).

Muhammad Ilyas *See* TABLIGHI JAMAT.

Muhammad Taraghay ibn Shah Rukh ibn Timur *See* ULUGH BEG.

Muhammad Touré *See* SONGHAY.

Muhammadiyya Indonesian reform movement founded by Kiyai Haji Ahmad Dahlan in 1912, during the period of Dutch rule. It was committed to reform through social and educational programmes that were also directed at women. It continues to make an important contribution through its extensive network and programmes based on voluntary effort and well-administered committees.

Muhaqqiq-i Tusi *See* TUSI, NASIR AL-DIN MUHAMMAD IBN MUHAMMAD.

Muharram First month of the Muslim lunar year. The first ten days of the month are observed by the Shia as a period of remembrance, mourning the martyrdom of Imam HUSAYN IBN ALI, and are accompanied by devotional acts and gatherings. *See also* TAZIYA.

mujahidin *See* AFGHANISTAN; TALIBAN.

mujtahid *See* IJTIHAD.

mulhid Deviator, apostate, heretic. The word is derived from the Arabic verb *l-h-d* meaning 'to deviate, to incline'. It is also mentioned in the Quran (7:180 and 22:25), where it refers to those who deviate from the names and signs of God. Active use of the term started in the UMAYYAD period to refer to those who rebelled against the caliphs and thus deviated from the community. Since the early ABBASID period with the development of heresiographical works the term came to be applied particularly to anyone who was believed to have deviated from the accepted religious beliefs. Over time the term *mulhid* was extended to those who rejected a particular religious belief as well as to those who rejected religion in general, such as materialists and atheists.

mulla Persian variation of the Arabic honorific *mawla* ('master'). It is usually applied to religious scholars.

Mulla Sadra Shirazi (1571–1640) Known also as Sadr al-Din Shirazi. He is regarded as one of the most important scholars of Shia philosophy and theology in the SAFAWID period. His work represents a synthesis of Muslim philosophy, developing existing ideas and building a broader framework for integrating intuitive and rational modes of knowing. His systematization is often described as 'transcendent wisdom' and is an original contribution to Muslim thought.

Mumtaz Mahal (d. 1631) Wife of the MOGHUL emperor SHAH JAHAN. When she died in 1631, her husband built the TAJ MAHAL as a tribute to her role as a wife and mother and as a way of commemorating her commitment to a mystical and devotional life.

munajat A form of personal devotional prayer reflecting individual communication with God. Many such prayers are also literary compositions noted for their poetic qualities.

munazara A discussion in the form of a debate or disputation, particularly in legal or theological matters. As a literary form these writings are models of argumentation and persuasion to put across a point of view. In certain cultures they also took the form of poetry and served to entertain audiences and engage the public in the intellectual or moral issues of the day. In Muslim societies the practice also underlined the notion that disputation and differences could be resolved through debate and dialogue rather than denunciation or outright rejection.

al-Muqaddasi, Shams al-Din (d. 990) Influential early Muslim geographer and traveller. His writings sought to create a new geographical science that would encompass description and analysis of social and economic aspects of geography. To this end his work reflects the systematization of information as well as defining the then-existing realm of Islam.

muqarnas A decorative architectural feature in Muslim buildings which resembles an ornamental stalactite ceiling. Its design is based on seven prismatic forms and underlines the synthesis of art, architecture and geometry achieved by Muslim designers and craftsmen.

Muqatil ibn Sulayman (d. 767) One of the early exegetes of the Quran, who developed his methods of interpretation at a time when the genre was still in its formative phase. His interpretations and methods were not always acceptable to later scholars, who objected to what they considered his mystical readings of certain verses.

Muridiyya A Sufi order founded by AMADU BAMBA in the nineteenth century in West Africa. A distinctive feature was a group of followers known as the Bay Fall, who were seen as the most committed of the followers in their work and therefore occasionally exempted from observing traditional practices. Their most important centre is in Touba in Senegal and among the order's recent leaders was a woman called Sokhna Magat Diop.

Murjia Early religious movement that believed that sinners need not be judged by society in this life because they would be punished on the DAY OF JUDGEMENT. In the context of early divisions in Muslim history, they held the position that judgement on the protagonists should be deferred.

Musa *See* MOSES.

Musa al-Kazim (745–799) The seventh imam of the Imami Ithna Ashari Shia (*see* ITHNA ASHARIYYA). He was one of the sons of the sixth imam, JAFAR AL-SADIQ. The difference of views after Imam Jafar's death in 765 led to the emergence of the two major schools of the Shia, of which the Ithna Ashari believe Musa to have been the designated successor.

Musa al-Sadr (1928–1978) One of the leaders of the Imami Shia in Lebanon. He was known to his followers as Imam Musa. He organized a movement to give voice to the Lebanese Shia minority and became its active spokesman and national representative, particularly during the civil war that broke out in 1975. He disappeared during a visit to Libya in 1978 and is believed to have been killed.

musharaka A legal term in Muslim commercial transactions that is today applied to attempts being made in the modern Muslim world to define participation financing. It reflects a contractual partnership.

music The theoretical discussion of music among Muslims can be found in the writings of various early philosophers such as AL-KINDI, AL-FARABI and the IKHWAN AL-SAFA. Classical works on the tradition of poetry in the early Muslim community also refer to music, song and singers.

While this generally theoretical approach aimed at studying music as both an art and a science, virtually every culture to which Islam has spread possessed its own indigenous musical tradition. Thus there has developed across the Muslim world a very extensive repertoire of traditional and folk music influenced by other traditions, musical instruments and performers. Music and performance also received extensive patronage from rulers. When music was allied with acts of devotion or praise (of God, the Prophet Muhammad

The Kamancheh (Persian spike fiddle) player, seventeenth century.

and his family), a practice particularly prevalent among Sufis, objections were raised by some jurists and others with a puritanical attitude who sought to curtail the use of music in the service of faith. It is worth noting that in the cultures of Andalusia, North Africa and Central Asia musical forms such as those based on the *magma*, a literary genre transposed to a melodic form, were appropriated by Jews and Christians, who preserved such traditions in parts of the Muslim world where they continued to live even after the medieval period.

Musical traditions continue to thrive across the Muslim world, and the use of technology and the media has enabled many musicians from West Africa, the Middle East, the Indian subcontinent and Central Asia to gain great popularity among audiences all over the world.

Muslim, Abu al-Husayn ibn al-Hajjaj al-Qushayri (817–875) Along with AL-BUKHARI one of the two foremost Sunni collectors of HADITH. Born at Nishapur, in present-day Iran, Muslim travelled extensively in order to collect *hadith*. His collection, commonly referred to as the *Sahih Muslim*, contains 3,000 traditions and is ranked second in authority in Sunni Islam only to that of al-Bukhari. Muslim's *Sahih* is generally regarded as the most useful reference point among the six famous collections of *hadith*, owing in large part to its specific arrangement. Muslim gathered all versions of the same *hadith* in one place, which makes tracing of the numerous versions of *hadith*s, even when their chains of transmitters differ, much easier. The *Sahih* of Muslim is the subject of numerous commentaries. The most famous among them is that of al-Nawawi (d. 1277).

Muslim Brotherhood The name of a political party in Egypt, Jordan and other Arab states as well as a reformist movement in various parts of the Muslim world, actively engaged in promoting its ideas for the formation of Muslim society. It was formally founded in 1928 by Hassan AL-BANNA to oppose British as well as secular Egyptian rule and to establish Egypt as a Muslim state. Although subsequently banned in Egypt for its anti-government activities and acts of terrorism, it spread to other countries in the Middle East and Africa and became an influential vehicle for the expression of ideas that promoted the role of a political form of Islam. It continues to function as a party of opposition in Egypt and elsewhere.

Muslim League In 1906, Muslim leaders in India created an organization known as the All-India Muslim League. In the wider context of discussions with British imperial authorities on self-governance for India, this organization sought to represent and protect Muslim interests and rights as well as to cooperate with the larger political body, the All-India National Congress.

As sentiment among Muslims in India shifted to seek nationhood within a separate state, the now renamed Muslim League under the leadership of Muhammad Ali JINNAH became the primary advocate of an independent state of Pakistan. After the partition of British-ruled India and the creation of the two states – India and Pakistan – the Muslim League led Pakistan through its early development and has since continued, though not always in power, as a political party among others, within the vagaries of Pakistan's struggle for political stability and democratic governance.

Muslim World League *See* RABITA AL-ALAM AL-ISLAMI.

Mustafa Barzani, Mulla (1902–1979) Influential modern leader of the Kurdish people. His family elders have served as shaykhs of the Sufi NAQSHBANDIYYA among the Kurds. Barzani made an unsuccessful attempt to proclaim a Kurdish People's Republic in 1945.

Mustafa Kemal (1881–1938) Known as Atatürk ('Father of the Turks'), he is regarded as the founder of the modern Turkish state and its secular orientation. He established his reputation as a military leader and patriot following the end of World War I by combating the humiliating terms imposed by the victorious Allies on the defeated OTTOMAN EMPIRE. He established a base in Ankara to organize opposition to the Ottoman caliph in Istanbul and tried to win back occupied territory. In 1923 he was elected president and head of government of the newly established Republic of Turkey. He undertook major programmes of modernization and secularization aimed at establishing an industrial state modelled on contemporary European countries. He also imposed changes that reflected his secular philosophy by disestablishing religious scholars and Sufi TARIQAS and banning public expressions of Muslim practice and law. He died in 1938 and his secular legacy and status as the founding figure of modern Turkey are still regarded as underpinning the political values of the state.

Mustaliyya The branch of the Shia Ismailis that accepted Mustali as imam after the death of Imam al-Mustansir in 1094. This caused a split among the Ismailis into two major branches, Mustali and Nizari (*see* ISMAILIYYA). The successors of Mustali held nominal power in Egypt until the end of the FATIMID dynasty. The subsequent line of imams is believed by the followers to have gone into concealment (SATR) and is represented by a supreme *dai* ('summoner'), *dai mutlaq*, appointed to guide the community. Its headquarters are in India and followers are to be found in many countries, but more particularly in the Indian subcontinent, East Africa and Yemen.

al-Mustansir Billah, Abu Jafar al-Mansur (1192–1242) ABBASID caliph, best known for his generous patronage of architecture and as the founder of the Mustansiriyya *madrasa* built between 1227 and 1238 in Baghdad. Al-Mustansir ruled between the two major Mongol assaults and was one of the last Abbasid caliphs of Baghdad before the city was sacked by the Mongols in 1258.

al-Mustansir Billah, Abu Tamim Maad (d. 1094) His reign of fifty-eight years represents one of the longest periods of rule in Muslim and Ismaili history. The magnificence of his court and the cultural and intellectual achievements of Cairo are reflected in contemporary accounts. On his death, the Ismaili community became divided over allegiance to a successor, giving rise to the Mustali and Nizari branches of Ismailism (*see* MUSTALIYYA; ISMAILIYYA).

mut'a A temporary marriage, believed to have been allowed under certain circumstances in early Muslim history but subsequently legitimized only in Imami Ithna Ashari law. It is regarded among the ITHNA ASHARIYYA as an irrevocable contract, including a precise definition of the period involved as well as the normal requirements of marriage.

al-Mutanabbi (915–955) The meaning of this pen name by which the poet Abu al-Tayyib Ahmad ibn al-Husayn is known has been debated widely. One interpretation is 'the one who claims to be a prophet'. He was certainly one of the most distinguished Arab poets. Claiming Yemeni origins, he travelled frequently, often in search of patronage, impressing rulers with his panegyrics. This gained him both admiration and support at various courts, but it is as an esteemed poet and supreme practitioner of classical Arabic verse that he is best remembered and still read widely. Towards the end of his life he is said to have been saddened by lack of appreciation and turned to participate in the politics of the time. He eventually returned to court service as a poet once more, but he was accidentally killed by looters during one of his many excursions.

Mutazila School of Muslim thought that flourished in the ninth century at the court of the ABBASID Caliph AL-MAMUN. Applying rationalist methods of discourse derived from Greek philosophy to questions of Muslim doctrine and Quranic interpretation, the Mutazila argued for the idea of the absolute unity of God, the justice of God, the temporality of creation, free will, and the createdness of the Quran. Al-Mamun supported their views and sought to impose them on other scholars. His policy was resisted and failed in its purpose, being reversed by his successor. The Mutazila produced some outstanding scholars, whose intellectual influence continued long after the movement's demise.

muwashshah A genre of poetry that developed in the ninth century in Andalusia and is acknowledged as a major development in Arabic literature but is also believed to have provided the context for the emergence of a tradition of Hispano-Arab poetry in Romance and Mozarabic.

Myanmar Southeast Asian country. Myanmar, known as Burma until 1968, has a Sunni Muslim minority representing an estimated 12 per cent of the 9 million population, the majority of whom are Buddhist. A military dictatorship has suppressed free expression of political and religious opinion, which it deems subversive, and has also carried out a campaign against Muslims, leading large numbers to cross the border into Bangladesh. Although Myanmar and Bangladesh have reached an agreement on the return of the refugees, many have elected not to return without a guarantee of safety.

mysticism *See* SUFISM.

N

Nabateans *See* THAMUD.

nabi Quranic term that defines the role of a figure whose vocation it is to preach the divine message within his community. It occurs in the Quran together with the more widely used term *rasul*, signifying a messenger who is the actual recipient of revelation and therefore establishes a new community. Generally a *nabi* is someone working within an established faith community and *rasul*, or messenger, is someone who brings a new revelation.

Nadir Shah Afshar (1688–1747) Nadir Shah ruled Iran between 1736 and 1747, after seizing the remnants of territory left by the disintegrating SAFAWID dynasty. In 1739 he sought to extend his control to Afghanistan and India and engaged in war against the OTTOMANS. During his rule he sought to reduce the power of Shia scholars and to balance the Sunni and Shia spheres of religious authority. He was eventually murdered by his own officers during a military campaign.

nafs The account of the creation of humanity in the Quran speaks of God animating the human material form by breathing His spirit into it. This endows humans with a spiritual dimension, completing their humanity. Elsewhere all beings are said to have been created out of one soul (*nafs*), often used interchangeably with spirit. Both carry a sense of the innermost self that helps define the fullness of being human. It is possible for the self to live up to its ultimate worthiness but also to trespass in a way that diminishes its value. ADAM's trespass is an example of such deviation. *Nafs* in this context can be seen as the seat where this striving takes place and where the soul seeks fulfilment through conformity with the divine will and acting in accordance with the highest spiritual and ethical values. It is as this totality of matter and spirit that human beings act out their destiny, which is governed by their actions throughout life.

Nahdat al-Ulama Indonesian Muslim organization which was created in 1926 in Java to defend the traditional forms of education through the PESANTREN system and to link the networks of traditional scholars in the country. They played an important role in resisting Dutch rule and policy but were often at odds with the more secular nationalist movement of the day. It continued to be influential through various regimes, retaining its strong emphasis on religious education. One of its major leaders, Abdul Rahman Wahid (b. 1940), served as president of Indonesia from 1999 to 2001.

Nahj al-Balagha Based on the sayings of the first Shia imam, ALI IBN ABI TALIB, this collection of speeches and sermons was compiled in its present form by SHARIF AL-RADI in the eleventh century. It is used extensively as a source of ideals, teaching and values and as a model of literary excellence and eloquence, and constitutes one of the most important texts in Shia devotional literature.

Najaf City in Iraq and the site of the mausoleum of Imam ALI IBN ABI TALIB. It is a centre of learning and of scholarship and one of the most important sites of pilgrimage among the Shia.

Najm al-Din Kubra (1145–1220) Regarded as the founder of the Kubrawiyya, a Sufi order that originated in Iran and Central Asia. His disciples are particularly noted for their work in spreading Sufism in many parts of Asia and for building on the many writings of their teacher.

Naqshbandiyya A Sufi order founded by Khwaja Baha al-Din Naqshband in the fourteenth century. It is widespread in most of Asia and particularly in Turkey, the Balkans and Central Asia. During the nineteenth century it became prominent in India, its influence spreading from there to Kurdistan and also into Daghistan, where it inspired resistance to European influence. Its devotional practices emphasize silent meditation and conformity to the traditions of Islam.

Nasir al-Din Tusi *See* TUSI, NASIR AL-DIN.

Nasir li-Din Allah Title used by several Zaydi imams and leaders in Yemen.

Nasir-i-Khusraw (d. 1078) A major intellectual and literary figure, Nasir-i-Khusraw wrote works on philosophy in Persian, integrating ideas of ancient philosophy with those of Islam. He is also famous for his poetry and his work of spreading Islam in the remote regions of Afghanistan and Central Asia on behalf of the Ismaili branch of Shia Islam.

Nasreddin Khoja Legendary character. Although his existence has never actually been proved, he is the subject of many humorous anecdotes dating to the sixteenth century.

Nasrids Last major Muslim dynasty of Spain which ruled from GRANADA. The foundation of the dynasty in 1232 is attributed to Muhammad I, who combined a strong religious outlook with military skills. In 1246 the dynasty made Granada its capital and its rule lasted until 1492 when the last Nasrid ruler left Spain for Morocco, ending seven centuries of Muslim rule in the region (*see* AL-ANDALUS). The Nasrids created in Granada some outstanding examples of palace, mosque and landscape architecture, including the ALHAMBRA.

nass Among the Shia the formal designation conferred by an existing imam upon his successor, appointed from among his sons or other male relatives who are descended directly from the first imam, ALI IBN ABI TALIB, and the Prophet's daughter,

FATIMA (*see* IMAM/IMAMA). Imam Ali is believed to have received his designation from the Prophet Muhammad.

Nasser, Gamal Abdel (1918–1970) While a colonel in the Egyptian army, Nasser led a coup in 1952 against King Farouk of Egypt and was subsequently elected president, a position he held until his death. His ideas on Arab nationalism and socialism were widely influential in the Arab world. Nasser's alliance with the Soviet Union during the Cold War created a reliance on arms and aid that, in the long run, became a handicap to Egyptian development and could not prevent defeat in 1967 by Israel. He restricted and suppressed the activities of various Muslim groups, including the MUSLIM BROTHERHOOD, but maintained a strong relationship with AL-AZHAR UNIVERSITY.

Nation of Islam The Nation of Islam movement arose among African-Americans in the 1930s. It was led by Farrad Mohammed, who linked their heritage to Muslim antecedents and organized his followers to develop a totally distinct identity from 'white' American culture. One of his representatives, Elijah Muhammad, took over the leadership of the movement following the sudden disappearance of Farrad in 1934. The movement's followers regarded him as a prophet representing Farrad, whom they believed was the Messiah. Elijah Muhammad developed the ideas of the Nation of Islam further and organized the followers around temples and communities in various cities. The dichotomy between 'black' and 'white' was emphasized and a total separation envisaged to establish the purity and superiority of the group's followers over against the dominant culture, which was believed to have victimized and oppressed black people through slavery and oppression.

One of the converts, MALCOLM X, became the movement's most effective spokesman and preacher, and membership grew dramatically in the 1960s. He was assassinated in 1965, a year after he left the movement.

Elijah Muhammad died in 1975 and was succeeded by his son Warith al-Din Muhammad, who chose to dismantle the distinctive organizations created by his father and to move closer to the traditions of Sunni Islam as head of a new group now called The Mosque Cares. Meanwhile leadership of the Nation of Islam was taken over by Minister Louis Farrakhan, who has continued to affirm the original principles of the movement and created controversy by taking positions on domestic and foreign policy that severely criticize trends in American society, maintaining the perspectives of the Nation of Islam espoused formerly by Elijah Muhammad. Both leaders have continued to evolve in their thinking and have adapted their respective groups to the changing conditions of American and international politics.

Natsir, Mohammad (1908–1993) Muslim intellectual from Indonesia, affiliated with Persatuan Islam, an organization committed to an active role for traditional Muslim ideals and institutions in the state. He was active as a writer, journalist and political activist in promoting the goals of the organization.

Navruz New Year according to the ancient Persian calendar. It is celebrated in the Persian-speaking world on 21 March each year.

al-Nawawi *See* MUSLIM, ABU AL-HUSAYN IBN AL-HAJJAJ AL-QUSHAYRI.

Nawbakhti, Abu Muhammad Imami Shia scholar of the tenth century who wrote works of philosophy and theology, including a study of all the Shia, reflecting the diversity of views that existed among them. He belonged to the influential Nawbakhti family, who played a prominent role in the affairs of the community.

Nazr al-Islam (1899–1976) Bengali poet and writer who is regarded as next in eminence in Bengali literature to Rabindranath Tagore. The themes of his poems range from the quest for political freedom and justice to praise of the Prophet.

Negus The ruler of Abyssinia at the time of the birth of Islam. In 615 the Prophet Muhammad sent a number of his followers to Abyssinia to escape persecution and they found refuge with the Negus, who refused to turn them over to the Meccans opposed to the growth of Islam.

Neoplatonism *See* PHILOSOPHY.

Niger West African republic. Niger gained independence from France in 1960. The majority of its ethnically diverse population of around 14 million is Muslim. They follow the Maliki SCHOOL OF ISLAMIC LAW and adhere to Sufi groups such as the QADIRIYYA. Islam was spread to the area through trade and missionary work, particularly by Sufi missionaries and traders.

Throughout its history the Niger region has been noted for the diversity of its influences, the erudition of its many noted scholars and its commercial links with

Yaama Mosque, Yaama, Niger.

neighbouring Muslim and African societies. This diverse pattern has continued in present-day Niger, opening Muslim society there to a variety of influences and developments from other parts of the Muslim world.

Nigeria West African state. Nigeria gained independence from Britain in 1960. It has one of the largest Muslim populations in Africa, comparable to that of Egypt. More than 50 per cent of the estimated 120 million population are Muslim. Though Muslims predominate in the northern Hausa-speaking region of the country, Islam cuts across ethnic lines and significant Muslim communities exist among the Yoruba and other Nigerian groups.

As with neighbouring Muslim states, Islam spread to the region through trade and Sufi influence. In the north it was consolidated during the *jihad* of UTHMAN DAN FODIO while its influence in the south was related to the growth of Muslim institutions from the time of the Muslim kingdom of MALI.

The British amalgamated the north and south to form Nigeria, as part of their colonization of West Africa. In 1954 they created a formal federation linking various regions and, after independence in 1960, the new nation constituted itself as a federal republic in 1963.

The history of Nigeria since then has been marked by civil war, several military coups, a temporary economic boom generated by oil revenues and much division among various political parties, ethnic groups and religions. The different Muslims of Nigeria are now in greater contact both with each other and with other Muslim states and organizations, and have sought to organize themselves to retain their sense of identity and institutional history against the backdrop of a divisive political climate, military rule and the growth of Christianity and its institutions and influence. Better education, particularly among women, has increased Muslims' participation in public life and engaged them in seeking to enhance their role in politics and the community. Several Muslim leaders have sought to impose the primacy of the SHARIA in regions where Muslims are in the majority but their actions have been opposed, occasionally with violence.

Night of Power *See* BARAKA; LAYLAT AL-QADR.

nikah Generally MARRIAGE, but also used specifically to denote the contract of marriage in Islamic law. The contract must be concluded by the bridegroom and the guardian of the bride. The guardian ensures that the contract is beneficial for the bride. The *nikah* is usually accompanied by the recitation of the Quran and additional edifying prayers, as well as celebrations and exchanges of gifts.

Nimatullahiyya Sufi order. This order originated with a Shia orientation. Its founder was Shah Ni'mat Allah, whose teachings and thought were greatly influenced by IBN AL-ARABI. His mausoleum in the province of Kirman, in Iran, is a major pilgrimage site. The contemporary leadership of the group has sought to extend their teachings and their practice of mysticism to the West.

ninety-nine names of God Muslim tradition came to preserve over time a list of ninety-nine names by which they could remember God. The Quran speaks of God as having 'the most beautiful names' (7:180).

niqab See HIJAB.

al-Nisa, Begum Ziba See MAKHFI.

Nizam al-Din Awliya (1243–1325) One of the most highly regarded Sufi figures of the subcontinent and a leading figure of the CHISHTIYYA order, whose work of preaching had an enormous impact on the diffusion of Sufism in India. Nizam al-Din Awliya is also noted for remaining free from political patronage and for maintaining his distance from the influence of the royal court. He is buried in Delhi, where his mausoleum attracts thousands of pilgrims.

Nizam al-Mulk (1018–1092) Vizier of the SALJUQ Sultan Alp Arslan in Iran. Though nominally vizier (chief minister), he exercised almost total control over the Saljuq Empire. Nizam al-Mulk is known for his institutionalization of Sunni education and law, through the creation of several MADRASAS in Iraq and Iran and by appointing noted scholars such as Abu Hamid Muhammad AL-GHAZALI to prominent professorships. He was also a patron of the arts and wrote a manual on statecraft. His death was attributed to the Nizari Ismailis of whose state based in Alamut, in present-day Iran, he had been an inveterate enemy. Other authorities attribute it to court intrigues of the time.

Nizami Ganjawi, Jamal al-Din Abu Muhammad (1141–1204) Nizami is regarded as one of the great poets in the Persian language. His major works are known collectively as *Khamsa* (*The Quintet*). Among the famous poems associated with him is the romance *Layla wa Majnun* (*see* LAYLA AND MAJNUN), which, like some of his other works, deals with the theme of love in both its human and mystical contexts. His poems incorporate ancient figures such as Alexander, and heroic figures from Iranian tradition, weaving them into larger themes cutting across cultures and traditions.

Nizaris See ISMAILIYYA.

Noah (Arabic, Nuh) Noah appears in the Quran as a prophetic figure who warns his people against the dire punishment that awaits wrongdoers.

nubuwwa The concept of PROPHECY. Although God is transcendent according to Muslim teaching, He has revealed Himself to humankind through the prophets, some of whom are also messengers, bringing revelation. Muhammad is believed to be the last, the 'seal of the Prophets'. The Quran includes references to many prophets and regards every society as having had access to such inspired individuals. All these figures are also believed to represent a continuing chain of communication from the One God.

Nuh See NOAH.

al-Numan, Qadi ibn Abi Abd Allah Muhammad ibn Mansur Judge and jurist. He was active in the FATIMID state in North Africa and Egypt during the tenth century. His work on law formed the foundation of the Ismaili interpretation and SCHOOL OF ISLAMIC LAW.

nur The symbol of divine light in the Quran. It is used in the *ayat an-nur* ('verse of light') (Quran 24:35) to describe the multilayered significance of signs in the cosmos that refer to the divine.

Nur Banu Valide Sultan (c. 1525–1583) Wife of the OTTOMAN Sultan Selim II. She was the mother of Sultan Murad III, hence her title *valide* sultan. Of non-Muslim origin, she was a figure of influence in the court and in the empire who helped to build and endow mosques and hospitals.

Nur Fazlullah (1843–1909) Shia scholar. He was regarded in his time as the MARJA AL-TAQLID. He was particularly involved in the debates surrounding the introduction of a constitution in Iran in the early part of the twentieth century. Nur Fazlullah argued against what he believed would be compromise in the SHARIA and religious authority of the jurist-scholars if a constitution were enacted. His opposition led to his execution by those who supported the constitutionalist movement.

Nur Jahan (1577–1645) MOGHUL queen. Nur Jahan was the wife of Emperor JAHANGIR and a powerful figure in the political life of the state. She was a highly educated woman, widely renowned for her knowledge of Persian. She was a leader of fashion as well as culture within the court.

Nurbakhshiyya Sufi order of Shia orientation. Its founder Muhammad Nurbakhsh (d. 1464) laid claim to being the MAHDI and also sought political influence and power. The order spread to parts of North India, where its followers were eventually assimilated into the Shia community.

Nurculuk Social movement in Turkey. It emphasized the teachings of Said NURSI (1876–1960), whose writings inspired its broad programme of social change based on an integrated view of faith and its role in modern society.

Nuri, Mirza Husayn Ali *See* BAHAIS.

Nursi, Shaykh Badi al-Zaman Said (c. 1876–1960) Religious leader during the later period of the OTTOMAN EMPIRE, also known in Turkish as Bediuzzaman Said Riza-Nursi. Nursi was of Kurdish origin, well educated and active in community life, particularly associated with the Sufi NAQSHBANDIYYA. While active in promoting educational and social reform, his views and activities were regarded with suspicion by the new secular regime and he was exiled in 1925. During his exile, he wrote *Risale-yi nur* (*Epistle of Light*), a commentary on the Quran combining science, tradition, theosophy and mysticism. It appealed widely to the educated elite of the time and inspired an intellectual and religious movement known as NURCULUK. He died in exile and his works and teaching led to an organized movement within Turkey, and also in Central Asia and in the West, that continues to be active to this day.

Nusayri *See* ALAWI.

O

Oman Gulf state. Its long history is linked to the Arabian peninsula from the time of the rise of Islam. Its present population of around 3 million is almost wholly Muslim, about equally divided between two major schools of Islam, the Ibadi and the Sunni. There is a small minority of Shia.

The presence of oil in Oman has given it prominence in regional affairs and has also led to changes in established patterns of social and economic life. The present ruler, Sultan Qaboos, has encouraged the development of schools and universities while attempting to maintain the traditional role of Islam in the legal and social life of the state.

Organization of the Islamic Conference (OIC) An organization consisting currently of fifty-six states and created to coordinate educational, cultural, social, economic and political activities among its Muslim members. The Islamic Development Bank, established in 1974, is one of the institutions affiliated with the OIC to encourage economic and social development.

Orientalism The tradition of Western scholarship with a focus on the study of the Orient, the East, in contrast to what was perceived to be its own distinctive pattern of civilization in the Occident or the West.

The late Edward Said argued in his well-known study *Orientalism* that such scholarship was intertwined with a hegemonic Eurocentrism that was reinforced during European colonization of the Muslim world and affected the way in which Islam and Muslims were represented.

Other scholars have argued that Orientalism played an important role in encouraging and enhancing sympathetic understanding of non-Western societies, including Muslims, and made possible the rise of a systematic scholarly tradition that is reflected in the many academic institutions of the Western world.

Ossetia Region of the RUSSIAN FEDERATION, formerly part of the Soviet Union. It has a significant minority of Muslims. Islam was introduced in the region under OTTOMAN influence and, in spite of severe persecution and forced migration under Soviet rule, the Muslim population was able to retain its religious identity.

Ottoman Empire The region known today as Anatolia in Turkey had become Islamized following the MONGOL invasion of the Muslim world in the thirteenth century. A growing Turkish principality led by Osman and then his successors (hence Ottomans) extended their rule by defeating the BYZANTINES and eventually capturing their capital Constantinople in 1453. They renamed it ISTANBUL and made it the centre of one of the largest and most enduring dynasties in Muslim history. At its height, the Ottomans had control over most of the Middle East and North Africa, parts of Central and Eastern Europe. This was a land and maritime empire that stretched from the Indian Ocean to the Black Sea.

Within Sunni Islam, the Ottoman sultan, as he was called, came to be regarded as caliph and protector of the SHARIA. His army, administration and government were the strongest and most efficient of the time, and the capital Istanbul became the most developed seat of culture, scholarship and science. The empire embraced many ethnic and religious groups, including the diverse schools of thought within Islam. It also provided a form of unity by its use of the Arabic language, a common administrative and institutional culture, a trade network and its patronage of Islam's important cities, such as MECCA, MEDINA and JERUSALEM. In architecture and the arts, the Ottomans developed the existing Muslim heritage. Among their mosques, palaces and other buildings, the style created by the famous architect Mimar SINAN articulated a specifically new expression of building and design.

In the later part of the eighteenth and the early nineteenth century the Ottoman Empire faced major opposition on several fronts. The SAFAWIDS disputed Ottoman sovereignty over neighbouring regions; Russia seized some territory; Egypt and Syria became autonomous under MUHAMMAD ALI; control over part of the Crimea and Eastern Europe was lost and several treaties had to be concluded to retain a degree of authority and control over existing territories. This was also a period of change and reform in the internal workings of the state as European influence and ideas of constitutional rule to restrict the absolute powers of the caliph began to penetrate the empire. Even though the caliph instituted some reforms, the process was slow and resistance to his authority and absolute power grew. When the Ottomans joined Germany and its allies in World War I, the British and the French wrested territory from them and by 1918 parts of Turkey were occupied. A revolt in its Arab territory, supported by the British, caused the loss of a significant part of the empire. National opposition to the humiliation continued to be directed against the caliph, and the Turkish parliament under the leadership of MUSTAFA KEMAL (Atatürk) sought to abolish Ottoman rule and its institutions, including the Caliphate. By the time this was formally accomplished in 1924, the empire had virtually ceased to exist and a new Turkish nation-state had emerged in its place.

Pakistan A modern state in Asia, it was created in 1947 to respond to the demands of Muslims in British-ruled India for their own homeland. It was envisaged by its founder Muhammad Ali JINNAH as a Muslim nation in which all faiths would be free and without distinction in the eyes of the state. At the time it consisted of two wings – West Pakistan and East Pakistan, now Bangladesh, which seceded in 1971, to emerge as a new nation-state. Pakistan has a population of over 160 million which includes a very small number of Christians, Hindus and Zoroastrians. Though most Muslims belong to the Sunni Hanafi SCHOOL OF ISLAMIC LAW, there is a significant Shia minor-

At the Dargah of Abdul Wahhab, Hyderabad, Pakistan.

ity. Both groups reflect the diversity of Muslim practice and historical heritage in the region. Pakistan contains many Sufi shrines and *khanqas* (sites of annual pilgrimage and commemoration). A long tradition of scholars and writers have left a considerable legacy.

Since its founding, Pakistan has fought with India on several occasions over the still-disputed territory of KASHMIR and internally has seen alternating periods of civilian and military governance. Its geopolitical position has given it a significant role in regional disputes, particularly in Afghanistan. While several regional languages such as Punjabi, Sindhi, Pashto and many others remain strong and vibrant, Pakistan has adopted Urdu as its national language. In 1977 the then military ruler, General Zia ul-Haq, instituted changes in Pakistan's legal and personal code intended to achieve greater conformity with traditional Muslim legal precepts. These included the so-called HUDUD ordinances, which carried stringent and severe punishments for criminal acts and were generally regarded as discriminatory against women. These have provoked much debate over the last three decades. Certain Muslim political parties have sought to extend and even intensify such practices, while others have challenged their validity and sought to oppose them.

Pakistan's involvement in supporting the Afghan resistance against Soviet occupation during the 1980s led to a large refugee influx from Afghanistan. Many young men came to be trained in religious-style camps often providing, in addition to military training, a narrow form of Muslim instruction. The TALIBAN, as these young men came to be called, eventually became a long-term source of conflict in Pakistan's border region with Afghanistan and this, as well as the insurgency in Kashmir, continues to be a source of tension as Pakistan seeks to play a constructive role to bring about peace in the region.

Palestine Region on the eastern Mediterranean coast which was conquered by Muslim armies from 634 to 640, and remained as part of the territories of various Muslim empires, except for a short period during the CRUSADES. The presence of Muslims, Christians and Jews reflected the long history of connection with holy places and pilgrimages in Palestine.

After the fall of the OTTOMAN EMPIRE and the end of World War I, the area was occupied by Britain. Both Christians and Jews lived there but Jewish immigration increased during and following Ottoman rule. After 1939 there was a further increase in immigration from Europe as Jewish refugees sought to escape persecution and genocide. A British undertaking to establish a Jewish state in Palestine led to several conflicts. The UN partition plan of 1947 envisaged the creation of two states in the region, but even before the official recognition of Israel in 1948 fighting had erupted and thereafter the region has seen a number of wars, ongoing low-level conflict and territorial disputes that have never been fully resolved, although more recent negotiations hold out hope for a settlement whereby the Palestinian and Israeli states could live in mutual recognition and peace.

The Palestinian Liberation Organization (PLO) under Yasser Arafat (1929–2004) maintained that Palestine should be a secular state. The PLO eventually recognized Israel in 1988 and agreed to a peace process, with the promise of greater autonomy, eventual statehood and a negotiated settlement over the status of East Jerusalem, which Palestinians regard as their capital. The Muslim party HAMAS has, however, rejected parts of this agreement and continued what it regards as a necessary armed struggle to achieve its goals. While the prospects for a peaceful resolution of the conflict and its underlying causes often seem slim, the volatility of the region, exacerbated by an unresolved festering crisis, makes the search for peace an issue demanding urgent global attention and commitment.

Panj Tan-i Pak The Five Pure Ones, referring, according to Shia tradition, to the five immediate members of the Prophet's family: the Prophet himself, his daughter FATIMA, his son-in-law and cousin ALI IBN ABI TALIB and their sons HASAN and HUSAYN IBN ALI. The idea of purity is based on a Quranic verse (33:33) that refers to the family of the Prophet.

Parvin E'tesami (1907–1941) Iranian writer and a pioneer of women's literary expression in modern Persian, who gave voice, within traditional models of poetry, to issues affecting women's place in public life. Her poetry reflects insights and articulates experiences from the perspective of women who are regarded as playing a marginal role in society and compelled to conform to these traditional standards.

pasha Turkish title given to military and civil leaders of high rank and reputation. It was one of the highest titles of honour in both the OTTOMAN EMPIRE and modern Turkey until 1934.

Pashto Language spoken in the southern region of Afghanistan and neighbouring regions of Pakistan. Literary works in Pashto can be traced back to oral epics, while a rich tradition of poetry including devotional and mystical works developed in the seventeenth and eighteenth centuries.

people *See* HUMAN BEINGS.

People of the Book *See* AHL AL-KITAB.

Persatuan Islam *See* NATSIR, MOHAMMAD.

Persian Official language of Iran. Of Indo-European origin, Persian was spoken widely in adjoining regions of Afghanistan and Tajikistan. The ancient language re-emerged in the Arabic script after the spread of Islam and became a major form of expression of literature, administration, court life and the arts in Iran, Central Asia, the Indian subcontinent and Turkey. The literary tradition in particular contains the best examples of philosophical, mystical and devotional writings on Islam.

pesantren Educational centres and boarding schools. These local institutions exist in Indonesia and Malaysia (where they are called *pondok*). They provide teaching in various Islamic subjects and training in farming, crafts and trade. As the most important Muslim educational institutions in the region, they provided continuity and learning during colonial rule. They are still of vital importance in their modern form for linking Muslim and national goals of education and have produced some of the country's leading religious and political figures.

The Shahnama (Epic of the Kings), Shiraz, c. 1492. A monument of Persian literature.

philanthropy *See* SADAQA; WAQ; ZAKAT.

Philippines A nation comprising some 7,000 islands in Southeast Asia, the Philippines has a population of 80 million, of which a significant minority found in the southern region of MINDANAO is Muslim. They consist of various ethnic groups who were generally marginalized during periods of Spanish and American rule. Since gaining independence in 1946, the Muslim population has agitated for recognition and autonomy, causing friction and violence in the region. In the 1970s various rebel groups began a period of violent resistance lasting until 1996, when an agreement was reached granting a degree of autonomy to the Muslim-dominated areas. Periodic conflict and violence, however, still continue in some areas, as members of various rebel groups link up with others to form wider networks of those committed to a global JIHAD.

philosophy Philosophical thought in Islam (*falsafa* in Arabic) grew out of attempts at discursive reflection on truths believed to be grounded in revelation but also intelligible by the disciplined use of human reason. While the methods and tools of *falsafa* were inspired primarily by the heritage of classical antiquity mediated through Christian scholarship, its fullest expressions were not restricted by either classical antecedents or the constraints of religious dogma.

The historical origins of this intellectual tradition are to be found in the encounter of scholars in the Muslim world of the time with translations of Greek, Pahlavi and Sanskrit (but principally Greek) philosophical texts. Patronage by Muslim rulers and the establishment of endowed institutions to promote translation and learning (such as the BAYT AL-HIKMA and AL-AZHAR UNIVERSITY, established in Baghdad and Cairo respectively during the ninth and tenth centuries) further stimulated interest in philosophical and scientific work.

Philosophy developed in the Islamic cultural context, and was written in Arabic and later in Persian. Some of the earliest translators of Greek texts into Arabic were Christians. The first major philosophers to work from the translated texts and write commentaries on them were Muslims, although they were soon followed by Jewish and Christian authors. In the twelfth and thirteenth centuries much of the Arabic heritage was translated into Latin and to an extent into Hebrew, promoting continual exchange between these traditions. The role of philosophy in these three faith communities represents a perspective through which the whole history of medieval philosophy linking Muslim, Christian and Jewish thought may be seen.

The first Muslim to be regarded as a philosopher in the formal sense is AL-KINDI (d. 866), who was a keen student of Greek philosophy as well as Indian arithmetic. The next major figure was AL-FARABI (d. 950). He was the first, in the Muslim context, to study the materials before him systematically and to proceed to give his own commentary on them. These materials were varied. They included early Christian-Arabic tracts on Aristotle, the works of Plato, the texts of Neoplatonism and of other ancient writers such as Porphyry, and commentaries written on Aristotle by Christian scholars of late antiquity. Even more importantly, al-Farabi was an early representative of what we now call the philosophy of religion, at least in its incipient form.

In the hands of the great Abu Ali IBN SINA (d. 1037), or Avicenna as he became known in the West, this process was taken considerably further. His chief aim was to harness philosophical thought to the principles of religion.

Ibn Sina's conclusions were not, in the eyes of several Muslim scholars, orthodox. While insisting that everything is eternally dependent on God – a major departure from Aristotle in the direction of religious doctrine – he also ascribed eternity to many other things besides, such as intellects, souls and the sublunary spheres. This was in keeping with the Aristotelian view of the eternity of the world, but was to create immense controversy, and to give the Sunni theologian Abu Hamid Muhammad AL-GHAZALI cause to declare Avicennan philosophy un-Islamic. But the idea of a Muslim orthodoxy was itself a product of circumstances, and a relatively late one at that. Ibn Sina's doctrine of the eternity of the world is in part a reflection of the openness of Muslim thought as late as his time, before the crystallization of such an 'orthodoxy', particularly in the Sunni world.

Ibn Sina's influence was considerable. Thomas Aquinas adopted his distinction between essence and existence as part of an argument for the existence of God. The Jewish philosopher of Spain, Abraham ibn Daud, followed him closely, with minor adaptations. Some of his works were translated into Latin and Hebrew. In the Muslim world, he was revered, especially in the Persian-speaking east, where his ideas became thoroughly absorbed into MYSTICISM. He was also widely admired for his vast medical knowledge and his work on the natural sciences.

Muslim Spain in the twelfth century was also a significant centre of philosophical activity. Ibn Bajja (d. 1139) commented extensively on al-Farabi's works on logic and also argued against Ibn Sina's view of the immortality of the soul. His student IBN TUFAYL (d. c. 1186) is best known as the author of *Hayy ibn Yaqzan*, a philosophical narrative that explores the divide between philosophical understanding and litera-list approaches to religion.

Ibn Tufayl's student IBN RUSHD (d. 1198), or Averroes as he came to be known in the West, became a gifted spokesman for philosophy in its defence against theologians. He also served as a judge in Seville, and later as chief judge (*qadi*) of Córdoba. His commentaries on Aristotle were translated into Latin and transmitted to Europe, where Dante referred to him as the 'Great Commentator'. His best-known works on the relation between philosophy and religion are *On the Harmony between Religion and Philosophy* and his defence of philosophy against the attack on it by Abu Hamid Muhammad AL-GHAZALI, the Sunni theologian and professor of law at the Nizamiyya College in Baghdad.

Another towering figure, born in Muslim Spain, who had enormous influence on the subsequent development of Muslim intellectual and mystical thought (Sufism), is IBN AL-ARABI (d. 1240). Among the major doctrines that represent a key strand in his multifaceted works are the concepts of the 'oneness of being' (*wahdat al-wujud*), the 'perfect man' (*al-insan al-kamil*) and the 'world of analogical imagination' (*alam al-mithal*). His thought links philosophy and mysticism into an original wisdom trad-ition.

Towards the eastern part of the Muslim world in Iran, the philosophical heritage of Ibn Sina and others took a different direction. It coalesced with Sufism (Muslim mysticism) and produced an intellectual school that included such creative figures as Shihab al-Din SUHRAWARDI (d. 1191), the founder of illuminationist (*ishraqi*) phil-osophy. The tradition flourished and received new impetus after a relatively long dormant period with the establishment of the Shia SAFAWID state in Iran (1501–1722). The intellectual and philosophical developments of the period are marked by the emergence of the 'school of Isfahan' that produced thinkers like MIR DAMAD (d. 1631) and MULLA SADRA (d. 1640). They developed further the tradition of Shia intellectual thought, drawing upon the contributions of Suhrawardi, Ibn al-Arabi and their successors and also the intellectual foundations laid down in the work of Nasir al-Din TUSI (d. 1274).

Muslim philosophers have thus played a significant role in the development of Muslim thought and religious education, an influence that has persisted in parts of the Muslim world until modern times. They also had an impact on intellectual developments in medieval and even Renaissance Europe. This universalism and cosmopolitanism remains a source of inspiration for the development of philosoph-ical inquiry among contemporary Muslim thinkers. *See also* MODERNIST MUSLIM THOUGHT.

pilgrimage The traditions of pilgrimage in Islam include the HAJJ, the major annual pilgrimage to sites in Mecca and surrounding areas, incumbent on Muslims who have the means and the capacity to undertake it; the UMRA, a minor version of the *Hajj* which can be undertaken at any time; visits to MEDINA, where the Prophet is buried, and to many other sites in the Muslim world visited for their significance in either regional or local terms or because they are associated with significant figures in Muslim history whose role has given them special religious status.

All pilgrims begin the *Hajj* in a purified state called *ihram*, wearing a simple garment of white, and commit themselves during the time of pilgrimage to avoid taking any life or committing acts of violence to others or to the environment. They are to practise abstinence by not displaying jewellery, shaving (for men), or having sexual relations.

The sequence of ritual actions performed by Muslims is based on revelation and the practice of the Prophet. Upon entering the precincts of al-Masjid al-Haram (the Sacred Mosque at Mecca), pilgrims perform the 'circling' of the KA'BA, seven circuits counter-clockwise. After acknowledging the Station of Abraham, the spot symbolizing the space of worship built in ancient times, the pilgrims cross to the two hills of Safa and Marwa and run or walk briskly between them. This ritual act signifies the running of Hagar, Abraham's second wife, as she sought water for their son ISHMAEL. According to Muslim tradition, Abraham had left Hagar and Ishmael there while on his mission for God. As food and water ran out, Hagar ran between the two hills, searching desperately for water in the blazing sun. Water miraculously sprang forth in a spot called the Well of Zam-Zam.

Next the pilgrims make for a place called Mina, some distance away, where they spend the night. The following morning they proceed to the plains of Arafat and spend the whole day there in prayer, remembrance and reading of the Quran. The ritual is called the 'standing', since pilgrims remain standing throughout the day. At sunset they go to Muzdalifa to spend the night. Before daybreak the next day, the pilgrims leave to return to Mina where they participate in the ritual stoning of three pillars, symbolizing the repudiation of evil by Abraham, who rejected all temptation put before him so that he might fulfil God's will by sacrificing his son. The theme is continued in the preparation of the festival that is to follow, which marks a formal end of each person's pilgrimage.

After offering a sacrifice and sharing the food with the needy and the poor, most pilgrims complete another circling of the Ka'ba.

The *Hajj* is a dramatic re-enactment of the beginnings of Islam. The rituals memorialize the ancient history of the Ka'ba, its founding as a sacred sanctuary by Abraham and its restoration by the Prophet Muhammad. The state of *ihram* underlines the equality of all Muslims, men and women, before God and their identity as a new community of believers. The days of the *Hajj* also represent a way of reaffirming one's commitment and sense of belonging and an opportunity to renew one's faith in the largest gathering of Muslims, before returning to daily life. Participation in the *Hajj* thus becomes a way of sharing in the founding experiences of the UMMA.

The concept of visiting, or *ziyarat*, as a form of pilgrimage is found across the Muslim world. While in modern times some Muslim groups have held this to be an innovation, there have been important shrines and locations visited by millions of Muslims throughout the period of their history. For the Shia in particular some of the important centres relate to the history of their IMAMS, while among Sufis places associated with founding figures or important teachers are visited in order to seek the 'blessing' associated with their spiritual status. These traditions remain deeply grounded in the local histories of Muslims and link them to a wider framework of devotional expression in Islam.

pir Term used to identify a spiritual teacher or a major Sufi figure. It is used extensively in South and Central Asia.

places of worship *See* SPACES OF GATHERING.

Plato (c. 428–347 BCE) In the Muslim philosophical tradition, Plato (known as Aflatun in Arabic) is perceived as being second in prestige to ARISTOTLE, although it is recognized that the two had much in common. Plato's works reached Muslim philosophers through translations and in various interpretations and constitute a major source and influence among many Muslim thinkers of the medieval period.

Pomaks Muslims of Bulgarian-speaking origin who live in Bulgaria and Macedonia. They converted to Islam in the OTTOMAN period, from the fifteenth century onwards.

pondok *See* PESANTREN.

prayer The Quran teaches multiple acts of personal and community prayer. These aspects of worship encompass the formal ritual prayer, the *salat*, acts of remembrance of God, *dhikr*, and prayers of supplication and praise, *dua*. Based on the experiences and example of the Prophet, they combine to represent the different forms of devotional expression in Islam.

The *salat* is the formal, ritual prayer. While Muslims may pray and remember God at any time, the evolution of the practice of the *salat* has led to its performance at traditional times: dawn, noon, afternoon, sunset, and late evening. It is to be preceded by an act of ablution. The cleansing involves the hands, the arms, the mouth, the nostrils and the feet. Where water is not available for ablution, the act may be performed symbolically, using sand or stone. The act of ablution links purity of the body to prayer as a means of purifying one's inner self.

On Friday Muslims are enjoined by the Quran to take part in a congregational midday prayer accompanied by a sermon. The first Muslims assembled in Medina, both for Friday congregational prayers and at other times, first in the courtyard of the Prophet's house and, as the community grew, in spaces which the Quran refers to as *masjid*, a place of prostration. The Arabic term *masjid* is the basis for the word 'mosque'.

Dhikr, remembrance of God, is also referred to in the Quran as an act of devotion and love. The example of the Prophet's early retreat and his acts of contemplation and personal meditation are seen as an important means of seeking a loving and personal relationship with God. Such remembrance can be practised at any time and in any place, though different spaces for such devotional acts evolved among Muslims in different parts of the world.

Dua consists of prayers of supplication that can be said in times of crisis or to fulfil individual and community needs and requests. All of these forms of devotion permit Muslims a means of communication with God and a constant reminder of the presence of God in their lives.

prophecy Muslims believe that God has communicated with human beings since the beginning of time, through messengers and prophets. Prophecy defines this role of communicating God's message which is divinely inspired. Revelation granted through prophecy enables human beings to have access to proper guidance as well as knowledge about God and His purpose for humanity. Man is asked to accept the message revealed through prophecy by reflecting on it and using the gift of the intellect to recognize its validity.

Muslim thinkers have argued in their works dealing with prophecy that its main characteristics were that prophets were the best of communicators to people in their own language, cultural context and behavioural norms, and were blessed with faith and conviction that enabled them to face opposition and even persecution.

Prophecy, according to Muslims, culminated in the revelations granted to Prophet Muhammad, who is regarded as the 'seal of the Prophets'. *See also* NUBUWWA.

Punjabi Language of Punjab, a region that straddles India and Pakistan. It has played an important role in the development of a rich and varied tradition of poetry and writings among Muslims in the region, including narrative poems that reflect some of the classical themes of Sufi literature.

purdah See HIJAB.

Q

qadi A Muslim judge, whose function according to law is to provide rulings and resolve disputes. Traditionally, the responsibility of the judge was to render judgements according to the recognized works and practice of each respective SCHOOL OF ISLAMIC LAW. Where the jurisdiction of traditional SHARIA courts continues to hold sway in the Muslim world, the office of the *qadi* is still of importance. *See also* ULAMA.

Qadiriyya Sufi order originating in the teachings of ABD AL-QADIR AL-JILANI in the twelfth century. Following his death his sons formalized the order and spread the teachings to most parts of the Muslim world. Local leaders, called *khalifas*, were responsible for each region and provided instruction and guidance. Today the Qadiriyya are found in several African and Asian Muslim communities.

al-Qaeda An organization led by Osama bin Laden, responsible for the attacks on the World Trade Center on September 11 2001 which killed over 3,000 people. Since then the organization has been condemned and prosecuted across virtually the whole world but has continued to preach its militant message against all those, Muslims and non-Muslims, whom it opposes, and to justify acts of violence against them in the name of what it regards as true Islam. Most Muslim leaders and scholars regard al-Qaeda as an extremist group whose views and practices are utterly opposed to the ethos of Islam.

Qajars Iranian dynasty that ruled from 1779 to 1923. It was during their rule that the first oil explorations and concessions began, which resulted in increasing Western attempts to influence Iran's development. In 1906 popular feeling led to the rise of a constitutional movement and the adoption of a constitution limiting the powers of the monarch, although this was suspended in 1911. A coup d'état led by REZA KHAN led to the overthrow of the dynasty.

qanun The idea of a system of rules and regulations eventually taken up by several past Muslim rulers to stand for state regulations or administration procedures. It became a highly systematized process under the OTTOMANS and was meant to complement the presence of the SHARIA in Muslim societies.

Qarawiyyin A mosque-university in Fez, Morocco. It was endowed in the ninth century by a pious Muslim woman, Fatima bint Muhammad al-Fihri, who had moved there with her family. The Qarawiyyin became a major seat of learning and scholarship, attracting renowned scholars. It has since been integrated into the national system of higher education in Morocco and continues to provide training for specialists in Islamic studies. Except for the mosque and the library, most of the educational facilities have been transferred elsewhere.

qasida Poetic form comparable to an ode. It appears in the literatures of many Muslim communities. A mono-rhymed poem, it was also used to express praise of God and to celebrate the Prophet.

Qasim Amin (1863–1908) Egyptian writer and social critic, particularly remembered for his writings on the emancipation of women. Although he died quite young, his efforts in the struggle to improve the living conditions of Egyptian women and thus increase their social participation and his constant struggle against those who favoured the traditional attitude towards women made him the most outspoken exponent of women's rights. His Egyptian patriotism is evident in his works written during his stay in Paris.

Qatar Gulf state bordered by Saudi Arabia and endowed with significant petroleum resources. Its majority population of Sunni Muslims adhere to the Wahhabi school of thought, but it also has a significant Shia minority.

The al-Thani family constitutes the ruling class and has governed the country since its formal independence as a separate nation-state in 1971.

Qayrawan A town in modern Tunisia but historically a capital city and the site of one of the oldest mosques and universities in North Africa.

qibla The direction of Mecca towards which Muslims face at the time of ritual prayer. It is often designated within a mosque by a MIHRAB, a decorated niche.

qiyas Analogical reasoning. One of the sources of jurisprudence in SUNNI legal practice. *See also* AL-SHAFII; SHARIA.

Qom A leading centre of Twelver Shia learning in Iran (*see* ITHNA ASHARIYYA), it is also the site of the important mausoleum of Hazrat-Masuma, the sister of the eighth imam. It contains major institutions for the training of students and is home to leading scholars and libraries. *See also* SAFAWIDS.

al-Quds *See* JERUSALEM.

Queen of Sheba *See* SHEBA, QUEEN OF.

Quran For Muslims, the Quran is the faithful and complete recording of all revelation that came in the form of divine inspiration to the Prophet Muhammad. The language of the revelation was Arabic, and the work of systematizing and organizing the text of the revelation is believed by Muslims to have been undertaken by the Prophet himself. Revelation came to him over a period of approximately twenty-two years and the process of revelation involved vision as well as audition.

The medium of revelation is described in the Quran as the 'spirit of Holiness', which brought the message to the Prophet. According to the Quran the angel GABRIEL was also a medium of revelation. It is this cumulative process revealed at successive intervals that is described specifically as the 'Quran'. The word literally means 'recitation', and it was in this recited form that the Prophet conveyed it to his followers.

During his lifetime this continuous revelation provided the basis on which both the Muslim faith and the Muslim community were developed by Muhammad. While most of the revelations were memorized by the followers, Muhammad also had scribes put them down in writing. Certain individuals in the growing community were noted for their powers of memory and recital, and they acted as teachers of the new converts.

Soon after the Prophet's death, attempts were made to establish a complete written text from these memorized and transcribed revelations. Since most of the transmission of the Quran among new converts was oral, it was important to establish a fixed, written version in order to avoid the risk of violating the sacred text and to prevent differences arising regarding its contents. On the basis of the previous systematization and arrangement, a written text was compiled and copies sent to all areas of the growing Muslim world. For Muslims, therefore, the Quranic text has existed unchanged for fourteen centuries and is believed to contain the complete message revealed to the Prophet.

The Quran is divided into 114 chapters, each called a *sura*. The number of verses in each chapter varies greatly, each verse being referred to as an *aya*. After the short opening *sura*, subsequent *suras* are arranged according to length, from longest to shortest. The chapter titles either indicate the main content or refer to a word or phrase from the text. All of the chapters, with the exception of *sura* 9, begin with the *basmala*: 'In the name of God, Most Beneficent, Most Merciful'. Chapters are also identified as having been revealed in Mecca or Medina or as containing verses revealed in both places. Thus, Muslims also recognize a chronological order of revelation.

Recitation is the key to understanding the impact of the Quran on its hearers. The Quran is meant to be recited, to be heard and to be experienced. It is impossible to convey the majesty and power of the Arabic recitation in any other language. The power of the 'word of God' for a Muslim lies in its impact not only on the mind, but also on the heart. The correct mode of recitation of the Quran is extremely important in maintaining this tradition, and it is regarded as an art form. Muslims often gather in groups and listen to practitioners, and there is even today an international annual competition to find the best reciters of the Quran.

The language of the Quran pervades all walks of Muslim life, influencing even the mode of writing Arabic and other languages used by Muslims who adopted the Arabic script, such as Persian, Turkish, Urdu, Hausa and Swahili.

The art of CALLIGRAPHY developed from the desire to represent the Quranic text in the most beautiful way using the aesthetic impulse of Muslim art. The written text is given the same devoted reverence as the art of recitation. Calligraphy, in all its elaborate forms, provides an experience for the eye just as correct recitation does for the ear. The art of calligraphy coupled with illumination and colouring has produced copies of the Quran that represent some of the most skilled creations of decorative art in Islam, which have in turn influenced the decoration of places of worship and the wider tradition of the arts in the Muslim world.

A variety of Quranic formulae, such as *Bismillah* ('in the name of God'), *Inshallah* ('If God wills'), *Subhanallah* ('Glory be to God'), are an integral part of the daily life of Muslims. Even the physical presence of the Quran is considered a source of blessing. Verses are recited during moments of personal and family crisis, occasions of celebration and joy, and the moments of birth and death. A copy of the Quran is given an honoured position in the house, where it is generally placed at a level higher than other belongings and furnishings. Muslims often carry a text from the Quran on their person in a small ornamental amulet.

The effort to understand the Quranic message gave rise to sciences related to linguistics and grammar, primarily of Arabic. Muslim scholars also devoted themselves to clarifying and explaining the Quran through works of exegesis known as *tafsir*. The study of the Quran has thus been at the heart of all Muslim scholarship and has given the intellectual and scientific endeavours of the Islamic world in the quest for new knowledge a great sense of unity, as well as reflecting the diversity of interpretation throughout the ages.

Quraysh Meccan tribe which rose to its position of power by controlling access to the pre-Islamic centres of pilgrimage. It rose to prominence under Fihr, who is said to have been among those who defended the KA'BA sanctuary from the attack of Yemeni tribes, eventually taking control of it. Thus during the time of the rise of Islam, the Ka'ba was in the hands of the Quraysh. Although the Prophet Muhammad was a member of the Quraysh clan of Banu Hashim, the tribe strongly opposed his message and sought initially to stop him from preaching, and then to assassinate him. His eventual success in winning over other tribes and the defeat of forces based in Mecca led the Quraysh to submit to his authority and convert to Islam. The Quraysh retained a prominent status in the early history of Muslims because of their association with the Prophet.

Qutb, Sayyid *See* SAYYID QUTB.

Qutb Minar Magnificent tower near Delhi, India, built in red sandstone. Construction of the Qutb Minar began at the end of the twelfth century and it was completed in its final form in the fourteenth century. Divided into five storeys, it serves as a free-standing minaret in part of a complex that includes a mosque.

R

Rabia al-Adawiyya (d. 801) One of the most celebrated women Sufi figures in early Islam. Sold into slavery as a child, she grew up to be an ascetic and a person of such great piety that she drew disciples around her. Rabia al-Adawiyya became famous for her teaching and her sayings, illustrating the themes of love and intimacy, and as a model of selfless devotion, an inspiration to future generations of mystics and seekers.

Rabita al-Alam al-Islami Muslim World League. It was founded in 1962 in Mecca under the auspices of the Kingdom of Saudi Arabia to promote and coordinate a spectrum of activities ranging from funding Muslim groups around the world to providing humanitarian relief, encouraging the standardization of practice and law within a traditionalist interpretation of Islam.

Rahman, Shaykh Mujibur *See* AWAMI LEAGUE.

Ramadan Ninth month of the Muslim CALENDAR marking the period of fasting. The Quran advocates fasting as a practice, in parallel with the tradition of other faith communities. The Quran is believed to have been first revealed during Ramadan. *See also* FASTING; LAYLAT AL-QADR; SAWM.

al-Raniri, Nur al-Din (d. 1658) A teacher and preacher who played an important role in the preaching and spread of Islam in the Malay world. His encyclopedic work *Bustan al-Salatin* (*The Garden of Kings*), although based on Arabic sources, was written in Malay.

Rashid al-Din, Fadl Allah ibn Imad al-Dawla (c. 1247–1318) The author of a major work of world history in which he included a detailed account of the history of the MONGOLS and their conquests. Especially important is his section on the life of Genghis Khan, for which he used a now lost Mongolian source. He was also an influential member of the Ilkhanid court which succeeded in establishing a dynasty after the initial period of Mongol invasion.

Rashid al-Din Sinan (d. 1193) Leader of the Ismaili Muslim community in Syria during the time of the CRUSADES. His organizational and diplomatic capabilities enabled the community to play an important role in the international affairs of the time. After his first visit to Alamut, in present-day Iran, he was sent by the then Imam Hasan Ala Dhikrihi al-Salam to Syria to serve the Ismaili community there.

Rashid Rida, Muhammad Rashid ibn Ali Rida (1865–1935) Rashid Rida is regarded as one of the major figures in the modern Sunni reform movement. He became a follower of MUHAMMAD ABDUH and founded a journal called *al-Manar*, which was devoted to interpretation of the sources of Muslim belief and practice and advocated the use of IJTIHAD (reasoning) as the means to tackle the new set of issues in social, political and economic life faced by Muslims in the early part of the twentieth century. He was also an advocate of Arab nationalism and viewed the Arabs as pivotal figures in restoring Islam to its former glory and eminence.

rasul See NABI.

rawzah-khvani The practice of remembering and mourning through narrative recitations the events related to the martyrdom of Imam HUSAYN IBN ALI and other Shia martyrs. It was developed in Iran in the sixteenth century and is practised widely by the Twelver Imami Shia (see ITHNA ASHARIYYA) all over the world and takes place in a variety of congregational spaces such as mosques, houses and HUSAYNIYYE, as well as in the streets and markets.

al-Razi, Abu Bakr Muhammad ibn Zakariyya (d. 925) Physician, alchemist and philosopher. Known as Rhazes in Latin, his translated works were influential in medieval Europe, particularly for the study of medicine. Al-Razi was a controversial figure among Muslim philosophers because he rejected the necessity of divine revelation and religion as a basis for understanding truth and argued that they were not necessary for the purposes of leading a truly moral life.

al-Razi, Abu Hatim Ahmad ibn Hamdan (d. 934) An important figure in the intellectual history of the early FATIMID period, writing on various religious subjects. He helped define the overall philosophical climate of the Ismaili community of this period.

al-Razi, Fakhr al-Din, Abu Abd Allah Muhammad ibn Umar (1149–1209) Theologian and exegete of the QURAN. He became one of the most noted scholars and teachers of theology in Central Asia. While his many books, some encyclopedic in their approach, concentrate on theology, philosophy and Quranic commentary, he was also a staunch polemicist and defended Sunni theology vigorously against the views of other philosophers.

Raziyya, Begum Jalalat al-Din Queen of the Muizzi dynasty of Delhi from 1236 to 1240 and the only woman to succeed to the throne during the period of Muslim rule in India.

recitation See TAJWID.

Reconquista (lit., 'Reconquest') The expulsion of Muslims from Spain and the establishment of Christian hegemony through conquest of all the territories once under Muslim rule. The process started officially with the beginning of the reign of Ferdinand and Isabella in 1474 and was completed in 1492. Muslims and Jews were permitted to remain in Spain only if they converted to Christianity.

reis effendi Under the OTTOMANS, this title was given to the official who served as secretary of state, in charge of maintaining official records related to matters of state. The post existed for more than three centuries until abolished in 1918.

revelation The revelations that came to Muhammad in the form of divine inspiration are believed by Muslims to be contained in the QURAN. The word Quran literally means 'recitation' or 'reading', and it was in recited form that the Prophet communicated it to his followers. Revelation came to Muhammad over a period of approximately twenty-two years in the form of powerful, jolting experiences that often left him shaken and cold. The process of revelation involved vision as well as hearing. The medium of revelation is described as a 'spirit of Holiness' (Quran 16:102). The angel GABRIEL acted as a mediator of revelation. The signs of Allah are described symbolically as a 'figure on the clear horizon' (Quran 81:20) who revealed to Muhammad the message. The Quranic conception of revelation involves a *tanzil* ('descent'), a universal process by which all previous revelations also come to have their specific terms as a *kitab* ('text' or 'book'). They all, including the Quran, have an original source, referred to as 'Umm al-Kitab' ('The Mother of the Book', Quran 43:1–5). All revelations are thus rooted in one transcendent primary source, which through inspiration becomes articulated to humanity. The Quran in Arabic represents the culmination of this process, completing and fulfilling previous revelations. It was a cumulative process revealed at intervals and appropriate times.

Reza Khan (1878–1944) The founder and first monarch (*shah*) of the Pahlavi dynasty in Persia (now Iran), Colonel Reza Khan came to power following a military coup in 1921 and quickly imposed his authority through the army across all regions and institutions in the country. He risked antagonizing rural-based Muslim scholars and leaders by imposing draconian measures of modernization and social policy. Following the intervention of British and Russian troops in 1941 he was forced to abdicate and died in exile in South Africa in 1944.

Rhazes *See* AL-RAZI, ABU BAKR MUHAMMAD IBN ZAKARIYYA.

riba Generally defined as 'usury' or 'interest', *riba* connotes, in the Quran, unlawful gain resulting from exploitative charges on accrued debt. It is not, however, meant to preclude lawful profit or gain. *See also* INTEREST; ISLAMIC BANKING.

al-ridda (lit., 'apostasy') A term associated with the wars against several tribes who, following the death of the Prophet Muhammad, refused to give ABU BAKR allegiance. The most famous of these battles was against the tribe of Tamim. Some *al-ridda* wars were against leaders of tribes that claimed prophecy in imitation of the Prophet.

Rifaiyya Sufi order. One of the earliest and most prevalent orders in the Middle East, its origins can be traced to the teachings of Ahmad al-Rifai (d. 1182). Among the various major Sufi groups that became dominant in medieval Muslim society, the Rifaiyya were always very prominent. They continue to be active in many parts of the Muslim world and among Muslims now living in Europe and the United States.

Rightly Guided Caliphs In the tradition of Sunni Islam, ABU BAKR, UMAR IBN AL-

KHATTAB, UTHMAN IBN AFFAN and ALI IBN ABI TALIB, the first four leaders of the Muslim community, are regarded as 'rightly guided' because of their personal commitment to the Prophet and for their exemplary role in building and guiding the Muslim community in its initial stages.

Riza-Nursi, Bediuzzaman Said *See* NURSI, SHAYKH BADI AL-ZAMAN SAID.

rubai (pl., *rubaiyyat*) A verse form employing a quatrain. It originated in Persian poetry devoted to expressing a variety of literary genres from mystical and philosophical to love poetry. Among the most famous examples in translation are the *Rubaiyyat of Omar Khayyam*.

Rum *See* BYZANTIUM.

Rumi, Jalal al-Din *See* JALAL AL-DIN RUMI.

Russian Federation The Russian Federation came into existence after the disintegration of the Soviet Union in 1991 and contains a significant Muslim population, mainly concentrated in the North Caucasus region (Kabardino-Balkaria, North OSSETIA, Chechen-Ingushetia (*see* INGUSH), DAGHISTAN, Adyghe and Karachai Cherkess) and in the republics of Tatarstan and Bashkortostan. The current Grand Mufti of Russia, Ravil Ismagilovich Gaynutdinov, is a TATAR. Muslims constitute the second largest religious denomination in Russia and are represented by both Shia and Sunni communities.

The Muslim populations of the Russian Federation form part of the culture and society of Central Asia and were forcibly incorporated into the Russian Empire in the nineteenth and twentieth centuries and subsequently into the Soviet Union. More recently, there have been signs of Islamic revival in all the republics, as peoples within the Federation seek to identify and redefine themselves in relation to their Muslim heritage. In some cases the tensions have resulted in conflict with the government in Moscow and demands for independence, particularly in CHECHNYA where it has taken on a violent and divisive form that has had to be severely repressed. The total population of all Muslims within the Russian Federation is estimated to be about 17 million. There are also large numbers of Muslims from other former Soviet republics who come to Russia as work migrants, forced migrants, refugees or displaced people. *See also* KAZAKHSTAN.

S

Saadia Gaon (882–942) Jewish philosopher recognized as a major figure in medieval Jewish thought who wrote in both Hebrew and Arabic. Known for his translation of the Bible into Arabic and his use of theological reasoning that drew from his knowledge of Muslim scholarship and ideas. Like many Muslim thinkers of the time, he was attracted to Neoplatonic philosophy, which he integrated into his interpretation of the Jewish tradition.

Saba One of the kingdoms of ancient South Arabia whose capital was Marib. In 580 a famous dam located near Marib collapsed. Saba is referred to as SHEBA in the Hebrew Bible and is associated with the Queen of Sheba, known as Bilqis in Muslim tradition.

Sabians A religious community mentioned in the Quran as one of the believing communities ('those who believe'), on a par with Jews and Christians. Muslim scholars identified them as a group originating in Hellenistic times with a prophet who had received a revelation.

sabil Literally, 'the way', but also a public water-house or fountain found in many traditional Muslim cities and towns. They were founded for the charitable purpose of dispensing free water, particularly for travellers, or in some instances as part of learning centres for children called *sabil kuttab* or for provision of water for animals. Often richly decorated, some of these have acquired the status of important architectural monuments.

al-Sabti, Abul Abbas (1130–1205) Sufi teacher renowned for his piety and charity. Al-Sabti's reputation as a saintly figure is reflected in the regular visitations to his mausoleum in present-day Morocco.

Sachal Sarmast (1739–1829) Noted mystic of Sind, present-day Pakistan, whose poetry composed in Sindhi is widely acknowledged for its mystical and devotional intensity. His tomb is a major centre of pilgrimage in the region.

Sa'd ibn Abi Waqqas (d. 671) An early convert to Islam who became famous for his military role in all the early battles fought by Muslims against their Meccan enemies. In 637, under the Caliph UMAR IBN AL-KHATTAB, he led the Muslim armies to victory against the Persians. He was appointed one of the governors of the growing Muslim Empire and was an active participant in the affairs of the community until his death.

Sa'd ibn Ibrahim Zaghlul (1858–1927) A disciple of MUHAMMAD ABDUH who was educated at AL-AZHAR UNIVERSITY and also in Europe. He went on to play an important role as jurist and state official during the period of British rule in Egypt. Sa'd Zaghlul led a political movement, the Wafd, to fight for Egyptian independence and remained the president of the party until his death.

sadaqa An act of voluntary giving. It is enjoined in the Quran as an ethical practice to alleviate the suffering of the poor and those unable to meet their needs. As reflected in the sayings attributed to the Prophet, such actions encompass giving as well as acts of generosity and kindness to animals and birds and tending the earth. *Sadaqa* is regarded as an expression of the social conscience in Islam. *See also* ZAKAT.

Sadat, Anwar (1918–1981) President of Egypt who succeeded Gamal Abdel NASSER. He was assassinated in 1981 by a group organized to undertake JIHAD who believed that he had betrayed the country by signing a peace accord with Israel, associating with the United States and suppressing Muslim groups who opposed his policies and were seeking to transform Egypt into an Islamic state.

Sadi, Shaykh (d. 1292) Well-known Sufi poet. He wrote some of the most popular collections of stories and narratives in Persian literature. The integration of diverse literary forms enabled him to frame moral and spiritual conflicts faced by human beings and the sources and examples of guidance available to them within the context of the ethical and moral traditions of Islam. A mausoleum and a statue in Shiraz, Iran, celebrate his contribution to the literature of his country. One of his famous poems which exemplifies universal values binding humanity is displayed in the entrance hall of the United Nations. It reads:

The children of humanity are each others' limbs
That share an origin in their creator.
When one limb passes its days in pain
The other limbs cannot remain easy.
You who feel no pain at the suffering of others,
It is not fitting for you to be called human.

Sadiyya Sufi order originating in the thirteenth and fourteenth centuries which spread widely in Egypt, Turkey and the Balkans. The order's founder, Sa'd al-Din Shaybani, played an important role in the history of DAMSACUS. Many of its members can still be found in Syria.

al-Sadr, Muhammad Baqir (1935–1980) Prominent Imami Shia leader in Iraq under the regime of Saddam HUSSEIN. He wrote extensively on how Muslim values could be integrated into everyday economic and social life. His activism and opposition to Saddam led to his imprisonment and eventual execution. Members of his family continue to play an active role as religious leaders in Iraq.

Sadr al-Din, Pir Preacher and missionary. Active during the fourteenth century, Pir Sadr al-Din is regarded as one of the most important figures in the conversion of Hindus in Sind and Gujarat to Nizari Ismaili Islam (*see* ISMAILIYYA). He continued a tradition of bridging the worlds of Indian and Muslim spirituality by linking traditional Hindu narratives and poetry in the vernacular to the Ismaili tradition.

Sadr al-Din Shirazi *See* MULLA SADRA SHIRAZI.

Sadyah Gaon *See* SAADIA GAON.

Safa One of two small hills (the other is Marwa) which are an integral part of the pattern of rituals in the annual *Hajj*. *See* HAJJ; PILGRIMAGE.

Safawids Dynasty that ruled in what is now Iran from 1501 to 1732, taking their name from Safi al-Din Ishaq, founder of the Safawiyya, a Sufi order whose leader claimed supreme religious and political authority. In time, they associated their form of Sufism with Twelver Imami Shiism (*see* ITHNA ASHARIYYA). Shah Ismail, a descendant of Safi al-Din, captured Tabriz in Iran, making it the capital of their dynasty. He united various groups and consolidated Twelver Imami Shiism as the dominant tradition of the new dynasty. This caused the migration of Shia scholars from Iraq to Iran. The growing power of the dynasty led to conflict with the OTTO-MANS. During the long reign of Shah Abbas I (1588–1629) the Safawid Empire expanded, leading to increased trade, growth of its cities and patronage of the arts. He established a new capital in Isfahan and consolidated the institutional role of Twelver Shia scholars in the life of the state. Isfahan and other cities in the empire grew in status, becoming important centres of learning, architecture and the arts. The period also gave rise to outstanding scholars of philosophy, law and mysticism and the further development of centres of learning and pilgrimage such as MASHHAD and QOM.

Disputes and rivalry between competing princes caused the decline of Safawid power and control over their empire, and by the middle of the eighteenth century rebellions had caused much of the territory to be lost, as the Ottomans and Russians also took advantage of Safawid weakness. The Safawid period continues to be renowned, however, for its outstanding achievements in art, architecture, law and philosophy, as well as in the medical and natural sciences, and for the splendour of its cities such as Isfahan.

safir Term used in Imami Shiism for those believed to have deputized for the twelfth imam following his occultation (*see* GHAYBA).

In Muslim history, particularly in medieval and modern times, the term is used in diplomatic contexts to refer to an ambassador.

sahaba *See* COMPANIONS OF THE PROPHET.

Sahifat al-Kamila al-Sajjadiyya The collection of prayers and supplications transmitted from Imam ZAYN AL-ABIDIN, imam of the Shia from 680 to 713. This has served as one of the most important sources for the Shia of personal, devotional prayer and an example of a life of great piety.

Sahl al-Tustari, Abu Muhammad ibn Abd Allah (818–896) Early mystical figure whose spiritual commentary on the Quran and practice of meditation to experience intimacy with God (DHIKR) made him important in the development of Sufi thought in the early period of Muslim history.

Sahnun, Abd al-Salam (777–854) Important Maliki scholar who lived in the North African city of Kairouan. He played a major role in the establishment of the Maliki SCHOOL OF ISLAMIC LAW and practice in the region. In addition to his scholarship, Sahnun was noted for his piety and his charitable acts.

Said al-Suada A well-known KHANQA or Sufi gathering place in Cairo. It is one of the few buildings to have survived from the FATIMID period and was subsequently converted to become the first space so designated and organized during the AYYUBID era. *Said al-suada* in Arabic means 'the supremely happy one'.

Said ibn Sultan (1791–1856) Ibadi ruler of Oman and Zanzibar, which he made the capital of his state in 1834. During his reign, the lucrative trade in slaves came to an end because of pressure from Europe. Prosperity, however, continued because of the clove trade and commerce with the interior of Africa.

Saladin *See* SALAH AL-DIN AL-AYYUB.

Salafiyya Reform movement initiated by JAMAL AL-DIN AL-AFGHANI and MUHAMMAD ABDUH in the nineteenth century. One of their major goals was to show that the original message and teachings of Islam could be reconciled with knowledge developed by contemporary science and thought. Appealing to the tradition of the 'elders' at the beginning of Islam, they argued for a return to what they perceived to be a spirit of openness and dynamic interpretation. In due course, however, among some of their followers, these ideas have been extended to emphasize the 'normativeness' of the original traditions and to show a lesser regard for the historical contexts and developments that govern Muslim practices and beliefs.

Salah al-Din al-Ayyub, al-Malik al-Nasir Abu al-Muzaffar Yusuf ibn Ayyub (1138–1193) Famous in the West as Saladin, founder of the AYYUBID dynasty that ruled Egypt between 1171 and 1250. He is mainly known for leading the fight against the CRUSADES, recapturing Jerusalem and ending Crusader control of the region in 1187. In 1171 he had taken control of Egypt and Syria from the Shia FATIMID dynasty and took upon himself the task of establishing and promoting Sunni institutions of learning and its legal tradition. Muslim historians viewed him as a heroic figure who defended Islam against the invaders. He is also regarded as a peacemaker; in 1192, following the Third Crusade, he agreed to a truce with Richard the Lionheart. When Salah al-Din died in 1193 he left behind a dynasty that survived for several decades. He is celebrated in Muslim military lore and in European medieval writings, and also in the fictional works of Sir Walter Scott, as embodying the values of chivalry.

Salam alaykum The traditional Muslim greeting: 'Peace be upon you.'

salat Term for the formal daily ritual PRAYER. It is said at prescribed times, generally dawn, noon, afternoon, sunset and late evening. It may be recited by oneself or with others. The Friday noon prayer is a congregational prayer. *Salat* is preceded by an act of ablution with water, or if water is not available, a symbolic cleansing may be performed. In congregation, prayer is performed behind an imam, with all facing the *qibla*, the direction of the KA'BA. The evolution of the form of the *salat*, based on the tradition of the Prophet and the practice of the Muslim community, reflects a well-defined framework, though each school of Muslim practice has developed its own set of variations. Consisting of units called *raka*, the prayer includes recitation from the QURAN of the opening *sura* (al-Fatiha) and other verses in a sequence that involves standing, bowing, prostration and silent praise and prayer. After the prayer is over, individuals in the congregation offer a greeting of peace to each other and call on God to bless the Prophet and his descendants.

Salih According to the Quran, Salih was a prophet sent to the THAMUD people, who were punished because of their rejection of the divine message.

Saljuqs Dynasty founded in 1038 by Tughril Beg, a military leader of Turkish origin who seized power from the BUYIDS. The Saljuqs ruled over a vast empire in Central and Western Asia. They reflected the rise in Muslim society of new groups being converted in Turkish-speaking areas and the further regionalization of rule by Muslims in different places. The Saljuqs consolidated the Sunni tradition and authority in regions under their control and its major SCHOOL OF ISLAMIC LAW, the Hanafi; they also created legal and educational institutions to balance and combat the influence of the Shia FATIMIDS and their successors in Iran and Syria.

Salman al-Farisi (d. c. 655–7) Persian convert to Islam and COMPANION OF THE PROPHET. Particularly in the Shia and mystical traditions, he is regarded as having been very close to the Prophet and his family, and as having come to recognize in Muhammad and Islam the message of true spirituality.

sama Spiritual gathering accompanied by music to engender spirituality and a heightened sense of devotion to God. Though condemned by some traditionalists, it is widely practised among Sufis and other esoterically orientated Muslim groups. *See also* MUSIC.

Samanids (819–1005) Early Iranian dynasty based in Central Asia. Their capital was BUKHARA, which became a major political and intellectual centre of the time. The dynasty is also noteworthy for its promotion of the Persian language and patronage of poets and writers of Persian.

Samarkand City in present-day Uzbekistan. Historically, it was the hub of the ancient Silk Road linking much of the eastern part of the Muslim world. It served as a trading, educational and cultural centre. The city flourished during the rule of TAMERLANE and his successors who built magnificent monuments, including mosques, *madrasas*, palaces and observatories. It was said that over 2,300 poets and artists lived in the city in the seventeenth century.

Samarra City in Iraq which became the capital of the ABBASID Empire during the ninth century. It subsequently became a site of pilgrimage for the Imami Shia because it contains the mausoleums of two of their imams, Ali al-Hadi and HASAN AL-ASKARI. The twelfth imam is also believed to have gone into occultation from here (*see* GHAYBA).

Archaeological remains and findings suggest a well-constructed and elaborate city. It was eventually abandoned and Baghdad was restored as the capital.

Samori Ture or **Touré** (1830–1900), Muslim leader of MANDÉ (Mandingo) origin. He created a small state in West Africa and established a policy often characterized by attempts to enforce certain Muslim practices upon the population. Faced with British and French armed forces he succumbed to defeat and died in exile.

Sana Ancient city and now capital of Yemen. Its history is linked to that of Islam from the earliest period. Its architectural heritage, including the multi-storey tower houses, unique in medieval Islam, its marketplace, mosques and public baths (*hammams*) have earned Sana an important place as an example of urban development in Muslim history.

Sanusiyya Reform movement founded by Sayyid Muhammad Ali al-Sanusi (1787–1859), a Berber influenced by WAHHABISM and SUFISM. The Sanusiyya played an active role in resisting Italian colonialism in North Africa. Under Muhammad al-Sanusi, known as the Great Imam, *zawiyas* (Sufi centres; *see* KHANQA) were established across North Africa and became centres of resistance against Italian occupation. Al-Sanusi saw his role as that of a teacher and leader of a revitalized Islam and wrote on a wide number of subjects to promote his vision of a TARIQA Muhammadiyya, the way of the Prophet Muhammad. Eventually, the movement spread into the Sahara and was organized further by his son and successor, known as Muhammad al-Mahdi. The Sanusis came into conflict with the French as they sought to extend their influence. They confronted the Italians after they invaded Libya in 1911–1912. After World War II, following an extensive period of resistance to Italian occupation, the then Sanusi leader Muhammad Idris became king of an independent LIBYA. In 1969 a coup led by military officers overthrew the monarchy and disestablished Sanusi political and spiritual authority.

Saqifa Bani Saida Refers specifically to a commercial space in Medina, where the Muslims of the time debated the question of who should occupy the position of authority, after the death of the Prophet. The debate is variously reported in the sources, reflecting the controversial and contested nature of the issue of succession.

Saracens A term coined in the medieval West and applied to the Muslim and Arab peoples of the Middle East. It derives from the Latin *saracenoi*, apparently the name of a nomadic tribe in the Middle East in the late Roman period.

Sarajevo Capital of Bosnia-Herzegovina. It came under OTTOMAN rule in the fifteenth century and became a major administrative and cultural centre, acquiring a distinctive identity through its architecture and multicultural population, Muslim and non-Muslim.

During the conflict in Bosnia between 1991 and 1995 the citizens of Sarajevo were subjected to heavy bombardment and atrocities, but they survived to rebuild its infrastructure and multi-faith character.

Sarekat Islam Party representing Muslim interests in Indonesia and Southeast Asia generally. The Kitab Sarekat al-Islam was established in 1912. Though an important player in the nationalist struggle for independence, it dwindled in significance after World War II.

al-Sarraj, Abu Nasr Abd, Allah ibn Ali (d. 988) The author of a major work on Sufism called the *Kitab al-Luma*, which became very influential in establishing an intellectual framework for mystical thought during its early development.

Sassanids Major pre-Islamic dynasty that ruled Persia and Mesopotamia from the third century until it was overthrown by Muslim armies that conquered the region in 651. Sassanid Persia was predominantly Zoroastrian. Its administrative and cultural heritage would have an important influence on the future course of events in the region as it came under Muslim rule.

Satan *See* IBLIS.

satr Literally, 'concealment'. Among the ISMAILIYYA, and particularly among the Mustali Ismailis, it connotes the belief that the Imam has chosen to conceal himself and is represented by an acknowledged leader from among the community.

Saudi Arabia Established in 1934 as a kingdom, it is ruled by the descendants of ABD AL-AZIZ IBN SAUD. Its roots date back to an alliance in 1744 between Muhammad ibn Abd al-Wahhab, leader of the Wahhabiyya (*see* WAHHABISM), and Muhammad ibn Saud, a tribal leader. In the early part of the twentieth century, much of Arabia, including Mecca and Medina, was captured under the leadership of

Corniche Mosque, Jeddah, Saudi Arabia.

Abd al-Aziz ibn Saud, who united the territory and brought to it the strict traditionalism of the Wahhabis. The population, estimated at 15 million, is 90 per cent Arab, of which 80 per cent are Sunni Muslims who follow the Hanbali SCHOOL OF ISLAMIC LAW. There is a significant Shia minority, found mostly in the eastern part of the country, and a smaller community of Mustali Ismailis in the region around Najran, bordering Yemen.

Muslim movements such as the MUSLIM BROTHERHOOD and others with similar aspirations have found support and refuge in Saudi Arabia, which has been active in promoting its traditions of Muslim practices and education elsewhere among Muslims. It has also promoted the building of mosques and religious centres among Muslims living in the West.

The Kingdom sees its greatest responsibility as being custodian of the holy places in Mecca and Medina and organizer of the HAJJ and the UMRA. While much has been done to ease and facilitate this, some Muslims have expressed concern about the cost of modernizing services to the neglect of historical places and buildings around Mecca, which hold long-standing associations and memories for the pilgrims who come from all over the world.

In the climate of conflict in the Middle East and elsewhere Saudi Arabia has sought to play an influential role, though its military and diplomatic alliance with the United States has caused opposition among some segments of its citizenry including members of AL-QAEDA, who believe that this represents a betrayal of Muslims and the sacred territories which the Saudis are considered to be holding in trust.

Sawda, Mirza Muhammad Rafi (1713–1781) Regarded as one of the great poets of Urdu, Sawda lived in Delhi and subsequently in Lucknow. Known for the versatility of his GHAZALS, he also wrote poetry in praise of the Shia imams.

Sawda bint Zama (d. 675) One of the earliest converts to Islam and the second wife of the Prophet, who married her in 621 after the death of KHADIJA. She is considered exemplary because of her generous nature and charitable spirit.

sawm or *siyam* Quranic term for fasting. Abstinence from food, drink and sexual activity is observed as a spiritual discipline from sunrise to sunset during the month of Ramadan. The fast is to be observed by adult Muslims unless they are sick, travelling, pregnant, menstruating or have just given birth. *See also* RAMADAN.

Saydawi, Shams al-Din Muhammad (d. 1506) A musician who is best known for providing musical notation, virtually unknown in Arabic music until his time. He also composed poetry of a devotional nature, set to music, and wrote didactic poetry emphasizing the ethical values of Islam.

Sayf al-Dawla, Abu al-Hassan Ali ibn al-Haya (916–967) Celebrated Muslim military leader, famous for his campaign against Byzantium and for representing the values of honour and chivalry associated with the warrior tradition among the Arabs. He was also a celebrated patron of the men of letters, scholars and poets who frequented his court.

sayyid Title of honour used for descendants of the Prophet Muhammad. It is usually given to those descended from the second grandson, HUSAYN IBN ALI, born to the Prophet's daughter FATIMA who was married to ALI IBN ABI TALIB.

Sayyid Qutb (1906–1966) Activist and leader of the MUSLIM BROTHERHOOD in Egypt. A teacher and administrator in the Ministry of Education, he spent time in the United States in the late 1940s, after which he joined the Muslim Brotherhood and rose to become its leader. Sayyid Qutb was deeply committed to the eradication of tendencies in Egypt that he regarded as bringing secular and Western influences into Muslim society. He was a severe critic of Muslim societies, which in his view had lapsed into a state of ignorance similar to pre-Islamic times, and believed that it was legitimate to overthrow them. In his various writings, including a commentary on the Quran, there is a strong defence of traditionalist Islam against the principles of modernity, assumed to have an eroding influence, and a strong insistence on the idea of social justice he considered to be embodied in Muslim legal practice and traditions. He is regarded by many scholars as being the ideologue of FUNDAMEN-TALISM among Muslims. Arrested in 1966, he was tried and executed by the Egyptian government of Gamal Abdul NASSER for alleged incitement to murder the head of state. His writings and views helped shape many of the tendencies that have become generally identified with ISLAMIST ideas.

schools of Islamic law (Arabic, *madhhab*) The process of systematizing and codifying law was undertaken by successive generations of Muslim scholars over three centuries in different regions of the world of Islam. Four separate and distinct schools finally emerged among the Sunni majority, while the various Shia groups developed their own schools of law. All recognize the Quran and the traditions of the Prophet (and in the case of the Shia, the imams as well) as roots of jurisprudence. The schools of the Shia advocated a stronger role for legal reasoning, beyond the principle of analogy as accepted by Sunni jurists. The four main Sunni schools are: Hanafi, founded by ABU HANIFA AL-NUMAN (d. 767), predominant in Central and Western Asia and India; (2) Maliki, founded in Medina by MALIK IBN ANAS (d. c. 796), predominant in Upper Egypt and North and West Africa; (3) Shafii, founded by Muhammad ibn Idris AL-SHAFII (d. c. 820), predominant in Egypt, East Africa and Southeast Asia and (4) Hanbali, founded by AHMAD IBN HANBAL (d. 855), predominant in Saudi Arabia. The three main Shia schools are Twelver Imami or Jafari (*see* ITHNA ASHARIYYA), ISMAILIYYA and ZAYDIYYA. The KHAWARIJ, represented today by the IBA-DIYYA, have their own school. In the AMMAN DECLARATION made in Jordan's capital in July 2005, the majority of Muslim leaders in the world joined in an agreement to affirm the legality and legitimacy of all these schools of law.

Sebuktegin of Ghazna Founder of the GHAZNAWID dynasty and father of MAH-MUD OF GHAZNA.

Segu Historic capital of the kingdom of the Bambara in Western Africa. It was captured by the followers of al-Hajj Umar Tal and integrated into the West African Muslim state that he created during the late nineteenth century. It became an important centre of learning and home of the renowned library of al-Hajj Umar and his family.

Selim I (1467–1520) The ninth OTTOMAN Sultan (r. 1512–1520). Selim, also known as 'the Grim', extended Ottoman control over Syria by defeating the Mamluks as well as gaining control of Mecca and Medina. He was also successful in conquering territory from the SAFAWIDS at the battle of Chaldiran in 1514.

Seljuks *See* SALJUQS.

Senegal West African republic. Senegal became independent in 1960, separating itself from the Mali Federation (made up of former colonies of French Sudan, later divided into MALI, CÔTE D'IVOIRE and Dahomey) in 1960. Islam spread to the region from the north and also as a result of the trans-Saharan trade. The majority of its population of about 11 million is Muslim. Despite its ethnic diversity (its population is divided into at least six major ethnic groups), the Muslims of Senegal share a common Sunni and Sufi heritage. Most of them belong to one of three Sufi orders: the TIJANIYYA, the MURIDIYYA and the QADIRIYYA. They continue to be influential in modern Senegalese affairs within the context of the country's emerging democratic and pluralistic framework. The first elected president of the country, Leopold Senghor, was a Christian. He stood down in 1980 and since then successive presidents and governments have tried to strengthen the tradition of elections and democratic governance.

Seven Sleepers The tale of the Seven Sleepers occurs in the Quran (18:9–26), when the 'Companions of the Cave', as they are called, seek refuge and are tried by God to prove their belief and commitment. It is the source of several important mystical interpretations in various Quranic commentaries.

Seville Spanish city. One of the capitals of the region once under Muslim rule (*see* AL-ANDALUS), now in Andalusia. It was first conquered around 716 and during its heyday was one of the most prosperous Muslim cities in the world. Various architectural elements survive to this day, including the famous Giralda bell tower of the Great Cathedral, originally a minaret.

Shaaban, Robert (1909–1962) Swahili poet and writer from Tanzania. His poetry is rich in content as well as in style and represents one of the best examples of classical Swahili poetry. The bulk of his work is devoted to the themes of freedom, equality and the struggle against any kind of oppression.

al-Shadhili, Abu al-Hasan (1197–1258) Founder of the Shadhiliyya TARIQA. His teachings and influence are still widespread. His teachings sought to instil spirituality as an internal part of Muslim traditions. He rejected asceticism. The Shadhiliyya are today mostly found in North Africa, Egypt and the Sudan.

shadow play A form of live theatre that is significant as a means of story-telling in many parts of the Muslim world, but particularly in Southeast Asia. It is used to educate as well as entertain, teaching people about their faith and its historic and ethical heritage, contextualized often in local idiom and narrative tradition.

shafaa or **tawassul** Arabic for intercession or mediation. The concept of intercession occurs in the Quran and has been developed in Muslim tradition to include intercession by the Prophet, the Shia imams and other figures of piety and closeness to God.

al-Shafii, al-Imam Abu Abd Allah Muhammad ibn Idris (767–820) Generally known as Imam Shafii, he is regarded as the foremost architect among early Muslim jurists of the Sunni synthesis of jurisprudence. After studying in Medina under MALIK IBN ANAS he moved to Baghdad where he wrote his most famous works, the *Kitab al-Umm* and the *Risala*, in which he synthesized existing and often rival views on juristic practice into one coherent framework. In his later years his views led to a significant difference of opinion with his teacher Malik. The achievement of al-Shafii was to record the essentials of legal thought which had remained fluid and based to an extent on oral transmission. He reduced these essentials to the four principal sources of law: the QURAN, the SUNNA as reflected primarily in documented prophetic traditions, *ijma*, the consensus of the community, and *qiyas*, the principle of analogy. Al-Shafii taught in many centres of learning of the Muslim world, but it is in Egypt, where he died, that he had the greatest success and from where the SCHOOL OF ISLAMIC LAW that bears his name developed further. *See also* USUL AL-FIQH.

Shafiiyya The SCHOOL OF ISLAMIC LAW that based its codification and practice on the teachings of AL-SHAFII. The majority of adherents of this school are found in Southeast Asia, East Africa and parts of Central Asia and the Middle East.

shah Title used primarily by Persian rulers until recent times. *See* individual entries below.

Shah, Abdul Latif (1689–1752) A scholar, saint and poet. His spiritual and mystical poetry features the love of God and the universality of the human race. The major themes of his poetry are drawn from Sufism and the collection of his poems is known as the *Risalo*. He is regarded as the foremost poet and exponent of the Sindhi language.

Shah Abbas SAFAWID ruler from 1588 to 1629 who established his capital in Isfahan and whose reign marked a period of military consolidation in Safawid rule and an expansion of its economic and political influence.

Shah Jahan (1592–1666) MOGHUL emperor who reigned from 1628 to 1657. He is particularly famous for building the TAJ MAHAL in memory of his wife, Mumtaz Mahal, and for the designing of the Peacock Throne.

Shah Sultan (d. 1577) Daughter of the Ottoman Sultan SELIM I. She married a high-ranking official and, after divorcing him, continued to be a major patron of the arts as well as a supporter of endowments to establish schools, mosques and *tekkes*, centres of Sufi life. The same title was also given to various other Ottoman princesses.

Shah Tahir al-Dakkani (d. 1549) Shia scholar and teacher. He was the son of the Ismaili imam of the time. Following his emigration to India, he was able to convert a prince, Burhan Nazim Shah, and his state, Ahmadnagar, to Shiism. He died in Ahmadnagar but his remains were later transferred to KARBALA.

Shah Wali Allah (1703–1762) Reformer, scholar and head of the Sufi NAQSHBAN-DIYYA order. His writings and work were aimed at revitalizing and reviving Islam in the Indian subcontinent. Among his major writings are a translation (into Persian) and commentary on the Quran and a study on Muslim legal tradition. He also established a school for Quranic studies.

shahada or ***kalima*** The affirmation of faith in Islam that 'There is no God but Allah and Muhammad is his Messenger.'

shahid The term connotes witnessing and is used by extension to mean 'martyr'. According to the Quran and Muslim tradition, those who die while striving for the cause of Islam receive divine blessing and benevolence.

Shahnama The *Epic of the Kings*. Written by the poet FIRDAWSI (940–1020), and believed to be the longest poem by a single author, the *Shahnama* portrays the history of Iran from ancient times to the rise of Islam. Firdawsi is said to have spent thirty years on its composition. *Shahnamakhani* is a term widely used in Persian-speaking countries and refers to competitions, festivals and recitations of the epic.

Shaltut, Muhammad (1893–1963) Principal of AL-AZHAR UNIVERSITY in Cairo who introduced major reforms in its curriculum, administration and direction of its programmes. His most significant contribution was in promoting IJTIHAD by adding new, modern subjects to the curriculum and in seeking to prevent al-Azhar from becoming a narrowly focused centre of learning in traditional religious and legal sciences. He also sought to reconcile legal schools within the Sunni, Shia and Ibadi traditions, but much of his work has since been undone by a more conservative leadership.

al-Sham *See* DAMASCUS.

Shamil, Imam (1796–1871) Shamil led a resistance movement against Russian rule and the occupation of DAGHISTAN using guerrilla tactics. His background and training as a scholar of the Quran and religious sciences led to his recognition by the ULAMA as their leader or imam. After the defeat of the Ottomans in the Crimean War he could no longer count on their support and the militarily superior Russian army exacted his surrender in 1859. The Russians sent him into exile, though later granted permission for a *Hajj*. He died while visiting Medina and is buried there.

Shahrastani, Abu al-Fath Muhammad Ibn Abd al-Karim (1086–1153) The author of a number of important works, including the *Kitab al-Milal wa al-Nihal*, a work of comparative religion which provides a wealth of information about contemporary religious groups in Islam and other faith communities. He also wrote an important work of commentary on the Quran.

Sharia Often translated as 'law', the word *sharia* derives from the Arabic for 'path' or 'way' and has the connotation of the total sum of duties, obligations and guidelines for Muslims. With the growth of the Muslim community, a common pattern or set of stipulations to guide the lives of the people was developed. Much of the early work in this field was carried out by Muslim thinkers who attempted to operate largely within the framework defined by the Quran and the Sunna as well as rational arguments to arrive at an understanding of the best mode of life in the light of the teachings of Islam in each time and place. The resulting framework is generally referred to as the Sharia. It encompasses the relationship of the individual Muslim with God and with other human beings as well as ETHICS and the ethical life generally. Thus it has the wider connotation of a comprehensive system that regulates aspects of life within the Muslim community as well as relationships with non-Muslims. At the political level the Sharia has in the past defined the nature of the Muslim state, the duties and responsibilities of the caliphs, the organization of institutions that would assure the security and well-being of its inhabitants, and the nature of relationships with both Muslim and non-Muslim states. At the social and personal level, it provides for rules and regulations affecting economic, social and family life. The Sharia also describes in detail the specifically religious duties incumbent on Muslims.

For the Sharia to be implemented fully, earlier Muslim states provided an organized system of courts and judges whose function it was to mediate disputes at all levels and to oversee the workings of the Sharia by administering justice through the courts. The individuals specializing in law were known as *fuqaha* or jurists (sing., *faqih*), whose task was to define and systematize special legal prescriptions within the Sharia. The totality of political, moral and social order in Islam was thus given specific definition. It was not meant, however, to be a fixed system of rigid rules and regulations. Within the Sharia there was always a wider purpose of *maslaha* (the public good), which enabled Muslim scholars to interpret and apply the Sharia in relation to existing conditions and places. Several schools of thought developed in various parts of the Muslim world, which applied the Sharia differently according to variation in human and geographical conditions. Some scholars tended to be stricter in their interpretation than others, but on the whole the Sharia continued to give the world of Islam, through its various schools, a common framework and code that governed personal, family and social practice. The Sharia, or more accurately, *fiqh*, its legal expression, did not constitute the only form of legal practice in most Muslim societies. Commercial, fiscal and state practices varied widely, as did the existence of indigenous traditions and local cultural practices. Those who therefore argue for the restoration of the Sharia are essentially seeking to enforce what they regard as affecting personal, social and perhaps communal legal practices. Others consider that such practices, like any other system of law, should be interpreted in the context of existing conditions and should be adapted without losing their moral impetus and values of social justice and equitable systems of governance. *See also* FIQH, SUNNA, USUL AL-FIQH.

sharif Arabic term signifying nobility. Within the Muslim tradition, the ideal of noble descent became associated with nearness to the Prophet, his immediate family and his clan, the Banu Hashim. They were accorded great respect and were often in positions of leadership and even acted as heads of state.

Sharif al-Radi, Abu al-Hasan Muhammad ibn Abi Ahmad (970–1016) A Shia leader, poet and scholar, Sharif al-Radi was active during the period of BUYID ascendancy under the ABBASIDS. In addition to his role as a scholar and a privileged public figure, he often served as a mediator in resolving disputes between Sunni and Shia. The brother of another famous scholar of Shia Islam, Sharif al-Murtada (d. 1044), he is best known for his anthology of the sayings, letters and sermons of Imam Ali (ALI IBN ABI TALIB) called *Nahj al-Balagha*.

Sharif al-Tilimsani Family of scholars. They were active in Tlemcen, present-day Algeria, during the fourteenth century and exercised great influence as specialists in law and Muslim thought in the region.

al-Shatibi, Muhammad (d. 1385) Andalusian scholar and jurist. He lived in Granada and was noted for his legal views on contextualizing Muslim law and reinterpreting established practices within the social and economic contexts of the time. He is said to have made a significant contribution by introducing greater flexibility in the adaptation of Sharia rules to the changed environment of Granada.

shatranj Arabized word from the Sanskrit *anga*, 'having four ranks', for a game considered to be the predecessor of chess. It was adopted early by Muslims and became a popular cultural pastime.

al-Shaybani, Abu Abd Allah Muhammad ibn al-Hasan (c. 750–803) Scholar and jurist who was known to be a student of ABU HANIFA AL NUMAN. Al-Shaybani grew up in Kufa, one of the centres of intellectual and scholarly activity of the time. He also travelled to Medina, where he studied with another important scholar of the early Muslim tradition, MALIK IBN ANAS. His teaching career at a young age so impressed his peers that he was appointed to important legal positions. Among those who admired his scholarship and legal acumen was the famous Abbasid caliph HARUN AL-RASHID, who harnessed his work in the service of the state, as new issues arose within the Muslim world that required legal and administrative solutions. His work also illustrates the complexity of the intellectual atmosphere among scholars of law and also underlines the legal pluralism of the time.

shaykh (lit., 'elder') Title of respect and authority associated with the head of a group. It was also adapted as a title for the spiritual leader of a Sufi TARIQA, others being the Persian PIR and the Arabic *murshid*.

Shaykh Husayn Sufi teacher and mystic active in Ethiopia during the thirteenth century. His preaching is believed to have been instrumental in the spread of Islam in the region. His tomb in the Bale region of Oroma is a major site of visitation.

Shaykh al-Ishraq *See* SUHRAWARDI, SHIHAB AL-DIN.

Shaykh al-Islam The official title given to the MUFTI of Istanbul during the OTTOMAN period. He was appointed by the caliph and regarded as the foremost Sunni religious scholar and authority of his time. The title had a long history but was applied mostly as a mark of honour until it became an official position within the state. The office and its title were abolished in 1924.

Shaykh al-Taifa *See* AL-TUSI, ABU JAFAR MUHAMMAD IBN AL-HASAN.

Sheba, Queen of Known as Bilqis in Arabic. There is a reference in the Quran to her visit to SOLOMON and acceptance of his faith. In Sufi tradition she is emblematic of the quality of wisdom and spirituality.

Shia Islam One of the major branches of Islam. The death of the Prophet Muhammad marked the end of his prophetic mission. In Muslim belief he had been the last of the prophets, who had completed the divinely entrusted task of making known God's final revelation. In order to discharge his mission effectively he combined in his person religious, political and military power. After his death the early Muslim community was faced with the question of how to maintain the sovereignty of the

Muslim state and further the continuity of Islam. The question involved them in discussion and dispute regarding the position of head of the newly established Muslim state. Those Muslims who believed that ALI IBN ABI TALIB, the Prophet's son-in-law, had been designated on the basis of divine guidance by the Prophet to lead the community, the UMMA, after the death of the Prophet eventually became known as the Shia.

Shia means 'followers' and refers to those who gave their support to Ali. During the eighth century these followers and others crystallized into a group with definite views about the question of authority, which they saw as being intimately linked to the issue of understanding and implementing Islam. They believed that the Prophet had specifically designated Ali as successor before his own death on the occasion of his FAREWELL PILGRIMAGE and that Ali was henceforth to represent a new institution called Imama. Such an institution was meant to guarantee protection and continuing implementation of the Islamic message, and to ensure that the message would continue to be interpreted for the *umma* by the person best suited to do so. The Imama was to continue among the descendants of the Prophet, through Ali and FATIMA, the daughter of the Prophet, in a direct succession. Each imam would be specifically designated by his predecessor to be responsible for the community after his death. The Shia, like other Muslims, continued nevertheless to affirm that there would be no more prophets after Muhammad. This belief in the Imama as an institution to complement and sustain the work of the Prophet Muhammad is integrated by the Shia in their profession of faith, embodied in the SHAHADA.

In addition to professing belief in the unity of God and the role of Muhammad as a messenger, the Shia also maintain that Ali, the commander of true believers, is the Friend (*Wali*) of God. Devotion to the imams thus becomes a cardinal act of faith among the Shia. The imam is believed also to possess divinely endowed knowledge and the capacity to provide spiritual guidance. This belief reflects the Shia view that in order to understand and implement the Quran and the SUNNA, it is necessary that the imam be divinely inspired. He can thus provide both material and spiritual leadership and it is within the mandate of the imam, where conditions permit, to ensure the welfare of the community in both domains. The imams also act as intercessors, as does Muhammad, seeking divine forgiveness and charity for persons who have sinned or are dead. In time, Shia thought developed the view that a true understanding of the Quran was not limited merely to the literal aspects of revelation. There was also an inner dimension to the Quranic verses that could be grasped through the teachings of the imams. The science of TAFSIR, the explanation of the outward significance and context of the Quran, was complemented among the Shia by the science of TA'WIL, the analysis of the inner dimension and deeper meanings of revelation. In this respect the Shia contributed greatly to the intellectual tradition in Islam and influenced the development of philosophical and mystical thought in Islam.

On the death of Ali in 661 the Imama devolved upon his eldest son HASAN IBN ALI and then passed to a younger son, Husayn. HUSAYN IBN ALI is one of the great tragic figures of early Islam. In order to combat the growing and oppressive rule of the UMAYYADS and to affirm his role as imam he refused to accept Yazid, Muawiyya's son and appointee, as the head of the Muslim community. Yazid sent troops to forestall any uprising, and in a brutal massacre Husayn and members of his family were put to death at Karbala in Iraq. This event shocked the Muslims, strengthened the opposition to the Umayyads, and rallied support to the cause of the imams who succeeded Husayn. These imams, though constantly persecuted, maintained an active role in the religious life of the community. They contributed a great deal to the developing sciences of law, philosophy and theology. In particular the sixth imam, JAFAR AL-SADIQ, played a key role in keeping alive the aspirations of the Shia. On his death the Shia split into two major divisions: one recognized the appointment of his son Ismail and continued to give allegiance to the successors of Ismail; the other supported a younger son, Musa al-Kazim. The former group is known as the ISMAILIYYA and the latter as ITHNA ASHARIYYA (or Twelvers). On occasion, because of the insistence on the rights of their imams to head the Muslim community and the emphasis on certain esoteric aspects of faith, each of these Shia groups has suffered persecution and been accused by other Muslims of holding heretical beliefs. *See also* ZAYDIYYA.

Shibli Numani (1857–1914) Muslim scholar in British India who became a leading figure at ALIGARH MUSLIM UNIVERSITY, where he developed an interest in Western literature. He travelled extensively, wrote on a wide variety of historical, legal and literary subjects and composed poetry in Urdu, some of which commemorates the martyrdom of Muslims at the hands of the British.

al-Shinqiti, Sid Ahmad ibn al-Amin (1872–1913) A Sufi and a scholar of Mauritanian origin, he was a collector of oral and folk poetry emanating from that region. His major work is called *al-Vasit* and includes a detailed description of the peoples and geography of Mauritania.

Shiraz City in present-day Iran. It originated as a centre of learning in the medieval period of Muslim history. It is famous for its mosques, *madrasas* and sanctuaries and as a burial place for famous poets such as HAFIZ and SADI.

shirk Associating other beings with God; polytheism. It is considered by Muslims to be an act of blasphemy.

Shuayb The Quran refers to Shuayb as a prophet sent to the people of Madyan, a town in north-western Arabia. According to medieval Muslim chronicles it was on the route from Hijaz to Syria. The Prophet Muhammad is said to have sent an expedition to the town. Muslim commentators have suggested that Shuayb could be Jethro, the father-in-law of Moses.

Shungwaya Site on the East African coast believed to be the centre for ten major Muslim groups who subsequently dispersed along the coast and are the ancestors of the Swahili-speaking population.

shura The Quranic concept of consultation which developed in Muslim tradition to reflect participation in legal and political decision making. The term was used to denote the process of consultation in pre-Islamic tribal times, and is also said to refer to the process by which consensus was achieved on contentious matters in early

Muslim history. The idea of *shura* has been revived in modern Muslim political discourse to encompass processes such as elections and democratic forms of governance. Thus, parliaments and national assemblies in many Muslim countries are referred to as Majlis-i Shura ('Consultative Council'). In more general terms, the concept has come to refer to the institutionalization of assemblies and representative forms of governance in the Muslim world, reflecting the pursuit of more participatory forms of democratic government and decision making.

Sibawayhi (d. c. 796) Grammarian and the founding figure of the systematic study of Arabic grammar. Also called Abu Bishr Amr ibn Uthman, Sibawayhi is believed to be of Persian origin. His major work is simply known as *al-Kitab* (*The Book*) and is considered the seminal study of Arabic grammar. It incorporated the work of previous scholars, consolidating the various principles that informed the study of Arabic for future generations.

Sicily Mediterranean island first captured by the Muslims in 652, though not integrated finally as Muslim territory until the ninth century. It was eventually lost to the Normans during the CRUSADES.

Sierra Leone West African nation. It has been linked to the diffusion of Islam in the region since the fifteenth century. About a third of the estimated 6 million population is Muslim.

Siffin, battle of In 657 a battle took place at Siffin in Arabia between the supporters of MUAWIYYA IBN ABI SUFYAN, the governor of Syria, and ALI IBN ABI TALIB, the Shia imam and the fourth caliph. When it became likely that Ali's army would be victorious, Ali agreed to arbitration, in keeping with Prophetic tradition, but lost the support of some parts of his army who disagreed and left his camp. They became known as the KHAWARIJ.

Sikandar Shah (d. 1390) Sultan of Bengal who, succeeding his father Ilyas Shah, the founder of the independent sultanate in Bengal, brought a long period of stability and prosperity to the country from 1358 to 1390. He is also famous as a great patron of architecture and the projects he commissioned and supported are among the best examples in the region.

Sikhs Religious community based on the teachings of Guru Nanak and other gurus who succeeded him. It emerged in the region of Punjab in north-west India and developed as a separate religious tradition, drawing from Islam as well as the religious and devotional traditions of India. The Sikhs came into conflict with MOGHUL rulers and were on occasion persecuted. They number today about 20 million and, though still found predominantly in India, also live in many other parts of the world.

silsila (lit., 'chain') In Sufism, a line of succession tracing the spiritual status of the current shaykh of the TARIQA through the founding figure Imam Ali (ALI IBN ABI TALIB) directly to the Prophet himself.

Simurgh Mythical king of the birds. Simurgh is associated in Farid al-Din ATTAR'S mystical work with the object of the spiritual quest. *See* SUFISM.

sin Transgression of various kinds against God or divine will for which there is punishment either in this life or the hereafter. God is, however, forgiving and is said to respond positively to those seeking forgiveness.

Sinan, Mimar (1490–1588) Turkish architect who built some of the best-known mosques, schools and other buildings in the OTTOMAN EMPIRE, particularly in Istanbul and other major cities. He was a convert to Islam and lived during the time of Sulayman the Magnificent (SULAYMAN I). He also directed the rebuilding of the Grand Mosque in Mecca, al-Masjid al-Haram.

Sinbad Sinbad the sailor is the narrator of a series of tales in the *Thousand and One Nights* (*see* ALF LAYLA WA LAYLA). His maritime adventures have become part of popular Western lore.

Sindhi Ancient Indo-Aryan language spoken by a majority of the inhabitants of Sind, now a province in Pakistan. Since the sixteenth century there has developed an elaborate literary tradition in Sindhi, preserved in both local and Arabic scripts, expressing a range of devotional, mystical and ethical ideals. The best examples are the poetry of Abdul Latif SHAH and SACHAL SARMAST.

Singapore Island nation off the Malay Peninsula. As a port, Singapore provided a trade link between the region and India. It was settled by Malay and Indian Muslims during the period of the growth of Islam in Southeast Asia.

During the nineteenth century large-scale immigration of Chinese took place after the island had been ceded to the British, and the Muslim Malay population eventually became a minority. Following a short period as part of a federal and independent Malaysia in 1963, Singapore seceded and became an independent nation-state in 1965. The Muslim population has begun to prosper thanks to Singapore's economic growth, and a number of national and local institutions provide a supportive framework for the promotion of education and culture among Muslims.

Sinkiang *See* XINJIANG.

sira A life narrative; applied particularly to the accounts of the Prophet's life (in full, *al-sira al-nabawiyya*). Biographies of the Prophet date back to the first centuries of Muslim history and continue to the present. Among the most famous works that are still regarded as important sources today are those of IBN ISHAQ, Ibn Hisham (d. c. 812), al-Waqidi (d. c. 822) and AL-TABARI. Most scholars agree that prior to the emergence of the written tradition of *sira* narratives about Muhammad were transmitted orally. European scholars generally regarded such narratives as unreliable for the purpose of constructing historically accurate accounts. However, more recent scholarship has been more receptive to such genres of recounted history. Reports that contain information about the life of Muhammad are also found in other collections of prophetic traditions and commentaries on the Quran. Most of these reports parallel the accounts in *sira* and commonly rely on the same authorities. The *sira* works of the early period, however, still remain the most important source of information about the life of the Prophet and the early history of Islam as preserved by Muslim historians. As with the study of other founding figures, such as in the Christian, Buddhist and Zoroastrian traditions, the *sira* material continues to receive widespread attention in many languages, making such accounts among the most popular in world literature, within and outside the Muslim world.

siyam *See* SAWM.

slavery The Quran sought to regulate the institution of slavery in the Muslim world as part of its vision of building a new society by encouraging emancipation of slaves and their conversion, a good example being BILAL, one of the earliest converts of African origin to Islam and the first MUEZZIN. It also mandated that Muslims could not be enslaved, hence the only legal manner in which new slaves continued to be obtained was through war and forced acquisition along trade routes. They served primarily as domestic servants or as soldiers. The institution of slavery is today prohibited in all Muslim countries, but remnants of the practice survive in a very few instances in some societies.

Sokoto Caliphate Kingdom in Hausaland in northern Nigeria. It was established around 1808 by UTHMAN DAN FODIO, a FULBE religious teacher who had been influenced by ideas which had begun to take hold through the spread of the QADIRIYYA and TIJANIYYA movements. His exposure to some WAHHABI beliefs, after completing the *Hajj*, led him to the conviction that the indigenous Hausa rulers were obstructing the practice of pure Islam in West Africa. This led to his declaration of a *jihad* in 1804, which was joined by Fulbe herdsman and Hausa peasants who had grievances against the rulers. Uthman assumed the title Commander of the Faithful and his two sons led the military campaign, until it succeeded in conquering territory which extended to Chad and Niger. After Uthman Dan Fodio's death in 1817 the Sokoto Caliphate remained a significant though somewhat weakened power until the British occupied Sokoto in 1904. Since Nigeria's independence in 1960 it has continued to play an important role in the development of civil society in the country.

Solomon (Arabic, Sulayman) According to the Quran he was a prophet and a king endowed with magical power and great wisdom.

Somalia State in the Horn of Africa with a population of about 10 million, almost all Muslim. Islam was first introduced in the tenth century by travellers, traders and missionaries as they moved along trade routes which crossed the region. Various Sufi groups established themselves and over time the various nomadic and pastoral peoples and ethnic groups were converted to Islam. During the nineteenth and early twentieth centuries several European powers sought control of the region as part of the scramble for Africa. British, French and Italian spheres of influence or protectorates were created.

In 1935 organized Somali resistance to colonial rule began. Following independence in 1960 a republican and representative democracy came into existence, but internal differences led to a military coup and the imposition of an ideological socialist state which adopted a policy of repression against religious leaders. Mounting opposition ousted it in 1991, and since then the country's ethnic and economic divisions have led to a continuing civil war. Although all Somalis share a common faith and language, the pattern of historical differences was exacerbated by colonial rule, a subsequent dictatorship and the activities of warlords, extremist influences from outside and militant groups allegedly acting on behalf of ideological Muslim goals.

A small part of the country, Somaliland, has sought to escape from the cycle of violence and civil war by organizing itself as an autonomous entity.

Songhay West African state in existence from c. 1450 to 1600. Muslim preachers and traders had spread Islam to this ancient region in the eleventh century. It flourished as part of other Muslim kingdoms such as MALI and as a separate Muslim empire established by Sunni Ali in the fifteenth century.

The empire flourished until 1591, when the ruler was defeated by invading Moroccan forces. Muslim culture and practice had united different groups and created a formidable state with a powerful economy based on trade and a rich educational environment that attracted many scholars. At its height, the kingdom's influence extended across the Niger valley to Senegal, the region comprising modern-day Niger and much of western Africa. One of its important rulers was Muhammad Touré (r. 1493–1528), who expanded Songhay territory and promoted trade and learning. 'Songhay' also denotes the language and people of this region.

Sow-Fall, Aminata (b. 1941) Together with Miriama BÂ, Aminata Sow-Fall has emerged as a leading woman writer in Senegal, writing in French as well as Wolof. Her writings are concerned with ethical themes and the role of women, interpreted from the perspective of a Muslim modernity.

spaces of gathering In addition to the mosque, there are various other spaces in which Muslim life and identity find devotional expression. Among the most significant of these are KHANQAS or *zawiyas*, places where Sufis live and also come together, individually or in congregations, to perform acts of devotion, prayer and contemplation. The burial places of saints are highly venerated and visited, for the blessing (BARAKA) associated with their piety and closeness to God. The Shia visit places associated with their imams, for acts of remembrance and commemoration, and all across the Muslim world there are numerous locations with strong regional and indigenous historical associations which allow believers to express their reverence and afford opportunities for congregational gatherings and festivals.

Spain *See* AL-ANDALUS.

Spanish Inquisition Institution established in 1478 by Ferdinand and Isabella of Aragon on the approval of Pope Sixtus IV to identify, punish and bring to repentance those insincere in their belief. Following the reconquest of Spain, which as AL-ANDALUS had been a multicultural and multi-faith land in which Jews, Muslims and Catholics lived harmoniously, non-Catholics were compelled either to convert to Catholicism or to flee their homes. In theory, the Inquisition was directed against those converts who were suspected of insincere conversion and non-conformity to the correct practice of the Catholic faith. In its implementation, it sought to bring those accused to trial by extracting their confessions to heresy. The punishment varied from a fine to execution, in severe cases.

Sudan Historically, the region south of the Sahara stretching from the Red Sea to the Atlantic and known as Bilad al-Sudan. It is today the name of an African state. Islam was introduced to the region through trading contacts as far back as the eleventh century. Its population of around 30 million are ethnically and regionally very diverse in character. Arabic is spoken mostly in the northern region, though it has over time come to exercise the role of a lingua franca. About a third of the population follows traditional tribal practices, while there are well-established Christian communities in the south. The rest are Sunni Muslims, aligned to Sufi TARIQAS, which spread to the region in medieval times and observe the traditions of the Maliki SCHOOL OF ISLAMIC LAW.

Before its modern formation, the Sudan was under occupation of the OTTOMAN EMPIRE from 1821 to 1880, and British administrators ruled it from 1898 to 1956. Since independence it has had a chequered political history. Under a regime seeking to create an Islamic state, the SHARIA was declared the sole basis of law in 1983, alienating the Sudanese in the south, most of whom belong to various African tribes and many of whom are Christians. An organized political party under the auspices of the MUSLIM BROTHERHOOD, led by Hassan al-Turabi, also entered into the fray, collaborating with those in power and arguing for a more dynamic ideal of an Islamic state, though in time it failed to pursue its own ideals of pluralism and reinterpretation of the Sharia. Since the 1980s the ongoing civil war between the north and the south has caused much suffering and curtailed the overall development of a rich and fertile region. Although a peace agreement has been negotiated between north and south, unrest and violence are increasingly present in various regions including DARFUR. The situation has raised an international outcry following violation of human rights and the displacement of several million people.

al-Suduq *See* IBN BABAWAYH.

Sufism Those Muslims who from the beginning have considered the teachings of the Quran and the example of the Prophet to mirror an inner and spiritual orientation to life have come to be known as Sufis. The name is derived from *tasawwuf*, the act of devoting oneself to a search for an inner life.

Sufis are also referred to as *faqir* or *dervish*, both meaning 'poor' (in spirit), words that have extended into Western languages. The word *sufi* may in part also be attributed to the wearing of *suf*, woollen garments, by early Muslim mystics.

The roots of Sufism lay in some of the early Muslims' experiences of the QURAN and their desire to understand the nature of the Prophet's religious experience: 'From God we are and to Him is our return' (Quran 2:156).

This and similar Quranic verses constituted the basis of what became the Sufi understanding of spiritual life. Sufis themselves often employed vivid imagery to describe their quest for religious meaning. The poet JALAL AL-DIN RUMI, whose *Math-*

nawi is considered one of the great classics of Sufi literature, began his work by citing the analogy of a flute, made out of reeds, playing soulfully:

> Listen to the reed as it tells a tale, complaining of separation, crying: 'Ever since I was torn from the reedbed, my complaint has brought tears to man and woman. Seek a heart torn by separation, that I may reveal the yearning of love.'

> All those torn asunder from their source, long for the day they were one with it.

Sufi Hat, twentieth century.

The central image of the flute or pipe, as it is used in this passage and elsewhere in Sufi literature, mirrors the yearning of the soul, which, like the reed from which the flute is made, has been separated from its source, namely God.

Since the major concern of Sufism was to enable individual Muslims to gain deep knowledge of God's will, it was felt that such seekers must embrace an inner life, a path of devotion and prayer that would lead to spiritual awakening.

In Sufism, therefore, the Sharia has had a counterpart called the TARIQA ('way') that complements and represents the meaning of observance. The *tariqa* is the journey and the discipline undertaken by a Muslim in the quest for knowledge of God, which leads ultimately to an experiential understanding of the true meaning of TAWHID ('divine unity'). From this early stage, when Sufism was no more than a very intense and personal quest for God on the part of certain Muslims, it developed into a system of mystical orders centring around the teachings of a leader. This gave rise to the establishment of several Sufi orders in Islam, named after their founding teachers but also tracing their spiritual genealogy back to the teachings of the Prophet and ALI IBN ABI TALIB, whom they considered to have been endowed with the special mission of explaining the esoteric and mystical dimension of Quranic teachings. By the thirteenth century these orders had grown and spread all over the Muslim world. Muslims were attracted from all walks of life and from all groups in Islam, among them Abu Hamid Muhammad AL-GHAZALI and IBN SINA. Later Jalal al-Din Rumi, IBN AL-ARABI and many other important figures across the Muslim world sought an experiential understanding of Islam by way of the Sufi path.

Among initiates within the orders, the path or way began with the acceptance of a teacher as a guide. His teaching was aimed at enabling the disciple to develop discipline through sometimes strict, ascetic practices and by meditation on certain formulas from the Quran, mostly attributes of God. By means of meditation, remembrance and contemplation, the Sufi passed through several spiritual 'stations', each representing the development of inner life, until finally through the experience of *fana* ('annihilation') the true meaning of spiritual union with God was realized. Sufism taught that at this point the Muslim devotee had reached a true understanding of Islam, having finished the *tariqa*, or path of discipline built on the Sharia.

The Sufi quest is described by the twelfth-century poet Farid al-Din ATTAR in a famous mystical poem called *Mantiq al-Tayr* (*The Conference of the Birds*). The poem depicts the quest of a large number of birds for the Simurgh, the mythic king of the birds. After many tribulations, and having crossed over seven valleys, thirty of the birds reach the end of their journey and come to the gate where the Supreme Majesty lives. The gatekeeper tests them and then opens the door. As they sit on the dais awaiting the king, an inner glow awakens in all of them at the same moment and they realize that the Simurgh has been with them all along, guiding them from within. They realize further that the goal of their quest was ultimately the recognition that their inner selves together represent the Simurgh (the Persian words *si murgh* mean 'thirty birds'). The parable thus illustrates the Sufi concept of the return of the soul to its original source – God Almighty – and the universal spiritual aspiration that provides a common bond and purpose among all human beings.

The Quranic admonition 'and seek to remember Allah often' (Quran 62:10) contributed to the practice of meditation, and the Quranic statement that 'In the messenger of God [Muhammad] you have a beautiful example of him whose hope is in God and the Last Day and who remembers God a great deal' (Quran 33:21) indicated an appropriate model for the Sufi quest. In addition, Sufis point to a saying attributed to Muhammad: 'There is a means for polishing everything that removes rust; what polishes the heart is the remembrance of God.' Nevertheless, certain Sufi observances, such as the use of music or dancing as aids to spiritual ecstasy and the veneration of Sufi leaders, were seen by some other Muslims as unacceptable. Conflicts with other groups and scholars in Islam have resulted, along with charges of heresy and unbelief.

On the whole, however, Sufism has been responsible for creating a deeper awareness of the spiritual dimension of Islam. Through the education provided in the various orders and their travels and preaching all over the Muslim world, the Sufis rendered invaluable service to the spread of Islam in Africa, the Indian subcontinent and Southeast Asia. They influenced Muslim piety and created the means to express it through their writings and works of art. Sufi poetry and literature in Arabic, Bengali, Persian, Turkish, Urdu, Sindhi, Swahili, Hausa and the languages of Indonesia and Malaysia represents the creative dimension of the synthesis of Islamic and local traditions and forms of cultural expression. Further, this literature provided people with a medium in their own language to express their particular sense of devotion and love for Islam and for the Prophet and to create a bridge for greater understanding of Islam among non-Muslims. On the other hand, a number of Muslims in the past, and even in the modern era, who have sought to restore Muslim practice to the norms of the Quran, have accused Sufism of causing degeneration in Islam. In addition to their contributions at the literary and cultural levels, some Sufi orders have also acted as vehicles for political and social movements.

To a significant extent, the national struggles in parts of the Muslim world in the nineteenth century derived their fervour from a common bond forged by allegiance to the Sufi orders. Sufism continues to be implemented in the daily devotional lives of Muslims in virtually all parts of the Muslim world, and increasingly among Muslims and converts living in the West.

Suhrawardi, Shihab al-Din (1154–1191) Known as Shaykh al-Ishraq – Teacher of Illumination – Suhrawardi initiated a new school of mystical and philosophical thought.

He was a prolific writer and his works elaborate the central theme of the primacy of immediate cognition as a tool for spiritual understanding. This intuitive mode differed from the existing notion of understanding based on Aristotelian ideas and, in his view, represented a distinct and alternative approach. Accused of heresy and subversion, he was executed by the order of al-Malik al-Zahir, son of SALAH AL-DIN, and so sometimes is called al-Maqtul, 'the Slain'.

suicide To kill oneself is condemned in the Quran and in Muslim tradition in general. Among Muslims in modern times, the ethical issue of suicide has emerged in relation to so-called 'suicide bombings' by individuals who see themselves as martyrs for various causes. Most Muslim schools reject such justification for suicide, pointing to the Quranic teaching that whoever kills another person '… it is as though he killed all humanity' (Quran 4:39).

Sulayhids A Muslim dynasty that ruled Yemen between 1047 and 1138 and was affiliated with the FATIMID Caliphate in Egypt. The founder of the dynasty was Ali ibn Muhammad al-Suhayli and it was at one point led by Queen Sayyida Arwa bint Ahmad.

Sulayman *See* SOLOMON.

Sulayman I (1494–1566) Known as Sulayman the Magnificent in the West, he was Sultan when the OTTOMAN EMPIRE reached the height of its splendour. He was known for his patronage of the arts and for supporting the work of SINAN in many architectural projects. His reputation for justice and law led to his being known as the 'Lawgiver' throughout the empire, for the codification of the new Ottoman law based on the Sharia, the canonical Islamic law, and the *qanun*, the secular law mainly derived from the decrees of the Sultan and the local practices of the vast territories he ruled.

sultan In Muslim history, the term sultan, meaning 'one who holds authority', came to be given primarily to those military commanders who, under various caliphal dynasties, acquired autonomy in domains under their control. As de facto rulers they were recognized by Sunni jurists, who tried to balance their notions of Muslim governance with the reality of political power, often obtained by usurpation.

Sundiata Epic oral narrative about Mali and its great ruler Keita Sundiata. It represents an integration of African traditional narratives and themes with those of the Muslim tradition.

Sunna The Arabic term *sunna* has since pre-Islamic times signified established custom, precedent, the conduct of life and cumulative tradition. In a general sense, such tradition encompasses knowledge and practices believed to have been passed down from previous generations and representing an authoritative, valued and continuing corpus of beliefs and customs.

In the context of early Muslim juridical and theological development, the word came to connote a more specific notion: that the actions and sayings of the Prophet Muhammad complemented the divinely revealed message of the Quran and embodied a paradigm and a model, constituting a source for establishing norms for Muslim conduct.

Early Muslim scholars further developed and elaborated the concept of the *sunnat al-Nabi* (Prophetic tradition) in their quest to capture as complete a picture of the Prophet's exemplary life as they could authenticate on the basis of the HADITH (accounts, traditions of the Prophet), of his words and deeds as transmitted by his companions and others from the first generation of Muslims.

This quest to memorialize the life of the Prophet and ground it in a historically verifiable process also led to a type of literary reconstruction of the narrative of the Prophet's life called SIRA. All these forms acted as reference points that would subsequently inform and inspire various Muslim communities of interpretation as they sought to ground their own juridical, doctrinal and historical identities in what they perceive to be the normative *sunna*. The Sunna is a multivalent concept, illustrating how different kinds of Muslim orientations and institutions have found literary formulation, expression, and codification in law, ethics, theology and mysticism.

The Sunna serves as a common template for all these Muslim groups and individuals, permitting them to represent a connection with the beginnings of Islam and acting as a common referent in the religious discourse of community formation and identity.

Sunni The Sunnis represent the majority of Muslims. For them, as for other Muslims, the SUNNA has a central significance, but because of their particular emphasis on the role of the Sunna in their tradition, they have been called Ahl al-Sunna or Sunnis. Conformity to past tradition and practice is thus the cornerstone of the Sunni interpretation of Islam.

The position of Sunnism became defined as a response to questions concerning authority and practice that had also given rise to the KHAWARIJ and the SHIA.

Much of the eventual content of Sunni thought developed as a result of its reactions to these other groups. In regard to practice, the Sunnis evolved a means of elaborating the SHARIA by which their scholars developed, in addition to the Quran and the Sunna, the concepts of *ijma* (consensus) and *qiyas* (analogy). According to *ijma*, consensus of most scholars on the validity of a practice, followed by common agreement on it, was sufficient to establish the validity of the practice in Sharia. According to *qiyas*, the validity of a practice could be tested by scholars employing reasoning and the drawing of analogies with other laws of the Sharia.

Nevertheless, certain minor areas of disagreement have led to variations in the interpretation of the Sharia. Each school has recognized the rights of the others to disagree on minor points of interpretation, and therefore all are considered as normative in Sunni Islam. Not all of these scholars have always been as tolerant towards other groups in Islam. The scholars in the Sunni tradition, generally referred to as *ulama* in Arabic or *mulla* in other languages, have acted as learned experts and teachers of Islam. They have received their training in a variety of schools, specializing in Quranic and legal sciences. In Sunni Islam they have played an important role as custodians of knowledge and protectors of the tradition.

Since the divine law was the basis on which a Muslim state was to be organized, the law in Sunni Islam also involved a definition of the nature of the state and politics. Like the Shia, the Sunni tradition accepted the necessity of having a head of state, generally referred to as *khalifa* (caliph). His role, as defined by jurists, was to act as the custodian of the state and the Sharia. Jurists developed elaborate theories that defined and circumscribed the conditions under which one could become a ruler and the duties and responsibilities that the ruler was to have.

Besides having its own specific systematization of matters related to the law and the state, Sunnism also defined itself in relation to the interpretation of doctrine. An interesting example in early Islam is the controversy regarding Muslim attitudes to the 'createdness' of the Quran. One group of Muslims, the MUTAZILA, believed that the Quran, since it could be considered as the speech or word of God, should be regarded as created. This position was based on their view that the concept of *tawhid* (the unity of God) implied that God was pure Essence, and that this belief would be violated if the Quran, the speech of God, were to be considered as uncreated and, therefore, part of this pure Essence. On this issue the Mutazila were supported in Baghdad by Caliph AL-MAMUN (r. 813–833), who set about imposing their view and persecuting those who rejected it. However, the viewpoint of the opposing Sunni majority who could not accept the idea of the createdness of the Quran and who believed instead in its eternal nature eventually gained acceptance after al-Mamun's death.

Subsequent Sunni scholars, the main ones being AL-ASHARI and AL-MATURIDI, used rational, theological tools to refute Mutazili arguments and defined Sunni theology regarding the nature of God and the Quran. Sunni theoretical thinking was consolidated into four major schools which came to command the allegiance of the majority of Sunni adherents.

Sunni Ali *See* SONGHAY.

sura Term denoting a chapter of the QURAN.

Surinam South American state. Although only 25–30 per cent of the less than 500,000 population is Muslim, this former Dutch colony, which gained autonomy in 1975, has the highest percentage of Muslims in South America, and for that matter the Western Hemisphere. While the ethnic population of Surinam is quite diverse, the majority of Muslims are Sunni who follow the Shafii SCHOOL OF ISLAMIC LAW. Islam was introduced to the region during the 1660s when Muslim slaves were brought by the Dutch from Africa. After slavery was abolished in 1863, thousands of indentured Muslims of Indian origin arrived in Surinam to work.

al-Suyuti, Abu al-Fadl Abd al-Rahman Ibn Abi Bakr (1445–1505) Among the most prolific of Sunni scholars, believed to be the author of numerous treatises, al-Suyuti was born and lived in Egypt. A scholar of law and theology, his writings were influential for their use in Shafii *madrasas* and other centres of learning. He is also recognized for his works on history. He made extensive use of HADITH in his commentary on the Quran and his biography of the Prophet. The biography is regarded as a model work in this genre. A practising Sufi, he is believed to have retired to a private and reclusive life at the age of forty.

Swahili East African language that emerged along the coast with the spread of Islam. It became the means of the expression of the historical heritage and literature of the Muslim peoples of the region. It was first written using the Arabic script. The use of that script diminished over time and the language is now expressed using the Roman script. Swahili is the national language of Tanzania and plays a dominant and unifying role in Kenya. It is also used extensively further along the coast in parts of Mozambique as well as in the interior, along the Congo.

Syria Historically, a region extending beyond what is the modern state of the same name to include adjoining regions. Today's Syria has a population of 15 million, 90 per cent of whom are of Arab origin and 70 per cent of whom are Sunni Muslims who follow the Hanafi SCHOOL OF ISLAMIC LAW. The rest are Shia, Alawis and a small percentage of DRUZE and Christians.

The region of Syria, which was part of the BYZANTINE Empire in the seventh cen-

At the Maqam of Hazrat Yahya, John the Baptist, inside the Grand Umayyad Mosque at Damascus.

tury, was conquered by Muslims in 636, and the UMAYYAD dynasty under Muawiyya made Damascus the capital of its newly established regime. It was a theatre of conflict during the time of the CRUSADES and, after the Muslims regained control of the region, it was ruled by the MAMLUKS. Then the OTTOMANS made it part of their possessions in the sixteenth century, creating autonomous regions governed by a *pasha*, the Turkish title for a governor. During the nineteenth century it became the scene of European and Ottoman rivalry and, after the end of World War I, was colonized by the French. It was not until 1946 that Syria became independent. After independence the country went through a succession of military coups until the Ba'ath Arab Socialist Party came to power in 1963. Since then it has been governed by the Ba'ath Party under absolute single-party rule.

A number of groups wishing to instil traditional religious institutions into public and political life have attempted unsuccessfully to resist the secularizing policies of the ruling party. In 1982 the government put down a rebellion organized by the MUSLIM BROTHERHOOD in Hama that was seeking to replace the existing order of the state with a Muslim one.

Syria engaged in the 1967 and 1973 wars against Israel, losing part of its territory, and has since been in regular conflict with Israel, though attempts to develop a peaceful solution to the conflict have been initiated in recent times.

T

al-Tabari, Abu Ja'far Muhammad ibn Jarir (839–923) Historian, Quranic commentator and legal scholar. He is best known for his voluminous work of history *Tarikh al-Rusul wa al-Muluk (History of Prophets and Kings)*, popularly known as *Tarikh al-Tabari*, an authoritative source for Muslim history up to his time. Equally popular is his commentary on the Quran.

Tabatabai, Muhammad Husayn (1901–1982) A Shia scholar of great influence whose works on the Quran and on philosophical themes are regarded as among his most enduring contributions to modern Muslim scholarship.

Tablighi Jamat A movement founded in India c. 1928 by Mawlana Muhammad Ilyas (1885–1944) to preach and spread the teachings of Islam in the Indian subcontinent as a way of reaching Muslims in marginal areas who were considered under threat from conversion movements from Hinduism and later Christianity. It also created the tradition of small volunteer groups preaching from door to door and travelling to remote parts of the country to undertake their work. Their activities have spread to different parts of the Muslim world and to countries in Europe, North America, the Caribbean and South America among Muslim communities who have migrated to those regions. In general this evangelical work draws its inspiration from the Sunni tradition of practice and thought.

tafsir (lit., 'explaining') The term refers to interpretation in general and more specifically to the explanation of Quranic verses (*see* QURAN), including many important typologies of interpretation in linguistic, legal, historical and theological terms. The practice of *tafsir* represents a wide spectrum across all Muslim communities, reflecting diverse interpretations, approaches and understandings. Many works of interpretation are found in local languages and indicate attempts by Muslims living in different regions to draw on past traditions but also to create contemporary works in response to specific circumstances.

al-Tahtawi, Rifa (1801–1873) One of the leading figures in the intellectual life of Muslim Egypt in the nineteenth century and the initiator of the *nahda* ('awakening') movement. A graduate of AL-AZHAR UNIVERSITY, he accompanied members of a military mission to France, where he studied European literature and thought, and on his return wrote an account of what he had observed and learned. He then became a major translator and head of a new school of languages which made available in

Arabic information on aspects of European military and scientific works. He subsequently taught at al-Azhar.

Taj Mahal Mausoleum built by the MOGHUL emperor SHAH JAHAN for his wife, Mumtaz Mahal, who died in 1631. It is located in Agra in northern India. Its architecture and design drew from existing buildings of the time, notably the tomb in Delhi of the second Moghul emperor, Humayun.

The Taj Mahal was built between 1632 and 1643. The architect and main calligrapher were among the best known in India at the time and the structure, together with its formal garden laid out in the *chahar bagh* ('four quadrant') style, represents according to general consensus an architectural creation of great purity and beauty. It is one of the most visited monuments in India.

Tajikistan Central Asian republic. Formerly part of the Soviet Union, it became independent in 1991. It has a diverse Muslim population of around 7 million people, including Sunni, Twelver Shia and Ismailis. The Tajik language is closely related to and influenced by Persian. Soon after independence conflict broke out among various groups, but since the restoration of peace Tajikistan has continued to promote internal development and a strong national identity.

tajwid (lit., 'making beautiful') Art of Quranic recitation. It was developed to articulate the importance accorded to the beauty of the Quran's recited form. Several styles

A women's gathering at a new mosque in Tajikistan.

of *tajwid* exist, ranging from a soft, slow and rhythmic monotone to a highly musical and emotive form. Aside from recitation which regularly forms part of ritual and personal prayer, certain occasions such as weddings, funerals, public ceremonies and the nights of the month of Ramadan also call for Quranic recitation. Public performance and competitions in *tajwid* are also very popular in Muslim societies.

takbir Term used to express God's greatness – *Allahu akbar*, 'God is great'.

Talha Ibn Ubayd Allah (d. 656) A COMPANION OF THE PROPHET and early convert to Islam. Unable to gain support for his candidacy as caliph, he eventually formed an alliance against ALI IBN ABI TALIB and was killed in battle.

Taliban A splinter group from among the *mujahidin* movement that resisted the Soviet Union's 1979–89 occupation of AFGHANISTAN. Drawing their support largely from students in various *madrasas*, they organized themselves into a military force based on a very narrow and conservative view of Islam. After 1994 they set out to remove the existing government and to impose control as well as their religious ideology and practices in various regions of Afghanistan and on such communities as the Shia which had different traditions of practice and observance of Islam. They continued to capture major cities and by 1999 had consolidated their control over major parts of the country. While viewed in its initial stage as a movement to restore order and Muslim values, it became apparent to most Afghans that the Taliban were seeking to impose, by force if necessary, a strict code of behaviour based on extremely restrictive rules that affected women in particular and the social life of most Afghanis in general. They also sought to control the drug trade for their own means, combat foreign influence and draw support from bands of fighters from different Muslim countries who had come to Afghanistan ostensibly to oust the Soviet troops. In 2001 their religious leader, Mullah Omar, ordered the destruction of two ancient statues of the Buddha and intensified the persecution of representatives of various Shia groups and Sufis. Such destructive tendencies, allied to support of radicalized groups led by Osama bin Laden, who made his headquarters in Afghanistan, caused the Taliban to be virtually isolated in international circles. The events of 11 September 2001 further emphasized their threat outside Afghanistan and cata-lysed international opposition to the regime, including that of many Muslim nations and leaders. An American-led force invaded Afghanistan and in alliance with the Afghan opposition groups finally defeated the Taliban, who fled into remote mountain regions or sought refuge in neighbouring Pakistan. Though sub-dued and replaced by a new government selected in a lengthy but generally peaceful participatory election process, the Taliban have constantly sought to reorganize and reassert themselves through attacks and suicide missions against international peacekeeping forces. They continue to be a disruptive force in Afghanistan and Pakistan and pose a constant threat to progress towards greater stability and devel-opment in the region.

Tamerlane (1336–1405) Conqueror and founder of the Timurid dynasty, more properly Timur-i Lang (Timur the Lame) ibn Taraghay Barlas. The Chaghatayids of his native Kish region traced their lineage to Genghis Khan. Timur was to use this claim to great advantage. After uniting the Chaghatayid tribes under his rule, he succeeded in establishing his authority over Transoxiana, with his capital in Samarkand. Between 1379 and 1402 Timur embarked on a series of major military conquests in a number of daring campaigns which included, but were not limited to, Iran, Iraq, Kurdistan, Azerbaijan, India and Anatolia. A ruthless commander with a skilful grasp of politics, his campaigns led to the conquest of much of Central Asia and by 1392 he was planning to invade Persia. In 1398, following the conquest of Persia, he entered India, where he sacked and razed Delhi. Two years later he was threatening the Mamluks of Egypt. Having devastated the armies of most of these countries, he set his sights upon the conquest of China. In 1405 he died in pursuit of this, his ultimate goal.

Most observers regard his method of conquest as chaotic, given the size of the areas he wished to control. He seemed to go from one region to the other without any concerted strategy and was unable to establish a lasting or effective administrative structure for the territories he conquered, an important reason for the subsequent disintegration of his empire. Most of the conquered territories were recaptured and the rest were divided among his various successors.

Timur ruled for thirty-five years and the kingdom that he carved out eventually became a region of significant development in culture, architecture, science and trade within Central Asia. His reputation extended to Europe, leading the English playwright Christopher Marlowe to write his famous play *Tamerlane* around 1587.

Tanzania East African state. It consists of the former British trust territory of Tanganyika and the islands of Zanzibar and Pemba. Although Islam is believed to have been established on the east coast of Africa as early as the ninth century, its influence and expansion in the region dates to a later period. It is estimated that approximately 90 per cent of Zanzibar's population and 40 per cent of the mainland's is Muslim, numbering about 15–20 million in all. The Muslim communities reflect considerable diversity; Sunni groups predominate, but there are significant Ibadi and Shia communities. Swahili is the national language of Tanzania.

Tanzimat (lit., 'regulations') Collective title given to a series of reforms enacted by the OTTOMAN Sultan Abd al-Majid (Turkish, Abdülmecit) I (1823–1861), beginning with the Gulhane Decree in 1839.

The changes which were instituted included enforcement of dress regulations such as the substitution of the fez for the turban, elimination of the legal distinction between Muslims and Dhimmi (*see* AHL AL-DHIMMA), removal of foreign trade restrictions, establishment of military service for Muslims, elimination of confiscation laws and the introduction of certain practices derived from civil laws, particularly in cases involving the death penalty.

The impetus behind the reforms was the perceived need to modernize and reorganize a bureaucracy whose weaknesses had become apparent in its encounter with European influence and expansionist designs on Ottoman domains.

taqīyya (lit., 'guarding oneself') In Shiism, the practice of not openly expressing one's faith and religious affiliation as a form of self-protection in situations of compulsion or persecution.

taqwa The human quality that encompasses the concept of the ideal ethical value in the Quran is summed up in the term *taqwa*, which, in its various forms, occurs over two hundred times in the text. It represents, on the one hand, the moral grounding that underlies human actions, while on the other hand it signifies the ethical conscience which makes human beings aware of their responsibilities to God and society. Applied to the wider social context *taqwa* becomes the universal ethical mark of a truly moral community.

Tariq ibn Ziyad Muslim general who led the conquest of the Iberian Peninsula by crossing the Straits of Gibraltar in 711. The hilly location where his troops were gathered, Jabal Tariq, came to be known as Gibraltar. His forces were able to achieve a strong foothold, leading to the establishment of the first region in Europe under Muslim control. *See* AL-ANDALUS.

tariqa (lit., 'path') Term referring both to the esoteric expression of Islam in general and to esoteric or Sufi groups organized under a spiritual leader called imam or shaykh.

The earliest Sufi *tariqa* was the QADIRIYYA, which established the model adopted by subsequent groups. The concept of *tariqa* suggests a dimension of Islam for those who seek a deeper level of spirituality than that which is achieved by following the SHARIA alone. It is meant to complement the ritual observance of the faith with an understanding of its inner and esoteric dimensions.

Tartar *See* TATAR.

tasawwuf *See* SUFISM.

Tashkent Capital of present-day UZBEKISTAN. Conquered by Muslims in 751, it became an outpost of Islam against the Turks. It was governed by the SAMANIDS from 819 to 996 and then given over to the Turks, who eventually ceded it to the Chaghatay Mongols who ruled in the thirteenth and fourteenth centuries. From 1370 to 1506, the Timurid Empire (*see* TAMERLANE) held Tashkent, which then fell to the Shaybanids. The Khanate of Khokand annexed it in 1865. It was under Russian control from 1914 until the creation of the new Republic of Uzbekistan in 1991.

Tatar Also Tartar. In contemporary times, this is the name of a Turkic-speaking people who live along the region of the central course of the Volga River. They are mainly concentrated in the Republic of Tatarstan of the RUSSIAN FEDERATION, but have also settled in other regions of Russia and the former Soviet Union.

The Tatars, after being driven out of Mongolia, migrated westwards with other Turkic peoples. The word 'Mongol' was also held to define them collectively, and under Genghis Khan the epithet 'Tatar' came to be replaced by it. Under Russian and then Soviet occupation, the region of Tatarstan evolved as a multicultural society combining the presence of Islam with Orthodox Christianity. Soviet impositions such as the Cyrillic script cut off the Muslim Tatars from contact with other Muslim traditions. Tatarstan more recently became a province within the new Russian Federation, since when its Muslim population has sought to revive its religious and cultural heritage.

tawassul *See* SHAFAA.

tawhid (lit., 'oneness') The Quranic concept of the unity of God, a cardinal Muslim belief. It is also expressed in the first part of the SHAHADA: *'La ilaha illa allah'*.

ta'wil (lit., 'interpretation') While signifying the interpretation of the Quran in general, it has specifically come to mean an allegorical interpretation of the inner meaning of scripture. Such interpretation has come to have central importance in Shiism, and particularly among esoteric groups such as the Sufis and the Shia Ismailis, where it is linked to the role of a living imam as interpreter and guide to the spiritual, inner meaning of Islam.

Tawrat Quranic term for the Torah. The Pentateuch of the Hebrew Bible is recognized in Islam as a divinely revealed scripture, thus the inclusion of Jews as 'People of the Book' (*see* AHL AL-KITAB).

Taziya (lit., 'consolation') A Shia festival held during the first ten days of Muharram, the first month in the Muslim calendar (*see* ASHURA), culminating in a passion play, also called *taziya*, in commemoration of the tragic martyrdom of HUSAYN IBN ALI at KARBALA. The term also refers to a model of Husayn's tomb. These models may be elaborate and permanent structures in the home or they may be temporarily constructed for the Ashura ceremonies and for use in street processions.

Teungku Kuala *See* ABDUR RAUF AL-SINGKILI.

Thabit ibn Qurra (826–901) A Sabaean from Harran, appointed astronomer by the ABBASIDS. He was also a physician, mathematician and philosopher. His work in Syriac is believed to have been a major source for the religion of the Sabaeans, a people who lived in what today is Yemen. His work in the fields of mathematics, medicine and philosophy served as a model for Muslim intellectuals of the time.

Thamud According to the Quran, the Thamud were a people to whom the Prophet Salih gave divine revelation. They have been identified as the Nabateans whose capital was Petra, in what is today Jordan, and who had a colony in Arabia. They were punished for rejecting the revelation and the city is believed to have been destroyed by an earthquake and a thunderbolt. The Arabs called the ruins 'the cities of Salih' (Mada'in Salih) and their civilization has been referred to as 'Thamudic'.

theatre In pre-modern times, many Muslim societies had traditions of oral performance and various texts suggest that such performances constituted examples of a theatrical tradition. In modern times many Muslim states promote theatre and outstanding playwrights are found writing in several languages across the Muslim world.

theology *See* KALAM.

Thousand and One Nights, A *See* ALF LAYLA WA LAYLA.

Tijaniyya Sufi TARIQA. It was founded by Abu al-Abbas Ahmad al-Tijani (1737–1815), whose followers claimed that he had been commanded by the Prophet in a dream to found the movement. Because of the patronage of the then ruler of Morocco, Ahmad al-Tijani was able to establish his teaching in North Africa, from where it subsequently spread to other African centres of Muslim influence.

Timbuktu Town in MALI founded in the twelfth century. IBN BATTUTA visited the town in 1352 and described the life of the Muslim society of the time and the high level of cultural and educational institutions. Timbuktu has passed into legend as a crossroads of the trans-Sahara trade and as a centre of Muslim civilization in Africa famous for its libraries and scholars.

Timur, Timurids *See* TAMERLANE.

Tipu, Sultan (1710–1799) Muslim ruler of Mysore in western India from 1783 until his death. He was an opponent of the presence in India of the British, who eventually removed him from power. He died resisting the British as they sought control over his territory.

tiraz Type of textile woven extensively in the medieval Muslim world, particularly under the rule of the FATIMIDS in Cairo. They have been seen by subsequent scholars as representing an important industry, and their designs as historical documents illustrating facets of economic and social life in Muslim societies.

al-Tirmidhi, Abu Isa Muhammad ibn Musa (d. 892) Famous for his commentary on the Quran and his collection of HADITH. His commentary is regarded as being one of the most authoritative in Sunni Islam. He was a student of AL-BUKHARI, another renowned scholar and compiler of *hadith*. Al-Tirmidhi's collection *al-Jami al-Sahih* is counted among the six most authoritative Sunni collections. It consists of about 4,000 traditions and includes a section in which he explains his method of classification. He is also the compiler of a smaller collection solely devoted to the virtues of the Prophet Muhammad.

tolerance Muslims believe that God has communicated with humanity from the beginning of time by way of revelations and messengers. None has been neglected, though not all religions or messengers are always known to us. Those with whom God has communicated are referred to as the 'People of the Book' (AHL AL-KITAB). It is this broad spirit of inclusiveness and mutual acceptance that has generally guided Muslims in their relations with other religions, though in the course of history this has not necessarily prevented conflict between Muslims and people of different religious background.

The principle of tolerance and peaceful coexistence is also based on the Prophet's own early efforts to build common ground with Jews and Christians through an agreement sometimes referred to as the Constitution of Medina, which afforded status and rights to them. It laid out the ground rules for permitting non-Muslims to practise their faith freely, retain their religious organization and maintain their places of worship and local authority.

The Quran also teaches that God's grace and salvation are for all:

> Those who believe in God and His revelations, Jews, Christians, Sabians, whosoever believes in God and the Day of Judgement and does good, will have their reward from God, they should have no fear nor should they grieve. (Quran 2:62)

There is also an emphasis on the righteous, those who are 'morally aware'. In the course of Muslim intellectual and cultural history this openness to other traditions led to an enabling climate of exchange in which artistic, musical, architectural and literary traditions were nurtured. Literature in different languages provided an important bridge to unite people in Muslim societies within a common cultural matrix.

Perhaps the most important historical examples were to be found in Andalusia in Spain (*see* AL-ANDALUS), ruled by Muslims for over 700 years, and FATIMID Egypt in the tenth and eleventh centuries, for most of which time there was a spirit of harmonious collaboration between Jews, Christians and Muslims which led to the flowering of brilliant cosmopolitan civilizations, ultimately destroyed in the case of Spain by the reconquering of Spain for Christianity and the resulting SPANISH INQUISITION after 1492.

The global Muslim community includes members of most ethnic groups and nationalities found in the world. Among the early followers of the Prophet there were Arabs, but also others of different racial background, Persians and Africans to cite two examples. BILAL, the first MUEZZIN, was black. The worldwide spread of Islam has ever since encompassed groups of considerable ethnic and racial diversity. Among the more than one billion Muslims today, about one-fifth of humanity, about 15 per cent are of Arab origin, though not all Arabs are Muslim, there being substantial Arab Christian minorities in the Middle East and elsewhere. Among other groups the largest are Bengali, Punjabi, Javanese, Iranian, Turkish, Hausa, Malay, Azeri, Fulan, Uzbek, Pushtun, Berber, Kurdish and Chechen, all numbering in the hundreds of thousands, if not millions. Somewhat smaller groups are found in various parts of East and West Africa, the Balkans, various Indian Ocean islands, and parts of Europe and North America.

Torah *See* TAWRAT.

trade The Prophet Muhammad was a merchant by profession and Mecca, the city of his birth, was a centre of trade along some of the caravan routes that crossed Arabia. Commerce and trade became one of the dominant aspects of Muslim life and society. Trade routes and commerce linked regions and people across the Silk Road, the Sahara, the Indian Ocean and the Mediterranean and extended as far east as China and north to the borders of Spain. Prosperous Muslim cities were noted for their markets, goods and mercantile practices, exchanging a vast number of goods. Trade prompted economic prosperity and involved important non-Muslim groups such as Jewish and Chinese merchants and later many Europeans, particularly during the OTTOMAN, SAFAWID and MOGHUL periods.

The Muslim hegemony of trade was eventually eroded by the maritime discovery of the New World, the resulting influx of wealth into Europe and the growth of European economies which in turn fuelled expansion and eventually the colonization of many Muslim regions.

Most Muslim countries today, with the exception of a few oil-rich states, are regarded as part of the developing world and their role in international trade and global economy, while extensive, is by no means dominant. Attempts to create regional trade and economic growth have generally not led to significant benefits and many poor Muslim countries in Africa and Asia have been disadvantaged by the failure to reach internationally valid and equitable free trade agreements.

transcendent wisdom *See* MULLA SADRA SHIRAZI.

translation The first important translation movement in Muslim history was in the ninth century when a vast corpus of work from the classical and ancient heritage of Greece, Iran and India was translated into Arabic. This made available to Muslims the vast intellectual and scientific works of the past, enabling them to interpret, adapt and build further an intellectual and scientific tradition appropriate to their needs and time.

Works of Muslim scholarship in Arabic were eventually translated into Latin and nurtured intellectual development in Europe.

travel Travel writing emerged as an important genre among Muslims, particularly among geographers and scholars who travelled great distances in pursuit of their goals. Beginning in the ninth century, Muslim writers embarked on a series of major works detailing the geography and lifestyle of many of the world's contiguous regions. Travel writing associated with the HAJJ and other lesser religious pilgrimages was also an important feature. Two well-known accounts of the medieval period are those of NASIR-I-KHUSRAW and IBN BATTUTA.

Trinidad and Tobago Caribbean island state. Trinidad and Tobago gained independence from Britain in 1962. The islands' million-strong population is ethnically diverse, with a minority of Muslims of African and Asian descent.

Tuareg BERBER people who inhabit an area spreading from Algeria and Libya to northern Nigeria and from Fazzan to Timbuktu. A matriarchal and nomadic people, their distinctive lifestyle and cultural practices have been considerably threatened in recent times by both drought and modernization.

Tughril Beg (d. 1063) The first SALJUQ ruler, who ended BUYID control of Baghdad in 1055 and consolidated Saljuq control over Iraq and Persia.

Tulunids Egyptian dynasty of independent governors who ruled from 868 to 905. The so-called Tulunid period is often referred to as a golden age because of the prosperity of Egypt at this time. An important monument dating back to this period is the famous Ibn Tulun mosque in Cairo.

Tunisia North African republic. It won independence from France in 1956 and has a population of over 10 million, a majority of whom are Sunni Muslim who follow the

Maliki SCHOOL OF ISLAMIC LAW. Islam was introduced into the region in the eighth century and has been the state religion since independence.

Turhan Sultan, Hadice (d. 1683) OTTOMAN Queen Mother, whose son Mehmed IV reigned during the latter half of the seventeenth century. She is best known for her architectural patronage of several important monuments, among them a large mosque complex in Istanbul which included a school for children.

Turkey Republic created out of the former OTTOMAN EMPIRE in 1924. The majority of its 70 million inhabitants are Sunni Muslim who follow the Hanafi SCHOOL OF ISLAMIC LAW. However, there is a substantial Shia minority which is often referred to as the ALEVI.

The region has historically been a bridge between European and Asian cultures and civilization, and its people became part of the world of Islam in phases from the eighth century onwards. The apex of their engagement was the creation of the Ottoman Empire, which during its long history became the dominant power in Asia and Europe. At the beginning of the twentieth century the empire, which was beginning a process of disintegration, went through a period of change that resulted in the creation of a secular republic, divesting itself of the role and institutions that linked it to the Islamic world and setting its sights on emulating the emerging tradition of European nation-states. Following a policy of secularization, Westernization and modernization of its culture, language and economy, Turkey has emerged as a modern nation-state linked to Europe but tied economically to its Muslim neighbours. More recently, within the framework of democratic governance, Turkey elected as its ruling party the Islamic Welfare Party, which has pledged to revive and integrate the country's Islamic heritage in public and political life. In its more immediate future, Turkey has the problems of integrating into the European Community, resolving its conflict with Greece over CYPRUS and creating structures that allow for a civil society in which the diverse Muslim heritage of its people is balanced with its secular, political commitment.

Turkish One of the Turkic group of languages, to which Uzbek, Uyghur, etc. also belong. It is the national language of Turkey and has employed the Latin alphabet since 1924.

Turkmenistan Central Asian republic, part of the Soviet Union before becoming independent in 1991. Approximately 70 per cent of its 4 million people are Sunni Muslims who follow the Hanafi SCHOOL OF ISLAMIC LAW.

al-Tusi, Abu Jafar Muhammad ibn al-Hasan (995–1067) A scholar in the Imami ITHNA ASHARIYYA Shia tradition, well known for his compilation of the traditions attributed to Shia imams. He is known also as Shaykh al-Taifa, an honorific title reflecting his stature as a mystical scholar. Born and educated in Tus, northeastern Iran, he later moved to Baghdad to further his education. He eventually gained a reputation and attracted hundreds of students. His works on theology and jurisprudence paved the way for the emergence of a strong legal tradition within the Imami Shia community.

Tusi, Nasir al-Din Muhammad ibn Muhammad (1201–1274) Scholar and scientist, known as Muhaqqiq-i Tusi (the Authoritative) in Shia literature. His reputation rests on his studies in philosophy and his research in astronomy. A great defender of rationalist discourse, he spent time among the Nizari Ismailis in Alamut, in present-day Iran, where he contributed significantly to their intellectual and doctrinal works. He describes the spiritual journey that led him to Alamut in his autobiographical work *Sayr wa Suluk (Contemplation and Action)*, in which he explains how he found consolation in an esoteric understanding of Islam. Though displaced by the MONGOL invasion, he continued his scientific and philosophical pursuits and authored several important treatises, including *The Nasirean Ethics*.

Twelver Imami Shia *See* ITHNA ASHARIYYA.

Uganda East African state. Islam was first introduced to Uganda in the nineteenth century. Though accurate statistics on religious groups in the country do not exist it is thought that as many as one in four of the 25 million population of Uganda are Muslims. Uganda joined the ORGANIZATION OF THE ISLAMIC CONFERENCE in the 1970s and through a credit provided by the Islamic Development Bank established a Muslim university in the town of Mbale.

Between 1971 and 1979 the dictator Idi Amin led a brutal regime that devastated the country's economy and resulted in the killing and expulsion of many of its intellectuals as well as its Asian community. Since his downfall Uganda has enjoyed a greater degree of stability and prosperity, though some regions are still threatened by rebellions and violence.

ulama (lit., '[the] learned'; sing., *alim*) Religious scholars in the Muslim tradition. Since the ABBASID period of Muslim history religious scholars have been regarded as the guardians of the faith and recognized for their learning. Their role was to explain the relevance of the law to everyday life and to comment on nuances of the law affecting specific contexts, social groups and individuals. Their significance in institutional terms has varied across history, but in general most Muslim rulers and states afforded them their protection and institutional support. Within the Sunni tradition they are still regarded as representing authority in matters of religious law and doctrine. A similar role is played by learned scholars in other Muslim schools, though the pattern of institutionalization of this role varies, particularly among the Shia and Sufi traditions.

There are at least three recognized categories of *ulama* in Sunnism: (1) *Faqih*, an expert in legal aspects of the faith functioning in a non-official capacity whose expertise and the weight assigned to whose opinion may vary considerably. (*See also* WILAYAT AL-FAQIH.) (2) *Mufti*, legal expert, sometimes but not always acting in an official capacity, whose rendered opinion is not legally binding but carries considerable authority. (3) *Qadi*, judge appointed by the state whose judgement is considered binding.

The *ulama* have also played an important role as educators, both independently and as teachers in MADRASAS and mosques.

Ulugh Beg (1394–1449) Muhammad Taraghay ibn Shah Rukh ibn Timur, known as Ulugh Beg, was a grandson of the great conqueror TAMERLANE, born to his eldest son

Shah Rukh. His policies and efforts led to Central Asia becoming a major centre of Muslim architecture and learning. He was the governor of SAMARKAND until 1447, a period during which the city was transformed into a seat of education, science and the arts. After the death of his father Shah Rukh he lost control of Samarkand to his young brother, but maintained his hold over the city of Balkh. Ulugh Beg is particularly well known for his interest in astronomy and for the observatory and other monuments he built in Samarkand and elsewhere. The Samarkand observatory was believed to be undertaking the most advanced astronomical calculations of the time.

Umar, ibn al-Farid (1181–1235) Well-known and influential mystic whose writings on mystic love are considered to be model expressions of poetic imagery. Later Sufis regarded him as 'Sultan al-Ashiqin' ('the Prince of Lovers').

Umar ibn Abd al-Aziz ibn Marwan (Umar II) (680–720) UMAYYAD caliph who ruled from 717 to 720. He attempted to reverse the harsh policies of his predecessor Suleiman by giving rights to non-Arabs, reducing taxes and curtailing military expenditure. Historians have acknowledged his piety and good governance towards the subjects under Muslim rule during his time.

The strength and attraction of Islam, Umar believed, lay in unity and he therefore insisted that Islam could not continue under the auspices of an Arab-dominated power and hierarchy.

Umar ibn al-Khattab (592–644) Designated by ABU BAKR as the second caliph, the first to assume the title Commander of the Faithful, under whom the rapidly expanding Islamic Empire conquered the rest of the Arabian Peninsula and significant areas of the Persian (Sassanian) and BYZANTINE Empires.

Umar had once plotted to kill Muhammad because he perceived him to be a troublemaker, but, persuaded by the example of his sister's devotion to the new faith, he converted. After his conversion Umar became one of the most loyal followers of the Prophet, giving his daughter Hafsa to him in marriage. During his reign he initiated the dating of the CALENDAR from the year of the migration to Medina (*hijra*) and organized the *diwan*, a register of Muslims according to which the ever-increasing wealth coming to Medina was distributed. Umar is said to have lived a life of devotion and simplicity. His administrative measures and fiscal policies greatly influenced the organization of the Muslim state in the subsequent period. He died at the hands of a disgruntled servant who killed him as an act of revenge.

Umar Khayyam (1048–1123) Well known as Omar Khayyam and renowned for his *rubaiyyat* (quatrains), freely translated and made famous in Edward Fitzgerald's nineteenth-century English translation. He is, however, better known within the Muslim community as a mathematician, astronomer and commentator on philosophy.

Umayyads The Umayyads, famous as 'the first dynasty', ruled in Damascus from 661 to 750, deriving their name from the QURAYSH clan of Banu Umayya.

Recognizing that they had come to power through force, the Umayyads combined a policy of ruthless suppression of dissent with attempts to seek validation and legitimacy as rulers defending and promoting Islam.

The dynasty came to power when Muawiyya (d. 680), governor of Syria and nephew of UTHMAN IBN AFFAN, challenged ALI IBN ABI TALIB's claim to the Caliphate. Ali's agreement to submit the dispute to arbitration led to the defection of the KHAWARIJ and his subsequent murder by one of their party in 661. It was during the Umayyad period that Islam expanded into Europe in the west and into India in the east. A distinctive Muslim culture began to take shape as Arabic replaced Greek and Persian as the official language, currency was issued and several Muslim spaces for prayer were constructed that became architectural points of reference, such as al-Masjid al-Aqsa and the Dome of the Rock in Jerusalem and the Great Mosque in Damascus. The Umayyads' role in extending Muslim rule into former Byzantine and Samarian territories reflects a significant transition in the emergence of a new culture and civilization, fashioned out of the confluence of different cultures and linked to the new faith of Islam. While they were brutal in suppressing internal opposition and in maintaining military control over their subjects, Muslim identity in its various forms, legal, historical and cultural, was beginning to take shape and a large non-Arab population came to be assimilated into the growing empire. There was also fierce opposition to the Umayyads and to what was perceived as their unjust rule, factors that eventually combined to lead to the downfall of the dynasty.

The dynasty ruled through fourteen caliphs until it was overthrown by the ABBASIDS, who moved the capital of the Caliphate to Baghdad. Only one of the Umayyad princes, Abd al-Rahman, avoided execution, escaping to Spain where he established a Spanish Umayyad dynasty at CÓRDOBA.

The Umayyad dynasty of Spain ruled from 756 to 1031, becoming known as the 'Western Caliphate' and initiating a period of Muslim rule and culture in AL-ANDALUS.

Umm Kulthum (1898–1975) Egyptian singer, performer and actor who became one of the most famous Arabic artists of her time. She was the daughter of an imam from a poor village, from whom she learned religious songs which she performed at various gatherings and occasions.

umma (lit., 'people') Used about forty times in the Quran to refer to people of a certain religious community, such as the '*umma* of Abraham', the word has come to represent the concept of the Muslim community as a whole, not separated by nationalistic boundaries or political divisions, although this has always been an ideal rather than a reality in the course of Muslim history.

Umra The lesser pilgrimage to Mecca, performed as an act of piety at any time except during the eighth to tenth days of Dhu al-Hijja, the last month of the Muslim CALENDAR during which the main pilgrimage, the HAJJ, is undertaken. Pilgrims undergo the same ritual purification, donning of the IHRAM and observation of prohibitions that apply during the *Hajj*. The *Umra* consists of ceremonies which take place as part of the greater pilgrimage within the area of the Grand Mosque of Mecca, al-Masjid al-Haram. These rituals include seven circumambulations of the

KA'BA, drinking water from the Well of Zam-Zam and running (or walking quickly) seven times between the hills of Safa and Marwa. At the end of these rituals, the hair is cut or shaved, at which time the state of ritual purification is ended. *See also* HAJJ; PILGRIMAGE.

United Arab Emirates Federation of small Arab Emirates in the Gulf formed in 1971. Before 1971 the emirates were known individually as Abu Dhabi, Ajman, Dubai, Al Fujayrah, Ra´s al-Khaymah, Ash Shariqah, and Umm al-Qaywayn. The government is composed of ruling families and representatives of the commercial elite from each individual state, who often serve in high administrative positions. The population is predominantly Sunni but the Shia compose an estimated 20 per cent of it. Its oil resources have enabled the UAE to modernize their societies, encouraging a large number of migrant workers to contribute to the economy. Dubai is its most important city.

United Kingdom The long history of relations between the United Kingdom and the Muslim world dates back to the Crusades and the chivalrous tradition evoked in the name of both Richard the Lionheart and Saladin (*see* SALAH AL-DIN). During the nineteenth century trading contacts with the East India Company brought a small number of Muslims to English ports. Subsequently, as the Muslim population increased, the first formal mosque in Britain was erected in Woking in 1889. A sig-

Ismaili Centre, London.

nificant growth in Muslim immigration occurred after World War II, when many Muslims from British colonies in Asia, Africa and the Caribbean made their homes in the United Kingdom. Since then many other Muslim migrants have settled in Britain and today the UK's Muslim population numbers over 1.5 million, reflecting the cultural, ethnic and linguistic diversity of the Muslim world. The majority have roots in Bangladesh, India or Pakistan, though there is also representation from Afghanistan, Iran and other Middle Eastern states, various African countries, eastern Europe, the Caribbean, Central Asia and Turkey. Each Muslim community has established its own institutions and organizations, including mosques, welfare centres and schools, and various bodies exist at a national level to coordinate activities on behalf of the country's wider Muslim population. Recent acts of terrorism have focused attention on a small number of young Muslim *jihadists* and the British government is working with various Muslim representatives to develop greater awareness of citizenship, community and individual responsibility to act within the laws and traditions of the state, to encourage Muslims to participate in national life, and to provide better education, particularly for Muslim women.

Muslims are represented at all levels of British society, including academia, government, media, the arts, the professions, philanthropy and commerce, and have also contributed to the development of Islamic scholarship and awareness through the creation of research institutes and educational centres.

United States of America Although Muslims represent only 3 per cent of the 300 million population of the United States, Islam is believed to be the fastest growing religious tradition in the country owing to immigration and conversion. It is estimated that approximately one-third of the conversions are among African-Americans.

The Muslim community in the United States is a heterogeneous one, made up of immigrants from virtually every part of the Muslim world, African-Americans, European converts and visiting students, diplomats, business people etc. It is estimated that one-fifth of the African slaves brought to the United States during the seventeenth to nineteenth centuries were Muslims. The first wave of Muslim immigration began in 1875 from what was then Syria, a region which now encompasses modern Syria, Lebanon, Jordan and Palestine. The second wave took place from the 1920s to the beginning of World War II. The law then changed to allow only 'Negroids' and 'Caucasians' to enter the United States, and Arabs did not fall into either of these categories.

The third wave, dating from the mid-1940s to the mid-1960s, comprised for the most part Palestinians leaving the recently established state of Israel, Egyptians moving away from Nasser's confiscation policies, Iraqis departing after the revolution of 1948 and Muslims from Eastern Europe trying to escape hardship and persecution under communist regimes. Muslim immigration continues as a consequence of instability in many parts of the Muslim world. The events of 11 September 2001 focused attention on any Muslim groups expressing radical views, and the Muslim community in general came under intense scrutiny largely due to the activities of some fringe minorities. The majority of Muslims in the

United States see themselves as loyal citizens living in a religiously plural society. The extraordinary growth of Muslim numbers has resulted in increased building programmes and education initiatives. The US Muslim community relates to the global Muslim community in many ways and almost every SCHOOL OF ISLAMIC LAW is represented.

universities There is a long tradition of higher learning in the Muslim world, as illustrated by the founding of major educational institutions such as the *jami* (the Friday mosque), mosque universities and *madrasas* – colleges of higher studies, primarily in law and theology. Some of these institutions have survived and developed further in our day. Studies of the curriculum and teaching in these institutions indicate that a wide variety of subjects were taught and endowments established to support professors, students and libraries. Universities also acted as networks to link Muslim scholars from different parts of the world. It is thought that Muslim patterns of university life and education influenced the rise and development of medieval universities in Europe.

In the modern period there has been a very significant growth in university construction in virtually all Muslim countries. Many of these institutions are state-supported, though in some cases private universities are funded by endowments or local philanthropists. The quality of these institutions within an international framework is uneven, and many Muslim students still wish to pursue higher education abroad, mostly in North America, continental Europe, the United Kingdom and Australia. As Muslim countries and societies seek to develop the capacity and human resources to meet the challenges of development, education will have a key role to play in building further on an already established tradition supporting the pursuit of knowledge in all its forms.

Urdu Language closely related to various languages of the Indo-Aryan family, spoken on the Indian subcontinent. It is today the national language of Pakistan, written in the Arabic script. Its rich tradition of poetry and other literary works constitutes a major vehicle for the promotion of the heritage of Muslims in Pakistan and elsewhere.

usul al-fiqh (lit., 'the sources or roots of jurisprudence') For the Sunnis, these consist of the QURAN, SUNNA, QIYAS (analogical reasoning) and IJMA (consensus). For the Shia, special emphasis is placed on the role of the living imam or, among the ITHNA ASHARIYYA and MUSTALIYYA, those who represent the absent imam (*see* GHAYBA; SATR).

Uthman Dan Fodio (Arabic, Uthman ibn Fudi) (1754–1817) Religious leader, reformer, Sufi shaykh and scholar of West Africa. He was trained in the study of Islam as a youth and was an active member of the QADIRIYYA Sufi order. His opposition to what he regarded as non-Islamic practices among Muslims of the region brought him into conflict with local ruling authorities. He declared a JIHAD against them and sought to extend the religious and political hegemony of Islam in the region that currently forms part of northern Nigeria. The eventual success of his mission led to the establishment of the SOKOTO CALIPHATE, which unified the region and led to the development of a strong commercial and intellectual Muslim society in this predominantly Hausa-speaking area. His *jihad* also sparked similar movements in other parts of West Africa.

Uthman ibn Affan (d. 656) The third caliph and an early convert to Islam. He had been appointed by his predecessor, UMAR IBN AL-KHATTAB, on his deathbed. Although the first half of his reign was peaceful, his perceived favouritism towards his own clan, the UMAYYADS, resulted in trouble and rebellion throughout the quickly expanding Muslim-held territories. The opposition to him eventually turned militant and he was killed by rebels who stormed his palace. Among his achievements is believed to be the compilation of a standardized text of the Quran, based on the consensus of other COMPANIONS OF THE PROPHET.

Uzbekistan Central Asian republic. Uzbekistan has an estimated population of 26 million, 75 per cent of whom are Sunni Muslims of the Hanafi SCHOOL OF ISLAMIC LAW. Cities of medieval splendour such as BUKHARA, SAMARKAND and Khiva lie within its borders and represent the most prestigious centres of Muslim culture and influence in Central Asia. Islam was introduced into the area during the seventh century.

verse of light *See* BARAKA; NUR.

violence *See* EXTREMISM.

virtue *See* IHSAN.

visiting *See* ZIYARAT.

wahdat al-wujud (lit., 'unity of existence') A philosophical articulation of the principle of unity as expounded by IBN AL-ARABI.

Wahhabism The form and interpretation of Islam which is the basis for the official Sunni doctrine in the Kingdom of SAUDI ARABIA. It developed out of the reform movement led by Muhammad ABD AL-WAHHAB (1703–1792) in the eighteenth century. His alliance with Muhammad ibn Saud brought him a political base and support from which to launch a JIHAD against all those he believed to have strayed from the correct practice and those who disagreed with his interpretation. He advocated the use of compulsion to enforce the practices of the faith and denounced 'innovations' that had developed since the first generation of Muslims.

Esoteric interpretations, especially the practices of the Sufis, were attacked as well as prayer for the intercession of saints, the commemoration of the saints and visiting of tombs. All such beliefs and practices were eradicated and denounced as *shirk* ('association'), as they were opposed to the foundational belief of Wahhabism concerning the 'unity of God'. Although generally confined to the Arabian Peninsula under the leadership of Wahhabi scholars, the influence of Wahhabism has grown through its promotion in other regions.

Wahid, Abdul Rahman *See* NAHDAT AL-ULAMA.

wahy (lit., 'inspiration') Term which refers to 'divine inspiration' as the mode by which the Quran was revealed to the Prophet Muhammad. *Wahy* also refers to divine inspiration as a source to which the Prophet had continuous access and by which were also inspired the 'holy sayings' (*hadith qudsi* – *see* HADITH) considered to be transmitted in Muhammad's words, but not included in the text of the Quran. Muslims regard the Prophet's entire life and actions as being under the influence of *wahy*.

walaya Additional pillar of the ISMAILIYYA and DRUZE communities, expressed as 'Love and Devotion for God, the Prophets and the imam'.

waqf A charitable trust established in perpetuity for a pious or philanthropic purpose, the underlying principle of which is assignation of one's property for charitable use. The property and any profit from it are used only for the benefit of persons or public institutions acting with charitable intent.

Waraqa ibn Nawfal *See* AHL AL-FATRA.

Whirling Dervishes Popular name given to the followers of the MEVLEVI Sufi order, who perform a ritual whirling dance, accompanied by flute and drum music, as a form of spiritual exercise. Among the Mevlevi (from *mawlana*, 'our master') the dance and music evoke a wealth of mystical symbolism drawn from JALAL AL-DIN RUMI's thought and writings. Although the order was banned in Turkey during the changes instituted under MUSTAFA KEMAL (Atatürk), their activities are now permitted and the dance officially sanctioned and seen as an important cultural tradition.

wilayat al-faqih The concept of the guardianship of the jurist in Imami Shiism. The concept was developed by Ayatollah KHOMEINI during the 1970s in lectures delivered in Najaf, Iraq, where he was exiled. It has been institutionalized in modern Iran following the Islamic revolution of 1979 to represent the authoritative role of the jurists in the Consultative Assembly as significant partner in the decision-making process of the nation.

Wolof African language spoken by a large number of Muslims in West Africa, primarily in the Senegambia region. The vitality and evolution of Wolof literature were inspired by a long tradition of oral stories and tales that were among the first to be published in the West. As a result, several Senegalese discovered the value of the tradition and made it their own. In addition, the emergence of a modern tradition of film-making generated greater development and creativity in Wolof. Wolof literature expresses the heritage of Muslims in all their diversity in its West African context.

Xian Provincial capital in the Shaanxi province of China. This ancient city also served as one of the gateways to the Silk Road and adopted Muslim culture as part of its heritage. It is the site of an important complex of Muslim buildings including a mosque.

Xinjiang Province in north-western China. It is believed that Muslims first came to the region as early as 750 but it was not until two centuries later that Sufi missionaries and the actions of Muslim rulers caused the religion to become widespread. Over the next few centuries Xinjiang was at times governed by Muslim rulers and at others acknowledged the authority of the Chinese emperor. Despite the latter's political control, the cultural and economic influences in the region came from its Muslim trading ties because of its contiguity to Central Asia.

In the twentieth century an attempt to create a Turkish Islamic Republic of Eastern Turkestan was suppressed, and there was persecution of Muslims. Under communist rule during the Cultural Revolution, religious practice and expression were curtailed and even banned.

At present there is a greater degree of religious freedom in China within what is called the Xinjiang Uyghur Autonomous Province. However, according to many accounts a large-scale influx of Chinese settlers from other regions has compromised the cultural integrity of the region and created support for Muslim political activism.

Y

Yahya *See* JOHN THE BAPTIST.

Yaqub *See* JACOB.

Yathrib *See* MEDINA.

Yazid ibn Muawiyya (642–683) Yazid inherited the role of UMMAYAD caliph from his father MUAWIYYA IBN ABI SUFYAN and immediately found himself immersed in the conflicts generated by the imposition of Umayyad rule over an expanding Muslim world. During his brief rule from 680 until his death he tried to deal with one dimension of the problem by suppressing support for HUSAYN IBN ALI, the Prophet's grandson. In a siege ordered by Yazid, Husayn and several of his family and followers were massacred. The incident has caused Yazid's name to be forever infamous in Muslim historiography and Shia memory.

Conservation of old Sana, Yemen.

Yemen Country in the southern part of the Arabian Peninsula. The majority of its 12 million people are Zaydi Shia.

Approximately 90 per cent of the population is of Arab origin, making Yemen almost homogeneous both ethnically and religiously. The present Republic of Yemen was created in 1990.

Yemen converted to Islam in 628, and its Zaydi orientation developed in the ninth century. *See* ZAYDIYYA.

Yunus, Muhammad *See* GRAMEEN BANK.

Yusuf *See* JOSEPH.

Z

Zahir al-Din Muhammad *See* BABUR.

Zahiris A SCHOOL OF ISLAMIC LAW in the medieval period of Islam which insisted on a literal interpretation of the SHARIA and SUNNA as a basis for its systematization of doctrine and legal practice in Islam. Among its foremost exponents was the eleventh-century Spanish Muslim scholar IBN HAZM. The school eventually passed out of existence.

zakat Giving of a portion of one's wealth. The Quran ordained *zakat* as a way of purifying one's wealth and as a form of obligatory giving for very specific causes. In Muslim legal practice, the amount due is based on percentage formulas applied against certain types of wealth, such as the produce of land, livestock, precious metals and financial investments. *See also* SADAQA.

Zamakhshari, Abu al-Qasim Mahmud ibn Umar (1075–1144) Persian grammarian of Arabic best known for his commentary on the Quran. Although Zamakhshari's rationalist exegesis became unacceptable to those seeking a more orthodox interpretation, his reputation as a grammarian and his authoritative analysis of the language of the Quran assured his reputation as a scholar and Quranic exegete.

Zam-Zam, Well of *See* HAJJ; PILGRIMAGE; UMRA.

zawiya *See* KHANQA.

Zayd ibn Ali (d. 740) A grandson of Imam Husayn (*see* HUSAYN IBN ALI) who developed a following that considered him to be an imam (*see* ZAYDIYYA). They followed his lead in combating what they regarded as the unjust rule of the UMAYYADS. Zayd led several revolts against Umayyad authority but was unsuccessful. He died fighting against the Umayyad governor of Kufa in Iraq.

Zayd ibn Thabit (d. 665) A COMPANION OF THE PROPHET, he served as his secretary and is known for assisting in the collection of the Quran.

Zaydiyya Branch of Shia Islam which recognized ZAYD IBN ALI as an imam. Zaydi states were established in Tabaristan (in Persia) and in YEMEN, the latter surviving until its overthrow in 1963. Zaydis are distinguished from other schools of Shiism by their own SCHOOL OF ISLAMIC LAW and theology. They recognize a non-dynastic imamate through the lineage of ALI IBN ABI TALIB based on the criteria of political and religious competence. As a consequence, Zaydis are willing to recognize more than one imam at a time or none at all. Today Zaydis are dominant only in North Yemen.

Zayn al-Abidin (c. 659–713) The imam of the Shia who succeeded after the martyrdom of his father, Imam Husayn (*see* HUSAYN IBN ALI). He had been with his father at KARBALA but escaped death at the hands of the UMAYYAD army. He lived in Medina, where his exemplary piety and commitment to helping the poor earned him a close following among the early Shia. His recitation of prayers has been preserved as a model of personal piety and devotion. He designated his son MUHAMMAD AL-BAQIR as next imam. *See also* SAHIFAT AL-KAMILA AL-SAJJADIYYA.

Zaytuna Mosque-university complex in Tunis and one of the earliest examples in Muslim history in which the mosque came to be complemented by the establishment of a centre of learning. While it is not known exactly when the first programmes of instruction started, there are indications that Zaytuna was a centre of increasing influence in the medieval period.

In the modern period it serves as a university with responsibility for training religious scholars and for the promotion of materials for the instruction of Islam in the state school system.

al-Zayyati, Hasan *See* LEO AFRICANUS.

ziyarat (lit., 'visiting') In its widest application, visiting the tomb of the Prophet and the holy sites in Mecca and Medina (*see* PILGRIMAGE). In Shiism and Sufism the term also refers to visiting the tombs of imams, saints and martyrs as places of BARAKA (blessing) and spiritual intercession.

Zoroastrianism The major religion of Persia and parts of Central Asia until it was replaced by the spread of Islam. Small Zoroastrian communities survived under Muslim rule in Iran and subsequently in India, where many had migrated following the Muslim conquest. The religion's followers are called Zoroastrians.

Chronology of Muslim History

570	Birth of the Prophet Muhammad (traditionally accepted date); 'Year of the Elephant'
595	Muhammad's marriage to Khadija
610	Muhammad receives first revelation
613	Period of public preaching begins
615	Muhammad sends a group of Muslims to Abyssinia to escape persecution
616–618	Boycott of the Prophet's family by leaders of the Quraysh opposed to him
620	Death of Khadija; death of Abu Talib, the Prophet's uncle
622	The *hijra*; establishment of a Muslim community in Medina; base year of the Muslim calendar; the Prophet undertakes important social and economic reforms in building the new Muslim community
623	Fatima, daughter of the Prophet, marries Ali ibn Abi Talib
624	Battle of Badr; Muslims are victorious over the Meccan Quraysh
625	Battle of Uhud
628	Unsuccessful siege of Medina by combined force of Meccans and Bedouins (Battle of the Ditch); battle of Hunayn; Treaty of Hudaybiyya gives Muslims the right to make the pilgrimage to Mecca; the Prophet sends messengers to the rulers of Egypt, Persia, Byzantium and the Yemen with an invitation to accept Islam
629	The Prophet leads the pilgrimage to Mecca
630	Mecca submits to the authority of the Prophet; a general amnesty is declared and the Ka'ba is rededicated to the worship of Allah
632	Tribal conversions throughout Arabia; the Prophet leads expedition to Tabuk; the Prophet's farewell pilgrimage; the declaration of Ghadir Khumm and the year of his death
632–634	Caliphate of Abu Bakr
633	Expeditions against Syria and Iraq; conquest of southern Mesopotamia
634	Muslim army defeats Byzantines at battle of Anjadyan in Palestine; Umar becomes caliph on the death of Abu Bakr
634–644	Caliphate of Umar ibn al-Khattab
636	Byzantine forces defeated at the battle of Yarmuk
637	Conquest of Syria; Sassanian army defeated at the battle of Qadisiyya (Iraq); Muslim authority extends over the Fertile Crescent; Jerusalem comes under Muslim rule
638	Invasion of Egypt
640	Battle of Nihavand results in collapse of Sassanian rule in Egypt
644–656	Uthman succeeds Umar as caliph

651	First delegation of Muslims believed to have visited the court of the Chinese emperor
655	Muslim navy defeats the Byzantine fleet off the coast of Lycia
656	The assassination of Uthman
656–660	Civil war breaks out; Battle of the Camel; Caliphate of Ali
657–660	Ali settles in Kufa; Muawiyya, governor of Syria, challenges the authority of Ali resulting in the battle of Siffin; after arbitration fails, Muawiyya rejects Ali's authority and proclaims himself ruler
661	Assassination of Ali; with the forcible assumption of rule by Muawiyya (r. 661–680) the period of the Rightly Guided Caliphs comes to an end
661–750	A group of Muslims called Khawarij secede from the rest of the community; Umayyad dynastic Caliphate based in Damascus; period of major territorial expansion begins
661–680	Uqba ibn Nafi founds Qayrawan in North Africa (Tunisia)
680	Yazid succeeds Muawiyya and suppresses attempts to restore authority to Husayn, son of Ali and grandson of the Prophet; Husayn and his followers are massacred at Karbala, intensifying opposition by supporters who collectively are called Shia
705	Construction of Great Mosque of Damascus
712	Tariq ibn Ziyad lands in Spain, initiating a period of Muslim control and influence; Córdoba becomes the seat of government in Spain; Muslim conquest of Sind in India under Muhammad ibn Qasim; Muslims gain control of Transoxiana and conquer Central Asia (Samarkand, Balkh, Bukhara)
713	Death of the Shia Imam Ali Zayn al-Abidin; some adherents follow one of his sons, Zayd, so beginning Zaydi Shia; the rest accept Muhammad al-Baqir as Imam
719	Narbonne, in France, is captured by Muslim forces
732	Charles Martel turns back Muslim advance at Tours and Poitiers; founding of the mosque of Xian in China
742	Abbasid revolution begins with the Hashimiyya movement led by Abu Muslim in Khurasan
747	Abbasids consolidate power
750	Umayyad Caliphate ends
751	Islam spreads into Central Asia following victory over the Chinese at the battle of the Talas River
756–1031	Rule of Umayyad dynasty initiated in Spain, established by Abd al-Rahman
762	Baghdad is founded by al-Mansur as capital of Abbasid Caliphate
765	First free public hospital in Muslim world founded in Baghdad; death of the sixth Shia imam, Jafar al-Sadiq, results in Shia split over the imamate and the emergence of what subsequently became the Ismailis and Ithna Asharis
767	Death of Abu Hanifa, eponym of the Hanafi school of Islamic law
778	Unsuccessful campaign under Charlemagne to recapture Spain
786–809	Caliphate of Harun al-Rashid; height of Abbasid influence and culture; city of Fez founded by Idris II in 789
795	Death of Malik ibn Anas, founder of the Maliki school of Islamic law
809	Death of Harun al-Rashid; accession of Amin to Abbasid Caliphate
813–833	Caliphate of al-Mamun, son of Harun al-Rashid; period of translation of classical works of philosophy, medicine, etc. into Arabic begins

820	Death of Muhammad ibn Idris al-Shafii, founder of Shafii school of Islamic law
827	Aghlabids begin campaign to capture Sicily; harassment and persecution of Muslim scholars who do not conform to Caliph al-Mamun's institution of *mihna* in support of Mutazili doctrines
848	Ahmad ibn Hanbal is imprisoned for opposing al-Mamun's policy
855	Death of Ahmad ibn Hanbal, founder of Hanbali school of Islamic law
864–928	Hasan ibn Zayd establishes Zaydi Shia state in Daylam
866	Death of philosopher al-Kindi
870	Capture of Malta; death of al-Bukhari, scholar and compiler of *hadith*
874	The eleventh imam of the Ithna Ashari Shia dies and his son Muhammad al-Mahdi goes into lesser occultation (*ghayba*)
877	Death of Yaqub Layth in Sistan; accession of Amr ibn Layth
909–972	Ismaili Fatimids overthrow Aghlabids in Ifriqiyya and establish a state in North Africa
929	Abd al-Rahman takes the title of caliph in Córdoba; Muslim world exists under three Caliphates: Abbasids, Fatimids and Spanish Umayyads
935	Death of Sunni theologian al-Ashari
969	The Fatimids conquer Egypt and establish Cairo as their capital; al-Azhar University is founded
1037	Death of philosopher and physician Ibn Sina (Avicenna)
1037–1063	Tughril Beg rules in western Iran as first sultan of the Saljuq dynasty
1038–1194	Saljuqs control most of Asia Minor for much of this period (1038–1157, Khurasan; 1053–1194, western Iran); independent principality emerges in northeast Anatolia under Malik Danishmand
1055	Founding of al-Nizamiyya *madrasa* and college in Baghdad
1071	Alp Arslan captures Byzantine Emperor Romanos Diogenes at Manzikert
1086–1147	Almoravids depose the king of Granada; Almoravid rule in al-Andalus (Muslim Spain)
1090	Hasan i-Sabbah obtains control of the Alamut fortress on behalf of the Fatimids in northern Persia
1094	Death of the Fatimid Caliph al-Mustansir; Ismaili movement divides into the Nizari and the Mustali
1095	Pope Urban II launches First Crusade to capture the Holy Land
1099	First Crusade ends; the Fatimids are defeated at Acre and the Crusaders take Jerusalem
1099–1291	The Crusades continue
1100	Christian kingdom of Jerusalem established under Baldwin
1111	Death of theologian and scholar al-Ghazali
1118–1157	Sultanate of Sanjar, son of Malikshah; Muslim Empire breaks up into independent states under sultanates of Nishapur, Baghdad and Konya with power in the hands of independent Atabegs in Syria, Azerbaijan, and northern Iraq; Ghaznawids become vassal state
1123	Death of Persian poet, astronomer and mathematician Omar Khayyam
1143	Translation of the Quran into Latin
1166	Almoravids capture Santarém, Badajoz, Porto, Évora and Lisbon; death of Sufi Abd al-Qadir al-Jilani, founder of the Qadiriyya order
1171–1193	Saladin establishes the Ayyubid dynasty in Egypt; construction begins on the Great Mosque of Seville

1187	Saladin defeats the Crusaders at the battle of the Horn of Hattin and takes Jerusalem
1198	Death of physician and philosopher Ibn Rushd (Averroes)
1200	Ghurids in eastern Afghanistan begin expansion into Khurasan and northern India
1204	The Fifth Crusade
1218	Mongols invade Turkestan; Khwarazm-Shah Ala al-Din Muhammad kills envoys of Chingiz Khan as spies, provoking Mongol retaliation
1225	Mongol Empire divided among Ogeday in Qaragorum, Batu in Khwarazm, Orda in Siberia, Chaghatay III in Transoxiana and eastern Turkestan, and Toluy in Mongolia
1227	Death of Chingiz Khan
1250	Mamluk dynasty established in Egypt
1254	Almohads driven out of Spain; Muslims hold power only in Granada; arrival of Islam in Southeast Asia
1258	Hulagu Khan sacks Baghdad and establishes the Mongol Il-Khanid dynasty in Persia with its capital at Tabriz
1273	Death of Jalal al-Din Rumi, author of the *Mathnawi*
1281–1328	Yusuf I is Nasrid ruler in Spain
1300	Ottoman rule established in Bithynia under Osman I ibn Ertoghril
1301	Establishment of small Muslim states in Indonesia
1325–1353	Construction of the Alhambra; travels of Ibn Battuta through the world of Islam
1328	Osman defeats Byzantines at Baphaeon; death of Hanbali jurist and theologian Ibn Taymiyya
1333–1354	Expansion of the Ottoman state into Anatolia and Balkans; formation of the Janissaries
1354	Muslim states established in Arakan in Burma (Myanmar)
1361–1389	Sufi Safawid order established in Azerbaijan
1362–1389	Rule of Ottoman Murad I, who takes title sultan
1395–1400	Conquest of western Persia and Iraq by Timur (Tamerlane)
1396	Ottoman victory over Byzantines at the battle of Nicopolis
1398–1399	Timur sacks Delhi and conquers north India; Delhi sultanate ends
1443	John Hunyadi leads Crusade against Turks and occupies the Balkans
1447–1448	Aq-Qoyunlu reach height of power under Uzun Hasan, conquering the Qara-Qoyunlu and controlling Persia, Azerbaijan and Iraq
1450–1459	Portugal seizes ports in Morocco
1453–1478	Ottoman conquest of Constantinople, renamed Istanbul
1458–1519	Safawids establish authority in north-west Iran, Azerbaijan and eastern Anatolia
1478	Establishment of Spanish Inquisition
1479	Mosque of Demak is built in Indonesia
1492	Ferdinand and Isabella end Muslim rule in Spain; surrender of the Alhambra
1497	Babur, founder of the Moghul Empire, captures Samarkand; construction of Bayezid mosque in Istanbul
1497–1503	The East African Muslim Ibn Majid guides Vasco da Gama's ship to India; Portuguese gain trade supremacy in the Indian Ocean

1498	Muhammad Shaybani, khan of the Siberian Mongol state, overcomes Timurids and establishes Uzbek dynasty in Transoxiana and Khwarazm
1500	Ahmad Gran challenges Christian Ethiopia; Muslims conquer Nubia
1501–1524	Shah Ismail establishes the Safawid dynasty in Azerbaijan and takes Iran and Mesopotamia; Twelver Imami Shiism is established as the official school of the state
1506–1603	Muslim sultanates replace Hindu institutions in Sumatra and Java
1514	The battle of Chaldiran between the Ottomans and the Safawids
1517	Ottoman conquest of Mamluk Egypt
1520–1566	Rule of Sultan Sulayman II ('the Magnificent'); height of Ottoman power
1521	Belgrade falls to Ottomans
1526	Babur establishes Moghul dynasty in India after defeating Lodi Sultan in Delhi; Louis of Hungary is killed at the battle of Mohacs; Ottomans control Hungary; the battle of Panipat in India
1529	Shia tradition and practice become dominant in region under Safawid rule
1530	Beginning of Muslim kingdom of Aceh in Sumatra
1538	Ottomans defeat Holy League at the battle of Preveza, taking naval control of the Mediterranean
1542	Francis Xavier arrives in India
1556–1605	Islam spreads to Java, the Moluccas and Borneo; Spain seizes the Philippines, including Muslim principalities in Mindanao; Moghul Emperor Akbar in Delhi; flowering of Moghul culture
1568	Alpujarra uprising of the Moriscos in Spain
1571–1603	King Idris Aloma makes Kanem-Bornu a power in the central Sahara
1591	Songhai Empire of Gao weakened by antipathy between Muslims and followers of traditional African religions
1596	Agra becomes Moghul capital
1598	Shah Abbas establishes Isfahan as Safawid capital
1600–1850	Long period of forced migration of hundreds of thousands of Africans as slaves to the Americas, including Mandé- and Wolof-speaking Muslims from West Africa as part of the Atlantic slave trade
1607–1636	Great age of Sufism in Aceh in Sumatra; Manchu dynasty alienates Chinese Muslims
1613–1646	Sultan Agung controls most of Java from Mataram; Islamization of Southeast Asia continues; ruler of Muslim state in Java takes the title sultan
1632–1643	Shah Jahan builds the Taj Mahal at Agra
1638	New capital built at Delhi (Shahjahanabad)
1638–1654	Murad IV retakes Baghdad from the Safawids
1639	Treaty of Qasr-i Shirin turns Caucasus and Azerbaijan over to the Safawids; boundaries are established between the two empires
1640	Death of Mulla Sadra (Sadr al-Din), Persian theologian and philosopher
1641	Dutch conquer Malacca in Southeast Asia
1642	Chinese Muslim scholar Wang Tai-Yu publishes the *Cheng Chiao Chen Chuan* (*Veritable Explanation of True Religion*), expressing common ground between Muslim and Confucian belief
1644	Climax of campaign of conversion of Muslims to Orthodox Christianity which began under Peter the Great; mosques and Quranic schools destroyed
1668	Zanzibar becomes part of the Omani sultanate

1680	First Fulani war results in establishment of a Muslim state in the Fulani region of West Africa
1684	Holy Alliance formed against the Ottomans by Austria, Poland, Venice and the Papacy
1730–1740	French gain concessions in North Africa
1739	Peace of Belgrade concludes Ottoman war with Austria and Russia; Ottomans receive northern Serbia and Belgrade and regain supremacy in the Black Sea region; Russia receives Azov
1747	Ahmad Shah establishes autonomous rule in Afghanistan; Nadir Shah is murdered by Afshar and Qajar leaders
1750	Muhammad Karim Khan Zand of Shiraz becomes ruler of Persia
1750–1779	Beginning of Wahhabi reform movement in Arabia through alliance of Muhammad ibn Abd al-Wahhab and tribal chief Muhammad ibn Saud
1758–1760	England establishes trade with Persia
1770	Ottoman fleet destroyed by Russians in battle of Cheshme; Catherine II imposes Russian rule over Crimean Tatars; Third Fulani War establishes Islam in Futa Toro
1783	Muslims rebel against Chinese emperor
1791	Death of Ma (Muhammad) Ming-hsin, founder of the 'New Sect' in China
1794–1924	Qajar dynasty in Shiraz replaces the Zand dynasty and extends rule throughout Persia
1798–1801	French enter Egypt under Napoleon Bonaparte; England and Russia forge alliance with the Ottomans
1801	Fath Ali Shah signs treaty with British East India Company against France and Afghanistan; Dutch control Muslim sultanates on Java and Sumatra
1803	Delhi falls to the British, although direct rule does not begin until 1857
1804	Wahhabis seize control of Mecca and Medina in Arabia; the French are forced out of Egypt by the Ottomans under Muhammad Ali; Uthman dan Fodio, supported by Fulani and Hausa groups, eventually forms Caliphate of Sokoto in 1808
1805–1848	Muhammad Ali initiates struggle for Egyptian independence by seizing power and gaining Ottoman recognition as governor; reform measures begin; British rule is established throughout India
1828	First government printing press in Egypt
1821	Founding of Khartoum, capital of Sudan
1823	Muslims revolt in Xinjiang
1833	Ottoman–Russian Treaty of Hünkâr İskelesi
1834	French colonial rule in Algeria
1837	Muhammad Ali al-Sanusi founds Sanusiyya movement in Libya
1839	Period of reforms in Ottoman Empire begins
1842	Druze revolt in Lebanon; British are forced out of Afghanistan by Amir Dost Muhammad
1848	France incorporates Algeria
1853	Founding of the Babi sect and the onset of the Bahai movement
1854	The Council of Tanzimat initiates reforms in Turkey; Ferdinand de Lesseps receives concession to build Suez Canal
1856–1872	The Tijaniyya spreads in West Africa; Ma Te-hsin leads an independence movement among Chinese Muslims in Yunnan

1856–1857	War between Persia and Britain results in independence for Afghanistan
1857	The Indian Mutiny breaks out
1858	Ottoman land reforms; end of Moghul domination
1859	Construction of Suez Canal begins
1861	First modern constitution enacted by a Muslim country is promulgated by Muhammad al-Sadiq in Tunisia
1863–1893	Tijani Empire stretches from Niger to Senegal
1864	Independent Muslim kingdom of Xinjiang established in north-west China
1866	Dar al-Ulum founded at Deoband in British India
1869	Opening of the Suez Canal
1870	Jamal al-Din al-Afghani initiates reform activity in Cairo
1871–1879	Creation of the Majlis-i ahkam-i adliyye, Ottoman legislative body
1873–1910	Aceh War in Sumatra opposing Dutch expansion in Indonesia
1875–1876	Rebellions in Bulgaria, Bosnia and Herzegovina
1881	The 'Mahdi' appears in the Sudan
1876	Constitution based on parliamentary government is promulgated for the Ottoman Empire
1876–1878	Serbia and Montenegro declare war against Ottoman and Serbian forces; armistice after Ottomans occupy Russia; Sultan Abd al-Aziz is deposed; brief sultanate of Murad V (also deposed)
1881–1882	Rebellion in Egypt results in British occupation; France occupies Tunisia
1881	The 'Mahdi' calls for *jihad* in the Sudan
1884	In Paris al-Afghani with Muhammad Abduh publishes *al-Urwa al-Wuthqa*, a journal of modern Muslim reform and political opinion
1885	Muhammad al-Mahdi initiates a reform movement in the Sudan and captures Khartoum from the British; Sultan Muhammad Shah becomes forty-eighth Imam of the Ismailis; Uganda becomes the scene of intense rivalry among Catholic and Protestant Christian missions and Muslims for control and conversion of the Kabaka and his people
1891	Masqat (Muscat) and Oman become British protectorates
1891–1892	Shia Ulama join in tobacco revolts in Iran, resulting in cancellation of British concession
1892–1905	Muhammad Abduh initiates reforms at al-Azhar but faces opposition
1898	Autonomy for Crete under Greek governor; *al-Manar* is published in Cairo as a journal of Muslim opinion; Lord Kitchener defeats the Mahdists; Britain colonizes Nigeria, including Sokoto, the Muslim kingdom in the north
1900–1908	Construction of the Hijaz railway to Mecca
1905–1906	Constitutional revolution in Iran
1906	Formation of All-India Muslim League to seek political rights for Indian Muslims; Sinai peninsula is ceded to Britain
1907	Revolution in Iran fails and the country is divided into Russian and British spheres of influence
1908	Young Turks Revolution; restoration of the 1876 constitution in the Ottoman Empire; Shah Muhammad Ali of Iran dissolves parliament and executes opposition leaders
1908–1909	Young Turks lead rebellion; deposition of Sultan Abd al-Hamid of Turkey; Turkish nationalism is advocated by Ziya Gökalp; Austria annexes Bosnia and Herzegovina; Bulgaria declares independence

1909	Civil war in Iran forces Shah to flee to Russia; emergence of the Muhammadiyya reform movement in Indonesia
1909–1918	Constitutional sultanate of Mehmed V; discovery of oil in Iran leads to creation of Anglo-Persian Oil Company; formation of Muslim League in Southeast Asia
1912	First Balkan War; Ottomans lose Adrianople and Thessalonika
1912–1913	France and Spain form protectorates in Morocco
1914–1918	World War I; Ottomans are allied with Germany and Austria; Egypt is made a British protectorate
1916	Sykes-Picot agreement delimits English and French interests in the Middle East
1916–1918	Arabs under the Sharif of Mecca revolt against Ottoman rule; emir of Bukhara issues manifesto promising extensive reform and freedoms; independence of the Yemen
1917	Balfour Declaration; Russians withdraw from Iran; T. E. Lawrence leads Arab army against the Ottomans; Osmania College established in Hyderabad; Russian revolution begins
1918	Ottomans leave Iraq after defeat by the British and sign the Armistice, conceding defeat and eventually agreeing to dismantling their possessions in the Middle East and Eastern Europe
1919	Sad Zaghlul, leader of the Wafd Party for Egyptian independence, is arrested by the British; popular rebellion quashed by occupation troops; Damascus falls to the British
1919–1922	After Greek invasion of Anatolia, gathering of nationalistic fighting forces under Mustafa Kemal (Atatürk); Turkish war of independence against the Allies; Conference of the League of Nations declares Syria and Lebanon a French mandate; France occupies Damascus and overthrows Faysal's government; independence for Hijaz; Bolsheviks occupy Rasht in Iran
1920	Emirate of Bukhara comes to an end; People's Republic of Bukhara declared; Soviet Republic of Gilan is proclaimed; Basmachi Muslim resistance group in Central Asia is driven by Russians into rural areas and eventually crushed; Turkish national assembly proclaims constitution in Ankara
1921	Coup d'état in Iran by Reza Khan, a colonel of the Cossack Brigade; Abd Allah ibn Husayn is made king of Transjordan; Iraq becomes a constitutional monarchy under Faysal ibn Husayn; Turks repel Greek invasion at battle on the Sakaarya
1922	Independent Kingdom of Egypt is formed with Ahmad Fuad I as king; proclamation of Egyptian constitution; the Republic of Lebanon is created under French mandate
1922–1924	Rebellion by Iraqi Kurds against the British mandate; Reza Khan becomes prime minister in Iran
1923	The Ottoman sultanate is abolished by Mustafa Kemal; Mehmed VI flees Istanbul; Abdülmecit II is declared caliph without any authority; proclamation of the Turkish Republic with Mustafa Kemal as president; Transjordan is recognized as an autonomous state under British mandate
1924	The caliphate is abolished in Turkey; Turkey adopts civil law, marking its secularist direction
1925	University of Tehran is founded

1925–1926   Reza Khan ends the Qajar dynasty in Iran, proclaiming himself Shah and establishing the Pahlavi dynasty; Abd al-Aziz ibn Saud conquers Mecca and is proclaimed King of the Najd and Hijaz, establishing the Wahhabi kingdom

1926   Four closely controlled republics created by the Soviet Union in Central Asia: Uzbekistan, Turkmenistan, Kazakhstan and Kyrgyzstan; Turkey becomes formally a secular state and replaces Arabic script with the Latin alphabet

1928   Muslim Brotherhood is founded by Hassan al-Banna in Egypt; Mawlana Muhammad Ilyas founds the Tablighi movement in India

1932   Iran becomes independent

1935   Iran becomes the official name of Persia

1936   Formal removal of British–French mandate and proclamation of the Republic of Syria

1938   Oil is discovered in Saudi Arabia

1939–1945   World War II

1941   Reza Shah is forced to abdicate in favour of his son Muhammad Reza Shah following British and Russian invasion of Iran; Abu al-Ala Mawdudi founds the Jamaat-i-Islami in India

1942–1945   Japanese occupation of Indonesia; formation of Partai Muslimin Indonesia

1944   An Eastern Turkestan Republic free of Chinese control is proclaimed in Xinjiang; Albania is declared a republic under a communist government

1945   Foundation of Arab League; proclamation of Indonesian independence

1946   British and French troops withdraw from much of the Middle East; Lebanon and Syria become independent and the Kingdom of Jordan is established

1947   End of the British Palestine mandate as the UN sanctions partition of the country and the establishment of the state of Israel; formation of Muslim Pakistan after partition of British India; violence mars Indian independence as partition takes effect

1948   First Arab–Israeli War

1949   Communists triumph in China; assassination of Hassan al-Banna, founder of the Muslim Brotherhood

1950   Enlargement of the Prophet's mosque is begun in Medina

1951   Kingdom of Libya becomes independent

1952   Revolution in Egypt deposes King Faruq; constitutional monarchy established in Jordan

1953   Egypt is declared a republic by Gamal Abdel Nasser; death of King Abd al-Aziz ibn Saud of Saudi Arabia; Western-led coup deposes Mosaddeq in Iran and restores the monarchy; Xinjiang Uyghur Autonomous Region created within the People's Republic of China

1954   Algerian war of independence against France

1956   Nasser nationalizes the Suez Canal; the Suez Crisis ensues as Britain, France and Israel attack Egypt; Tunisia wins autonomy from France and then independence; Kingdom of Morocco becomes independent under Muhammad V

1957   In Tunisia the Bey is deposed and the country becomes a republic under President Bourguiba; Malaysia becomes independent; Karim Aga Khan becomes imam of the Ismailis, succeeding his grandfather Sultan Muhammad Shah, Aga Khan III; Muslim Dawa Party is established in Iraq led by Ayatollah Muhammad Baqir al-Sadr

1958   Ayub Khan establishes military rule in Pakistan

1958–1963 Abd al-Karim Qasim leads revolution in Iraq, toppling the monarchy and establishing a republic; strong anti-religious campaigns in the Soviet Union under Khrushchev

1960 Mali and Senegal gain independence from France

1962 Creation of the Yemeni Arab Republic

1963 Algeria wins independence under President Ben Bella; civil war in Cyprus; Zanzibar gains independence from British rule

1964 The Sultan of Zanzibar is overthrown and the country is merged with Tanganyika to form Tanzania

1965 Assassination of Malcolm X; death of Sayyidina Tahir, head of the Bohoras, who is succeeded by Mohammed Burhanuddin; Indo-Pakistan war

1966 Execution of Sayyid Qutb

1966–1976 During the Cultural Revolution in China mosques as well as other religious buildings are defaced and practice of the faith repressed

1967 Proclamation of the People's Republic of South Yemen; third Arab–Israeli War results in Jerusalem, the West Bank, Gaza and the Sinai Peninsula coming under Israeli control; mosques and churches are closed in Albania as all forms of public worship are banned by the Communist Party

1969 Colonel Muammar al-Qaddafi leads a coup in Libya, ending the monarchy of King Idris

1971 Pakistan and India clash again as civil war between West and East Pakistan breaks out, leading to the eventual secession of East Pakistan as Bangladesh

1973 Morocco adopts constitution

1973 King Zahir Shah of Afghanistan is overthrown; fourth Arab–Israeli War; Israel continues to occupy the Sinai, the Golan Heights and the West Bank

1974 Turkish intervention in Cyprus leads to the emergence of an autonomous Turkish-Cypriot zone

1975 Civil war begins in Lebanon; death of Elijah Muhammad; Warith al-Din Muhammad II becomes leader of the Nation of Islam; Turkish Republic of Northern Cyprus is declared; Indonesia invades East Timor

1976 Professor Muhammad Yunus establishes the Grameen Bank to provide loans for the rural poor in Bangladesh

1977 Establishment of the Aga Khan Award for Architecture

1978 Disappearance of Imam Musa Sadr, religious leader of Lebanese Shiites and founder of Amal

1979 Iranian revolution deposes Shah Muhammad Reza Pahlavi; proclamation of the Muslim Republic of Iran; Soviet invasion of Afghanistan, following which a Muslim resistance movement, the *mujahidin*, is organized and thousands of Afghanis flee to Pakistan as refugees; the Grand Mosque of Mecca is captured by Saudi dissidents and held for two weeks until their capture and execution

1980–1988 Iran–Iraq War

1981 Assassination of Egyptian President Anwar Sadat

1982 In China a climate of religious tolerance returns and many mosques and other places of worship are reopened; Israel invades Lebanon

1987 Muslim Brotherhood in Egypt forms a coalition known as the Muslim Alliance that wins several seats in parliament; military coup deposes Bourguiba in Tunisia; the Intifada movement begins among Palestinians

1988 Publication of Salman Rushdie's *The Satanic Verses* leads to violent protests;

	Egyptian writer Naguib Mahfouz wins Nobel Prize for Literature; Benazir Bhutto becomes the first woman prime minister of Pakistan but is deposed less than two years later
1989	Soviet troop withdrawal from Afghanistan begins, followed by a struggle for power among various groups; a *fatwa* is issued by the Ayatollah Khomeini denouncing Salman Rushdie as an apostate; death of Ayatollah Khomeini; military coup in Sudan; Algerian Muslim movement Front Islamique du Salut (FIS – the Muslim Salvation Front) is legalized
1990–1991	Forces commanded by Saddam Hussein, Ba'athist leader of Iraq, invade Kuwait
1991	Civil war begins in Somalia; Iraqis are forced out of Kuwait by a Muslim–Western coalition; the collapse of communist power and the dismantling of the Soviet Union leads to the emergence of independent Muslim republics in Central Asia which, however, remain linked to the newly established Commonwealth of Independent States; Somalia and Sudan face severe drought and famine
1992	Continuing state of tension in Iraq between the government, the Shia community and the Kurdish population; Kurds revolt in Iraq; constitutional government is suspended in Algeria because of the growing power of Muslim parties, which are all banned; persecuted Muslims in Burma flee to Bangladesh; Bosnia-Herzegovina, a newly created state in former Yugoslavia, declares its independence; Serbian forces surround and attack the capital Sarajevo and initiate a campaign of 'ethnic cleansing' against Bosnian Muslims and Croats; the Aga Khan Award for Architecture ceremony is held in Samarkand, Uzbekistan
1993	Arab–Israeli peace talks begin; restoration work on the Dome of the Rock in Jerusalem begins
1994	Agreement to begin peace process between Israel and the Palestinian Authority; the first annual Festival of Sacred Music is held in Fez, Morocco
1995	Israeli prime minister Yitzhak Rabin is assassinated by a Jewish fundamentalist; massacre in Srebrenica, where an estimated 8,000 Bosnian Muslims are killed
1996	Establishment of Taliban in Afghanistan, which imposes a harsh and puritanical regime
1997	Mohammad Khatami becomes elected president of Iran; terror attacks on foreigners in Egypt; death of renowned musician and Qawwali singer Nusrat Fateh Ali Khan
1998	The Taliban pursue an expansionist policy, persecuting and killing many Shia; General Suharto resigns as president of Indonesia after thirty years in power
1999	King Hussein of Jordan dies and is succeeded by his son Abdullah; Morocco's King Hassan II dies and is succeeded by his son Mohammed VI; Abdelaziz Bouteflika elected president in Algeria, vowing to bring about reconciliation; NATO bombing halts Serbian policy of ethnic cleansing in Kosovo
2000	President Hafez Assad of Syria dies and is succeeded by his son Bashar; Second Intifada starts after breakdown of Israeli–Palestinian negotiations; Russian troops occupy Grozny, capital of Chechnya, and put down resistance; in Pakistan General Parvez Musharraf establishes military rule
2001	The Taliban government orders the destruction of the centuries-old Buddha

statues in Bamiyan; 9/11 attacks in the USA by al-Qaeda terrorists, whose leader, Osama bin Laden, declares global *jihad* from his base in Afghanistan; Afghanistan is invaded by American and international forces, who oust the Taliban and install Hamid Karzai as president

2002   al-Qaeda suicide bombings in Kuta, Bali, kill 202 people

2003   Invasion of Iraq by US-led coalition; Saddam Hussein deposed and the rule of the Ba'ath Party ended; Iranian author Shirin Ebadi awarded Nobel Prize for Peace for promotion of democracy and human rights; Prince Sadruddin Aga Khan, United Nations High Commissioner for Refugees 1965–1977, dies in Geneva

2004   Elections in Afghanistan lead to victory for Hamid Karzai; terrorist attack on Karbala during holy festival; Yasser Arafat dies in France and is replaced as chairman of PLO by Mahmud Abbas; a peace treaty is signed to bring to an end decades of conflict and turmoil in the Sudan, but rebellion and violence continue in Darfur province; continuing warfare among various groups in Somalia exacerbates the country's precarious political state and the devastating effects of famine; Indian Ocean tsunami hits several countries, including India, Indonesia, Malaysia, the Maldives and Sri Lanka, killing over 200,000 people and devastating coastal regions

2005   At the International Muslim Conference in Amman, Jordan, more than 170 religious leaders and scholars from forty countries gather and endorse the final declaration that whoever is an adherent of one of the eight schools of Muslim jurisprudence is a Muslim who cannot be declared or treated as an apostate or infidel, and whose life, honour and property are inviolable; in Palestine the first democratic elections are won by Mahmud Abbas, which leads to reopening of peace negotiations with Israel; Rafik Hariri, former Lebanese prime minister, killed by car bomb, leading eventually to the resignation of Syria-installed government; conservative Mahmoud Ahmadinejad wins presidential elections in Iran, whose nuclear aspirations become a cause for concern in the West; King Fahd of Saudi Arabia dies and is replaced by his half-brother, Prince Abdullah; Israel withdraws from the West Bank and Gaza Strip; a devastating earthquake kills more than 70,000 people in the mountainous region of Kashmir in Pakistan

2006   Hundreds of Muslim pilgrims killed in a crush during *Hajj*; Hamas wins the first multi-party elections in Palestine and Ismail Haniya becomes new prime minister; Sunni terrorists in Iraq blow up the golden dome of Samarra's al-Askariyya Shrine; the situation in Iraq continues to deteriorate as sectarian conflict and suicide bombings intensify; Saddam Hussein is tried for murder and executed

The bibliography is intended primarily for the general reader interested in Islam, but should also be of use to those who wish to focus on more specialized areas and topics.

A bibliography of this nature is by definition selective. It therefore aims to list significant and representative titles and to be as comprehensive and balanced as possible in its scope.

In compiling this bibliography a historical approach has been taken and the works are arranged under broad subject headings to facilitate access across areas of Muslim history and civilization. Some titles may be included in more than one category. While an alphabetical arrangement may have been more useful to some, the present arrangement has been chosen to highlight topics that illustrate the broad range of developments across time and space.

The titles are divided and subdivided as follows:

Reference: handbooks, dictionaries, encyclopaedias

Adamec, Ludwig W. *Historical Dictionary of Islam*. Historical Dictionaries of Religions, Philosophies, and Movements, 37. Lanham, MD: Scarecrow Press, 2001

Adamson, Peter and Richard C. Taylor. *Cambridge Companion to Arabic Philosophy*. Cambridge: Cambridge University Press, 2005

Bakhtiar, Laleh, ed. and trans. *Encyclopedia of Islamic Law: A Compendium of the Views of the Major Schools*. Chicago, IL: ABC International Group, 1996

Bosworth, Clifford Edmund. *The Islamic Dynasties: A Chronological and Genealogical Handbook*. Islamic Surveys, 5. Edinburgh: Edinburgh University Press, 1967

——. *The New Islamic Dynasties: A Chronological and Genealogical Manual*. Edinburgh: Edinburgh University Press, 1996

E. J. Brill's First Encyclopaedia of Islam, 1913–1936. 9 vols. Ed. T. Houtsma et al. Leiden: E. J. Brill, 1987. Reprint of the *Encyclopaedia of Islam*, 1st edn., originally published 1913–1938

Coughlin, Kathryn M., ed. *Muslim Cultures Today: A Reference Guide*. Westport, CT: Greenwood Press, 2006

Encyclopaedia Iranica. Ed. Ehsan Yarshater. London: Routledge & Kegan Paul, 1982. Ongoing multi-volume work, now published under the patronage of the International Union of Academies, New York: Encyclopaedia Iranica Foundation

The Encyclopaedia of Islam. New edn. 12 vols. Prepared by a number of leading orientalists. Ed. C. E. Bosworth et al. Leiden: E. J. Brill, 1960–2002. Also available in online format from E. J. Brill

The Encyclopaedia of Islam. New edn. Supplement 1980. Prepared by a number of leading orientalists. Ed. C. E. Bosworth. Leiden: E. J. Brill, 1980–2004

Encyclopaedia of Islam Three. Ed. Marc Gaborieau et al. Leiden: E. J. Brill, 2007. Also available in online format from E. J. Brill

Esposito, John L., ed. *The Islamic World: Past and Present*. Abdulaziz Sachedina, Tamara Sonn and John O. Voll, associate editors. 3 vols. New York: Oxford University Press, 2004

——. *The Oxford Dictionary of Islam*. Oxford: Oxford University Press, 2003

——. *The Oxford Encyclopaedia of the Modern Islamic World*. 4 vols. New York: Oxford University Press, 1995

al-Faruqi, Ismail R. and Lois Lamya al-Faruqi. *The Cultural Atlas of Islam*. New York: Macmillan, 1986

Federspiel, Howard M. *A Dictionary of Indonesian Islam*. Monographs in International Studies Southeast Asia Series, 94. Athens, OH: Center for International Studies, Ohio University, 1995

Ferguson, John. *An Illustrated Encyclopedia of Mysticism and the Mystery Religions*. New York: Seabury Press, 1977

Freeman-Grenville, G. S. P. *The Islamic and Christian Calendars: AD 622–2222 (AH 1–1650): A Complete Guide for Converting Christian and Islamic Dates and Dates of Festivals*. Revised edn. of *Muslim and Christian Calendars*. Reading, UK: Garnet, 1995

Freeman-Grenville, G. S. P. and Stuart Christopher Munro-Hay. *Historical Atlas of Islam*. Revised and expanded edn. New York: Continuum International, 2002

Geddes, Charles L. *Guide to Reference Books for Islamic Studies*. Bibliographic Series, American Institute of Islamic Studies, 9. Denver, CO: American Institute of Islamic Studies, 1985

Glasse, Cyril. *Concise Encyclopaedia of Islam*. Revised edn. London: Stacey International, 2001

Hillauer, Rebecca. _Encyclopedia of Arab Women Filmmakers_. Trans. Allison Brown, Deborah Cohen and Nancy Joyce. Cairo: American University in Cairo Press, 2005

Index Islamicus 1665–1905: A Bibliography of Articles on Islamic Subjects in Periodicals and other Collective Publications. Comp. W. H. Behn. Millersville, PA: Adiyok, 1989

Index Islamicus Supplement 1665–1980, vol. 2, part 1: _A Bibliography of Articles on Islamic Subjects in Periodicals and other Collective Publications_. Comp. W. H. Behn. Millersville, PA: Adiyok, 1995

Index Islamicus 1605 [and ongoing]: _A Catalogue of Articles on Islamic Subjects in Periodicals and Other Collective Publications_. Cambridge: W. Heffer, 1958–. Subsequently published by Mansell, 1981–, and Bowker, 1992–

Index Islamicus 1906. CD-Rom version. East Grinstead: Bowker-Saur, 1998. Now published by E. J. Brill. Also available online from E. J. Brill

Index Islamicus 2001 [and ongoing]: _New Books, Articles and Reviews on Islam and the Muslim World_. Comp. G. J. Roper and C. H. Bleany. Leiden: E. J. Brill, 2001–

Jenkins, Everett, Jr. _The Muslim Diaspora: A Comprehensive Reference to the Spread of Islam in Asia, Africa, Europe and the Americas_, vol. 1. Jefferson, NC: McFarland & Co., 1999

Joseph, Suad et al., eds. _Encyclopedia of Women and Islamic Cultures_, 4 vols. Leiden: E. J. Brill, 2003–2007

Kennedy, Hugh, ed. _An Historical Atlas of Islam_. 2nd revised edn. Leiden: E. J. Brill, 2002

Khan, Masood Ali and S. Ram, eds. _Encyclopaedia of Sufism_. 12 vols. New Delhi: Anmol Publications, 2003

Khan, Muhammad Akram. _Islamic Economics and Finance: A Glossary_. 2nd edn. Routledge International Studies in Money and Banking, 23. New York: Routledge, 2003

Leaman, Oliver, ed. _Companion Encyclopaedia of Middle Eastern and North African Film_. London: Routledge, 2001

——. _The Quran: An Encyclopedia_. London: Routledge, 2006

Martin, Richard C., ed. _Encyclopedia of Islam and the Muslim World_. 2 vols. New York: Macmillan Reference USA, 2004

Mattar, Phillip, ed. _Encyclopedia of the Modern Middle East and North Africa_. 2nd edn. 4 vols. Detroit: Thompson Gale, 2004

McAuliffe, Jane Dammen, ed. _The Cambridge Companion to the Quran_. Cambridge: Cambridge University Press, 2006

——. _Encyclopaedia of the Quran_. 6 vols. Leiden: E. J. Brill, 2001–2006. Also available on CD-Rom

Meisami, Julie Scott and Paul Starkey, eds. _Encyclopedia of Arabic Literature_. 2 vols. London: Routledge, 1998

Meri, Joseph W., ed. _Medieval Islamic Civilization: An Encyclopedia_. 2 vols. New York: Routledge, 2006

Mir, Mustansir. _Dictionary of Quranic Terms and Concepts_. Garland Reference Library of the Humanities, 693. New York: Garland, 1987

Nanji, Azim A., ed. _The Muslim Almanac: A Reference Work on the History, Faith, Culture, and Peoples of Islam_. Detroit: Gale Research, 1996

Netton, Ian Richard. _A Popular Dictionary of Islam_. London: Curzon Press, 1992

Newby, Gordon D. _A Concise Encyclopedia of Islam_. Oxford: Oneworld, 2002

Nicolle, David. _Historical Atlas of the Islamic World_. London: Mercury Books, 2004

Nurbakhsh, Javad. _Sufi Symbolism: The Nurbakhsh Encyclopaedia of Sufi Terminology: Farhang-e Nurbakhsh_. Trans. Leonard Lewisohn and Terry Graham. 15 vols. London: Khaniqahi-Nimatullahi Publications, 1984

Petersen, Andrew. *Dictionary of Islamic Architecture*. London: Routledge, 1996

Qazi, M. A., comp. *Concise Dictionary of Islamic Terms*. Revised and enlarged by Mohammed Said el-Dabbas. Lahore: Kazi Publications, 1979

Rahman, Afzalur. *Muhammad: Encyclopaedia of Seerah*. 5 vols. London: Muslim Schools Trust, 1981–1987

Rahman, H. U. *A Chronology of Islamic History, 570–1000 CE*. Revised edn. London: Ta-Ha Publishers, 1995

Rippin, Andrew, ed. *The Blackwell Companion to the Quran*. Malden, MA: Blackwell, 2006

Robinson, Francis. *Atlas of the Islamic World since 1500*. Oxford: Phaidon Press, 1982

Ronart, Stephan, and Nandy Ronart. *Concise Encyclopaedia of Arabic Civilization*, vol. 1: *The Arab East*; vol. 2: *The Arab West*. Amsterdam: Djanbatan, 1959–1966

Roolvink, Roelof, comp. *Historical Atlas of the Muslim Peoples*. Amsterdam: Djambatan, 1957

Ruthven, Malise with Azim Nanji. *Historical Atlas of the Islamic World*. Oxford: Oxford University Press, 2004. Published in the US as *Historical Atlas of Islam* by Harvard University Press

Shaikh, Farzana, ed. *Islam and Islamic Groups: A Worldwide Reference Guide*. Harlow: Longman, 1992

Shorter Encyclopaedia of Islam. Edited on behalf of the Royal Netherlands Academy by H. A. R. Gibb and J. H. Kramer and published in 1953. Repr. Leiden: E. J. Brill, 1974

Simon, Reeva S., Phillip Mattar and Richard W. Bulliet, eds. *The Encyclopedia of the Modern Middle East*. 4 vols. New York: Macmillan Reference USA, 1996

Singh, N. K. and A. M. Khan, eds. *Encyclopaedia of the Muslims: Tribes, Castes and Communities*. 4 vols. New Delhi: Global Vision, 2001

Van Donzel, E., comp. *Islamic Desk Reference*. Compiled from *The Encyclopaedia of Islam*. Leiden: E. J. Brill, 1994

Weekes, Richard V., ed. *Muslim Peoples: A World Ethnographic Survey*. 2 vols. 2nd edn. London: Aldwych Press, 1984

History

General surveys, history and civilization

Abun-Nasr, Jamil M. *A History of the Maghrib in the Islamic Period*. Cambridge: Cambridge University Press, 1987

Aghaie, Kamran Scot. *The Martyrs of Karbala: Shii Symbols and Ritual in Modern Iran*. Seattle: University of Washington Press, 2004

Ahmed, Akbar S. *Discovering Islam: Making Sense of Muslim History and Society*. Revised edn. with a new foreword by Lawrence Rosen. London: Routledge, 2002

——. *Islam Today: A Short Introduction to the Muslim World*. London: I. B. Tauris, 1999

——. *Living Islam: From Samarkand to Stornoway*. London: BBC Books, 1993

Ali, Syed Ameer. *The Spirit of Islam: History of the Evolution and Ideals of Islam, with a Life of the Prophet*. London: Methuen and Co., 1965. First published by Christophers, London, 1922

Arberry, A. J. *Aspects of Islamic Civilization as Depicted in the Original Texts*. London: Allen & Unwin, 1964

Armstrong, Karen. *Islam: A Short History*. London: Weidenfeld & Nicolson, 2000

Aslan, Reza. *No God but God: The Origins, Evolution, and Future of Islam*. London: William Heinemann, 2005

Auchterlonie, Paul, ed. *Introductory Guide to Middle Eastern and Islamic Bibliography*. Middle East Libraries Research Guides, 5. Oxford: Middle East Libraries Committee, 1990

Ayoub, Mahmoud. *The Crisis of Muslim History: Religion and Politics in Early Islam*. Oxford: Oneworld, 2003

Bannerman, Patrick. *Islam in Perspective: An Introduction to Islamic Society, Politics and Law*. London: Routledge for the Royal Institute of International Affairs, 1988

Bartley, Paula. *Medieval Islam*. London: Hodder & Stoughton, 1993

Berkey, Jonathan P. *The Formation of Islam: Religion and Society in the Near East, 600–1800*. Themes in Islamic History, 2. Cambridge: Cambridge University Press, 2003

Bernards, Monique and John Nawas, eds. *Patronate and Patronage in Early and Classical Islam*. Islamic History and Civilization, Studies and Texts, vol. 61. Leiden: E. J. Brill, 2005

Black, Antony. *The History of Islamic Political Thought: From the Prophet to the Present*. Edinburgh: Edinburgh University Press, 2001

Blichfeldt, Jan-Olaf. *Early Mahdism: Politics and Religion in the Formative Period of Islam*. Leiden: E. J. Brill, 1985

Bloom, Jonathan and Sheila Blair. *Islam: A Thousand Years of Faith and Power*. New York: TV Books, 2000

Bogle, Emory C. *Islam: Origin and Belief*. Austin: University of Texas Press, 1998

Bosworth, Clifford Edmund. *The Arabs, Byzantium and Iran: Studies in Early Islamic History and Culture*. Variorum Collected Studies Series, CS529. Brookfield, VT: Variorum, 1996

Bosworth, C. Edmund, ed. *The Turks in the Early Islamic World*. Formation of the Classical Islamic World, 9. Aldershot: Ashgate, 2007

Brown, Daniel. *A New Introduction to Islam*. Malden, MA: Blackwell, 2004

Bulliet, Richard W. *Conversion to Islam in the Medieval Period: An Essay in Quantitative History*. Cambridge, MA: Harvard University Press, 1979

——. *Islam: The View from the Edge*. New York: Columbia University Press, 1994

Cole, Juan R. I., ed. *Comparing Muslim Societies: Knowledge and the State in a World Civilization*. Comparative Studies in Society and History Book Series. Ann Arbor, MI: University of Michigan Press, 1992

Collins, Roger. *The Arab Conquest of Spain, 710–797*. A History of Spain. Oxford: Blackwell, 1989

Cragg, Kenneth. *The House of Islam*. 2nd edn. Religious Life of Man. Belmont, CA: Dickenson Publishing, 1975

Crone, Patricia. *Meccan Trade and the Rise of Islam*. Oxford: Blackwell, 1987

——. *Medieval Islamic Political Thought*. Edinburgh: Edinburgh University Press, 2004

Crone, Patricia and Michael Cook. *Hagarism: The Making of the Islamic World*. Cambridge: Cambridge University Press, 1977

Crone, Patricia and Martin Hinds. *God's Caliph: Religious Authority in the First Centuries of Islam*. Cambridge: Cambridge University Press, 1986

Dabashi, Hamid. *Authority in Islam: From the Rise of Muhammad to the Establishment of the Ummayads*. New Brunswick, NJ: Transaction Publishers, 1989

Daftary, Farhad. *The Assassin Legends: Myths of the Ismailis*. London: I. B. Tauris, 1994

——. *Ismaili Literature: A Bibliography of Sources and Studies*. London: I. B. Tauris/Institute of Ismaili Studies, 2004

——. *Ismailis in Medieval Muslim Societies*. Ismaili Heritage Series, 12. London: I. B. Tauris/Institute of Ismaili Studies, 2005

——. *The Ismailis: Their History and Doctrines*, 2nd edn. Cambridge: Cambridge University Press, 2007

——. *A Short History of the Ismailis: Traditions of a Muslim Community*. Islamic Surveys. Edinburgh: Edinburgh University Press, 1998

Daftary, Farhad, ed. *Medieval Ismaili History and Thought*. Cambridge: Cambridge University Press, 1996

Daniel, Norman. *Islam and the West: The Making of an Image*. Edinburgh: University of Edinburgh Press, 1960. Repr. 1966

Denny, Frederick Mathewson. *An Introduction to Islam*. 2nd edn. New York: Macmillan, 1994

Donner, Fred M. *Narratives of Islamic Origins: The Beginnings of Islamic Historical Writing*. Studies in Late Antiquity and Early Islam, 14. Princeton, NJ: Darwin Press, 1998

Donner, Fred McGraw. *The Early Islamic Conquests*. Princeton, NJ: Princeton University Press, 1981

Dunn, Ross E. *The Adventures of Ibn Battuta: A Muslim Traveler of the 14th Century*. Revised edn. with a new preface. Berkeley: University of California Press, 2005

Ede, David et al., eds. *Guide to Islam*. Boston: G. K. Hall, 1983

Endress, Gerhard. *Islam: An Historical Introduction*. 2nd edn. Trans. Carole Hillenbrand. New Edinburgh Islamic Surveys. Edinburgh: Edinburgh University Press, 2002. 1st edition published under the title: An Introduction to Islam, 1988

Engineer, Asghar Ali. *The Origin and Development of Islam: An Essay on Its Socio-Economic Growth*. Bombay: Orient Longman, 1980

Esposito, John L. *Islam: The Straight Path*. 3rd edn. New York: Oxford University Press, 1998. Revised and updated with a new epilogue, 2005

Esposito, John L., ed. *Oxford History of Islam*. Oxford: Oxford University Press, 1999

Ezzati, Abdul-Fazl. *Introduction to the History and Spread of Islam*. 2nd revised edn. London: News and Media Books, 1978

al-Faruqi, Ismail R. and Lois Lamya al-Faruqi. *The Cultural Atlas of Islam*. New York: Macmillan, 1986

Freeman-Grenville, G. S. P. and Stuart Christopher Munro-Hay. *Islam: An Illustrated History*. New York: Continuum, 2006

Gabrieli, Francesco. *Muhammad and the Conquest of Islam*. Trans. Virginia Luling and Rosamund Linell. London: Weidenfeld & Nicolson, 1968

Ghazanfar, S. M. *Islamic Civilization: History Contributions, and Influence: A Compendium of Literature*. Lanham, MD: Scarecrow Press, 2006

Gibb, H. A. R. *Islam: A Historical Survey*. 2nd edn. Oxford: Oxford University Press, 1962

——. *Studies on the Civilization of Islam*. Ed. Stanford J. Shaw and William P. Polk. London: Routledge & Kegan Paul, 1962

Goitien, S. D. *Jews and Arabs: Their Contact through the Ages*. Revised edn. New York: Schocken, 1964

——. *A Mediterranean Society: The Jewish Communities of the Arab World as Portrayed in the Documents of the Cairo Geniza*. 5 vols. Berkeley: University of California Press, 1967

——. *Studies in Islamic History and Institutions*. Leiden: E. J. Brill, 1966

Gordon, Matthew S. *The Rise of Islam*. Greenwood Guides to Historic Events in the Medieval World. Westport, CT: Greenwood Press, 2005

Grimwood-Jones, Diana, ed. *Middle East and Islam: A Bibliographical Introduction*. Revised edn. Bibliotheca Asiatica, 15. Zug, Switzerland: Inter-Documentation Co., 1979

Grimwood-Jones, Diana, Derek Hopwood and J. D. Pearson, eds. *Arab Islamic Bibliography*. Based on Giuseppe Gabrieli's *Manuale di Bibliografia Musulmana*. Hassocks, UK: Harvester Press, 1977

Guillaume, Alfred. _Islam_. 2nd edn. Harmondsworth: Penguin, 1956

Halm, Heinz. _The Arabs: A Short History_. Trans. Allison Brown and Thomas Lampert. Princeton, NJ: Markus Wiener, 2007

———. _The Empire of the Mahdi: The Rise of the Fatimids_. Trans. Michael Bonner. Leiden: E. J. Brill, 1996

———. _Shiism_. Trans. J. Watson and Marian Hill. 2nd edn. New Edinburgh Islamic Surveys. Edinburgh: Edinburgh University Press, 2004

Hawting, Gerald R. _The First Dynasty of Islam: The Umayyad Caliphate A.D. 661–750_. 2nd edn. London: Routledge, 2000

———. _The Idea of Idolatry and the Emergence of Islam_. Cambridge Studies in Islamic Civilization. Cambridge: Cambridge University Press, 1999

Heyneman, Stephen P. _Islam and Social Policy_. Nashville, TN: Vanderbilt University Press, 2004

el-Hibri, Tayeb. _Reinterpreting Islamic Historiography: Harun al-Rashid and the Narrative of the Abbasid Caliphate_. Cambridge Studies in Islamic Civilization. Cambridge: Cambridge University Press, 1999

Hillenbrand, Carole. _The Crusades: Islamic Perspectives_. Edinburgh: Edinburgh University Press, 1999

Hinds, Martin. _Studies in Early Islamic History_. Ed. Jere Bacharach, Lawrence I. Conrad, and Patricia Crone. Studies in Late Antiquity and Early Islam, 4. Princeton, NJ: Darwin Press, 1996

Hitti, Philip K. _History of the Arabs from the Earliest Times to the Present_. Rev. 10th edn. London: Macmillan, 1970. Repr. with a new preface by Walid Khalidi Macmillan, 2002

Hodgson, Marshall G. S. _The Order of Assassins: The Struggle of the Early Nizari Ismailis against the Islamic World_. s-Gravenhage: Mouton, 1955. Repr. AMS Press, 1980

———. _The Venture of Islam: Conscience and History in World Civilization_. 3 vols. Chicago: University of Chicago Press, 1974

Holt, P. M., Anne K. S. Lambton and Bernard Lewis, eds. _The Cambridge History of Islam_. 2 vols. Cambridge: Cambridge University Press, 1970

Horrie, Chris and Peter Chippindale. _What is Islam?_ London: W. H. Allen, 1990

Hourani, Albert Habib. _A History of the Arab Peoples_. London: Faber & Faber, 1991

Hourani, George F. _Arab Seafaring in the Indian Ocean in Ancient and Early Medieval Times_. Revised and expanded by John Carswell. Princeton, NJ: Princeton University Press, 1995

Hoyland, Robert, ed. _Muslims and Others in Early Islamic Societies_. Formation of the Classical Islamic World, 18. Aldershot: Ashgate, 2004

Humphreys, R. Stephen. _Islamic History: A Framework for Inquiry_. Revised edn. London: I. B. Tauris, 1991

Hurgronje, C. Snouck. _Islam: Origin, Religious and Political Growth and Its Present State_. New Delhi: Mittal Publications, 1989

Jafri, S. H. M. _The Origins and Early Development of Shia Islam_. London: Longman, 1979

Jeffrey, Arthur, ed. _Islam: Muhammad and His Religion_. Library of Liberal Arts. Indianapolis: Bobbs-Merrill, 1958

Kapstein, N. J. G. _Muhammad's Birthday Festival: Early History in the Central Muslim Lands and Development in the Muslim West until the 10th/16th Century_. Leiden: E. J. Brill, 1993

Kasravi, Ahmad. _On Islam and Shiism_. Costa Mesa, CA: Mazda Publishers, 1990

Kelly, Marjorie, ed. _Islam: The Religious and Political Life of a World Community_. New York: Praeger for the Foreign Policy Association, 1984

Kennedy, Hugh. *The Court of the Caliphs: The Rise and Fall of Islam's Greatest Dynasty.* London: Weidenfeld & Nicolson, 2004
——. *The Prophet and the Age of the Caliphates: The Islamic Near East from the Sixth to the Eleventh Century.* A History of the Near East. London: Longman, 1986
Kister, M. J. *Concepts and Ideas at the Dawn of Islam.* Variorum Collected Studies Series, CS584. Aldershot: Ashgate, 1997
——. *Society and Religion from Jahiliyya to Islam.* Variorum Collected Studies Series, CS327. Brookfield, VT: Variorum, 1990
Kozlowski, Gregory C. *The Concise History of Islam and the Origin of Its Empires.* Acton, MA: Copley, 1991
Kraemer, Joel L. *Humanism in the Renaissance of Islam: The Cultural Revival During the Buyid Age.* Studies in Islamic Culture and History, 7. Leiden: E. J. Brill, 1986
Laiou, Angeliki K. and Roy Parviz Mottahedeh., eds. *The Crusades from the Perspective of Byzantium and the Muslim World.* Washington, DC: Dumbarton Oaks Research Library and Collection, 2001
Lambton, Ann K. S. *State and Government in Medieval Islam: An Introduction to the Study of Islamic Political Theory: The Jurists.* London Oriental Series, 36. Oxford: Oxford University Press, 1981
Lapidus, Ira. M. *A History of Islamic Societies.* 2nd edn. Cambridge: Cambridge University Press, 2002
Lecker, Michael. *The 'Constitution of Medina': Muhammad's First Legal Document.* Studies in Late Antiquity and Early Islam, 23. Princeton, NJ: Darwin Press, 2004
Lewis, Bernard. *Arabs in History.* 4th edn. London: Hutchinson, 1966
——. *Islam in History: Ideas, People and Events in the Middle East.* 2nd edn. Chicago: Open Court, 1993
Lewis, Bernard, ed. and trans. *Islam, from the Prophet Muhammad to the Capture of Constantinople.* 2 vols. Documentary History of Western Civilization. New York: Harper & Row, 1974
Lippman, Thomas W. *Understanding Islam: An Introduction to the Moslem World.* New York: New American Library, 1982
Little, Donald P., ed. *Essays on Islamic Civilization: Presented to Niyazi Berkes.* Leiden: E. J. Brill, 1976
Madelung, Wilferd. *Religious Schools and Sects in Medieval Islam.* Variorum Collected Studies Series, CS213. London: Variorum Reprints, 1985
——. *The Succession to Muhammad: A Study of the Early Caliphate.* Cambridge: Cambridge University Press, 1997
Martin, Richard C. *Islam: A Cultural Perspective.* Englewood Cliffs, NJ: Prentice-Hall, 1982
Mathe, Jean. *The Civilization of Islam.* Trans. David Macrae. Geneva: Editions Minerva, 1980
McNeil, William H. and Marilyn Robinson Waldman, eds. *The Islamic World.* Readings in World History. New York: Oxford University Press, 1973
Momen, Moojan. *An Introduction to Shii Islam: The History and Doctrines of Twelver Shiism.* New Haven: Yale University Press, 1985
Morgan, David. *Medieval Persia, 1040–1797. A History of the Near East.* Harlow: Longman, 1988
Mortimer, Edward. *Faith and Power: The Politics of Islam.* London: Faber & Faber, 1987
Mottahedeh, Roy P. *Loyalty and Leadership in an Early Islamic Society.* Princeton, NJ: Princeton University Press, 1980

Mourad, Suleiman Ali. *Early Islam between Myth and History: Al-Hasan al-Basri (d. 110SH/728CE) and the Formation of His Legacy in Classical Scholarship*. Islamic Philosophy, Theology and Science, Texts and Studies, 62. Leiden: E. J. Brill, 2006

Muir, Sir William. *The Caliphate: Its Rise, Decline and Fall: From Original Sources*. London: Darf, 1984. First published 1891

Nasr, Seyyed Hossein. *The Heart of Islam: Enduring Values for Humanity*. San Francisco: HarperCollins, 2002

——. *Islam: Religion, History and Civilization*. San Francisco: HarperCollins, 2002

Nasr, Seyyed Hossein. Hamid Dabashi and Seyyed Vali Reza Nasr, eds. *Expectation of the Millennium: Shiism in History*. Albany: State University of New York Press, 1999

Newman, Andrew J. *The Formative Period of Twelver Shiism: Hadith as Discourse between Qum and Baghdad*. London: Curzon Press, 2000

Norcliffe, David. *Islam: Faith and Practice*. Brighton: Sussex Academic Press, 1999

Peters, F. E. *A Reader on Classical Islam*. Princeton, NJ: Princeton University Press, 1994

Poonawala, Ismail K. *Biobibliography of Ismaili Literature*. Malibu, CA: Undena, 1977

Rahman, Fazlur. *Islam*. 2nd edn. Chicago: University of Chicago Press, 1979

——. *Islamic Methodology in History*. Karachi: Central Institute of Islamic Research, 1965

Richards, D. S., ed. *Islamic Civilization, 950–1150*. A Colloquium Published under the Auspices of the Near Eastern History Group and the Near Eastern Center, University of Pennsylvania. Papers on Islamic History, 3. London: Cassirer, 1973

Riddell, Peter G. and Peter Cotterell. *Islam in Conflict: Past, Present, and Future*. Leicester: Inter-Varsity Press, 2003. First published in the US as *Islam in Context*

Robinson, Chase F., ed. *Islamic Historiography*. Themes in Islamic History, 1. Cambridge: Cambridge University Press, 2003

Robinson, Francis. *The Cambridge Illustrated History of the Islamic World*. Cambridge: Cambridge University Press, 1996

Robinson, Neal. *Islam: A Concise Introduction*. London: Curzon Press, 1999

Rosenthal, Franz. *A History of Muslim Historiography*. 2nd revised edn. Leiden: E. J. Brill, 1968

Sanders, Paula. *Ritual, Politics, and the City in Fatimid Cairo*. SUNY Series in Medieval Middle East History. Albany: State University of New York Press, 1994

Sardar, Ziauddin. *Muslim Civilization*. 2nd edn. London: Mansell, 1987

Saunders, J. J. *A History of Medieval Islam*. London: Routledge & Kegan Paul, 1965

Savory, R. M., ed. *Introduction to Islamic Civilization*. Cambridge: Cambridge University Press, 1976. Repr. 1979

Schacht, Joseph, ed., with C. E. Bosworth. *The Legacy of Islam*. 2nd edn. Oxford: Clarendon Press, 1974

Schimmel, Annemarie. *Islam: An Introduction*. Albany: State University of New York Press, 1992. Translation of *Der Islam*

Shaban, Mohammad A. *Islamic History: A New Interpretation*. 2 vols. Cambridge: Cambridge University Press, 1971–1976

Sonn, Tamara. *A Brief History of Islam*. Blackwell Brief Histories of Religion. Malden, MA: Blackwell, 2004

Sourdel, Dominique. *Medieval Islam*. Trans. J. Montgomery Watt. London: Routledge & Kegan Paul, 1983. Originally Published by Presses Universitaires de France, 1979

Southern, R. W. *Western Views of Islam in the Middle Ages*. Cambridge, MA: Harvard University Press, 1962

Spuler, Bertold. *The Muslim World: A Historical Survey.* 4 vols. Trans. F. R. C. Bagley. Leiden: E. J. Brill, 1960–1981

Stern, S. M. *History and Culture in the Medieval Muslim World.* Variorum Collected Studies Series, CS200. London: Variorum Reprints, 1984

Tabatabai, Allamah Sayyid Muhammad Husayn. *Shiite Islam.* Trans. and ed. with an introduction and notes by Seyyed Hossein Nasr. Persian Studies Series, 5. London: Allen & Unwin, 1975

Taha, Abdulwahid Dhannun. *The Muslim Conquest and Settlement of North Africa and Spain.* London: Routledge, 1989

Tayob, Abdulkader. *Islam: A Short Introduction.* Oxford: Oneworld, 1999

Tsugitaka, Sato, ed. *Muslim Societies: Historical and Comparative Aspects.* London: RoutledgeCurzon, 2004

Turner, Bryan S., ed. *Islam: Critical Concepts in Sociology.* 4 vols. London: Routledge, 2003

Turner, Colin. *The Muslim World.* Sutton Pocket Histories. Stroud: Alan Sutton, 2000

Udovitch, A. L., ed. *The Islamic Middle East, 700–1900: Studies in Economic and Social History.* Princeton Studies on the Near East. Princeton, NJ: Darwin Press, 1981

Vaziri, Mostafa. *The Emergence of Islam: Prophecy, Imamate and Messianism in Perspective.* New York: Paragon House, 1992

Von Grunebaum, Gustave Edmond. *Classical Islam: A History, 620–1258.* Trans. Katherine Watson. London: Allen & Unwin, 1970

Von Grunebaum, Gustave Edmond, ed. *Unity and Variety in Muslim Civilization.* Chicago: University of Chicago Press, 1955

Waardenburg, Jacques. *Islam: Historical, Social, and Political Perspectives.* Religion and Reason, 40. Berlin: Walter de Gruyter, 2002

Waardenburg, Jacques, ed. *Muslim Perceptions of Other Religions: A Historical Survey.* New York: Oxford University Press, 1999

Waines, David. *An Introduction to Islam.* 2nd edn. Cambridge: Cambridge University Press, 2003

Walker, Benjamin. *Foundations of Islam: The Making of a World Faith.* London: Peter Owen, 1998

Walker, Paul E. *Exploring an Islamic Empire: Fatimid History and Its Sources.* Ismaili Heritage Series, 7. London: I. B. Tauris/Institute of Ismaili Studies, 2002

Watt, William Montgomery. *Early Islam: Collected Articles.* Edinburgh: Edinburgh University Press, 1990

——. *Islam and the Integration of Society.* International Library of Sociology and Social Reconstruction. London: Routledge & Kegan Paul, 1961

——. *Islamic Political Thought: The Basic Concepts.* Edinburgh: Edinburgh University Press, 1968

——. *The Majesty that Was Islam: The Islamic World, 661–1100.* Great Civilization Series. London: Sidgwick & Jackson, 1974

——. *A Short History of Islam.* Oxford: Oneworld, 1996

Williams, John Alden, ed. *Themes of Islamic Civilization.* Berkeley: University of California Press, 1971

——. *The World of Islam.* Austin: University of Texas Press, 1994

Zaman, Muhammad Qasim. *Religion and Politics under the Early Abbasids: The Emergence of the Proto-Sunni Elite.* Islamic History and Civilization, Studies and Texts. Leiden: E. J. Brill, 1997

Modern period and contemporary issues

Abdul Rauf, Imam Feisal. *What's Right with Islam: A New Vision for Muslims and the West.* San Francisco: HarperSanFrancisco, 2004

Abootalebi, Ali Reza. *Islam and Democracy: State–Society Relations in Developing Countries, 1980–1994.* Comparative Studies in Democratization. New York: Garland, 2000

Abou el Fadl, Khaled. *Islam and the Challenge of Democracy.* Ed. Joshua Cohen and Deborah Chasman. Princeton, NJ: Princeton University Press, 2004

Abu-Rabi, Ibrahim M. *Intellectual Origins of Islamic Resurgence in the Modern Arab World.* SUNY Series in Near Eastern Studies. Albany: State University of New York Press, 1996

el-Affendi, Abdelwahab, ed. *Rethinking Islam and Modernity: Essays in Honour of Fathi Osman.* Leicester: Islamic Foundation/Maghreb Centre for Research and Translation, London, 2001

Ahmed, Akbar S. *Discovering Islam: Making Sense of Muslim History and Society.* London: Routledge & Kegan Paul, 1988

——. *Islam Today: A Short Introduction to the Muslim World.* London: I. B. Tauris, 1999

——. *Postmodernism and Islam: Predicament and Promise.* London: Routledge, 1992

Ahmed, Akbar S. and Hastings Donnan, eds. *Islam, Globalization and Postmodernity.* London: Routledge, 1994

Ajami, Fuad. *The Vanished Imam: Musa al Sadr and the Shia of Lebanon.* Ithaca, NY: Cornell University Press, 1986

Akhtar, Shabbir. *A Faith for All Seasons: Islam and Western Modernity.* London: Bellew, 1990

Algar, Hamid. *Religion and State in Iran, 1785–1906: The Role of the Ulama in the Qajar Period.* Berkeley: University of California Press, 1969

Amin, Camron Michael, Benjamin C. Fortna and Elizabeth Frierson. *The Modern Middle East: A Sourcebook for History.* Oxford: Oxford University Press, 2006

Arjomand, Said Amir. *The Turban for the Crown: The Islamic Revolution in Iran.* Studies in Middle Eastern History. New York: Oxford University Press, 1988

Arkoun, Mohammed. *Rethinking Islam Today: Common Questions, Uncommon Answers.* Trans. and ed. Robert D. Lee. Occasional Papers Series. Boulder: Westview Press, 1994

——. *The Unthought in Contemporary Islamic Thought.* London: Saqi Books/Institute of Ismaili Studies, 2002

Ayubi, Nazih N. M. *Political Islam: Religion and Politics in the Arab World.* London: Routledge, 1991

al-Azmeh, Aziz. *Islam and Modernities.* 2nd edn. London: Verso, 1996

Bennett, Clinton. *Muslims and Modernity: An Introduction to the Issues and Debates.* London: Continuum, 2005

Binder, Leonard. *Islamic Liberalism: A Critique of Development Ideologies.* Chicago: University of Chicago Press, 1988

Boullata, Isa J. *Trends and Issues in Contemporary Arab Thought.* Albany: State University of New York Press, 1990

Brown, Daniel W. *Rethinking Tradition in Modern Islamic Thought.* Cambridge Middle East Studies, 5. Cambridge: Cambridge University Press, 1996

Bulliet, Richard W. *Islam: The View from the Edge.* New York: Columbia University Press, 1994

Bunt, Gary R. *Islam in the Digital Age: E-Jihad, Online Fatwas and Cyber Islamic Environments.* Critical Studies on Islam. London: Pluto Press, 2003

——. *Virtually Islamic: Computer-Mediated Communication and Cyber Islamic Environments.* Religion, Culture and Society. Cardiff: University of Wales Press, 2000

Burgat, François. *Face to Face with Political Islam*. London: I. B. Tauris, 2003

Burke, Edmund, III and Ira M. Lapidus, eds. *Islam, Politics and Social Movements*. Comparative Studies on Muslim Societies, 5. Berkeley: University of California Press, 1988

Carré, Olivier, ed., with an introduction by Imtiaz Ahmad. *Islam and the State in the World Today*. Translation of *L'Islam et l'état dans le monde d'aujourd'hui*. London: Sangam, 1988

Choudhury, G. W. *Islam and the Modern Muslim World*. London: Scorpion, 1993

Clarke, Peters B., ed. *New Trends and Developments in the World of Islam*. London: Luzac Oriental, 1998

Cleveland, William L. *A History of the Modern Middle East*. 2nd edn. Boulder: Westview Press, 2000

Cohn-Sherbok, Dan, ed. *Islam in a World of Diverse Faiths*. Library of Philosophy and Religion. Basingstoke: Macmillan, 1991

Cole, Juan R. I. and Nikki R. Keddie, eds. *Shiism and Social Protest*. New Haven: Yale University Press, 1986

Cooke, Miriam and Bruce B. Lawrence, eds. *Muslim Networks: From Hajj to Hip Hop*. Islamic Civilization and Muslim Networks. Chapel Hill: University of North Carolina Press, 2005

Cooper, John, Ronald L. Nettler and Mohamed Mahmoud, eds. *Islam and Modernity: Muslim Intellectuals Respond*. London: I. B. Tauris, 1998

Cornell, Vincent J., ed. *Voices of Islam*. 5 vols. Praeger Perspectives. Westport, CT: Praeger, 2007

Cragg, Kenneth. *The Call of the Minaret*. 3rd edn. Oxford: Oneworld, 2000

——. *Counsels in Contemporary Islam*. Islamic Surveys, 3. Edinburgh: Edinburgh University Press, 1965

Crone, Patricia. *God's Rule: Government and Islam*. New York: Columbia University Press, 2004

Davidson, Lawrence. *Islamic Fundamentalism*. Greenwood Press Guides to Historic Events of the Twentieth Century. Westport, CT: Greenwood Press, 1998

Demant, Peter Robert, with a foreword by Asghar Ali Engineer. *Islam vs. Islamism: The Dilemma of the Muslim World*. Westport, CT: Praeger, 2006

Dessouki, Ali E. Hillal. *Islamic Resurgence in the Arab World*. New York: Praeger, 1982

Donohue, John J. and John L. Esposito, eds. *Islam in Transition: Muslim Perspectives*. New York: Oxford University Press, 1982

Eickelman, Dale F. and Jon W. Anderson, eds. *New Media in the Muslim World: The Emerging Public Sphere*. Indiana Series in Middle East Studies. Bloomington: Indiana University Press, 1999

Eickelman, Dale F. and James Piscatori. *Muslim Politics*. 2nd edn. Princeton Studies in Muslim Politics. Princeton, NJ: Princeton University Press, 2004

Enayat, Hamid. *Modern Islamic Political Thought: The Response of the Shii and Sunni Muslims to the Twentieth Century*. London: Macmillan, 1982

Ernst, Carl W. and Bruce B. Lawrence, eds. *Following Muhammad: Rethinking Islam in the Contemporary World*. Islamic Civilization and Muslim Networks. Chapel Hill: University of North Carolina Press, 2003

Esack, Farid. *On Being a Muslim: Finding a Religious Path in the World Today*. Oxford: Oneworld, 1999

Esposito, John L. *The Islamic Threat: Myth or Reality?* New York: Oxford University Press, 1995

Esposito, John L., ed. *Islam and Development: Religion and Sociopolitical Change*. Contemporary Issues in the Middle East. Syracuse, NY: Syracuse University Press, 1980
———. *Islam and Politics*. 4th edn. Contemporary issues in the Middle East. Syracuse, NY: Syracuse University Press, 1998
———. *Political Islam: Revolution, Radicalism, or Reform?* Boulder: Lynne Rienner, 1997
———. *Voices of Resurgent Islam*. New York: Oxford University Press, 1983
Esposito, John L. and François Burgat, eds. *Modernizing Islam: Religion in the Public Sphere in Europe and the Middle East*. London: C. Hurst & Co., 2003
Esposito, John and John O. Voll. *Islam and Democracy*. New York: Oxford University Press, 1996
Faksh, Mahmud A. *The Future of Islam in the Middle East: Fundamentalism in Egypt, Algeria and Saudi Arabia*. Westport, CT: Praeger, 1997
Fischer, Michael M. J. *Iran: From Religious Dispute to Revolution*. Harvard Studies in Cultural Anthropology, 3. Cambridge, MA: Harvard University Press, 1980
Fischer, Michael M. J. and Mehdi Abedi. *Debating Muslims: Cultural Dialogues in Postmodernity and Tradition*. New Directions in Anthropological Writing. Madison: University of Wisconsin Press, 1990
Gibb, H. A. R. *Modern Trends in Islam*. Haskell Lecture in Comparative Religion. Beirut: Librairie du Liban, 1947
Haddad, Yvonne Yazbeck. *Contemporary Islam and the Challenge of History*. Albany: State University of New York Press, 1982
Haddad, Yvonne Yazbeck and John L. Esposito, eds., with Elizabeth Hiel and Hibba Abugideiri. *The Islamic Revival since 1988: A Critical Survey and Bibliography*. Bibliographies and Indexes in Religious Studies, 45. Westport, CT: Greenwood Press, 1997
Haddad, Yvonne Yazbeck, Byron Haines and Ellison Findly, eds. *The Islamic Impact*. Syracuse, NY: Syracuse University Press, 1984
Hafez, Kai, ed., with a foreword by Mohammed Arkoun and Udo Steinbach. *The Islamic World and the West: An Introduction to Political Cultures and International Relations*. Trans. Mary Ann Kenny. Social, Economic and Political Studies of the Middle East and Asia, 71. Leiden: E. J. Brill, 2000
Halliday, Fred. *Islam and the Myth of Confrontation: Religion and Politics in the Middle East*. New edn. London: I. B. Tauris, 2003
Harik, Judith Palmer. *Hezbollah: The Changing Face of Terrorism*. London: I. B. Tauris, 2004
Hefner, Robert W., ed. *Remaking Muslim Politics: Pluralism, Contestation, Democratization*. Princeton Studies in Muslim Politics. Princeton, NJ: Princeton University Press, 2005
Hiskett, M. *Some to Mecca Turn to Pray: Islamic Values and the Modern World*. St Albans: Claridge Press, 1993
Hourani, Albert, Philip S. Khoury and Mary C. Wilson, eds. *The Modern Middle East: A Reader*. London: I. B. Tauris, 1993
Hunter, Shireen. *The Politics of Islamic Revivalism: Diversity and Unity*. Indiana Series in Arab and Islamic Studies. Bloomington: Indiana University Press for the Center for Strategic and International Studies, Washington, DC, 1988
Hunter, Shireen, with a foreword by Marc Gopin. *The Future of Islam and the West: Clash of Civilization or Peaceful Coexistence?* Westport, CT: Praeger, 1998
Hunter, Shireen T. and Huma Malik, eds., with a foreword by Ahmedou Ould-Abdallah. *Modernization, Democracy and Islam*. Westport, CT: Praeger, 2005. Published in cooperation with the Center for Strategic and International Studies, Washington, DC
Islam: Enduring Myths and Changing Realities. Special edition of *Annals of the American*

Academy of Political and Social Science, vol. 588 (July 2003), ed. Aslam Syed. Thousand Oaks, CA: Sage Publications, 2003

Ismael, Tareq Y. and Jacqueline S. Ismael, with contributions from Kamel S. Abu Jaber et al. *Politics and Government in the Middle East and North Africa*. Miami: Florida International University Press, 1991

Ismail, Salwa. *Rethinking Islamist Politics: Culture, the State and Islamism*. London: I. B. Tauris, 2003

Karim, Karim H. *Islamic Peril: Media and Global Violence*. Revised edn. Montreal: Black Rose Books, 2003

Kedourie, Elie. *Islam in the Modern World and other Studies*. London: Mansell, 1980

Kettani, M. A. *Muslim Minorities in the World Today*. Institute of Muslim Minority Affairs, Monograph Series, 2. London: Mansell, 1986

Khalid, Fazlun M., ed., with Joanne O'Brien. *Islam and Ecology*. London: Cassell, 1992

Khan, M. A. Muqtedar, ed. *Islamic Democratic Discourse: Theory and Philosophical Perspectives*. Global Encounters: Studies in Comparative Political Theory. Lanham, MD: Lexington Books, 2006

Khatami, Mohammed. *Hope and Challenge: The Iranian President Speaks*. Trans. Alidad Mafinezam. Binghamton, NY: Institute of Global Cultural Studies, SUNY, 1997

Khuri, Richard K. *Freedom, Modernity, and Islam: Towards a Creative Synthesis*. London: Athlone Press, 1998

Kurzman, Charles, ed. *Liberal Islam: A Sourcebook*. New York: Oxford University Press, 1998

——. *Modernist Islam, 1840–1940: A Sourcebook*. Oxford: Oxford University Press, 2002

Lahoud, Nelly and Anthony H. Johns, eds. *Islam in World Politics*. London: Routledge, 2005

Lane, Jan-Erik and Hamadi Redissi. *Religion and Politics: Islam and Muslim Civilisation*. Aldershot: Ashgate 2004

Lapidus, Ira M. *Contemporary Islamic Movements in Historical Perspective*. Policy Papers in International Affairs, 18. Berkeley: Institute of International Studies, University of California, 1983

Lawrence, Bruce B. *Defenders of God: The Fundamentalist Revolt against the Modern Age*. Studies in Comparative Religion. Columbia, SC: University of South Carolina Press, 1995. Originally published by Harper & Row, 1989

——. *Shattering the Myth: Islam Beyond Violence*. Princeton Studies in Muslim Politics. Princeton, NJ: Princeton University Press, 1998

Levtzion, Nehemia and John O. Voll. *Eighteenth Century Reform and Renewal in Islam*. Syracuse, NY: Syracuse University Press, 1987

Lewis, Bernard. *The Political Language of Islam*. Chicago: University of Chicago Press, 1988

——. *What Went Wrong: The Clash between Islam and Modernity in the Middle East*. London: Weidenfeld & Nicolson, 2002

Mackintosh-Smith, Tim. *The Hall of a Thousand Columns: Hindustan to Malabar with Ibn Battuttah*. London: John Murrray, 2005

Manger, Leif, ed. *Muslim Diversity: Local Islam in Global Contexts*. NIAS Studies in Asian Topics, 26. London: Curzon Press, 1999

Mehran, Kamrava, ed. *The New Voices of Islam: Reforming Politics and Modernity: A Reader*. London: I. B. Tauris, 2006

Milton-Edwards, Beverly. *Islam and Politics in the Contemporary World*. Cambridge: Polity Press, 2004

Moaddel, Mansoor. *Islamic Modernism, Nationalism, and Fundamentalism: Episode and Discourse*. Chicago: University of Chicago Press, 2005

Moaddel, Mansoor and Kamran Talattof, eds. *Contemporary Debates in Islam: An Anthology of Modernist and Fundamentalist Thought.* Basingstoke: Macmillan, 2000

Moghissi, Haideh, ed. *Muslim Diaspora: Gender, Culture, and Identity.* New York: Routledge, 2006

Mohammadi, Ali, ed. *Islam Encountering Globalization.* London: RoutledgeCurzon, 2002

Mottahedeh, Roy. *The Mantle of the Prophet: Religion and Politics in Iran.* Oxford: Oneworld, 2001. Originally published with the subtitle *Learning and Power in Modern Iran* by Chatto & Windus, 1985

Moussalli, Ahmad S. *The Islamic Quest for Democracy, Pluralism, and Human Rights.* Gainesville: University Press of Florida, 2001

——. *Moderate and Radical Islamic Fundamentalism: The Quest for Modernity, Legitimacy, and the Islamic State.* 2nd revised edn. Gainesville: University Press of Florida, 1999

Moussalli, Ahmad S., ed. *Islamic Fundamentalism: Myths & Realities.* Reading, UK: Ithaca Press, 1998

Munson, Henry, Jr. *Islam and Revolution in the Middle East.* New Haven: Yale University Press, 1988

Murden, Simon W. *Islam, the Middle East, and the New Global Hegemony.* The Middle East in the International System. Boulder: Lynne Rienner, 2002

Nakash, Yitzak. *Reaching for Power: The Shia in the Modern Arab World.* Princeton, NJ: Princeton University Press, 2006

Nanji, Azim, ed. *Mapping Islamic Studies: Genealogy, Continuity and Change.* Berlin: Mouton de Gruyter, 1997

Nasr, Seyyed Hossein. *Islam and the Plight of Modern Man.* London: Longman, 1975

——. *Traditional Islam in the Modern World.* London: Kegan Paul International, 1987

Nasr, Seyyed Vali Reza. *Islamic Leviathan: Islam and the Making of State Power.* Religion and Global Politics. New York: Oxford University Press, 2001

——. *The Shia Revival: How Conflict Within Islam will Shape the Future.* New York: Norton, 2006

Norton, Augustus Richard. *Hezbollah: A Short History.* Princeton Studies in Muslim Politics. Princeton, NJ: Princeton University Press, 2007

Norton, Augustus Richard, ed. *Civil Society in the Middle East.* 2 vols. Social Economic and Political Studies of the Middle East, 50. Leiden: E. J. Brill, 1995–1996

Ozdalga, Elizabeth and Sune Persson, eds. *Civil Society, Democracy and the Muslim World.* Papers presented at the conference held at the Swedish Research Institute in Istanbul, 28–30 Oct. 1996. Transactions (Swedish Research Institute in Istanbul), vol. 7. Istanbul: Swedish Research Institute in Istanbul, 1997

Piscatori, James P. *Islam in a World of Nation-States.* Cambridge: Cambridge University Press/Royal Institute of International Affairs, 1986

Poole, Elizabeth. *Reporting Islam: Media Representation of British Muslims.* London: I. B. Tauris, 2002

Rahman, Fazlur. *Islam and Modernity: The Transformation of an Intellectual Tradition.* Chicago: University of Chicago Press, 1982

Ramadan, Tariq. *Islam, the West and Challenges of Modernity.* Trans. Said Amghar. Leicester: Islamic Foundation, 2001

——. *Western Muslims and the Future of Islam.* Oxford: Oxford University Press, 2004

Rashid, Ahmed. *Jihad: The Rise of Militant Islam in Central Asia.* New Haven: Yale University Press, 2002

——. *Taliban: Islam, Oil and the New Great Game in Central Asia.* London: I. B. Tauris, 2002

Rejwan, Nissim, ed. *The Many Faces of Islam: Perspectives on a Resurgent Civilization*. Gainesville: University Press of Florida, 2000

Roy, Olivier. *Globalized Islam: The Search for a New Ummah*. CERI Series in Comparative Politics and International Studies. London: C. Hurst & Co., 2004

Ruthven, Malise. *Islam in the World*. 2nd edn. London: Penguin, 2000

Saad-Ghorayeb, Amal. *Hizbullah: Politics and Religion*. Critical Studies on Islam. London: Pluto Press, 2002

Sachedina, Abdulaziz. *The Islamic Roots of Democratic Pluralism*. New York: Oxford University Press, 2001

Safi, Omid, ed. *Progressive Muslims: On Justice, Gender, and Pluralism*. Oxford: Oneworld, 2003

Said, Edward W. *Covering Islam: How the Media and the Experts Determine How We See the Rest of the World*. Revised edn. London: Vintage, 1997

Sajoo, Amyn B., ed. *Civil Society in the Muslim World: Contemporary Perspectives*. London: I. B. Tauris/Institute of Ismaili Studies, 2002

Salvatore, Armando. *Islam and the Political Discourse of Modernity*. Reading, UK: Ithaca Press, 1997

Sardar, Ziauddin. *Future of Muslim Civilisation*. 2nd edn. Islamic Futures and Policy Studies. London: Mansell, 1987

Sayeed, Khalid B. *Western Dominance and Political Islam: Challenge and Response*. Albany: State University of New York Press, 1995

Schaebler, Brigit and Leif Stenberg, eds., with a foreword by Roy Mottahedeh. *Globalization and the Muslim World: Culture, Religion, and Modernity*. Modern Intellectual and Political History of the Middle East. Syracuse, NY: Syracuse University Press, 2004

Schulze, Reinhard. *A Modern History of the Islamic World*. Trans. Azizeh Azodi. London: I. B. Tauris, 2000

Shadid, Anthony. *Legacy of the Prophet: Despots, Democrats and the New Politics of Islam*. Boulder: Westview Press, 2001

Sidahmed, Abdel Salam and Anoushiravan Ehteshami, eds. *Islamic Fundamentalism*. Boulder: Westview Press, 1996

Simons, Thomas W. Jr. *Islam in a Globalizing World*. Stanford, CA: Stanford Law and Politics, 2003

Smith, Wilfred Cantwell. *Islam in Modern History*. Princeton, NJ: Princeton University Press, 1957

Soroush, Abdolkarim. *Reason, Freedom and Democracy in Islam: Essential Writings of Abdolkarim Soroush*. Trans. and ed. and with a critical introduction by Mahmoud Sadri and Ahmad Sadri. Oxford: Oxford University Press, 2000

Stowasser, Barbara Freyer, ed. *The Islamic Impulse*. Washington, DC: Georgetown University Center for Contemporary Arab Studies, 1987

Taji-Farouki, Soha and Basheer M. Nafi, eds. *Islamic Thought in the Twentieth Century*. London: I. B. Tauris, 2004

Tamimi, Azzam and John L. Esposito, eds. *Islam and Secularism in the Middle East*. London: C. Hurst & Co., 2000

Tapper, Richard, ed. *Islam in Modern Turkey: Religion, Politics, and Literature in a Secular State*. London: I. B. Tauris/SOAS, University of London, 1991

Tibi, Bassam. *The Challenge of Fundamentalism: Political Islam and the New World Disorder*. Comparative Studies in Religion and Society, 9. Berkeley: University of California Press, 1998

——. *Islam between Culture and Politics*. 2nd edn. Basingstoke: Palgrave Macmillan/Weatherhead Center for International Affairs, Harvard University, 2005

——. *Islam and the Cultural Accommodation of Social Change*. Trans. Clare Krojzl. Boulder: Westview Press, 1990. Translation of *Islam und das Problem der Kulturellen Bewältigung Sozialen Wandels*, published at Frankfurt am Main, in 1985

Tibi, Bassam, with a foreword by Peter von Sivers. *The Crisis of Modern Islam: A Preindustrial Culture in the Scientific-Technological Age*. Trans. Judith von Sivers. Salt Lake City: University of Utah Press, 1988. Translation of *Die Krise des Modernen Islams*, published in Munich, 1981

Voll, John Obert. *Islam: Continuity and Change in the Modern World*. Boulder: Westview Press, 1982

Waardenburg, Jacques, ed. *Islam and Christianity: Mutual Perceptions since the Mid-20th Century*. Leuven: Peeters, 1998

Watt, William Montgomery. *Islamic Fundamentalism and Modernity*. London: Routledge, 1988

Westerlund, David and Ingvar Svanberg. *Islam Outside the Arab World*. London: Curzon Press, 1999

Zaman, Muhammad Qasim. *The Ulama in Contemporary Islam: Custodians of Change*. Princeton Studies in Muslim Politics. Princeton, NJ: Princeton University Press, 2002

Zia, Rukhsana, ed. *Globalization, Modernization and Education in Muslim Countries*. Education – Emerging Goals in the New Millennium. New York: Nova Science Publishers, 2006

Zubaida, Sami. *Islam, The People and the State: Political Ideas and Movements in the Middle East*. Revised pbk. edn. London: I. B. Tauris, 1993

Regional

Middle East, Iran and Turkey

Abd-Allah, Umar F., with a foreword and postscript by Hamid Algar. *The Islamic Struggle in Syria*. Berkeley: Mizan Press, 1983

Aghaie, Kamran Scot. *The Martyrs of Karbala: Shii Symbols and Ritual in Modern Iran*. Seattle: University of Washington Press, 2004

Arberry, A. J. *The Legacy of Persia*. Oxford: Clarendon Press, 1953

Bayat, Mangol. *Iran's First Revolution: Shiism and the Constitutional Revolution of 1905–1909*. Studies in Middle Eastern History. New York: Oxford University Press, 1991

Berkes, Niyazi. *The Development of Secularism in Turkey*. Montreal: McGill University Press, 1964. Published in facsimile edition by C. Hurst & Co., London, 1998

Choueiri, Youssef M., ed. *A Companion to the History of the Middle East*. Malden, MA: Blackwell, 2005

Esposito, John L. and François Burgat, eds. *Modernizing Islam: Religion in the Public Sphere in the Middle East and Europe*. London: C. Hurst & Co., 2003

Fisher, W. B. et al., eds. *Cambridge History of Iran*. 7 vols. Cambridge: Cambridge University Press, 1968–1991

Frye, Richard N. *The Heritage of Persia*. New York: North American Library, 1963

Gilsenan, Michael. *Recognizing Islam: Religion and Society in the Modern Middle East*. Revised edn. London: I. B. Tauris, 2005. Distributed by Palgrave Macmillan in the USA and Canada. Originally published in 1982 by Croom Helm

Glubb, Sir John Bagot. *The Great Arab Conquests*. London: Hodder & Stoughton, 1963
——. *A Short History of the Arab Peoples*. London: Hodder & Stoughton, 1969
Hammudi, Hadi Hasan. *Oman, the State, the Development and the Modern Times*. London: New Reydman Publishing, 2005
Humphrey, Michael. *Islam: Multiculturalism and Transnationalism: From the Lebanese Diaspora*. London: Centre for Lebanese Studies/I. B. Tauris, 1998
İnalcık, Halil. *The Ottoman Empire: The Classical Age, 1300–1600*. Trans. Norman Itzkowitz and Colin Imber. History of Civilisation. London: Weidenfeld & Nicolson, 1973
Jahanbakhsh, Forough. *Islam, Democracy and Religious Modernism in Iran (1953–2000): From Bazargan to Soroush*. Social, Economic and Political Studies of the Middle East and Asia. Leiden: E. J. Brill, 2001
Kasaba, Resat. *The Ottoman Empire and the World Economy: The Nineteenth Century*. SUNY Series in Middle Eastern Studies. Albany: State University of New York Press, 1988
Keddie, Nikki R. with a contribution from Yann Richard. *Modern Iran: Roots and Results of Revolution*. Rev. updated edn. New Haven: Yale University Press, 2003
Kennedy, Hugh, ed. *The Historiography of Islamic Egypt (c. 950–1800)* The Medieval Mediterranean, 31. Leiden: E. J. Brill, 2000
Koprulu, Mehmed Fuad. *The Origins of the Ottoman Empire*. Trans. and ed. Gary Leiser. Albany: State University of New York Press, 1992
Lewis, Bernard. *The Emergence of Modern Turkey*. 3rd edn. New York: Oxford University Press, 2002
——. *Islam in History: Ideas, People and Events in the Middle East*. New revised and expanded edn. Chicago: Open Court, 1993
——. *Studies in Classical Ottoman Islam: (7th–16th Centuries)*. London: Variorum Reprints, 1976
Littlefield, David W. *The Islamic Near East and North Africa: An Annotated Guide to Books in English for Non-Specialists*. Littleton, CO: Libraries Unlimited, 1977
Loeffler, Reinhold. *Islam in Practice: Religious Beliefs in a Persian Village*. Albany: State University of New York Press, 1988
Mir-Hosseini, Ziba and Richard Tapper. *Islam and Democracy in Iran: Eshkevari and the Quest for Reform*. Library of Modern Middle East. London: I. B. Tauris, 2006
Monshipouri, Mahmood. *Islamism, Secularism and Human Rights in the Middle East*. Boulder: Lynne Rienner, 1998
Morony, Michael G. *Iraq after the Muslim Conquest*. Princeton, NJ: Princeton University Press, 1984
Munson, Henry, Jr. *Islam and Revolution in the Middle East*. New Haven: Yale University Press, 1988
Petrushevsky, I. P. *Islam in Iran*. Trans. Hubert Evans. London: Athlone Press, 1985
Pope, Hugh, and Nicole Pope. *Turkey Unveiled: Attaturk and After*. London: John Murray, 1997
Salibi, Kamal S. *Syria under Islam: Empire on Trial, 634–1097*. Delmar, NY: Caravan Books, 1977
Sauvaget, J. *Introduction to the History of the Muslim East: A Bibliographical Guide*. Based on the 2nd edn. as recast by Claude Cahen. Berkeley: University of California Press, 1965
Savory, Roger. *Iran under the Safavids*. Cambridge: Cambridge University Press, 1980
Shankland, David. *Islam and Society in Turkey*. Huntingdon, UK: Eothen Press, 1999
Silverburg, Sanford R. *Middle East Bibliography*. Scarecrow Area Bibliographies, 1. Metuchen, NJ: Scarecrow Press, 1992

Udovich, A. L., ed. *The Islamic Middle East, 700–1900: Studies in Economic and Social History.* Princeton Studies on the Near East. Princeton, NJ: Darwin Press, 1981

Westerlund, David and Ingvar Svanberg, eds. *Islam Outside the Arab World.* London: Curzon Press, 1999

Wilkinson, John C. *The Imamate Tradition of Oman.* Cambridge Middle East Library. Cambridge: Cambridge University Press, 1987

Africa

Abun-Nasr, Jamil M. *A History of the Maghrib in the Islamic Period.* Cambridge: Cambridge University Press, 1987

el-Affendi, Abdelwahab. *Turabi's Revolution: Islam and Power in Sudan.* London: Grey Seal, 1991

Atterbury, Anson P. *Islam in Africa: Its Effects – Religious, Ethical, and Social – upon the People of the Country.* London: Darf, 1987. Originally published by Putnam's, 1899

Azumah, John Alembillah. *The Legacy of Arab-Islam in Africa: A Quest for Inter-Religious Dialogue.* Oxford: Oneworld, 2001

Bakari, Mohamed and Saad S. Yahya, eds. *Islam in Kenya: Proceedings of the National Seminar on Contemporary Islam in Kenya.* Nairobi: Mewa Publications, 1995

Bravmann, Rene A. *African Islam.* Washington, DC: Smithsonian Institution Press, 1983

Brenner, Louis. *West African Sufi: The Religious Heritage and Spiritual Search of Cerno Bokar Saalif Taal.* Berkeley: University of California Press, 1984

Brenner, Louis, ed. *Muslim Identity and Social Change in Sub-Saharan Africa.* Bloomington: Indiana University Press, 1993

Burgat, François and William Dowell. *The Islamic Movement in North Africa.* Middle East Monograph Series. Austin: Center for Middle Eastern Studies, University of Texas at Austin, 1992

Clarke, Peter B. *West Africa and Islam: A Study of Religious Development from the 8th to the 20th Century.* London: Edward Arnold, 1982

Cruise O'Brien, Donal B. and Christian Coulon, eds. *Charisma and Brotherhood in African Islam.* Oxford Studies in African Affairs. Oxford: Clarendon Press, 1988

Daly, M. W., ed. *The Cambridge History of Egypt,* vol. 1: *Islamic Egypt, 640–1517,* ed. Carl F. Petry; vol. 2: *Modern Egypt, from 1517 to the End of the Twentieth Century,* ed. M. W. Daly. Cambridge: Cambridge University Press, 1998

Eickelman, Dale F. *Knowledge and Power in Morocco: The Education of a Twentieth-Century Notable.* Princeton Studies on the Near East. Princeton, NJ: Princeton University Press, 1985

——. *Moroccan Islam: Tradition and Society in a Pilgrimage Center.* Modern Middle East Series, 1. Austin: University of Texas Press, 1976

Gbadamosi, T. G. O. *The Growth of Islam among the Yoruba, 1841–1908.* Ibadan History Series. London: Longman, 1978

Harrison, Christopher. *France and Islam in West Africa, 1860–1960.* African Studies Series, 60. Cambridge: Cambridge University Press, 1988

Hiskett, Mervyn. *The Course of Islam in Africa.* Edinburgh: Edinburgh University Press, 1994

——. *The Development of Islam in West Africa.* London: Longman, 1984

Hunwick, John and Eve Trout Powell. *The African Diaspora in the Mediterranean Lands of Islam.* Princeton, NJ: Markus Wiener, 2002

Karrar, Ali Salih. *The Sufi Brotherhoods in the Sudan.* London: C. Hurst & Co., 1992

Kasozi, Abdu B. *The Spread of Islam in Uganda*. Nairobi: Oxford University Press/Islamic African Centre, Khartoum, 1986

King Noel Q., Arye Oded and Abdul Kasozi. *Islam and Confluence of Religion in Uganda*. Tallahassee, FL: American Academy of Religion, 1973

Kritzeck, James and William H. Lewis, eds. *Islam in Africa*. New York: Van Nostrand Reinhold Co., 1969

Levtzion, Nehemia. *Islam in West Africa: Religion, Society and Politics to 1800*. Variorum Collected Studies Series, CS462. Aldershot: Variorum, 1994

Levtzion, Nehemia and Humphrey J. Fisher, eds. *Rural and Urban Islam in West Africa*. Boulder: Lynne Rienner, 1987

Levtzion, Nehemia, and Randall L. Pouwels, eds. *The History of Islam in Africa*. Athens, OH: Ohio University Press, 2000

Lewis, I. M., ed. *Islam in Tropical Africa*. Studies presented and discussed at the Fifth International African Seminar, Ahmadu Bello University, Zaria, Nigeria, January 1964. Oxford: Oxford University Press for the International African Institute, 1966

Mahida, Ebrahim Mahomed. *History of Muslims in South Africa: A Chronology*. Durban: Arab Study Circle, 1993

Mandivenga, Ephraim C. *Islam in Zimbabwe*. Gweru, Zimbabwe: Mambo Press, 1983

Oded, Arye. *Islam and Politics in Kenya*. Boulder: Lynne Rienner, 2000

——. *Islam in Uganda: Islamization through a Centralized State in Pre-colonial Africa*. New York: Halsted Press, 1974

Ofori, P. E. *Islam in Africa South of the Sahara: A Select Bibliographic Guide*. Nendeln, Liechtenstein: KTO, 1977

Peel, J. D. Y. and C. C. Stewart, eds. *Popular Islam South of the Sahara*. Manchester: Manchester University Press/International African Institute, 1985

Pouwels, Randall Lee. *Horn and Crescent: Cultural Change and Traditional Islam on the East African Coast, 800–1900*. African Studies Series, 53. Cambridge: Cambridge University Press, 1987

Quinn, Charlotte A. and Frederick Quinn. *Pride, Faith, and Fear: Islam in Sub-Saharan Africa*. Oxford: Oxford University Press, 2003

Robinson, David. *Muslim Societies in African History*. New Approaches to African History. Cambridge: Cambridge University Press, 2004

Rosander, Eva Evers and David Westerlund. *African Islam and Islam in Africa: Encounters between Sufis and Islamists*. London: C. Hurst & Co., 1997, in co-operation with the Nordic Africa Institute, Uppsala, Sweden

Sanneh, Lamin O. *The Crown and the Turban: Muslims and West African Pluralism*. Boulder: Westview Press, 1997

Simone, T. Abdou Maliqalim. *In Whose Image? Political Islam and Urban Practices in Sudan*. Chicago: University of Chicago Press, 1994

Sullivan, Denis J. and Sana Abed-Kotob. *Islam in Contemporary Egypt: Civil Society vs. the State*. Boulder: Lynne Rienner, 1999

Taha, Abdulwahid Dhannun. *The Muslim Conquest and Settlement of North Africa and Spain*. London: Routledge, 1989

Tayob, Abdulkader. *Islam in South Africa: Mosques, Imams and Sermons*. Gainesville: University Press of Florida, 1999. Published in association with Religion in Africa, a series of the Association for the Study of Religions

——. *Islamic Resurgence in South Africa: The Muslim Youth Movement*. Cape Town: University of Cape Town Press, 1995

Trimingham, J. Spencer. *A History of Islam in West Africa*. London: Oxford University Press for the University of Glasgow, 1962
———. *The Influence of Islam upon Africa*. 2nd edn. Arab Background Series. London: Longman, 1980
———. *Islam in East Africa*. Oxford: Clarendon Press, 1964
———. *Islam in Ethiopia*. London: Frank Cass, 1965. Originally published by Oxford University Press, 1952
———. *Islam in the Sudan*. London: Frank Cass, 1965. Originally published by Oxford University Press, 1949
———. *Islam in West Africa*. Oxford: Clarendon Press, 1959
Willis, John Ralph, ed. *Studies in West African Islamic History*, vol. 1: *The Cultivators of Islam*. London: Frank Cass, 1979
Zoghby, Samir M., comp. *Islam in Sub-Saharan Africa: A Partially Annotated Guide*. Washington, DC: Library of Congress, 1978

Asia
Ahmad, Aziz. *Islamic Modernism in India and Pakistan, 1857–1964*. London: Oxford University Press and the Royal Institute of International Affairs, 1967
———. *Studies in Islamic Culture in the Indian Environment*. Oxford: Clarendon Press, 1964. Repr. Delhi: Oxford University Press, 1999
Ahmed, Rafiuddin. *The Bengal Muslims, 1871–1906: A Quest for Identity*. Delhi: Oxford University Press, 1981
Atkin, Muriel. *The Subtlest Battle: Islam in Soviet Tajikistan*. Philadelphia Papers. Philadelphia: Foreign Policy Research Institute, 1989
Baldick, Julian. *Imaginary Muslims: The Uwaysi Sufis of Central Asia*. New York: New York University Press, 1993
Banu, U. A. B. Razia Akter. *Islam in Bangladesh*. International Studies in Sociology and Social Anthropology, 58. Leiden: E. J. Brill, 1992
Bayly, Susan. *Saints, Goddesses and Kings: Muslims and Christians in South Indian Society, 1700–1900*. South Asian Studies Series, 43. New York: Cambridge University Press, 1989
Berlie, Jean A. *Islam in China: Hui and Uyghurs between Modernization and Cinicization*. Bangkok: White Lotus Press, 2004
Boland, B. J. and I. Farjon. *Islam in Indonesia: A Bibliographical Survey 1600–1942, with post-1945 Addenda*. Bibliographical Series Koninklijk Institute Voor Taal, Landen Volkenkunde, 14. Dordrecht: Foris Publications, 1983
Bosworth, Clifford Edmund. *The Ghaznavids: Their Empire in Afghanistan and Eastern Iran, 994–1040*. 2nd edn. Beirut: Librairie du Liban, 1973
———. *The Later Ghaznavids: Splendour and Decay. The Dynasty in Afghanistan and Northern India, 1040–1186*. Persian Studies Series, 7. Edinburgh: Edinburgh University Press, 1977
Bowen, John R. *Muslims through Discourse: Religion and Ritual in Gayo Society*. Princeton, NJ: Princeton University Press, 1993
Dillon, Michael. *China's Muslim Hui Community: Migration, Settlement and Sects*. London: Curzon Press, 1999
———. *China's Muslims*. Images of Asia. Hong Kong: Oxford University Press, 1996
Eaton, Richard M. *Essays on Islam and Indian History*. New Delhi: Oxford University Press, 2000
———. *The Rise of Islam and the Bengal Frontier, 1204–1760*. Berkeley: University of California Press, 1993

Eaton, Richard M., ed. *India's Islamic Traditions, 711–1750*. Themes in Indian History. New Delhi: Oxford University Press, 2003

Eickelman, Dale F. *The Middle East and Central Asia: An Anthropological Approach*. 4th edn. Upper Saddle River, NJ: Prentice-Hall, 2002

Eliraz, Giora. *Islam in Indonesia: Modernism, Radicalism, and the Middle East Dimension*. Brighton: Sussex Academic Press, 2004

Engineer, Asghar Ali, ed. *Islam in India: The Impact of Civilizations*. New Delhi: Indian Council for Cultural Relations, Shipra Publications, 2002

——. *Islam in South and South-East Asia*. Delhi: Ajanta Publications, 1985

Esposito, John L., ed. *Islam in Asia: Religion, Politics, and Society*. New York: Oxford University Press, 1987

Fiderspiel, Howard M. *Indonesian Muslim Intellectuals of the Twentieth Century*. Southeast Asia Background Series, 8. Singapore: Institute of Southeast Asian Studies, 2006

——. *Islam and Ideology in the Emerging Indonesian State: The Persatuan Islam (PERSIS), 1923–1957*. Social, economic and political studies of the Middle East and Asia, 78. Leiden: E. J. Brill, 2001

——. *Sultans, Shamans, and Saints: Islam and Muslims in Southeast Asia*. Honolulu: University of Hawaii Press, 2007

——. *The Usage of Traditions of the Prophet in Contemporary Indonesia*. Monographs in Southeast Asian Studies. Tempe, AZ: Program for Southeast Asian Studies, Arizona State University, 1993

Gammer, Moshe and David J. Wasserstein, eds. *Daghestan and the World of Islam*. Helsinki: Finnish Academy of Science and Letters, 2006

Gillette, Maris Boyd. *Between Mecca and Beijing: Modernization and Consumption among Urban Chinese Muslims*. Stanford, CA: Stanford University Press, 2000

Gross, Jo-Ann, ed. *Muslims in Central Asia: Expressions of Identity and Change*. Durham, NC: Duke University Press, 1991

Haghayeghi, Mehrdad. *Islam and Politics in Central Asia*. New York: St Martin's Press, 1995

Hardy, P. *The Muslims of British India*. Cambridge South Asian Studies, 13. Cambridge: Cambridge University Press, 1972

Haroon, M. *Muslims of India: Their Literature on Education, History, Politics, Socio-Economic and Communal Problems*. Delhi: Indian Bibliographies Bureau, 1989

Hasan, Mushirul. *Islam in the Subcontinent: Muslims in a Plural Society*. New Delhi: Manohar, 2002

Hasnain, Nadeem, ed. *Islam and Muslim Communities in South Asia*. New Delhi: Serial Publications, 2006

Hassan, Riaz. *Faithline: Muslim Conceptions of Islam and Society*. Oxford: Oxford University Press, 2002

Hefner, Robert W. *Civil Islam: Muslims and Democratization in Indonesia*. Princeton Studies in Muslim Politics. Princeton, NJ: Princeton University Press, 2000

Hiro, Dilip. *Between Marx and Muhammad: The Changing Face of Central Asia*. London: HarperCollins, 1994

Hitchcock, Michael. *Islam and Identity in Eastern Indonesia*. Hull: Hull University Press, 1996

Hooker, M. B. *Indonesian Islam: Social Change through Contemporary Fatwa*. Crows Nest, Australia: Asian Studies Association of Australia/Allen & Unwin and University of Hawaii Press, 2003

Hooker, M. B., ed. *Islam in South-East Asia*. Leiden: E. J. Brill, 1983

Ikram, S. M. *History of Muslim Civilization in India and Pakistan: A Political and Cultural History.* 9th edn. Lahore: Institute of Islamic Culture, 2000

Israeli, Raphael. *Islam in China: Religion, Ethnicity, Culture, and Politics.* Lanham, MD: Lexington Books, 2002

Israeli, Raphael, with a preface by C. E. Bosworth. *Muslims in China: A Study in Cultural Confrontation.* Scandinavian Institute of Asian Studies Monograph Series, 29. London: Curzon Press, 1980

Israeli, Raphael, with Lyn Gorman. *Islam in China: A Critical Bibliography.* Bibliographies and Indexes in Religious Studies, 29. Westport, CT: Greenwood Press, 1994

Khan, Dominique-Sila. *Crossing the Threshold: Understanding Religious Identities in South Asia.* London: I. B. Tauris/Institute of Ismaili Studies, 2004

Kim, Kay Khoo, Elinah Abdullah and Weng Meng Hao, eds. *Malays/Muslims in Singapore: Selected Readings in History, 1819–1965.* Selangor: Pelanduk Publications, 2006

Lawrence, Bruce B., ed. *The Rose and the Rock: Mystical and Rational Elements in the Intellectual History of South Asian Islam.* Durham, NC: Duke University Press, 1979

Lelyveld, David. *Aligarh's First Generation: Muslim Solidarity in British India.* Princeton, NJ: Princeton University Press, 1978

Leslie, Donald Daniel. *Islam in Traditional China: A Short History to 1800.* Canberra: Canberra College of Advanced Education, 1986

Lipman, Jonathan N. *Familiar Strangers: A History of Muslims in Northwest China.* Studies on Ethnic Groups in China. Seattle: University of Washington Press, 1997

Madan, T. N. *Muslim Communities of South Asia: Culture, Society and Power.* 3rd enlarged edn. Contributions to Indian Sociology. Occasional Studies, 6. New Delhi: Manohar/Book Review Literary Trust, 2001

Majul, Cesar Adib. *Muslims in the Philippines.* Quezon City: University of Philippines Press for the Asian Center, 1999. Reprint of the 2nd edn., 1973

Marsden, Magnus. *Living Islam: Religious Experience in Pakistan's North-West Frontier.* Cambridge: Cambridge University Press, 2005

McAmis, Robert Day. *Malay Muslim: The History and Challenges of Resurgent Islam in Southeast Asia.* Grand Rapids, MI: William. B. Eerdmans, 2002

McChesney, R. D. *Waqf in Central Asia: Four Hundred Years in the History of a Muslim Shrine, 1840–1889.* Princeton, NJ: Princeton University Press, 1991

Metcalf, Barbara D. *Islamic Contestations: Essays on Muslims in India and Pakistan.* New Delhi: Oxford University Press, 2004

——. *Islamic Revival in British India: Deoband, 1860–1900.* Princeton, NJ: Princeton University Press, 1982

Mitsuo, Nakamura, Sharon Siddique and Omar Farouk Bajunid, eds. *Islam and Civil Society in Southeast Asia.* ISEAS Series on Islam. Singapore: Institute of Southeast Asian Studies, 2001

Mohiuddin, Momin. *Muslim Communities in Medieval Konkan (610–1900 A.D.).* New Delhi: Sundeep Prakashan, 2002

Mousavi, Sayed Askar. *The Hazaras of Afghanistan: An Historical, Cultural, Economic and Political Study.* London: Curzon Press, 1998

Mutalib, Hussin. *Islam and Ethnicity in Malay Politics.* South-East Asian Social Science Monograph. New York: Oxford University Press, 1990

Nanji, Azim. *The Nizari Ismaili Tradition in the Indo-Pakistan Subcontinent.* Delmar, NY: Caravan Books, 1978

Nathan, K. S. and Mohammad Hashim Kamali. *Islam in Southeast Asia: Political, Social and Strategic Challenges for the 21st Century*. Singapore: Institute for Southeast Asian Studies, 2005

Ngata, Judith. *The Flowering of Malaysian Islam: Modern Religious Radicals and their Roots*. Vancouver: University of British Columbia Press, 1984

Osman, Mohd Taib. *Islamic Civilization in the Malay World*. Kuala Lumpur: Dewan Bahasa dan Pustaka and the Centre for Islamic History, Art and Culture, Istanbul, 1997

Poliakov, Sergei P. *Everyday Islam; Religion and Tradition in Rural Central Asia*. Trans. Anthony Olcott. Ed. and introduced by Martha Brill Olcott. Armonk, NY: M. E. Sharpe, 1992

Polonskaya, Ludmila and Alexei Malashenko. *Islam in Central Asia*. Reading, UK: Ithaca Press, 1994

Porter, Donald J. *Managing Politics and Islam in Indonesia*. London: RoutledgeCurzon, 2002

Rashid, Ahmed. *The Resurgence of Central Asia: Islam or Nationalism?* London: Zed Books, 1994

Riddell, Peter G. *Islam and the Malay-Indonesian World: Transmission and Responses*. London: C. Hurst & Co., 2001

Robinson, Francis. *Islam, South Asia, and the West*. New Delhi: Oxford University Press, 2007

Ro'i, Yaacov, ed. *Democracy and Pluralism in Muslim Eurasia*. Cummings Center Series, 19. London: Frank Cass, 2004

Roy, Olivier. *Islam and Resistance in Afghanistan*. 2nd edn. Cambridge: Cambridge University Press, 1990

Ruffin, Holt M. and Daniel C. Waugh. *Civil Society in Central Asia*. Seattle: University of Washington Press/Civil Society International, 1999

Saleh, Fauzan. *Modern Trends in Islamic Theological Discourse in 20th Century Indonesia: A Critical Study*. Social, Economic and Political Studies of the Middle East and Asia, 79. Leiden: E. J. Brill, 2001

Schimmel, Annemarie. *Islam in the Indian Subcontinent*. Leiden: E. J. Brill, 1980

Shaikh, Farzana. *Community and Consensus in Islam: Muslim Representation in Colonial India, 1860–1947*. Cambridge South Asian Studies. Cambridge: Cambridge University Press/Orient Longman, 1989

Siddiqui, Iqtidar Hussain. *Islam and Muslims in South Asia: Historical Perspective*. Delhi: Adam Publishers & Distributors, 1987

Starr, S. Frederick, ed. *Xinjiang: China's Muslim Borderland*. Studies of Central Asia and the Caucasus. Armonk, NY: M. E. Sharpe, 2004

Troll, Christian W., ed. *Muslim Shrines in India: Their Character, History and Significance*. Islam in India: Their Studies and Commentaries, 4. Delhi: Oxford University Press, 1989

Uddin, Sufia M. *Constructing Bangladesh: Religion, Ethnicity and Language in an Islamic Nation*. Islamic Civilization & Muslim Networks. Chapel Hill: University of North Carolina Press, 2006

Wolpert, Stanley. *A New History of India*. 7th edn. Oxford: Oxford University Press, 2004

Wong, How Man and Adel A. Dajani. *Islamic Frontiers of China: Silk Road Images*. London: Scorpion, 1990

Woodward, Mark R., ed. *Toward a New Paradigm: Recent Developments in Indonesian Islamic Thought*. Tempe, AZ: Program for Southeast Asian Studies, Arizona State University, 1996

Europe

Abbas, Tahir, ed. *Muslim Britain: Communities under Pressure*. London: Zed Books, 2005

Ahmad, Aziz. *A History of Islamic Sicily*. Islamic Surveys, 10. Edinburgh: Edinburgh University Press, 1975

Ahmed, S. M., ed. *Islam in the U. S. S. R., Turkey and Europe*. Allahabad: Abbas Manzil Library, 1956

Akiner, Shirin. *Islamic Peoples of the Soviet Union (with an Appendix on the non-Muslim Turkic Peoples of the Soviet Union)*. London: Kegan Paul International, 1983

Allievi, Stefano, and Jorgen Nielsen, eds. *Muslim Networks and Transnational Communities in and across Europe*. Muslim Minorities, 1. Leiden: E. J. Brill, 2003

Ansari, Humayun. *'The Infidel Within': Muslims in Britain since 1800*. London: C. Hurst & Co., 2004

Banks, David R. and Michael Frassetto, eds. *Western Views of Islam in Medieval and Early Modern Europe: Perception of Other*. New York: St Martin's Press, 1999

Bennigsen, Alexandre and Chantal Lemercier-Quequejay. *Islam in the Soviet Union*. London: Pall Mall Press/Central Asian Research Centre, 1967

Bennigsen, Alexandre and S. Enders Wimbush. *Muslims of the Soviet Empire: A Guide*. London: C. Hurst & Co., 1985

———. *Mystics and Commissars: Sufism in the Soviet Union*. London: C. Hurst & Co., 1985

Bringa, Tone. *Being Muslim the Bosnian Way: Identity and Community in a Central Bosnian Village*. Princeton Studies in Muslim Politics. Princeton, NJ: Princeton University Press, 1995

Cardini, Franco. *Europe and Islam*. Trans. Caroline Beamish. The Making of Europe. Malden, MA: Blackwell, 2001

Chejne, Anwar G. *Islam and the West. The Mariscos: A Cultural and Economic History*. Albany: State University of New York Press, 1983

———. *Muslim Spain, Its History and Culture*. Minneapolis: University of Minnesota Press, 1974

Daniel, Norman. *Islam, Europe and Empire*. Edinburgh: Edinburgh University Press, 1966

———. *Islam and the West: The Making of an Image*. Edinburgh: Edinburgh University Press, 1960

Djait, Hichem. *Europe and Islam*. Trans. Peter Heinegg. Berkeley: University of California Press, 1985

Dozy, Reinhart Pieter Anne. *Spanish Islam: A History of the Moslems in Spain*. Trans. with a biographical introduction and additional notes by Francis Griffin Stokes. London: Chatto & Windus, 1913

Eickelman, Dale F. *Russia's Muslim Frontier: New Directions in Cross-Cultural Analysis*. Indiana Series in Arab and Islamic Studies. Bloomington: Indiana University Press, 1993

Fierro, Maribel and Julio Samso, eds. *The Formation of al-Andalus, Part 2: Language, Religion, Culture and the Sciences*. Formation of the Classical Islamic World, 47. Aldershot: Ashgate, 1998

Fletcher, Richard. *Moorish Spain*. London: Weidenfeld & Nicolson, 1992

Frank, Allen J. *Muslim Religious Institutions in Imperial Russia: The Islamic World of Novou-zensk District and the Kazakh Inner Horde, 1780–1910*. Leiden: E. J. Brill, 2001

Friedman, Francine. *The Bosnian Muslims: Denial of a Nation*. Boulder: Westview Press, 1996

Geaves, Ron. *The Sufis of Britain: An Explanation of Muslim Identity*. Cardiff: Cardiff Academic Press, 2000

Gerholm, Tomas and Yngve Georg Lithman, eds. *The New Islamic Presence in Western Europe*. London: Mansell, 1988

Glick, Thomas F. *Islamic and Christian Spain in the Early Middle Ages*. Princeton, NJ: Princeton University Press, 1979

Goody, Jack. *Islam in Europe*. Cambridge: Polity Press/Blackwell, 2004

Haddad, Yvonne Yazbeck, ed. *Muslims in the West: From Sojourners to Citizens*. Oxford: Oxford University Press, 2002

Haddad, Yvonne Yazbeck and Jane Idleman Smith, eds. *Muslim Minorities in the West: Visible and Invisible*. Walnut Creek, CA: Altamira Press, 2002

Harvey, Leonard Patrick. *Islamic Spain 1250 to 1500*. Chicago: University of Chicago Press, 1990

——. *Muslims in Spain: 1500 to 1614*. Chicago: University of Chicago Press, 2005

Hourani, Albert. *Islam in European Thought*. Cambridge: Cambridge University Press, 1991

Hunter, Shireen T., ed., with a foreword by Charles Buchanan. *Islam, Europe's Second Religion: The New Social, Cultural, and Political Landscape*. Westport, CT: Praeger/Greenwood, 2002. Published in cooperation with the Center for Strategic and International Studies, Washington, DC

Imamuddin, S. M. *Some Aspects of the Socio-Economic and Cultural History of Muslim Spain 711–1492 A.D.* Leiden: E. J. Brill, 1965. Revised and enlarged edn: *Muslim Spain, 711–1492 A. D.: A Sociological Study*. Medieval Iberian Peninsula; Texts and Studies, 2. Leiden: E. J. Brill, 1981.

Jayyusi, Salma Khadra, ed. *The Legacy of Muslim Spain*. 2 vols. Handbook of Oriental Studies; the Near and Middle East, 12. Leiden: E. J. Brill, 1992. Published in paperback in 2 vols., 1994

Joly, Daniele and Jorgen Nielsen. *Muslims in Britain: An Annotated Bibliography 1960–1984*. Bibliographies in Ethnic Relations, 6. Coventry: Centre for Research in Ethnic Relations, University of Warwick, 1985

Kennedy, Hugh. *Muslim Spain and Portugal: A Political History of al-Andalus*. Harlow: Longman, 1996

Laurence, Jonathan and Justin Vaisse. *Integrating Islam: Political and Religious Challenges in Contemporary France*. Washington, DC: Brookings Institution Press, 2006

Lewis, Bernard and Dominique Schnapper, eds. *Muslims in Europe*. 2nd edn. Social Change in Western Europe. London: Pinter, 1995

Lewis, Philip. *Islamic Britain: Religion and Politics and Identity among British Muslims*. New edn. London: I. B. Tauris, 2002

Malik, Jamal, ed. *Muslims in Europe: From the Margins to the Centre*. Religionswissenschaft: Forchung und Wissenschaft, 1. Munster: Lit Verlag, 2004

Marechal, Brigitte et al., eds. *Muslims in the Enlarged Europe: Religion and Society*. Muslim Minorities, 2. Leiden: E. J. Brill, 2003

Marin, Manuela, ed. *The Formation of al-Andalus: Part 1: History and Society*. Formation of the Classical Islamic World, 46. Aldershot: Ashgate, 1998

Matar, Nabil. *Islam in Britain, 1558–1685*. Cambridge: Cambridge University Press, 1998

Metcalf, Barbara Daly, ed. *Making Muslim Space in North America and Europe*. Berkeley: University of California Press, 1996

Metcalfe, Alex. *Muslims and Christians in Norman Sicily: Arabic Speakers and the end of Islam*. Culture and Civilization in the Middle East. London: RoutledgeCurzon, 2003

Meyerson, Mark D. *Muslims of Valencia in the Age of Fernando and Isabel: Between Coexistence and Crusade*. Berkeley: University of California Press, 1991

Nielsen, Jorgen S. *Muslims in Western Europe.* 3rd edn. New Edinburgh Islamic Surveys. Edinburgh: Edinburgh University Press, 2004
——. *Towards a European Islam.* Migration, Minorities and Citizenship. Basingstoke: Macmillan/Centre for Research in Ethnic Relations, University of Warwick, 1999
Nonneman, Gerd, Tim Niblock and Bogdan Szajkowski, eds. *Muslim Communities in the New Europe.* Reading, UK: Garnet, 1996
Norris, H. T. *Islam in the Balkans: Religion and Society between Europe and the Arab World.* London: C. Hurst & Co., 1993
Pilkington, Hilary and Galina Yemelianova, eds. *Islam in Post-Soviet Russia: Public and Private Faces.* London: RoutledgeCurzon, 2003
Pinson, Mark, ed., with a foreword by Roy P. Mottahedeh. *The Muslims of Bosnia-Herzegovina: Their Historic Development from the Middle Ages to the Dissolution of Yugoslavia.* Harvard Middle Eastern Monographs, 28. Cambridge, MA: Center for Middle Eastern Studies, Harvard University, 1993
Poulton, Hugh and Suha Taji-Farouki, eds. *Muslim Identity and the Balkan State.* London: C. Hurst & Co./Islamic Council, 1997
Ramadan, Tariq. *Western Muslims and the Future of Islam.* Oxford: Oxford University Press, 2004
Robson, Glenna. *Muslims in Manchester.* Salford: Sacred Trinity Centre, 1986
Rodinson, Maxime. *Europe and the Mystique of Islam.* Trans. Roger Veinus. London: I. B. Tauris, 1988. Originally published in Paris as *La fascination de l'Islam* in 1980
Ro'i, Yaacov. *Islam in the Soviet Union: From the Second World War to Gorbachev.* London: C. Hurst & Co., 2000
Seddon, Mohammad Siddique, Dilwar Hussain and Nadeem Malik. *British Muslims between Assimilation and Segregation: Historical, Legal and Social Realities.* Markfield: Islamic Foundation, 2004
Shadid, W. A. R. and P. S. Van Koningsveld. *Religious Freedom and the Position of Islam in Western Europe: Opportunities and Obstacles in the Acquisition of Equal Rights* [with an extensive bibliography]. Kampaen: Kok Pharos Publishing House, 1995
Sonyel, Salahi Ramadan. *The Muslims of Bosnia: Genocide of a People.* Markfield: Islamic Foundation, 1994
Taha, Abdulwahid Dhannun. *The Muslim Conquest and Settlement of North Africa and Spain.* London: Routledge, 1989
Vakhabov, Abdulla. *Muslims in the U.S.S.R.* Moscow: Novosti Press Agency Publishing House, 1980
Waardenburg, Jacques. *Muslims and Others: Relations in Context.* Religion and Reason, 41. Berlin: Walter de Gruyter, 2003
Wasserstein, David J. *The Caliphate in the West: An Islamic Political Institution in the Iberian Peninsula.* Oxford: Clarendon Press, 1993
Watt, W. Montgomery. *The Influence of Islam on Medieval Europe.* Islamic Surveys, 9. Edinburgh: University of Edinburgh Press, 1972
Watt, W. Montgomery, with additional sections on literature by Pierre Cachia. *A History of Islamic Spain.* Edinburgh: Edinburgh University Press, 1965
Yemelianova, Galina M. *Russia and Islam: A Historical Survey.* Studies in Russia and East European History and Society. Basingstoke: Palgrave Macmillan, 2002

North America, Australia

Akbarzadeh, Shahram and Samina Yasmeen, eds. *Islam and the West: Reflections from Australia*. Sydney: University of New South Wales Press, 2005

Ba-Yunus, Ilyas and Kassim Kone. *Muslims in the United States*. Westport, CT: Greenwood Press, 2006

Barrett, Paul M. *American Islam: The Struggle for the Soul of a Religion*. New York: Farrar, Straus and Giroux, 2007

Elkholy, Abdo A. *The Arab Moslems in the United States: Religion and Assimilation*. New Haven: College & University Press, 1966

Haddad, Yvonne Yazbeck, ed. *The Muslims of America*. Religion in America Series. New York: Oxford University Press, 1991

Haddad, Yvonne Yazbeck and Adair T. Lummis. *Islamic Values in the United States: A Comparative Study*. New York: Oxford University Press, 1987

Haddad, Yvonne Yazbeck and Jane Idleman Smith. *Mission to America: Five Islamic Sectarian Communities in North America*. Gainesville: University Press of Florida, 1993

Haddad, Yvonne Yazbeck and Jane Idleman Smith, eds. *Muslim Communities in North America*. SUNY Series in Middle Eastern Studies. Albany: State University of New York Press, 1994

Kabir, Nahid Afrose. *Muslims in Australia: Immigration, Race Relations and Cultural History*. Studies in Anthropology, Economy and Society. London: Kegan Paul, 2004

Kahera, Akel Ismail. *Deconstructing the American Mosque: Space, Gender, and Aesthetics*. Austin: University of Texas Press, 2002

Lee, Martha F. *The Nation of Islam: An American Millenarian Movement*. Syracuse, NY: Syracuse University Press, 1996

Marsh, Clifton E. *From Black Muslims to Muslims: The Resurrection, Transformation and Change of the Lost-Found Nation of Islam in America, 1930–1995*. 2nd edn. Lanham, MD: Scarecrow Press, 1996

McCloud, Aminah Beverly. *African-American Islam*. New York: Routledge, 1995

Metcalf, Barbara Daly, ed. *Making Muslim Space in North America and Europe*. Berkeley: University of California Press, 1996

Richardson, E. Allen. *Islamic Cultures in North America: Patterns of Belief and Devotion of Muslims from Asian Countries in the United States and Canada*. New York: Pilgrim Press, 1981

Saeed, Abdullah and Akbarzadeh Shahram, eds. *Muslim Communities in Australia*. Sydney: University of New South Wales Press, 2001

Smith, Jane Idleman. *Islam in America*. Columbia Contemporary American Religion Series. New York: Columbia University Press, 1999

Turner, Richard Brent. *Islam in the African-American Experience*. 2nd edn. Bloomington: Indiana University Press, 2003

Waugh, Earle H., Baha Abu-Laban and Regula B. Qureshi, eds. *The Muslim Community in North America*. Edmonton: University of Alberta Press, 1983

The Quran and *hadith*

Abdul-Raof, Hussein. *Exploring the Quran*. Dundee: Al-Maktoum Institute Academic Press, 2003

——. *Quran Translation: Discourse, Texture and Exegesis.* Culture and Civilization in the Middle East. London: Curzon Press, 2001

Abu-Hamdiyyah, Mohammed. *The Quran: An Introduction.* London: Routledge, 2000

Ambros, Arne A. with Stephan Prochazka. *A Concise Dictionary of Koranic Arabic.* Wiesbaden: Reichert Verlag, 2004

——. *The Nouns of Koranic Arabic Arranged by Topics: A Companion Volume to the 'Concise Dictionary of Koranic Arabic'.* Wiesbaden: Reichert Verlag, 2006

Anees, Munawar A. and Alia N. Athar. *Guide to Sira and Hadith Literature in Western Languages.* East-West University Islamic Studies. London: Mansell, 1986

Awde, Nicholas, trans. and ed. *Women in Islam: An Anthology from the Quran and Hadiths.* London: Curzon Press, 2000

Ayoub, Mahmoud Mustafa. *The Quran and Its Interpreters.* 2 vols. Albany: State University of New York Press, 1984

al-Azami, Muhammad Mustafa. *The History of the Quranic Text. From Revelation to Compilation: A Comparative Study with the Old and New Testaments.* Leicester: UK Islamic Academy, 2003

——. *Studies in Early Hadith Literature.* 3rd edn. Indianapolis: American Trust Publications, 1992

Baljon, J. M. S. *Modern Muslim Koran Interpretation, 1880–1960.* Leiden: E. J. Brill, 1968. First published 1961

Barazangi, Nimat Hafez. *Woman's Identity and the Quran: A New Reading.* Gainesville: University Press of Florida, 2004

Barlas, Asma. *'Believing Women' in Islam: Unreading Patriarchal Interpretations of the Quran.* Austin: University of Texas Press, 2002

Bell, Richard. *Bell's Introduction to the Quran.* Revised, enlarged and ed. W. Montgomery Watt. Edinburgh: Edinburgh University Press, 1970

——. *A Commentary on the Quran.* 2 vols. Ed. Edmund Bosworth and M. E. J. Richards. Journal of Semitic Studies Monographs, 14. Manchester: University of Manchester Press, 1991

Bennabi, Malik, with an introduction by Mohamed el-Tahir el-Mesawi. *The Quranic Phenomenon: An Essay of a Theory on the Quran.* A new annotated translation. Kuala Lumpur: Islamic Book Trust, 2001

Berg, Herbert. *The Development of Exegesis in Early Islam: The Authenticity of Muslim Literature from the Formative Period.* London: Curzon Press, 2000

Binark, Ismet and Halit Eren. *World Bibliography of Translations of the Meaning of the Holy Quran: Printed Translations, 1515–1980.* Ed. and introduced by Ekmeleddin Ihsanoglu. Bibliographic Research Centre for Islamic History, Art and Culture; Bibliographical Series, 1. Istanbul: Research Centre for Islamic History, Art and Culture, 1986

Boullata, Issa J., ed. *Literary Structures of Religious Meaning in the Quran.* Curzon Studies in the Quran. London: Curzon Press, 2000

Burton, John. *The Collection of the Quran.* Cambridge: Cambridge University Press, 1977

——. *An Introduction to the Hadith.* Islamic Surveys. Edinburgh: Edinburgh University Press, 1994

Cilardo, Agostino. *The Quranic Term Kalala: Studies in Arabic Language and Poetry, Hadit, Tafsir, and Fiqh: Notes on the Origins of Islamic Law.* Edinburgh: Edinburgh University Press, 2005

Cook, Michael. *The Koran: A Very Short Introduction.* Oxford: Oxford University Press, 2000

Cragg, Kenneth. *The Event of the Quran: Islam in Its Scripture.* Oxford: Oneworld, 1994 Originally Published by Allen & Unwin, London, 1971

——. *The Mind of the Quran: Chapters in Reflection.* London: Allen & Unwin, 1973

——. *Muhammad in the Quran: The Task and the Text.* London: Melisende, 2001

Draz, M. A. *Introduction to the Quran.* London: I. B. Tauris, 2000

Esack, Farid. *Quran, Liberation and Pluralism: An Islamic Perspective of Interreligious Solidarity against Oppression.* Oxford: Oneworld, 1997

——. *The Quran: A Short Introduction.* Oxford: Oneworld, 2002

——. *The Quran – A User's Guide: A Guide to Its Key Themes, History and Interpretation.* Oxford: Oneworld, 2005

The Essential Koran: The Heart of Islam. An Introductory Selection of Readings from the Quran. Trans. and introduced by Thomas Cleary. New York: HarperCollins, 1993

Federspiel, Howard M. *The Usage of Tradition of the Prophet in Contemporary Indonesia.* Monographs in Southeast Asian Studies. Tempe, AZ: Program for Southeast Asian Studies. Arizona State University, 1993

Gatje, Helmut. *The Quran and Its Exegesis. Selected Texts with Classical and Modern Muslim Interpretations.* Trans. and ed. Alford T. Welch. London: Routledge & Kegan Paul, 1976

al-Ghazali, Muhammad. *Journey through the Quran: The Content and Context of the Suras.* Trans. Aisha Bewley; abridged by Abdalhaqq Bewley. London: Dar Al Taqwa, 1998

——. *A Thematic Commentary on the Quran.* Trans. Ashur A. Shamis. Herndon, VA: International Institute of Islamic Thought, 2000

Goldziher, Ignaz, with an introduction on Goldziher and *hadith* from *Geschichte des Arabischen Schrifttums* by Fuat Sezgin. *Schools of Koranic Commentators.* Ed. and trans. Wolfgang H. Behn. Wiesbaden: Harrassowitz, 2006. First published as *Die Richtungen der islamischen Koranuslegung,* Leiden, 1920

Graham, William A. *Divine Word and Prophetic Word in Early Islam: A Reconstruction of the Sources, with Special Reference to the Divine Saying on Hadith Qudsi.* The Hague: Mouton, 1977

Guillaume, Alfred. *The Traditions of Islam: An Introduction to the Study of the Hadith Literature.* New York: Books for Libraries, 1980. Originally published by Clarendon Press, Oxford, 1924

Gwynne, Rosalind Ward. *Logic, Rhetoric and Legal Reasoning in the Quran: God's Arguments.* RoutledgeCurzon Studies in the Quran. London: RoutledgeCurzon, 2004

Haleem, Muhammad Abdel. *Understanding the Quran: Themes and Style.* London: I. B. Tauris, 1999

Hasan, Vazeer. *The Study of the Quran by Non-Muslim Scholars.* New Delhi: Adam Publishers & Distributors, 2005

Hawting, Gerald R. and Abdul-Kader A. Shareef, eds. *Approaches to the Quran.* Routledge/SOAS Series on Contemporary Politics and Culture in the Middle East. London: Routledge, 1993

Ibn Warraq, ed. *The Origins of the Koran: Classic Essays on Islam's Holy Book.* Amherst, NY: Prometheus Books, 1998

——. *What the Koran Really Says: Language, Text, and Commentary.* Amherst, NY: Prometheus Books, 2002

Izutsu, Toshihiko. *Ethico-Religious Concepts in the Quran.* McGill Institute of Islamic Studies, McGill Islamic Studies, 1. Montreal: McGill University Press, 1966

——. *God and Man in the Koran.* Studies in the Humanities and Social Relations. New York:

Books for Libraries, 1980. Originally published by the Keio Institute of Cultural and Linguistic Studies, Japan, 1964

Jeffery, Arthur, with a preface by Gerhard Bowering and Jane Dammen McAuliffe. *The Foreign Vocubulary of the Quran*. Texts and Studies on the Quran, 3. Leiden: E. J. Brill, 2007

———. *The Quran as Scripture*. New York: Russell F. Moore, 1957

Juynboll, G. H. A. *The Authenticity of the Tradition Literature: Discussions in Modern Egypt*. Leiden: E. J. Brill, 1969

———. *Muslim Tradition: Studies in Chronology, Provenance and Authorship of Early Hadith*. Cambridge: Cambridge University Press, 1983

———. *Studies on the Origins and Uses of Islamic Hadith*. Variorum Collected Studies Series, CS550. Brookfield, VT: Variorum, 1996

Kassis, Hanna E. *A Concordance of the Quran*. Berkeley: University of California Press, 1983

Keeler, Annabel. *Sufi Hermeneutics: The Quran Commentary of Rashid al-Din Maybudi*. Quranic Studies Series, 3. Oxford: Oxford University Press/Institute of Ismaili Studies, 2006

Khui, Abu al-Qasim ibn Ali Akbar. *The Prolegomena to the Quran*. Trans. and introduced by Abdulaziz A. Sachedina. New York: Oxford University Press, 1998

Kropp, Manfred S., ed. *Results of Contemporary Research on the Quran: The Question of a Historio-Critical Text of the Quran*. Beiruter Texte und Studien, 100. Beirut: Orient-Institut, 2007

Lane, Andrew J. *A Traditional Mutazilite Quran Commentary: The Kashshaf of Jar Allah al-Zamakhshari*. Texts and Studies on the Quran, 2. Leiden: E. J. Brill, 2006

Lawrence, Bruce. *The Quran: A Biography*. Books that Shook the World. London: Atlantic Books, 2006

Luxenberg, Christoph. *The Syro-Aramaic Reading of the Koran: A Contribution to the Decoding of the Language of the Koran*. Berlin: Verlag Hans Schiler, 2007

Madigan, Daniel A. *The Quran's Self-Image: Writing and Authority in Islam's Scripture*. Princeton, NJ: Princeton University Press, 2001

McAuliffe, Jane Dammen. *Quranic Christians: An Analysis of Classical and Modern Exegesis*. Cambridge: Cambridge University Press, 1991

McAuliffe, Jane Dammen, ed. *The Cambridge Companion to the Quran*. Cambridge: Cambridge University Press, 2006

Mir, Mustansir. *Dictionary of Quranic Terms and Concepts*. Garland Reference Library of the Humanities, 693. New York: Garland, 1987

Motzki, Harald, ed. *Hadith: Origin and Developments*. Formation of the Classical Islamic World, 28. Aldershot: Ashgate, 2004

Nelson, Kristina. *The Art of Reciting the Quran*. Cairo: American University in Cairo Press, 1985

Newman, Andrew J. *The Formative Period of Twelver Shiism: Hadith as Discourse between Qum and Baghdad*. London: Curzon Press, 2000

Nurbakhsh, Javad. *Traditions of the Prophet: Ahadith*. 2 vols. Trans. and ed. Leonard Lewisohn and Ali-Reza Nurbakhsh. New York: Khaniqahi-Nimatullahi, 1981–1983

Parrinder, Geoffrey. *Jesus in the Quran*. New York: Oxford University Press, 1977

Penrice, John. *A Dictionary and Glossary of the Koran, with Copious Grammatical References and Explanations of the Text*. Totowa, NJ: Rowman & Littlefield, 1976

Powers, David S. *Studies in Quran and Hadith: The Formation of the Islamic Law of Inheritance*. Berkeley: University of California Press, 1986

Qutb, Sayyid. *In the Shade of the Quran: Fi Zilal al Quran*. Trans. and ed. M. A. Salahi and A. A. Shamis. London: Islamic Foundation, 1999

Rahman, Afzalur. *Quranic Sciences*. London: Muslim Schools Trust, 1981

Rahman, Fazlur. *Major Themes of the Quran*. 2nd edn. Minneapolis: Bibliotheca Islamica, 1989

Rippin, Andrew. *The Quran and Its Interpretative Tradition*. Variorum Collected Studies Series, CS715. Aldershot: Ashgate, 2001

Rippin, Andrew, ed. *Approaches to the History of the Interpretation of the Quran*. London: Oxford University Press, 1988

——. *The Blackwell Companion to the Quran*. Malden, MA: Blackwell, 2006

——. *The Quran: Formative Interpretation*. Formation of Classical Islamic World, 25. Aldershot: Ashgate, 1999

——. *The Quran: Style and Contents*. Formation of the Classical Islamic World, 24. Aldershot: Ashgate, 2001

Robinson, Neal. *Discovering the Quran: A Contemporary Approach to a Veiled Text*. London: SCM Press, 1996

Saeed, Abdullah. *Interpreting the Quran: Towards a Contemporary Approach*. London: Routledge, 2006

Saeed, Abdullah, ed. *Approaches to the Quran in Contemporary Indonesia*. Quranic Studies Series, 2. Oxford: Oxford University Press/Institute of Ismaili Studies, 2005

Saleh, Walid A. *The Formation of the Classical Tafsir Tradition: The Quran Commentary of al-Thalabi (d. 427/1035)*. Texts and Studies on the Quran, 1. Leiden: E. J. Brill, 2004

Sells, Michael. *Approaching the Quran: The Early Revelations*. 2nd edn. Ashland, OR: White Cloud Press, 2007

Shah-Kazemi, Reza. *The Other in the Light of the One: The Universality of the Quran and Interfaith Dialogue*. Cambridge: Islamic Texts Society, 2006

Siddiqi, Muhammad Zubayr. *Hadith Literature: Its Origin, Development and Special Features*. Ed. and revised Abdal Hakim Murad. Cambridge: Islamic Texts Society, 1993

Stowasser, Barbara Freyer. *Women in the Quran, Traditions, and Interpretations*. New York: Oxford University Press, 1994

Tabatabai, Allama Sayyid M. H. *The Quran in Islam: Its Impact and Influence on the Life of Muslims*. Trans. Assadullah ad-Dhaakir Yate. London: Zahra Publications, 1987

Taji-Farouki, Suha, ed. *Modern Muslim Intellectuals and the Quran*. Quranic Studies Series, 1. Oxford: Oxford University Press/Institute of Ismaili Studies, 2004

Turner, Colin, ed. *The Koran: Critical Concepts in Islamic Studies*. 4 vols. London: RoutledgeCurzon, 2004

Von Denffer, Ahmad. *Hadith: A Select and Annotated Guide to Materials in the English Language*. 2nd edn. Islamic Studies Bibliographies Series, 1. Leicester: Islamic Foundation, 1985

Wadud, Amina. *Quran and Woman: Reading the Sacred Text from a Woman's Perspective*. 2nd edn. Oxford: Oxford University Press, 1999. Revised edn. of *Quran and Woman*, Kuala Lumpur, 1992

Wansbrough, John E. *Quranic Studies: Sources and Methods of Scriptural Interpretation*. Oxford: Oxford University Press, 1977

Watt, W. Montgomery. *Companion to the Quran: Based on the Arberry Translation*. London: Allen & Unwin, 1967

——. *Muhammad's Mecca: History in the Quran*. Islamic Surveys. Edinburgh: Edinburgh University Press, 1988

Wilcox, Lynn. *Women and the Holy Quran: A Sufi Perspective*, vol. 1. Riverside, CA: M. T. O. Shahmaghsoudi, 1998

Wild, Stefan. *Self-Referentiality in the Quran*. Diskurse der Arabistik, 11. Wiesbaden: Harrassowitz, 2006

Wild, Stefan, ed. *The Quran as Text*. Islamic Philosophy, Theology, and Science; Texts and Studies, 27. A symposium on the 'Quran as Text' held in Bonn in Nov. 1993. Leiden: E. J. Brill, 1996

The Wisdom of the Quran. Oxford: Oneworld, 2000

The Quran in translation

The Glorious Koran: A Bi-lingual Edition with English Translation, Introduction and Notes. Trans. Muhammad Marmaduke Pickthall. London: Allen & Unwin, 1976. First published 1938

The Holy Qur-an: Text, Translation & Commentary. Trans. Abdullah Yusuf Ali. 2 vols. Lahore: Shaikh Muhammad Ashraf, 1969. First published 1938

The Holy Quran. Arabic Text, with English Translation and Commentary. 4th edn. Trans. S. V. Mir Ahmed Ali. Elmhurst, NY: Tahrike Tarsile Quran, 1995

An Interpretation of the Quran: English Translation of the Meanings: A Bilingual Edition. Trans. Majid Fakhry. New York: New York University Press, 2002

The Koran Interpreted. 2 vols. Trans. A. J. Arberry. London: Allen & Unwin, 1955

The Koran: A Translation. Trans. with notes by N. J. Dawood. 4th revised edn. London: Allen Lane, 1974

The Meaning of the Glorious Koran: An Explanatory Translation. Trans. Marmaduke Pickthall. London: Everyman's Library. First published by Alfred A. Knopf, 1930

The Message of the Quran. Trans. and explained by Muhammad Asad. Gibraltar: Dar al-Andalus, 1980

The Quran. Trans. T. B. Irving. Battleboro, VT: Amana Books, 1985

al-Quran: A Contemporary Translation. Trans. Ahmed Ali. Revised edn. Princeton, NJ: Princeton University Press, 1993

The Quran: The First Poetic Translation. Trans. Fazlollah Nikayin. Skokie, IL: Ultimate Books, 2000

The Quran: A Modern English Version. Trans. Majid Fakhry. Reading, UK: Garnet, 1997

The Quran: A New Interpretation. Textual Exegesis by Muhammad Baqir Behbudi. English trans. Colin Turner. In English with Arabic text. London: Curzon Press, 1997

The Quran: A New Translation. Trans. Thomas Cleary. Chicago: Starlatch Press, 2004

The Quran: A New Translation. Trans. M. A. S. Abdel Haleem. Oxford: Oxford University Press, 2004

The Quran: Translated, with a Critical Re-arrangement of the Surahs. Trans. Richard Bell. 2 vols. Edinburgh: T. & T. Clark, 1960. First published 1937

The Quran: With a Phrase-by-Phrase English Translation. Trans. Ali Quli Qarai. London: ICAS Press, 2004

The Prophet Muhammad

Andrae, Tor. *Mohammed: The Man and His Faith*. Trans. Theophil Menzel. London: Allen & Unwin, 1989

Armstrong, Karen. *Muhammad: A Biography of the Prophet*. New edn. London: Phoenix, 2001

——. *Muhammad: Prophet for Our Time*. Eminent Lives. London: HarperPress, 2006

———. *Muhammad: A Western Attempt to Understand Islam*. London: Victor Gollancz, 1991

Azzam, Abd al Rahman. *The Eternal Message of Muhammad*. Trans. Caesar E. Farah. Cambridge: Islamic Texts Society, 1993

Bodley, R. V. C. *The Messenger: The Life of Mohammed*. London: R. Hale, 1946

Cook, Michael. *Muhammad*. New York: Oxford University Press, 1983

Dashti, Ali. *Twenty-Three Years: A Study of the Prophetic Career of Mohammad*. Trans. F. R. C. Bagley. London: Allen & Unwin, 1985

Dermenghem, Emile. *Muhammad and the Islamic Tradition*. Trans. Jean M. Watt. Woodstock, NY: Overlook Press, 1981. Originally published by Harper in 1958

Forward, Martin. *Muhammad: A Short Biography*. Oxford: Oneworld, 1998

Glubb, John Bagot (Glubb Pasha). *The Life and Times of Muhammad*. London: Hodder & Stoughton, 1970

Haykal, Muhammad Husayn. *The Life of Muhammad*. Trans. from the 8th edn. by Ismail R. al-Faruqi. Indianapolis: North American Trust Publications, 1976

Ibn Ishaq, Muhammad. *The Life of Muhammad: A Translation of (Ibn) Ishaq's Sirat Rasul Allah*. Trans. with an introduction and notes by Alfred Guillaume. London: Oxford University Press, 1955

———. *The Making of the Last Prophet: Kitab al-Mubtada*. First section of *Sirat Rasul Allah*. Reconstructed by Gordon Darnell Newby. Columbia, SC: University of South Carolina Press, 1989

Ibn Kathir. *The Life of the Prophet Muhammad*. Translation of *al-Sira al-Nabawiyya*. 4 vols. Trans. Trevor Le Gassick. Great Books of Islamic Civilization. Reading, UK: Garnet, 2000

Ibn Warraq, ed. *The Quest for the Historical Muhammad*. Amherst, NY: Prometheus Books, 2000

Kelen, Betty. *Muhammad: The Messenger of God*. New York: Pocket Books, 1977

Khan, Muhammad Zafrulla. *Muhammad: Seal of the Prophets*. London: Routledge & Kegan Paul, 1980

Lings, Martin. *Muhammad, His Life Based on the Earliest Sources*. London: Allen & Unwin/Islamic Texts Society, 1983

Motzki, Harald, ed. *The Biography of Muhammad: The Issue of Sources*. Islamic History and Civilization, Studies and Texts, 32. Leiden: E. J. Brill, 2000

Muir, Sir William. *The Life of Mohammed: From Original Sources*. Revised by T. H. Weir. New York: AMS Publications, 1975. First published by John Grant, Edinburgh, 1923

Peters, F. E. *Muhammad and the Origins of Islam*. SUNY series in Near Eastern Studies. Albany: State University of New York Press, 1994

Rahman, Afzalur. *Muhammad: Blessing for Mankind*. London: Muslim School Trust of London, 1979

Ramadan, Tariq. *The Messenger: The Meaning of the Life of Muhammad*. New York: Oxford University Press, 2007

Rauf, Mohd Abdul. *The Life and Teaching of the Prophet Muhammad*. London: Longman, 1964

Rodinson, Maxime. *Mohammed*. Trans. Anne Carter. Harmondsworth: Penguin, 1971

Rogerson, Barnaby. *The Prophet Muhammad*. London: Little, Brown, 2003

Rubin, Uri, ed. *The Life of Muhammad*. Formation of the Classical Islamic World, 4. Aldershot: Ashgate, 1998

Salahi, M. A. *Muhammad: Man and Prophet: A Complete Study of the Life of the Prophet of Islam*. Shaftsbury: Element Books, 1995

Warren, Ruth. *Muhammad, Prophet of Islam*. London: Franklin Watts, 1965

Watt, W. Montgomery. *Muhammad at Mecca*. Oxford: Clarendon Press, 1953
———. *Muhammad at Medina*. Oxford: Clarendon Press, 1956
———. *Muhammad: Prophet and Statesman*. London: Oxford University Press, 1961
Zeitlin, Irving M. *The Historical Muhammad*. Cambridge: Polity Press, 2007

Thought and practice: philosophy, intellectual life, religious life, faith and practice

Abbas, Shemeem Burney. *The Female Voices in Sufi Ritual: Devotional Practices of Pakistan and India*. Austin: University of Texas Press, 2003
Abu-Rabi, Ibrahim M., ed. *The Blackwell Companion to Contemporary Islamic Thought*. Blackwell Companion to Religion. Malden, MA: Blackwell, 2006
Abu-Zahra, Nadia. *The Pure and the Powerful: Studies in Contemporary Muslim Society*. Reading, UK: Garnet, 1997
Ahmad, Zaid. *The Epistemology of Ibn Khaldun*. Culture and Civilization in the Middle East. London: RoutledgeCurzon, 2003
Amin, Mohamed. *Pilgrimage to Mecca*. Washington, DC: Islamic Center, 1980
Andrae, Tor. *In the Garden of Myrtles: Studies in Early Islamic Mysticism*. Trans. Birgitta Sharpe. SUNY Series in Muslim Spirituality in South Asia. Albany: State University of New York Press, 1987
Arberry, A. J. *Aspects of Islamic Civilization: As Depicted in the Original Text*. London: Allen & Unwin, 1964
———. *An Introduction to the History of Sufism*. London: Longman, 1942
———. *Sufism, An Account of the Mystics of Islam*. New York: Harper Torchbook, 1970. Originally published by Allen & Unwin, 1950
Arjomand, Said Amir. *Authority and Political Culture in Shiism*. Albany: State University of New York Press, 1988
Arnaldez, Roger. *Averroes: A Rationalist in Islam*. London: Allen & Unwin, 2000
al-Attas, Syed Muhammad Naquib. *Islam and the Philosophy of Science*. Kuala Lumpur: International Institute of Islamic Thought and Civilization, International University of Malaysia (ISTAC), 1989
———. *Prolegomena to the Metaphysics of Islam: An Exposition of the Fundamental Elements of the Worldview of Islam*. Kuala Lumpur: International Institute of Islamic Thought and Civilization, International University of Malaysia (ISTAC), 1995
Ayoub, Mahmoud. *Islam: Faith and Practice*. Markham: Open Press, 1989
———. *Redemptive Suffering in Islam: A Study of the Devotional Aspects of Ashura' in Twelver Shiism*. Religion and Society, 10. The Hague: Mouton, 1978
al-Azmeh, Aziz. *Arabic Thought and Islamic Societies*. Exeter Arabic and Islamic Series. London: Croom Helm, 1986
———. *Ibn Khaldun: An Essay in Reinterpretation*. London: Frank Cass, 1982
Baali, Fuad and Ali Wardi. *Ibn Khaldun and Islamic Thought-Styles: A Social Perspective*. Albany: State University of New York Press, 1988
Bakar, Osman, with a foreword by Seyyed Hossein Nasr. *Classification of Knowledge in Islam: A Study of Islamic Philosophy of Science*. Cambridge: Islamic Texts Society, 1998
Bakhtiar, L. *Sufi: Expressions of the Mystic Quest*. London: Thames & Hudson, 1976
Baldick, Julian. *Mystical Islam: An Introduction to Sufism*. London: I. B. Tauris, 1989
Bashir, Shahzad. *Messianic Hopes and Mystical Visions: The Nurbakshiya between Medieval*

and Modern Islam. Studies in Comparative Religion. Columbia, SC: University of South Carolina Press, 2003

Bello, Iysa A. *The Medieval Islamic Controversy between Philosophy and Orthodoxys: Ijma and Tawil in the Conflict between Al-Ghazali and Ibn Rushd.* Islamic Philosophy and Theology, Texts and Studies, 3. Leiden: E. J. Brill, 1989

Bowen, Donna Lee and Evelyn A. Early, eds. *Everyday Life in the Muslim Middle East.* 2nd edn. Indiana Series in Middle East Studies. Bloomington: Indiana University Press, 2002

Brockopp, Jonathan E., ed., with a foreword by Gene Outka. *Islamic Ethics of Life: Abortion, War and Euthanasia.* Studies in Comparative Religion. Columbia, SC: University of South Carolina Press, 2003

Burckhardt, Titus. *An Introduction to Sufi Doctrine.* Trans. D. M. Matheson. Wellingborough: Thorsons, 1976. Originally published in 1959

Butterworth, Charles E., ed. *The Political Aspects of Islamic Philosophy: Essays in Honor of Muhsin S. Mahdi.* Harvard Middle East Monographs, 27. Cambridge, MA: Center for Middle Eastern Studies, Harvard University Press, 1992

Chittick, William C. *The Heart of Islamic Philosophy: The Quest for Knowledge in the Teaching of Afdal al-Din Kashani.* Oxford: Oxford University Press, 2001

——. *Ibn Arabi: Heir to the Prophets.* Makers of the Muslim World. Oxford: Oneworld, 2005

——. *Imaginal Worlds: Ibn al-Arabi and the Problem of Religious Diversity.* Albany: State University of New York Press, 1994

——. *The Self-Disclosure of God: Principles of Ibn al-Arabi's Cosmology.* SUNY Series in Islam. Albany: State University of New York Press, 1998

——. *The Sufi Path of Knowledge: Ibn al-Arabi's Metaphysics of Imagination.* Albany: State University of New York Press, 1989

——. *Sufism: A Short Introduction.* Oxford: Oneworld, 2000

Chittick, William C., trans. *Faith and Practice of Islam: Three Thirteenth-Century Sufi Texts.* Albany: State University of New York Press, 1992

Cook, Michael. *Commanding Right and Forbidding Wrong in Islamic Thought.* Cambridge: Cambridge University Press, 2000

——. *Forbidding Wrong in Islam: An Introduction.* Themes in Islamic History. Cambridge: Cambridge University Press, 2003

Corbin, Henry. *Alone with the Alone: Creative Imagination in the Sufism of Ibn Arabi.* Trans. Ralph Manheim. Bollingen Series, 91. Princeton, NJ: Princeton University Press, 1969. Repr. with a new preface by Harold Bloom, 1997

——. *Avicenna and the Visionary Recital.* Trans. Willard Trask. Irving, TX: University of Dallas Press, 1980

——. *Cyclical Time and Ismaili Gnosis.* Islamic Texts and Contexts. London: Kegan Paul International/Islamic Publications, 1983

——. *History of Islamic Philosophy.* Trans. Liadain Sherrard with the assistance of Phillip Sherrard. London: Kegan Paul International/Islamic Publications for the Institute of Ismaili Studies, 1993

——. *Temple and Contemplation.* Trans. Philip Sherrard with the assistance of Liadain Sherrard. London: Kegan Paul International/Islamic Publications, 1986

——. *The Voyage and the Messenger: Iran and Philosophy.* Trans. Joseph Rowe. Berkeley: North Atlantic Books, 1998

Cornell, Vincent J. *Realm of the Saint: Power and Authority in Morrocan Sufism.* Austin: University of Texas Press, 1998

Daiber, Hans. *Bibliography of Islamic Philosophy.* 2 vols. Leiden: E. J. Brill, 1999

Danner, Victor. *The Islamic Tradition: An Introduction*. Amity, NY: Amity House, 1988

Davidson, Herbert A. *Alfarabi, Avicenna, and Averroes, on Intellect: Their Cosmologies, Theories of the Active Intellect, and Theories of Human Intellect*. New York: Oxford University Press, 1992

Dhanani, Alnoor. *The Physical Theory of Kalam: Atoms, Space, and Void in Basrian Mutazili Cosmology*. Leiden: E. J. Brill, 1994

Eaton, Charles Le Gai, with a foreword by Seyyed Hossein Nasr. *Remembering God: Reflections on Islam*. Chicago: ABC International Group, 2000

Eaton, Richard Maxwell. *Sufis of Bijapur, 1300–1700: Social Roles of Sufis in Medieval India*. Princeton, NJ: Princeton University Press, 1978

Eickelman, Dale F. and James Piscatori, eds. *Muslim Travellers; Pilgrimage, Migration and the Religious Imagination*. London: Routledge, 1990

Elad, Amikam. *Medieval Jerusalem and Islamic Worship: Holy Places, Ceremonies, Pilgrimage*. 2nd edn. Islamic History and Civilization, Studies and Texts, 8. Leiden: E. J. Brill, 1999

Elkaisy-Friemuth, Maha. *God and Humans in Islamic Thought: Abd al-Jabbar, Ibn Sina and al-Ghazali*. Culture and Civilization in the Middle East. London: Routledge, 2006

Ernst, Carl W. *Eternal Garden: Mysticism and Politics at a South Asian Sufi Center*. 2nd edn. New Delhi: Oxford University Press, 2004

——. *The Shambhala Guide to Sufism*. Boston: Shambhala Publications, 1997

Ernst, Carl W. and Bruce B. Lawrence. *Sufi Martyrs of Love: The Chisti Order in South Asia and Beyond*. Basingstoke: Palgrave Macmillan, 2002

Fakhry, Majid. *Averroes (Ibn Rushd): His Life, Works and Influence*. Great Islamic Thinkers. Oxford: Oneworld, 2001

——. *Ethical Theories in Islam*. 2nd expanded edn. Islamic Philosophy, Theology and Science, Texts and Studies, 8. Leiden: E. J. Brill, 1994

——. *Al-Farabi, Founder of Islamic Neoplatonism: His Life, Work and Influence*. Great Islamic Thinkers. Oxford: Oneworld, 2002

——. *A History of Islamic Philosophy*. 2nd edn. Studies in Oriental Culture, 5. London: Longman, 1983

——. *Islamic Philosophy, Theology and Mysticism: A Short Introduction*. Oxford: Oneworld, 1997

Fatemi, Nasrollah S., Faramarz S. Fatemi and Fariborz S. Fatemi. *Sufism: Message of Brotherhood, Harmony and Hope*. Cranbury, NJ: A. S. Barnes & Co., 1976

Fluehr-Lobban, Carolyn. *Islamic Society in Practice*. Gainesville: University Press of Florida, 1994

Frank, Richard M. *Al-Ghazali and the Asharite School*. Duke Monographs in Medieval and Renaissance Studies, 15. Durham, NC: Duke University Press, 1994

——. *Philosophy, Theology and Mysticism in Medieval Islam: Texts and Studies on the Development and History of Kalam*, vol. 1. Ed. Dimitri Gutas. Aldershot: Ashgate, 2005

Galston, Miriam. *Politics and Excellence: The Political Philosophy of Alfarabi*. Princeton, NJ: Princeton University Press, 1990

Geaves, Ron. *Aspects of Islam*. London: Darton Longman & Todd, 2005

——. *The Sufis of Britain: An Exploration of Muslim Identity*. Cardiff: Cardiff Academic Press, 2000

Goodman, Lenn E. *Avicenna*. London: Routledge, 1992

——. *Islamic Humanism*. Oxford: Oxford University Press, 2003

Green, Nile. *Indian Sufism since the Seventeenth Century: Saints, Books, and Empires in the Muslim Deccan*. London: Routledge, 2006

Guellouz, Ezzedine. *Mecca: The Muslim Pilgrimage.* New York: Paddington Press, 1979

Gumley, Frances and Brian Redhead. *The Pillars of Islam: An Introduction to the Islamic Faith.* London: BBC Books, 1990

Gutas, Dimitri. *Avicenna and the Aristotelian Tradition: Introduction to Reading Avicenna's Philosophical Works.* Islamic Philosophy and Theology, Texts and Studies, 4. Leiden: E. J. Brill, 1988

Hahn, Lewis Edwin, Randall E. Auxier and Lucian W. Stone, eds. *The Philosophy of Seyyed Hossein Nasr.* Library of Living Philosophers, 28. Chicago: Open Court, 2001

Haleem, Harfiyah Abdel. *Islam and the Environment.* London: Ta-Ha Publishers, 1998

Hammoudi, Abdellah. *A Season in Mecca: Narrative of a Pilgrimage.* Trans. Pascale Ghazaleh. New York: Hill and Wang, 2006

Hashmi, Sohail H., ed. *Islamic Political Ethics: Civil Society, Pluralism, and Conflict.* Ethikon Series in Comparative Ethics. Princeton, NJ: Princeton University Press, 2002

Hawting, Gerald, ed. *The Development of Islamic Ritual.* Formation of the Classical Islamic World, 26. Aldershot: Ashgate, 2006

Heath, Peter. *Allegory and Philosophy in Avicenna (Ibn Sina): With a Translation of the Book of the Prophet Muhammad's Ascent to Heaven.* Middle Ages Series. Philadelphia: University of Pennsylvania Press, 1992

Hirtenstein, Stephen and Michael Tiernan, eds. *Muhyiddin Ibn Arabi: A Commemorative Volume.* Shaftesbury: Element Books for the Muhyiddin ibn Arabi Society, 1993

Hourani, Albert. *Arabic Thought in the Liberal Age, 1798–1939.* Cambridge: Cambridge University Press, 1983. First published by Oxford University Press, 1979

Hourani, George F. *Islamic Rationalism: The Ethics of Abd al-Jabbar.* Oxford: Clarendon Press, 1971

——. *Reason and Tradition in Islamic Ethics.* Cambridge: Cambridge University Press, 1985

Hourani, George F., ed. and comp. *Essays in Islamic Philosophy and Science.* Studies in Islamic Philosophy and Science. Albany: State University of New York Press for the Society for the Study of Islamic Philosophy and Science, 1975

Hovannisian, Richard G., ed. *Ethics in Islam.* Proceedings of the Ninth Giorgio Levi Della Vida Conference, 1983. Malibu: Undena Publications, 1985

Hurgronje, C. Snouck. *Mekka in the Latter Part of the 19th Century: Daily Life, Customs and Learning. The Moslims of the East-Indian Archipelago.* Trans. J. H. Monahan, with an introduction by Jan Just Witkam. Leiden: E. J. Brill, 2007

Hyder, Syed Akbar. *Reliving Karbala: Martyrdom in South Asian Memory.* Oxford: Oxford University Press, 2006

Izutsu, Toshihiko. *Concept of Belief in Islamic Theology: A Semantic Analysis of Iman and Islam.* Tokyo: Keio Institute of Cultural and Linguistic Studies, 1965

——. *Sufism and Taoism: A Comparative Study of Key Philosophical Concepts.* Tokyo: Iwanami Shoten, 1983

Izutsu, Toshihiko, with a foreword by William C. Chittick. *Creation and Timeless Order of Things: Essays in Islamic Mystical Philosophy.* Ashland, OR: White Cloud Press, 1994

Jackson, Sherman A. *On the Boundaries of Theological Tolerance in Islam: Abu Hamid al-Ghazali's Faysal al-Tafriqa Bayna al-Islam wa al-Zandaqa.* Studies in Islamic Philosophy, 1. Karachi: Oxford University Press, 2002

Karamustafa, Ahmet T. *Sufism: The Formative Period.* New Edinburgh Islamic Surveys. Edinburgh: Edinburgh University Press, 2007

Kemal, Salim. *The Philosophical Poetics of Al Farabi, Avicenna and Averroes: The Aristotelian Reception.* Culture and Civilization in the Middle East. London: RoutledgeCurzon, 2003

Khalidi, Tarif. *Arabic Historical Thought in the Classical Period*. Cambridge Studies in Islamic Civilization. Cambridge: Cambridge University Press, 1994

Knysh, Alexander. *Ibn Arabi in the Later Islamic Tradition: The Making of a Polemical Image in Medieval Islam*. SUNY Series in Islam. Albany: State University of New York Press, 1999

———. *Islamic Mysticism: A Short History*. Themes in Islamic Studies, 1. Leiden: E. J. Brill, 2000

Kraemer, Joel. *Philosophy in the Renaissance of Islam: Abu Sulayman al-Sijistani and his Circle*. Studies in Islamic Culture and History, 8. Leiden: E. J. Brill, 1986

Lawson, Todd, ed. *Reason and Inspiration in Islam: Theology, Philosophy and Mysticism in Muslim Thought: Essays in Honour of Hermann Landolt*. London: I. B. Tauris/Institute of Ismaili Studies, 2004

Leaman, Oliver. *Averroes and His Philosophy*. Oxford: Clarendon Press, 1988

———. *A Brief Introduction to Islamic Philosophy*. Malden, MA: Polity Press/Blackwell, 1999

———. *An Introduction to Classical Islamic Philosophy*. 2nd edn. Cambridge: Cambridge University Press, 2002. Revised edn. of *An Introduction to Medieval Islamic Philosophy*, published 1985

Lewisohn, Leonard, ed. *The Heritage of Sufism*. 3 vols. Oxford: Oneworld, 1999

Lewisohn, Leonard and Christopher Shackle, eds. *Attar and the Persian Sufi Tradition: The Art of Spiritual Flight*. London: I. B. Tauris/Institute of Ismaili Studies, 2006

Lings, Martin. *What is Sufism?* Berkeley: University of California Press, 1975

Mahdi, Muhsin. *Ibn Khaldun's Philosophy of History: A Study in the Philosophic Foundation of the Science of Culture*. London: Allen & Unwin, 1957

Mahdi, Muhsin, with a foreword by Charles E. Butterworth. *Al Farabi and the Foundation of Islamic Political Philosophy*. Chicago: University of Chicago Press, 2001

Marmura, Michael E., ed. *Islamic Theology and Philosophy: Studies in Honor of George F. Hourani*. Albany: State University of New York Press, 1984

Martin, Richard C. and Mark R. Woodward, with Dwi S. Atmaja. *Defenders of Reason in Islam: Mutazilism from Medieval School to Modern Symbol*. Oxford: Oneworld, 1997

Mason, Herbert W. *Al-Hallaj*. Curzon Sufi Series. London: Curzon Press, 1995

Massignon, Louis. *The Passion of al-Hallaj, Mystic and Martyr of Islam*. 4 vols. Trans. Herbert Mason. Bollingen Series, 98. Princeton, NJ: Princeton University Press, 1982

McGinnis, John, ed., with David C. Reisman. *Interpreting Avicenna: Science and Philosophy in Medieval Islam*. Proceedings of the Second Conference of the Avicenna Study Group, Mainz, 2002. Islamic Philosophy, Theology and Science, Texts and Studies, 56. Leiden: E. J. Brill, 2004

Meier, Fritz. *Essays on Islamic Piety and Mysticism*. Trans. John O'Kane with Bernd Radtke. Islamic History and Civilization, Studies and Texts, 30. Leiden: E. J. Brill, 1999

Messick, B. *The Calligraphic State: Textual Domination and History in a Muslim Society*. Berkeley: University of California Press, 1993

Mitha, Farouk. *Al-Ghazali and the Ismailis: A Debate on Reason and Authority in Medieval Islam*. Ismaili Heritage Series, 5. London: I. B. Tauris/Institute of Ismaili Studies, 2001

Moosa, Ebrahim. *Ghazali and the Poetics of Imagination*. Islamic Civilization and Muslim Networks. Chapel Hill: University of North Carolina Press, 2005

Morewedge, Parviz, ed. *Islamic Philosophy and Mysticism*. Studies in Islamic Philosophy and Science. Delmar, NY: Caravan Books, 1981

———. *Neoplatonism and Islamic Thought*. Studies in Neoplatonism, Ancient and Modern, 5. Albany: State University of New York Press, 1992

Morris, J. W. *Wisdom of the Throne: An Introduction to the Philosophy of Mulla Sadra*. Princeton, NJ: Princeton University Press, 1981

Murata, Sachiko and William C. Chittick. *The Vision of Islam: The Foundations of Muslim Faith and Practice*. London: I. B. Tauris, 1996

Mutahhari, Ayatullah Murtaza. *Fundamentals of Islamic Thought: God, Man and the Universe*. Trans. R. Campbell. Contemporary Islamic Thought, Persian Series. Berkeley: Mizan Press, 1985

Nasir-i-Khushraw. *Knowledge and Liberation: A Treatise on Philosophical Theology*. A new edition and English translation of *Gushayish wa Rahayish* by Faquir M. Hunzai, with an introduction and commentary by Parviz Morewedge. London: I. B. Tauris/Institute of Ismaili Studies, 1998

Nasr, Seyyed Hossein. *The Heart of Islam: Enduring Values for Humanity*. San Francisco: HarperCollins, 2002

——. *Ideals and Realities of Islam*. 2nd edn. With added preface by Titus Burckhardt, new introduction by the author and supplementary bibliography. London: Aquarian Press, 1994. First published by Allen & Unwin, 1975

——. *An Introduction to Islamic Cosmological Doctrines: Conceptions of Nature and Methods used by Ikhwan Al-Safa, Al-Biruni, and Ibn Sina*. Revised edn. Albany: State University of New York Press, 1993

——. *The Islamic Intellectual Tradition in Persia*. Ed. Mehdi Amin Razavi. London: Curzon Press, 1996

——. *Islamic Life and Thought*. London: Allen & Unwin, 1981

——. *Islamic Philosophy from Its Origin to the Present: Philosophy in the Land of Prophecy*. SUNY Series in Islam. Albany: State University of New York Press, 2006

——. *Sufi Essays*. 2nd edn. Albany: State University of New York Press, 1991

——. *Three Muslim Sages: Avicenna – Suhrawardi – Ibn Arabi*. Harvard Studies in World Religions. Cambridge, MA: Harvard University Press, 1964

Nasr, Seyyed Hossein, ed. *Islamic Spirituality: Foundations*. World Spirituality, 19. London: Routledge & Kegan Paul, 1987

——. *Islamic Spirituality: Manifestations*. World Spirituality, 20. New York: SCM Press, 1991

Nasr, Seyyed Hossein, H. Dabashi and S. V. R. Nasr, eds. *Shiism: Doctrines, Thought, and Spirituality*. Albany: State University of New York Press, 1988

Nasr, Seyyed Hossein and Oliver Leaman, eds. *History of Islamic Philosophy*. 2 vols. Routledge History of World Philosophies, 1. London: Routledge, 1996

Netton, Ian Richard. *Al-Farabi and His School*. London: Curzon Press, 1999. Originally published by Routledge, 1992

——. *Muslim Neoplatonists: An Introduction to the Thought of the Brethren of Purity (Ikhwan al-Safa)*. London: Allen & Unwin, 1982

——. *Sufi Ritual: The Parallel Universe*. Curzon Sufi Series. London: Curzon Press, 2000

Nicholson, Reynold A. *The Mystics of Islam*. London: Routledge & Kegan Paul, 1966. First published 1914

——. *Studies in Islamic Mysticism*. Cambridge: Cambridge University Press, 1980. First published 1921

Nigosian, S. A. *Islam: Its History, Teaching, and Practices*. Bloomington: Indiana University Press, 2004. Previously published as *Islam: The Way of Submission*, Crucible, 1987

Padwick, Constance E. *Muslim Devotions: A Study of Prayer-Manuals in Common Use*. London: SPCK, 1961

Parens, Joshua. *An Islamic Philosophy of Virtuous Religions: Introducing Alfarabi*. Albany: State University of New York Press, 2006

Parkin, Davis and Stephen C. Headly, eds. *Islamic Prayer across the Indian Ocean: Inside and Outside the Mosque*. Curzon Indian Ocean Series. London: Curzon Press, 2000

Pearson, Michael N. *Pilgrimage to Mecca: The Indian Experience, 1500–1800*. Princeton, NJ: Markus Wiener, 1996

Peters, F. E. *The Hajj: The Muslim Pilgrimage to Mecca and the Holy Places*. Princeton, NJ: Princeton University Press, 1994

Pinault, David. *The Shiites: Ritual and Popular Piety in a Muslim Community*. New York: St Martin's Press, 1992

Razavi, Mehdi Amin. *Suhrawardi and the School of Illumination*. London: Curzon Press, 1997

Reinhart, A. Kevin. *Before Revelation: The Boundaries of Muslim Moral Thought*. SUNY series in Middle Eastern Studies. Albany: State University of New York Press, 1995

Reisman, David C. *The Making of the Avicennan Tradition: The Transmission, Contents, and Structure of Ibn Sina's al-Muhabatat (The Discussions)*. Islamic Philosophy, Theology and Science, Texts and Studies, 49. Leiden: E. J. Brill, 2002

Renard, John. *In the Footsteps of Muhammad: Understanding the Islamic Experience*. New York: Paulist Press, 1992

——. *Seven Doors to Islam: Spirituality and the Religious Life of Muslims*. Berkeley: University of California Press, 1996

Renard, John, trans., with a preface by Ahmet T. Karamustafa. *Knowledge of God in Classical Sufism: Foundations of Islamic Mystical Theology*. Classics of Western Spirituality. New York: Paulist Press, 2004

Renard, John, ed. *Windows on the House of Islam: Muslim Sources on Spirituality and Religious Life*. Berkeley: University of California Press, 1998

Riddell, Peter G. and Tony Street, eds. *Islam: Essays on Scripture, Thought and Society: A Festschrift in Honour of Anthony H. Johns*. (Transmission of Islam Conference, Canberra: 1993.) Islamic Philosophy, Theology and Science, Texts and Studies, 28. Leiden: E. J. Brill, 1997

Rippin, Andrew. *Muslims: Their Religious Beliefs and Practices*. 3rd edn. Library of Religious Beliefs and Practices. London: Routledge, 2005

Rispler-Chaim, Vardit. *Islamic Medical Ethics in the Twentieth Century*. Leiden: E. J. Brill, 1993

Rosenthal, Franz. *Muslim Intellectual and Social History: A Collection of Essays*. Variorum Collected Studies Series, CS309. Aldershot: Variorum, 1990.

Sachedina, Abdulaziz A. *Islamic Messianism: The Idea of Mahdi in Twelver Shism*. Albany: State University of New York Press, 1981

Saeed, Abdullah. *Islamic Thought: An Introduction*. London: Routledge, 2006

Sajoo, Amyn B. *Muslim Ethics: Emerging Vistas*. London: I. B. Tauris/Institute of Islamic Studies, 2004

el-Sakkakini, Widad. *First among Sufis: The Life and Thought of Rabia al-Adawiyya, the Woman Saint of Basra*. London: Octagon Press, 1982

Schimmel, Annemarie. *Mystical Dimensions of Islam*. Chapel Hill: University of North Carolina Press, 1975

——. *Spiritual Aspects of Islam*. Venice: Instituto per la Collabrorazione Culturale, 1962

Schubel, Vernon James. *Religious Performance in Contemporary Islam: Shii Devotional Rituals in South Asia*. Studies in Comparative Religion. Columbia, SC: University of South Carolina Press, 1993

Schuon, Frithjof. *Islam and the Perennial Philosophy*. Trans. J. Peter Hobson with a preface by Seyyed Hossein Nasr. London: World of Islam Festival Publishing Co., 1976

——. *Understanding Islam*. Trans. D. M. Matheson. London: Allen & Unwin, 1963

Sedgwick, Mark J. *Sufism: The Essentials*. Cairo: American University in Cairo Press, 2000

Sells, Michael A., ed. *Early Islamic Mysticism: Sufi, Quran, Miraj and Poetic and Theological Writings*. Trans., ed. and introduced by Michael A. Sells with a preface by Carl W. Ernst. Classics of Western Spirituality, 86. Mahwah, NJ: Paulist Press, 1996

Sharib, Zahurul Hassan. *The Sufi Saints of the Indian Subcontinent*. New Delhi: Munshiram Manoharlal, 2006

Sobhani, Ayatollah Jaffer. *Doctrines of Shii Islam: A Compendium of Imami Beliefs and Practices*. Trans. and ed. Reza Shah-Kazemi. London: I. B. Tauris/Institute of Ismaili Studies, 2001

Smith, Jane Idleman and Yvonne Yazbeck Haddad. *The Islamic Understanding of Death and Resurrection*. Albany: State University of New York Press, 1981

Smith, Margaret. *Al-Ghazali, The Mystic: A Study of the Life and Personality of Abu Hamid Muhammad al-Tusi al-Ghazali, Together with an Estimate of His Place in the History of Islamic Mysticism*. London: Luzac & Co., 1944

——. *An Introduction to Mysticism*. London: Sheldon Press, 1977. First published as *An Introduction to the History of Mystics*, 1931

——. *Rabia the Mystic and Her Fellow Saints in Islam: Being the Life and Teachings of Rabia al-Adawiyya al-Qaysiyya of Basra, Sufi Saint, ca A.H. 99–185, A.D. 717–801, Together with Some Account of the Place of the Women in Islam*. Cambridge: Cambridge University Press, 1928

——. *Studies in Early Mysticism in the Near and Middle East*. Oneworld Mysticism Series. Oxford: Oneworld, 1995. First Published by Sheldon Press, 1931

Smith, Wilfred Cantwell. *On Understanding Islam: Selected Studies*. The Hague: Mouton, 1981

Sonn, Tamara. *Interpreting Islam: Bandali Jawzi's Islamic Intellectual History*. New York: Oxford University Press, 1996

Stepaniants, M. T. *Islamic Philosophy and Social Thought (in the 19th and 20th Centuries)*. Lahore: People's Publishing House, 1989

Stern, S. M. *Studies in Early Ismailism*. Max Schloessinger Memorial Series, Monographs, 1. Leiden: E. J. Brill, 1983

Stroumsa, Sarah. *Freethinkers of Medieval Islam: Ibn al-Rawandi, Abu Bakr al-Razi, and their Impact on Islamic Thought*. Islamic Philosophy, Theology and Science, Texts and Studies, 35. Leiden: E. J. Brill, 1999

Trimingham, J. Spencer. *The Sufi Orders in Islam*. Oxford: Clarendon Press, 1971

Tritton, A. S. *Islam: Belief and Practices*. 2nd edn. London: Hutchinson's University Library, 1954

Urvoy, Dominique. *Ibn Rushd (Averroes)*. Trans. Olivia Stewart. Arabic Thought and Culture. London: Routledge, 1991

Van Ess, Josef. *The Flowering of Muslim Theology*. Cambridge, MA: Harvard University Press, 2006

Waines, David, ed. *Patterns of Everyday Life*. Formation of the Classical Islamic World, 10. Aldershot: Ashgate, 2002

Walker, Paul. *Early Philosophical Shiism: The Ismaili Neoplatonism of Abu Yaqub al Sijistani*. Cambridge Studies in Islamic Civilization. Cambridge: Cambridge University Press, 1993

Watt, W. Montgomery. *The Faith and Practice of al-Ghazali*. London: Allen & Unwin, 1953

——. *The Formative Period of Islamic Thought*. Oxford: Oneworld, 1998. First published by Edinburgh University Press, 1973

——. *Free Will and Predestination in Early Islam*. London: Luzac & Co., 1948

——. *Islamic Philosophy and Theology: An Extended Survey*. 2nd edn. Edinburgh: Edinburgh University Press, 1985

———. *Islamic Political Thought*. Islamic Surveys, 6. Edinburgh: Edinburgh University Press, 1968

———. *Muslim Intellectual: A Study of al-Ghazali*. Edinburgh: Edinburgh University Press, 1963

Wisnovsky, Robert. *Avicenna's Metaphysics in Context*. London: Duckworth, 2003

Wisnovsky, Robert, ed. *Aspects of Avicenna*. Princeton, NJ: Markus Wiener, 2001

Wolfe, Michael. *The Hadj: A Pilgrimage to Mecca*. London: Secker & Warburg, 1993

Wolfson, Harry Austryn. *The Philosophy of the Kalam*. Cambridge, MA: Harvard University Press, 1976

Yazdi, Mehdi Hairi, with a foreword by Seyyed Hossein Nasr. *The Principles of Epistemology in Islamic Philosophy: Knowledge by Presence*. Albany: State University of New York Press, 1992

Legal sciences

Abdul-Rauf, Feisal. *Islam: A Sacred Law: What Every Muslim Should Know about the Shariah*. New York: Qiblah Books, 2000

Abou el Fadl, Khaled. *And God Knows the Soldiers: The Authoritative and Authoritarian in Islamic Discourses*. Lanham, MD: University Press of America, 2001

———. *Rebellion and Violence in Islamic Law*. Cambridge: Cambridge University Press, 2001

———. *Speaking in God's Name: Islamic Law, Authority, and Women*. Oxford: Oneworld, 2001

Ali, Shaheen Sardar. *Gender and Human Rights in Islam and International Law: Equal before Allah, Unequal before Man?* The Hague: Kluwer Law International, 2000

Amin, Sayed Hassan. *Islamic Law in the Contemporary World: Introduction, Glossary and Bibliography*. Glasgow: Royston, 1985

Anderson, J. N. D. *Islamic Law in the Modern World*. Westport, CT: Greenwood Press, 1975. Originally published by New York University Press, 1959

Arabi, Oussama. *Studies in Modern Islamic Law and Jurisprudence*. Arab and Islamic Law Series, 21. The Hague: Kluwer Law International, 2001

al-Azmeh, Aziz, ed. *Islamic Law: Social and Historical Contexts*. London: Routledge, 1988

Bannerman, Patrick. *Islam in Perspective: A Guide to Islamic Society, Politics and Law*. London: Routledge for the Royal Institute of International Affairs, 1988

Bowen, John R. *Islam, Law and Equality in Indonesia: An Anthropology of Public Reasoning*. Cambridge: Cambridge University Press, 2003

Brockopp, Jonathan. *Early Maliki Law: Ibn Abd al-Hakam and His Major Compendium of Jurisprudence*. Studies in Islamic Law and Society, 14. Leiden: E. J. Brill, 2000

Burton, John. *The Sources of Islamic Law: Islamic Theories of Abrogation*. Edinburgh: Edinburgh University Press, 1990

Calder, Norman. *Interpretation and Jurisprudence in Medieval Islam*. Ed. Jawid Mojaddedi and Andrew Rippin. Variorum Collected Studies Series, CS862. Aldershot: Ashgate, 2006

———. *Studies in Early Muslim Jurisprudence*. Oxford: Clarendon Press, 1993

Cilardo, Agostino. *The Quranic Term Kalala: Studies in Arabic Language and Poetry, Hadit, Tafsir, and Fiqh: Notes on the Origins of Islamic Law*. Edinburgh: Edinburgh University Press, 2005

Cotran, Eugene and Adel Omar Sherif, eds. *Democracy, the Rule of Law and Islam*. CIMEL Book Series, 6. London: Kluwer Law International for CIMEL, 1999

Cotran, Eugene and Mai Yamani. *The Rule of Law in the Middle East and the Islamic World:*

Human Rights and the Judicial Process. London: I. B. Tauris/Centre of Islamic Studies and Middle Eastern Law, SOAS, University of London, 2000

Coulson, Noel J. A. *Conflicts and Tensions in Islamic Jurisprudence*. Chicago: University of Chicago Press, 1969

——. *A History of Islamic Law*. Islamic Surveys, 2. Delhi: Universal Law Publishing Co./ Edinburgh University Press, 1997. Originally published by Edinburgh University Press, 1964

Dalacoura, Katerina. *Islam, Liberalism and Human Rights: Implications for International Relations*. Revised edn. London: I. B. Tauris, 2003

Doi, Abdur Rahman I. *Shariah: The Islamic Law*. London: Ta-Ha Publishers, 1984

Dutton, Yasin. *The Origins of Islamic Law: The Quran, the Muwatta and Madinah Amal*. Culture and Civilization in the Middle East. London: Curzon Press, 1999

Dwyer, Daisy Hilse, ed. *Law and Islam in the Middle East*. New York: Bergin & Garvey, 1990

Edge, Ian D., ed. *Islamic Law and Legal Theory*. International Library of Essays in Law and Legal Theory, Legal Cultures, 7. Aldershot: Dartmouth, 1996

Esposito, John L. *Women in Muslim Family Law*. 2nd edn. Contemporary issues in the Middle East. Syracuse, NY: Syracuse University Press, 2001

Fyzee, Asaf Ali Asgar. *Outlines of Muhammadan Law*. 4th edn. Delhi: Oxford University Press, 1974

Gerber, Haim. *Islamic Law and Culture, 1600–1840*. Studies in Islamic Law and Society, 9. Leiden: E. J. Brill, 1999

Gleave, Robert and Eugenia Kermali, eds. *Islamic Law: Theory and Practice*. London: I. B. Tauris, 1997

Goldziher, Ignaz. *Introduction to Islamic Theology and Law*. Trans. Andras and Ruth Hamori with an introduction and additional notes by Bernard Lewis. Princeton, NJ: Princeton University Press, 1981

Haddad, Yvonne Yazbeck and Barbara Freyer Stowasser, eds. *Islamic Law and the Challenges of Modernity*. Walnut Creek, CA: Alta Mira Press, 2004

Hallaq, Wael B. *Authority, Continuity and Change in Islamic Law*. Cambridge: Cambridge University Press, 2001

——. *A History of Islamic Legal Theories: An Introduction to Sunni Usul-al-Fiqh*. Cambridge: Cambridge University Press, 1997

——. *Law and Legal Theory in Classical and Medieval Islam*.Variorum Collected Studies Series, CS474. Aldershot: Variorum, 1995

——. *The Origins and Evolution of Islamic Law*. Themes in Islamic Law, 1. Cambridge: Cambridge University Press, 2005

Hallaq, Wael B., ed. *The Formation of Islamic Law*. Formation of the Classical Islamic World, 27. Aldershot: Ashgate, 2004

Hasan, Ahmad. *The Early Development of Islamic Jurisprudence*. Islamabad: Islamic Research Institute, 1970

Heer, Nicholas, ed. *Islamic Law and Jurisprudence*. Seattle: University of Washington Press, 1990

Hodkinson, Keith. *Muslim Family Law: A Sourcebook*. London: Croom Helm, 1984

Hussain, Jamila. *Islamic Law and Society*. 2nd edn. Sydney: Federation Press, 1999

Iqbal, Safia. *Woman and Islamic Law*. 2nd revised edn. Delhi: Adam Publishers and Distributors, 1994

Issawi, Charles and Bernard Lewis, eds. *Law and Society in Islam*. Princeton Papers, 4. Special issue of the *Interdisciplinary Journal of Middle Eastern Studies*, spring 1996. Princeton, NJ: Markus Wiener, 1996

Izzi Dien, Mawil. *Islamic Law: From Historical Foundations to Contemporary Practice*. New Edinburgh Islamic Surveys. Edinburgh: Edinburgh University Press, 2004

Jackson, Sherman A. *Islamic Law and the State: The Constitutional Jurisprudence of Shihab-al-Din al-Qarafi*. Studies in Islamic Law and Society, 1. Leiden: E. J. Brill, 1996

Jaques, R. Kevin. *Authority, Conflict and the Transmission of Diversity in Medieval Islamic Law*. Studies in Islamic Law and Society, 26. Leiden: E. J. Brill, 2006

Kamali, Mohammad Hashim. *Islamic Law in Malaysia: Issues and Developments*. Kuala Lumpur: Ilmiah Publishers, 2000

——. *Principles of Islamic Jurisprudence*. 3rd revised and enlarged edn. Cambridge: Islamic Texts Society, 2003

——. *Punishment in Islamic Law: An Inquiry into the Huddud Bill of Kelantan*. Kuala Lumpur: Institut Kajan Dasar, 1995

Kerr, Malcolm H. *Islamic Reform: The Political and Legal Theories of Muhammad Abduh and Rashid Rida*. Berkeley: University of California Press, 1966

Khadduri, Majid. *The Islamic Conception of Justice*. Baltimore, MD: Johns Hopkins University Press, 1984

——. *War and Peace in the Law of Islam*. New York: AMS Press, 1979. First published by Johns Hopkins University Press, 1955

Khadduri, Majid and Herbert J. Liebesny, eds. *Origin and Development of Islamic Law*. Washington, DC: Middle East Institute, 1955. Repr. AMS Press, New York, 1984

Khan, M. A. *Islamic Jurisprudence: Islamic Laws in the Modern World*. London: Avon Books, 1996

Khare, R. S., ed. *Perspectives on Islamic Law, Justice, and Society*. Lanham, MD: Rowman & Littlefield, 1999

Kohlberg, Etan. *Belief and Law in Imami Shiism*. Variorum Collected Studies Series, CS339. Aldershot: Variorum, 1991

Kusha, Hamid R. *The Sacred Law of Islam: A Case Study of Women's Treatment in the Islamic Republic of Iran's Criminal Justice System*. Aldershot: Ashgate, 2002

Little, David, John Kelsay and Abdulaziz A. Sachedina. *Human Rights and the Conflict of Cultures: Western and Islamic Perspectives on Religious Liberty*. Studies in Comparative Religion. Columbia, SC: University of South Carolina Press, 1988

Lowry, E. Joseph, Devin J. Stewart and Shawkat M. Toorawa, eds. *Law and Education in Medieval Islam: Studies in Honor of Professor George Makdisi*. Warminster: Gibb Memorial Trust, 2004

Makdisi, George. *Religion, Law and Learning in Classical Islam*. Variorum Collected Studies Series, CS347. Aldershot: Variorum, 1991

Mallat, Chibli. *The Renewal of Islamic Law: Mohammad Baqer as-Sadr, Najaf and Shii International*. Cambridge Middle East Library, 29. Cambridge: Cambridge University Press, 1993

Mallat, Chibli and Jane Connors, eds. *Islamic Family Law*. Arab Islamic Laws Series. London: Graham & Trotman/Centre of Islamic and Middle Eastern Law, SOAS, University of London, 1990

Mayer, Ann Elizabeth. *Islam and Human Rights: Tradition and Politics*. 3rd edn. Boulder: Westview Press, 1999

Mir-Hosseini, Ziba. *Marriage on Trial: A Study of Islamic Family Law in Iran and Morocco*. Revised edn. London: I. B. Tauris, 2000

Motzki, Harald. *The Origins of Islamic Jurisprudence: Meccan Fiqh Before the Classical Schools.* Trans. Marion H. Katz. Islamic History and Civilization, Studies and Texts, 41. Leiden: E. J. Brill, 2002

an-Naim, Abdullahi Ahmad, with a foreword by John Voll. *Toward an Islamic Reformation: Civil Liberties, Human Rights, and International Law.* Contemporary Issues in the Middle East. Syracuse, NY: Syracuse University Press, 1990

an-Naim, Abdullahi Ahmad, ed. *Islamic Family Law in a Changing World: A Global Resource Book.* London: Zed Books, 2002

Nasir, Jamal J. *The Islamic Law of Personal Status.* 3rd revised and updated edn. Arab and Islamic Laws Series, 23. The Hague: Kluwer Law International, 2001

Pearl, David. *A Textbook on Muslim Personal Law.* 2nd edn. London: Croom Helm, 1987

Peletz, Michael G. *Islamic Modern: Religious Courts and Cultural Politics in Malaysia.* Princeton Studies in Muslim Politics. Princeton, NJ: Princeton University Press, 2002

Price, Daniel E. *Islamic Political Culture, Democracy and Human Rights: A Comparative Study.* Westport, CT: Praeger, 1999

Qaradawi, Yusuf. *The Lawful and the Prohibited in Islam.* Translation of *Al-Halal wal-Haram fil Islam* by Kamal el-Helbaway, M. Moinuddin Siddiqui and Syed Shukry. London: Shorouk International, 1985

Ramic, Sukrija (Husejn). *Language and the Interpretation of Islamic Law.* Cambridge: Islamic Texts Society, 2003

Rose Ismail. *Hudud in Malaysia: The Issues at Stake.* Kuala Lumpur: SIS Forum (Malaysia), 1995

Rosen, Lawrence. *The Anthropology of Justice: Law as Culture in Islamic Society.* Lewis Henry Morgan Lectures. Cambridge: Cambridge University Press, 1989

———. *The Justice of Islam: Comparative Perspectives on Islamic Law and Society.* Oxford: Oxford University Press, 2000

Sachedina, Abdulaziz. *The Just Ruler in Shiite Islam: The Comprehensive Authority of the Jurist in Imamite Jurisprudence.* New York: Oxford University Press, 1988

Saeed, Abdullah. *Islamic Banking and Interest: A Study of the Prohibition of Riba and Its Contemporary Interpretation.* 2nd edn. Studies in Islamic Law and Society, 2. Leiden: E. J. Brill, 1999

Sait, Siraj and Hilary Lim. *Land Law and Islam: Property and Human Rights in the Muslim World.* London: Zed Books, 2006

Schacht, Joseph. *An Introduction to Islamic Law.* 2nd edn. Oxford: Clarendon Press, 1964

———. *The Origins of Muhammadan Jurisprudence.* Oxford: Clarendon Press, 1950

Serajuddin, Alamgir Muhammad. *Sharia Law and Society: Tradition and Change in South Asia.* Karachi: Oxford University Press, 2001. First published by Asiatic Society of Bangladesh, 1999

Sonbol, Amira el-Azhary, ed. *Women, the Family and Divorce Laws in Islamic History.* Syracuse, NY: Syracuse University Press, 1996

Stewart, Devin J. *Islamic Legal Orthodoxy: Twelver Shiite Response to the Sunni Legal System.* Salt Lake City: University of Utah Press, 1998

Stewart, Devin J., Baber Johansen and Amy Singer. *Law and Society in Islam: Three Essays.* Princeton Series on the Middle East. Princeton, NJ: Markus Wiener, 1996

Tabatabai, Hossein Moderressi. *An Introduction to Shii Law: A Bibliographical Study.* London: Ithaca Press, 1984

Vogel, Frank E. *Islamic Law and Legal System: Studies of Saudi Arabia.* Studies in Islamic Law and Society, 8. Leiden: E. J. Brill, 2000

Vogel, Frank E. and Samuel L. Hayes III. _Islamic Law and Finance: Religion, Risk and Return_. Arab and Islamic Law Series. The Hague: Kluwer Law International, 1998

Von Grunebaum, Gustave Edmund. _Theology and Law in Islam_. Proceedings of the Second Giorgio Levi Della Vida Conference, 1969, Los Angeles, University of California. Wiesbaden: Harrassowitz, 1971

Weiss, Bernard G. _The Spirit of Islamic Law_. Athens, GA: University of Georgia Press, 1998

Weiss, Bernard G., ed. _Studies in Islamic Legal Theory_. Studies in Islamic Law and Society, 15. Leiden: E. J. Brill, 2002

Wheeler, Brannon M. _Applying the Canon in Islam: The Authorization and Maintenance of Interpretive Reasoning in Hanafi Scholarship_. SUNY Series Towards a Comparative Philosophy of Religions. Albany: State University of New York Press, 1996

Yanagihashi, Hiroyuki. _A History of the Early Islamic Law of Property: Reconstructing the Legal Development, 7th–9th Centuries_. Studies in Islamic Law and Society, 20. Leiden: E. J. Brill, 2004

Yanagihashi, Hiroyuki, ed. _The Concept of Territory in Islamic Law and Thought_. Islamic Area Studies, 2. London: Kegan Paul International, 2000

Yilmaz, Ihsan. _Muslim Laws, Politics and Society in Modern Nation States: Dynamic Legal Pluralism in England, Turkey, and Pakistan_. Aldershot: Ashgate, 2005

Zaid, Abdulaziz Mohammed. _Islamic Law of Bequest_. London: Scorpion, 1986

Zubaida, Sami. _Law and Power in the Islamic World_. London: I. B. Tauris, 2003

Economy and finance

Ahmad, Khurshid, ed. _Studies in Islamic Economics_. Jeddah: International Center for Research in Islamic Economics, King Abdul Aziz University, 1980

el-Ashker, Ahmed Abdel Fattah. _The Islamic Business Enterprise_. London: Croom Helm, 1987

el-Ashker, Ahmed and Rodney Wilson. _Islamic Economics: A Short History_. Themes in Islamic Studies, 3. Leiden: E. J. Brill, 2006

Bhacker, Reda. _Trade and Empire in Muscat and Zanzibar: Roots of British Domination_. London: Routledge, 1992

Bhuyan, Ayubur Rahman et al., eds. _Towards an Islamic Common Market_. Dhaka, Bangladesh: Islamic Economic Research Bureau, 1996

Chapra, M. Umer. _Islam and the Economic Challenge_. Islamic Economic Series, 17. Leicester: Islamic Foundation/International Institute of Islamic Thought, 1992

Choudhury, Masudul Alam. _Contributions to Islamic Economic Theory: A Study in Social Economics_. London: Macmillan, 1986

Ehrenkreutz, Andrew S. _Monetary Change and Economic History in the Medieval Muslim World_. Ed. Jere L. Bacharach. Variorum Collected Studies Series, CS371. Brookfield, VT: Variorum, 1992

Essid, Yassine. _A Critique of the Origins of Islamic Economic Thought_. Islamic History and Civilization, Studies and Texts, 11. Leiden: E. J. Brill, 1995

Faridi, F. R., ed. _Aspects of Islamic Economics and the Economy of Indian Muslims_. New Delhi: Institute of Objective Studies, 1993. Marketed by Qazi Publishers & Distributors

Ghazanfar, S. M., ed., with a foreword by Todd Lowry. _Medieval Islamic Economic Thought: Filling the 'Great Gap' in European Economics_. London: RoutledgeCurzon, 2003

Henry, Clement M. and Rodney Wilson, eds. _The Politics of Islamic Finance_. Edinburgh: Edinburgh University Press, 2004

Homoud, Sami Hassan. *Islamic Banking: The Adaptation of Banking Practice to Conform with Islamic Law*. London: Arabian Information, 1985

Ibrahim, Mahmood. *Merchant Capital and Islam*. Austin: University of Texas Press, 1990

Iqbal, Munawar, ed. *Islamic Banking and Finance: Current Developments in Theory and Practice*. Leicester: Islamic Foundation/Islamic Development Bank/Saudi Arabia and International Association for Islamic Economics, UK, 2001

Iqbal, Munawar and Ausaf Ahmad. *Islamic Finance and Economic Development*. Basingstoke: Palgrave Macmillan, 2005

Issawi, C. *Fertile Crescent, 1800–1914: A Documentary Economic History*. Studies in Middle East History. New York: Oxford University Press, 1988

Issawi, Charles, ed. *The Economic History of the Middle East, 1800–1914: A Book of Readings*. Chicago: University of Chicago Press, 1975. Originally published 1966

Jomo, K. S., ed. *Islamic Economic Alternatives: Critical Perspectives and New Directions*. London: Macmillan, 1992

Kamali, Mohammad Hashim. *Islamic Commercial Law: An Analysis of Futures and Options*. Cambridge: Islamic Texts Society, 2000

Khan, Javed Ahmad, comp. *Islamic Economics and Finance: A Bibliography*. London: Mansell, 1995

Khan, M. Fahim. *Essays in Islamic Economics*. Islamic Economic Series, 19. Leicester: Islamic Foundation, 1995

Khan, Muhammad Akram. *Glossary of Islamic Economics*. 2nd edn. Routledge International Studies in Money and Banking, 23. London: Routledge, 2003

——. *An Introduction to Islamic Economics*. New Delhi: Kitab Bhavan, 1999

Lewis, Mervyn K. and Latifa M. Algaoud. *Islamic Banking*. Cheltenham: Edward Elgar, 2001

Lowick, Nicholas. *Islamic Coins and Trade in the Medieval World*. Ed. Joe Cribb. Variorum Collected Studies Series, CS318. Ashgate: Variorum, 1990

Masters, Bruce. *The Origins of Western Economic Dominance in the Middle East: Mercantilism and the Islamic Economy in Aleppo, 1600–1750*. New York: New York University Press, 1988

Meenai. S. A. *The Islamic Development Bank: A Case Study of Islamic Co-operation*. London: Kegan Paul International, 1989

Morony, Michael G., ed. *Manufacturing and Labour*. Formation of the Classical Islamic World, 12. Aldershot: Ashgate, 2003

——. *Production and Exploitation of Resources*. Formation of the Classical Islamic World, 11. Aldershot: Ashgate, 2002

an-Nabhani, Taqiuddin. *The Economic System in Islam*. New Delhi: Milli Publications, 2002

Naqvi, Syed Nawab Haider. *Islam, Economics, and Society*. London: Kegan Paul International, 1994

Niblock, Tim, and Rodney Wilson, eds. *The Political Economy of the Middle East*, vol. 3: *Islamic Economics*. Elgar Reference Collection. Cheltenham: Edward Elgar, 1999

Nomani, Farhad and Ali Rehnema. *Islamic Economic Systems*. London: Zed Books, 1994

al-Omar, Fuad and Mohammed Abdel-Haq. *Islamic Banking: Theory, Practice and Challenges*. London: Zed Books, 1996

Rahman, Afzal-ur. *Banking and Insurance*. Economic Doctrines of Islam, 4. London: Muslim School Trust, 1979

Rahman, M. *Muslim World: Geography and Development*. Lanham, MD: University Press of America, 1987

Richards, D. S., ed. *Islam and the Trade of Asia: A Colloquium*. Oxford: Cassirer, 1970

Rodinson, Maxime. *Islam and Capitalism.* 2nd edn. Trans. Brian Pearce. Harmondsworth: Penguin, 1977

al-Saadi, Abdullah Jumaan. *Fiscal Policy in the Islamic State: Its Origins and Contemporary Relevance.* Trans. Ahmad al-Anani. Newcastle-under-Lyme: Lyme Books, 1986

Siddiqi, Muhammad Nejatullah. *Banking Without Interest.* Islamic Economics Series, 5. Leicester: Islamic Foundation, 1983

——. *The Role of the State in the Economy: An Islamic Perspective.* Islamic Economic Series, 20. Leicester: Islamic Foundation, 1996

Siddiqui, S. A. *Public Finance in Islam.* Lahore: Shaikh Muhammad Ashraf, 1948

Sudin, Haron and Bala Shanmugam. *Islamic Banking System: Concepts and Applications.* Petaling Jaya: Pelanduk Publications, 1997

Tamer, Sami. *The Islamic Financial System: A Critical Analysis and Suggestions for Improving Its Efficiency.* European University Studies Series, 5, Economics and Management, 3119. New York: Peter Lang, 2005

Vogel, Frank E. and Samuel L. Hayes III. *Islamic Law and Finance: Religion, Risk and Return.* Arab and Islamic Law Series. The Hague: Kluwer Law International, 1998

Warde, Ibrahim. *Islamic Finance in the Global Economy.* Edinburgh: Edinburgh University Press, 2000

Wilson, Rodney, ed. *Islamic Financial Markets.* London: Routledge, 1990

Architecture, built environment and the fine arts

Abou el-Fadl, Khaled M. *Conference of the Books: The Search for Beauty in Islam.* Lanham, MD: University Press of America, 2001

Aga Khan Trust for Culture. *Spirit & Life: Masterpieces of Islamic Art from the Aga Khan Museum Collection.* Published to accompany the exhibition 'Spirit & Life' at the Ismaili Centre, London, July–Aug. 2007. Geneva: Aga Khan Trust for Culture, 2007

Akbar, Jamel. *Crisis in the Built Environment: The Case of the Muslim City.* Singapore: Concept Media, 1988. Distributed by E. J. Brill

Akhtar, Nasim et al. *Islamic Art of India.* Published in conjunction with the exhibition 'Islamic Arts of India', held at the Islamic Arts Museum of Malaysia, 2002. Kuala Lumpur: Islamic Arts Museum of Malysia, 2002

Alexander, David. *The Art of War: Arms and Armour of the 7th to 19th Centuries.* The Nasser D. Khalili Collection of Islamic Art, 21. London: Nour Foundation/Azimuth Editions and Oxford University Press, 1992

Alfieri, Bianca Maria. *Islamic Architecture of the Indian Subcontinent.* London: Laurence King, 2000

Ali, Wijdan. *Contemporary Art from the Islamic World.* London: Scorpion for the Royal Society of Fine Arts, Amman, 1989

——. *Modern Islamic Art: Development and Continuity.* Gainesville: University Press of Florida, 1997

Allan, James W. *Islamic Ceramics.* Ashmolean-Christie's Handbooks. Oxford: Ashmolean Museum, 1991

Allan, James W., ed. *Islamic Art in the Ashmolean, Part One.* Oxford Studies in Islamic Art, 10. Oxford: Oxford University Press for the Board of Faculty of Oriental Studies, University of Oxford, 1995

Allan, James and Caroline Roberts, eds. *Syria and Iran: Three Studies in Medieval Ceramics.*

Oxford Studies in Islamic Art, 4. Oxford: Oxford University Press for the Board of Faculty of Oriental Studies, University of Oxford, 1987

Aslanapa, Oktay. *Turkish Art and Architecture*. London: Faber & Faber, 1971

Atil, Esin. *The Age of Sultan Suleyman the Magnificent*. Washington, DC: National Gallery of Art, 1987

——. *Ceramics from the World of Islam*. Freer Gallery of Art, Fiftieth Anniversary Exhibition. Washington, DC: Smithsonian Institution, 1973

——. *Renaissance of Islam: Art of the Mamluks*. Washington, DC: Smithsonian Institution, 1981

Atil, Esin, ed. *Islamic Art and Patronage: Treasures from Kuwait*. New York: Rizzoli International, 1990

Atil, Esin, W. T. Chase and Paul Jett. *Islamic Metalwork in the Freer Gallery of Art*. Washington, DC: Smithsonian Institution, 1985

Aziz, K. K. *The Meaning of Islamic Art: Exploration in Religious Symbolism and Social Relevance*. Lahore: al-Faisal, 2004

Baer, Eva. *The Human Figure in Islamic Art: Inheritance and Islamic Transformations*. Bibliotheca Iranica. Islamic Art and Architecture Series, 11. Costa Mesa, CA: Mazda, 2004

——. *Islamic Ornament*. Edinburgh: Edinburgh University Press, 1998

Baker, Patricia L. *Islam and the Religious Arts*. London: Continuum, 2004

Baker, Patricia L. and Barbara Brend, eds. *Sifting Sands, Reading Signs: Studies in Honour of Professor Geza Fehervari*. London: Furnace, 2006

Baker, Phillipa, ed. *Architecture and Polyphony: Building in the Islamic World Today*. Thames & Hudson/ Aga Khan Award for Architecture, 2004

Ball, Warwick and Leonard Harrow. *Cairo to Kabul: Afghan and Islamic Studies Presented to Ralph Pinder-Wilson*. London: Malisende, 2002

Banyani, Manijeh, Anna Contadini and Tim Stanley. *The Decorated Word: Qurans of the 17th to 19th Centuries*. The Nasser D. Khalili Collection of Islamic Art, 4/1–2. London: Nour Foundation/Azimuth Editions and Oxford University Press, 1999–2005

Barakat, Heba Nayel. *Al-Kalima*. Catalogue published in conjunction with the exhibition 'Al-Kalima' held at the Islamic Arts Museum of Malaysia, Dec. 2003. Kuala Lumpur: Islamic Arts Museum of Malaysia, 2003

Barry, Michael. *Colour and Symbolism in Islamic Architecture: Eight Centuries of the Tile-Maker's Art*. Contains 158 colour illustrations. London: Thames & Hudson, 1996

Bates, Michael L. *Islamic Coins*. American Numismatic Society Handbook, 2. New York: American Numismatic Society, 1982

Beg, Muhammad Abdul Jabbar. *Fine Arts in Islamic Civilization*. Kuala Lumpur: University of Malaysia Press, 1981

Behrens-Abouseif, Doris. *Islamic Architecture in Cairo: An Introduction*. Studies in Islamic Art and Architecture. Supplement to *Muqarnas*, vol. 3. Leiden: E. J. Brill, 1992

——. *Mamluks and Post-Mamluks Metal Lamps*. Supplement to *Annales islamologiques*, 15. Cairo: Institut français d'archéologie orientale, 1995

Behrens-Abouseif, Doris and Stephen Vernoit, eds. *Islamic Art in the 19th Century: Tradition, Innovation and Eclecticism*. Islamic History and Civilization, Studies and Texts, 60. Leiden: E. J. Brill, 2006

Bennett, James. *Crescent Moon: Islamic Art and Civilization in Southeast Asia*. Trans. Susan Piper et al. Adelaide: Art Gallery of South Australia/National Gallery of Australia, 2005

Bianca, Stefano. *Syria: Medieval Citadels between East and West*. Turin: Umberto Allemandi, 2007

Blair, Sheila S. *Islamic Calligraphy*. Edinburgh: Edinburgh University Press, 2006
——. *Islamic Inscriptions*. Edinburgh: Edinburgh University Press, 1998
Blair, Sheila S. and Jonathan M. Bloom. *The Art and Architecture of Islam 1250–1800*. Pelican History of Art. New Haven: Yale University Press, 1994
Blair, Sheila S. and Jonathan M. Bloom, eds. *Images of Paradise in Islamic Art*. Hanover, NH: Hood Museum of Art/Trustees of Dartmouth College, 1991
Bloom, Jonathan. *Minaret: Symbol of Islam*. Oxford Studies in Islamic Art, 7. Oxford: Oxford University Press for the Board of the Faculty of Oriental Studies, 1989
Bloom, Jonathan M., ed. *Early Islamic Art and Architecture*. Formation of the Classical Islamic World, 23. Aldershot: Ashgate, 2002
Bloom, Jonathan, and Sheila Blair. *Islamic Arts*. London: Phaidon Press, 1997
Brend, Barbara.. *Islamic Art*. London: British Museum Publications, 1991
Brookes, John. *Gardens of Paradise: The History and Design of the Great Islamic Gardens*. London: Weidenfeld & Nicolson, 1987
Broome, Michael. *A Handbook of Islamic Coins*. London: Seaby, 1985
Brosh, Naama. *Islamic Jewelry*. Jerusalem: Israel Museum, 1987
Bunce, Frederick W. *Islamic Tombs in India: The Iconography and Genesis of Their Design*. New Delhi: D. K. Printworld, 2004
Burckhardt, Titus, with a foreword by Seyyed Hossein Nasr. *Art of Islam: Language and Meaning*. Trans. J. Peter Hobson. London: World of Islam Festival Publishing Co., 1976
——. *Fez, City of Islam*. Trans. William Stoddart. Cambridge: Islamic Texts Society, 1992
Canby, Sheila R. *Islamic Art in Detail*. London: British Museum Publications, 2005
——. *Princes, Poets and Paladins: Islamic and Indian Paintings from the Collection of Prince Sadruddin Aga Khan*. London: British Museum Publications for the Trustees of British Museum, 1998
Cantacuzino, Sherban, ed. *Architecture in Continuity: Building in the Islamic World Today*. New York: Aperture for the Aga Khan Award for Architecture, 1985
Carboni, Stefano. *Glass from Islamic Lands*. London: Thames & Hudson/al-Sabah Collection, Kuwait National Museum, 2001
Carboni, Stefano and David Whitehouse with Robert H. Brill and William Gundenrath. *Glass of the Sultans*. New York: Metropolitan Museum of Art, 2001
Çelik, Zeynep. *Displaying the Orient: Architecture of Islam at Nineteenth-Century World's Fairs*. Berkeley: University of California Press, 1992
——. *The Remaking of Istanbul: Portrait of an Ottoman City in the Nineteenth Century*. Seattle: University of Washington Press, 1986
Clark, Emma. *The Art of the Islamic Garden*. Marlborough: Crowood Press, 2004
——. *Underneath Which Rivers Flow: Symbolism of the Islamic Garden*. London: Prince of Wales's Institute of Architecture, 1996
Clévenot, Dominique. *Ornament and Decoration in Islamic Architecture*. London: Thames & Hudson, 2000
Contadini, Anna. *Fatimid Art at the Victoria and Albert Museum*. London: V&A Publications, 1998
Content, Darek J., ed. *Islamic Rings and Gems: The Benjamin Zucker Collection*. London: Philip Wilson, 1987
Creswell, Sir K. A. C. *A Bibliography of the Architecture, Arts and Crafts of Islam to 1st January, 1960*. Cairo: American University of Cairo Press, 1961. First supplement, 1973; second supplement, 1984
——. *Early Muslim Architecture*. 2nd edn. 2 vols. Oxford: Oxford University Press, 1969

——. *A Short Account of Early Muslim Architecture*. Revised and supplemented by James W. Allen. Aldershot: Scolar Press, 1989

Critchlow, Keith. *Islamic Patterns: An Analytical and Cosmological Approach*. London: Thames & Hudson, 1976

Danby, Miles. *Moorish Style*. London: Phaidon Press, 1995

Daneshvari, Abbas. *Animal Symbolism in Warqa wa Gulshah*. Oxford Studies in Islamic Art, 2. Oxford: Oxford University Press for the Board of Faculty of Oriental Studies, University of Oxford, 1986

Davidson, Cynthia C. with Ismail Serageldin, eds. *Architecture Beyond Architecture: Creative and Social Transformation in Islamic Culture: The 1995 Aga Khan Award for Architecture*. London: Academy Editions/ Aga Khan Award for Architecture, 1995

Degeorge, Gérard and Yves Porter. *The Art of the Islamic Tile*. Trans. David Radzinowicz. Paris: Flammarion, 2002

Deroche, François. *The Abbasid Tradition: Qurans of the 8th to the 10th Centuries AD*. The Nasser D. Khalili Collection of Islamic Art, 1. London: Nour Foundation/Azimuth Editions and Oxford University Press, 1992

Dodds, Jerrilynn D., ed. *Al-Andalus: The Art of Islamic Spain*. New York: Metropolitan Museum of Art, 1992

Ettinghausen, Richard, ed. *Islamic Art in the Metropolitan Museum of Art*. New York: Metropolitan Museum of Art, 1972

Ettinghausen, Richard, Oleg Grabar and Marylyn Jenkins-Madina. *The Art and Architecture of Islam, 650–1250*. 2nd edn. New Haven: Yale University Press, 2001

Ettinghausen, Richard et al. *Prayer Rugs*. Catalogue of exhibition held at Textile Museum, Washington, DC, Sept. 1974. Washington, DC: Textile Museum, 1974

Evin, Ahmet. *Architecture Education in the Islamic World*. Proceedings of Seminar Ten in the Series 'Architectural Transformation in the Islamic World' held in Granada, Spain, 21–25 April 1986. Singapore: Concept Media for the Aga Khan Award for Architecture, 1986

Fathy, Hassan. *Architecture for the Poor: An Experiment in Rural Egypt*. Chicago: University of Chicago Press, 1973

Fehervari, Geza. *Ceramics of the Islamic World in the Tareq Rajab Museum*. London: I. B. Tauris, 2000

——. *Pottery of the Islamic World in the Tareq Rajab Museum*. Kuwait: Tareq Rajab Museum, 1998

Fehervari, Geza, with a foreword by Ralph Pinder-Wilson. *Islamic Metalwork of the Eighth to the Fifteenth Century in the Keir Collection*. London: Faber & Faber, 1976

Flood, Finbarr Barry. *The Great Mosque of Damascus: Studies on the Makings of an Umayyad Visual Culture*. Islamic History and Civilization, Studies and Texts, 33. Leiden: E. J. Brill, 2001

Frampton, Kenneth. *Modernity and Community: Architecture in the Islamic World*. London: Thames & Hudson/Aga Khan Award for Architecture, 2001

Frampton, Kenneth, Charles Correa and David Robson. *Modernity and Community: Architecture in the Islamic World*. With 296 illustrations, 82 in colour. London: Thames & Hudson/Aga Khan Award for Architecture, 2001

Freer Gallery of Art and Esin Atil. *Art of the Arab World* [Catalogue of an Exhibition]. Washington, DC: Smithsonian Institution, 1975

Frembgen, Jürgen Wasim. *The Friends of God: Sufi Saints in Islam. Popular Poster Art from Pakistan*. In cooperation with the Museum of Ethnology, Munich. Oxford: Oxford University Press, 2006

Frishman, Martin and Hasan-Uddin Khan, eds. _The Mosque: History, Architectural Development and Regional Diversity._ London: Thames & Hudson, 1994

Garlake, Peter S. _The Early Islamic Architecture of the East African Coast._ Memoir Number 1 of the British Institute of History and Archaeology in East Africa. Nairobi: Oxford University Press for the Institute, 1966

Gierlichs, Joachim and Annette Hagedorn, eds. _Islamic Art in Germany._ Mainz am Rhein: Verlag Philipp von Zabern, 2004

Gilsenan, Michael. _Studies in Medieval Islamic Art._ London: Variorum Reprints, 1976

Glassie, Henry. _Turkish Traditional Art Today._ Bloomington: Indiana University Press, 1993

Gonzalez, Valerie. _Beauty and Islam: Aesthetics in Islamic Art and Architecture._ London: I. B. Tauris/Institute of Ismaili Studies, 2001

Goodwin, Godfrey. _Sinan: Ottoman Architecture and Its Values Today._ London: Saqi Books, 1993

Grabar, Oleg. _The Alhambra._ London: Allen Lane, 1978

——. _Early Islamic Art, 650–1100._ Constructing the Study of Islamic Art, 1. Variorum Collected Studies Series, CS809. Aldershot: Ashgate, 2005

——. _The Formation of Islamic Art._ Revised and enlarged edn. New Haven: Yale University Press, 1987

——. _Islamic Art and Beyond._ Constructing the Study of Islamic Art, 3. Variorum Collected Studies Series, CS829. Aldershot: Ashgate, 2006

——. _Islamic Visual Culture, 1100–1800._ Constructing the Study of Islamic Art, 2. Variorum Collected Studies Series, CS825. Aldershot: Ashgate, 2006

——. _Jerusalem._ Constructing the Study of Islamic Art, 4. Variorum Collected Studies Series, CS821. Aldershot: Aldershot, 2005

——. _The Mediation of Ornament._ Bollingen Series, 35/38. Princeton, NJ: Princeton University Press, 1992

——. _Mostly Miniatures: An Introduction to Persian Painting._ Trans. Terry Grabar. Princeton, NJ: Princeton University Press, 2000

Grabar, Oleg and Cynthia Robinson, eds. _Islamic Art and Literature: Textuality and Visuality in the Islamic World._ Princeton, NJ: Markus Wiener, 2001

Gray, Basil. _Studies in Chinese and Islamic Art,_ vol. 2: _Islamic Art._ London: Pindar Press, 1987

Grube, Ernst J. _Islamic Pottery of the Eighth to the Fifteenth Century in the Keir Collection._ London: Faber & Faber, 1976

——. _Studies in Islamic Painting._ London: Pindar Press, 1995

——. _The World of Islam._ Landmarks of the World's Art. London: Paul Hamlyn, 1966

Grube, Ernst J., with Manijeh Bayani et al. _Cobalt and Lustre: The First Centuries of Islamic Pottery._ The Nasser D. Khalili Collection of Islamic Art, 9. London: Nour Foundation/Azimuth Editions and Oxford University Press, 1994

Grube, Ernst J., with Maria Fabris. _Muslim Miniature Paintings from the XIII to XIX Century from Collections in the United States and Canada: Catalogue of the Exhibition._ Venice: N. Pouzza, 1962

Guaita, Ovidio. _The Art of Living: Residential Architecture in the Islamic World._ Trans. Lawrence A. Taylor. Kuala Lumpur: Islamic Arts Museum of Malaysia, 2001

Hafiz, Huseyin Ayvansarayi. _The Garden of the Mosques: Hafiz Huseyin al-Ayvansarayi's Guide to the Muslim Monuments of Ottoman Istanbul._ Trans. and annotated by Howard Crane. Studies in Islamic Art and Architecture. Leiden: E. J. Brill, 2000

Hamilton, Alastair. _Arab Culture and Ottoman Magnificence in Antwerp's Golden Age._ Arcadian Series, 2. Oxford: Arcadian Library/Oxford University Press, 2001

Hasan, Perween. *Sultans and Mosques: The Early Muslim Architecture of Bangladesh.* London: I. B. Tauris, 2007

Hasson, Rachel. *Early Islamic Jewelry.* Jerusalem: L. A. Mayer Memorial Institute for Islamic Art, 1987

Hattstein, Markus and Peter Delius., eds. *Islam: Art and Architecture.* Cologne: Konnemann, 2000

Helms, Svend. *Early Islamic Architecture of the Desert: A Bedouin Station in Eastern Jordan.* Edinburgh: Edinburgh University Press, 1990

Herdeg, Klaus, with a preface by Oleg Grabar. *Formal Structure in Islamic Architecture of Iran and Turkistan.* New York: Rizzoli, 1990

Hill, Derek, with an introduction by Oleg Grabar. *Islamic Architecture and Its Decoration A.D. 800–1500: A Photographic Survey.* London: Faber & Faber, 1964

Hillenbrand Robert. *Islamic Architecture: Form, Function and Meaning.* Edinburgh: Edinburgh University Press, 1994

——. *Islamic Art and Architecture.* London: Thames & Hudson, 1999

——. *Studies in Medieval Islamic Architecture.* 2 vols. London: Pindar Press, 2001/2006

Hillenbrand, Robert, ed. *Persian Painting: From the Mongols to the Qajars.* London: I. B. Tauris, 2000

——. *Shahnama: The Visual Language of the Persian Book of Kings.* Visual Arts Research Institute Edinburgh, Occasional Papers 2. Aldershot: Ashgate, 2004

Hoag, John D. *Islamic Architecture.* History of World Architecture. New York: Harry N. Abrams, 1977

Holod, Renata, ed., with Darl Rastorfer (associate editor). *Architecture and Community: Building in the Islamic World Today: The Aga Khan Award for Architecture.* New York: Aperture for the Aga Khan Award for Architecture, 1983

Holod, Renata and Ahmet Evin, eds. *Modern Turkish Architecture.* Philadelphia: University of Pennsylvania Press, 1984

Holod, Renata and Hasan-Uddin Khan with Kimberly Mims. *The Mosque and the Modern World: Architects, Patrons and Designs since the 1950s.* Contains 446 illustrations. London: Thames & Hudson, 1997

Hourani, A. H. and S. M. Stern, eds. *The Islamic City: A Colloquium.* Papers on Islamic History, 1. Published under the auspices of the Near Eastern History Group, Oxford and the Near East Center, University of Pennsylvania. Oxford: Cassirer/University of Pennsylvania Press, 1970

Hussain, Mahmood, Abdul Rehman and James L. Wescoat, Jr, eds. *The Mughal Garden: Interpretation, Conservation and Implications.* Rawalpindi: Ferozsons, 1996

James, David. *After Timur: Qurans of the 15th and 16th Centuries.* The Nasser D. Khalili Collection of Islamic Art, 3. London: Nour Foundation/Azimuth Editions and Oxford University Press, 1992

——. *Islamic Art: An Introduction.* London: Hamlyn, 1974

——. *The Master Scribes: Qurans of the 10th to 14th Centuries AD.* The Nasser D. Khalili Collection of Islamic Art, 2. London: Nour Foundation/Azimuth Editions and Oxford University Press, 1992

——. *Qurans of the Mamluks.* London: Alexandria Press/Thames & Hudson, 1988

Jenkins, Marilyn and Manuel Keene. *Islamic Jewelry in the Metropolitan Museum of Art.* New York: Metropolitan Museum of Art, 1982

Jodidio, Philip, ed. *Iran: Architecture for Changing Societies.* An international seminar cosponsored by the Tehran Museum of Contemporary Art et al. Turin: Umberto Allemandi for the Aga Khan Award for Architecture, 2004

Jones, Jeremy, ed. *Bayt Al-Maqdis: Jerusalem and Early Islam*. Oxford Studies in Islamic Art, 9/2. Oxford: Oxford University Press for the Board of Faculty of Oriental Studies, University of Oxford, 1999

Kennedy, Hugh, ed. *Muslim Military Architecture in Greater Syria: From the Coming of Islam to the Ottoman Period*. History of Warfare, 35. Leiden: E. J. Brill, 2006

Khalili, Nasser D. *The Timeline History of Islamic Art and Architecture*. Bassingbourn, UK: Worth Press, 2005

Khalili, Nasser, D. B. W. Robinson and Tim Stanley with Manijeh Bayani. *Lacquer of the Islamic Lands*. 2 vols. The Nasser D. Khalili Collection of Islamic Art, 22. London: Nour Foundation/Azimuth Editions and Oxford University Press, 1996/1997

Khan, Gabriel Mandel. *Arabic Script: Styles, Variants, and Calligraphic Adaptations*. Trans. Rosanna M. Giammanco Frongia. New York: Abbeville Press, 2001

Khan, Geoffrey. *Bills, Letters and Deeds: Arabic Papyri of the 7th to 11th Centuries*. The Nasser D. Khalili Collection of Islamic Art, 6. London: Nour Foundation/Azimuth Editions and Oxford University Press, 1993

Khansari, Mehdi, M. Reza Moghtader and Minouch Yavari. *The Persian Garden: Echoes of Paradise*. Washington, DC: Mage, 1998

Khatibi, Abdelkebir and Mohammed Sijelmassi. *The Splendour of Islamic Calligraphy*. Trans. James Hughes. London: Thames & Hudson, 1976

King, G. R. D. *The Historical Mosques of Saudi Arabia*. London: Longman, 1986

Koch, Ebba. *The Complete Taj Mahal and the Riverfront Gardens of Agra*. London: Thames & Hudson, 2006

——. *Mughal Architecture: An Outline of Its History and Development (1526–1858)*. Munich: Prestel-Verlag, 1991. Distributed in the UK by Thames & Hudson

Komaroff, Lina and Stefano Carboni, eds. *The Legacy of Genghis Khan: Courtly Art in Western Asia, 1256–1353*. New York: Metropolitan Museum of Art, 2002

Kuban, Dogan. *Muslim Religious Architecture*. Part 1: *The Mosque and Its Early Development*; part 2: *Development of Religious Architecture in Later Periods*. Iconography of Religions. Leiden: E. J. Brill, 1974

Kuran, Aptullah. *The Mosque in Early Ottoman Architecture*. Publications of the Center for Middle Eastern Studies, 2. Chicago: University of Chicago Press, 1968

Lawton, John. *Samarkand and Bukhara*. Travel to Landmark Series. London: Tauris Parke Books, 1991

Leaman, Oliver. *Islamic Aesthetics: An Introduction*. New Edinburgh Islamic Surveys. Edinburgh: Edinburgh University Press, 2004

Lehrman, Jonas. *Earthly Paradise: Garden and Courtyard in Islam*. London: Thames & Hudson, 1980

Lentz, Thomas W. and Glenn D. Lowry. *Timur and the Princely Vision: Persian Art and Culture in the Fifteenth Century*. Los Angeles: Los Angeles County Museum of Art, 1989

Lifchez, Raymond, ed. *The Dervish Lodge: Architecture, Art and Sufism in Ottoman Turkey*. Comparative Studies in Muslim Societies, 10. Berkeley: University of California Press, 1992

Lings, Martin. *The Quranic Art of Calligraphy and Illumination*. London: World of Islam Festival Trust, 1976

——. *Splendours of Quran Calligraphy & Illumination*. Vaduz, Liechtenstein: Thesaurus Islamicus Foundation, 2005. Distributed by Thames & Hudson

Lowick, Nicholas M. *Coinage and History of the Islamic World*. Ed. Joe Cribb. Variorum Collected Studies Series, CS311. Aldershot: Variorum, 1990

——. *Islamic Coins and Trade in the Medieval World*. Ed. Joe Cribb. Variorum Collected Studies Series, CS318. Aldershot: Variorum, 1990

Macdougall, Elisabeth B. and Richard Ettinghausen. *The Islamic Garden*. Dumbarton Oaks Colloquium on the History of Landscape Architecture. Washington, DC: Dumbarton Oaks, Trustees for Harvard University, 1976

Maddison, Francis and Emilie Savage-Smith. *Science, Tools and Magic*. Part one: *Body and Spirit, Mapping the Universe*; part two: *Mundane Worlds*. The Nasser D. Khalili Collection of Islamic Art, 12. London: Nour Foundation/Azimuth Editions and Oxford University Press, 1997

Meinecke, Michael. *Patterns of Stylistic Changes in Islamic Architecture: Local Traditions versus Migrating Artists*. Hagop Kevorkian Series on Near Eastern Art and Civilization. New York: New York University Press, 1996

Merklinger, Elizabeth Schotten. *Sultanate Architecture of Pre-Mughal India*. New Delhi: Munshiram Manoharlal, 2005

Messick, Brinkley M. *The Calligraphic State: Textual Domination and History in a Muslim Society*. Berkeley: University of California Press, 1993

Metropolitan Museum of Art, introduced by Stuart Cary Welch. *The Islamic World*. New York: Metropolitan Museum of Art, 1987

Michell, George, ed. (text by Ernst Grube et al.). *Architecture of the Islamic World: Its History and Social Meaning*. With a complete survey of key monuments and 758 illustrations, 112 in colour. London: Thames & Hudson, 1978. Repr. 1987

Michell, George and Mark Zebrowski. *Architecture and Art of the Deccan Sultanates*. New Cambridge History of India, 1/7. New York: Cambridge University Press, 1999

Moughtin, J. C. *Hausa Architecture*. London: Ethnographica, 1985

Museum With No Frontiers. *Andalusian Morocco: A Discovery in Living Art*. Islamic Art in the Mediterranean. Madrid: Museum With No Frontiers, 2002

——. *Early Ottoman Art: The Legacy of the Emirates*. Islamic Art in the Mediterranean. Madrid: Museum With No Frontiers, 2002

——. *In the Lands of the Enchanted Moorish Maidens: Islamic Art in Portugal*. Islamic Art in the Mediterranean. Madrid: Museum With No Frontiers, 2001

——. *Mamluk Art: The Splendour and Magic of the Sultans*. Islamic Art in the Mediterranean. Madrid: Museum With No Frontiers, 2001

Nanji, Azim, ed. *Building for Tomorrow: The Aga Khan Award for Architecture*. London: Academy Editions, 1994

Nasr, Sayyed Hossein. *Islamic Art and Spirituality*. Ipswich: Gogonooza Press, 1987

Nath, R. *History of Mughal Architecture*, vol. 1. New Delhi: Abhinav Publications, 1982

Necipoglu, Gülru. *The Age of Sinan: Architecture in the Ottoman Empire*. London: Reaktion Books, 2005

——. *Architecture, Ceremonial, and Power: The Topkapi Palace in the Fifteenth and Sixteenth Centuries*. New York: Architectural History Foundation/MIT Press, 1991

O'Kane, Bernard. *Early Persian Painting: Kalila and Dimna Manuscripts of the Late Fourteenth Century*. London: I. B. Tauris, 2003

O'Kane, Bernard, ed. *The Iconography of Islamic Art: Studies in Honour of Robert Hillenbrand*. Edinburgh: Edinburgh University Press, 2005

Otto-Dorn, Katharina. *The Art and Architecture of the Islamic World*. Berkeley: University of California Press, 1991

Papadopoulo, Alexandre. *Islam and Muslim Art*. Trans. Robert Erich Wolf and ed. Nora Beeson and John P. O'Neill. Contains 1,118 illustrations, including 174 colour plates. London: Harry N. Abrams, 1980

Petruccioli, Attilio and Khalil K. Pirani, eds., with a foreword by Oleg Grabar. *Understanding Islamic Architecture*. London: RoutledgeCurzon, 2002

Petsopoulos, Yanni, ed. *Tulips, Arabesques and Turbans: Decorative Arts from the Ottoman Empire*. London: Alexandria Press, 1982

Pinder-Wilson, R., ed., with D. Barrett et al. *Paintings from Islamic Lands*. 4 vols. Oxford: Cassirer, 1969

Piotrovsky, Mikhail and John Vrieze. *Earthly Beauty, Heavenly Art: Art of Islam*. Amsterdam: Lund Humphries, 1999

Piotrovsky, M. B. and J. M. Rogers, eds. *Heaven on Earth: Art from Islamic Lands. Works from the State Hermitage Museum and the Khalili Collection*. Munich: Prestel, 2004

Porter, Venetia. *Islamic Tiles*. London: British Museum Publications, 1995

Porter, Venetia and Heba Nayel Barakat with Cecil Bresc. *Mightier than the Sword. Arabic Script: Beauty and Meaning*. Published in conjunction with the exhibition 'Mightier than the Sword – Arabic Script: Beauty and Meaning'. Kuala Lumpur: Islamic Arts Museum of Malaysia, 2004

Prochazka, Amjad Bohumil. *Determinants of Islamic Architecture*. Architecture of the Islamic Cultural Sphere, 1b. Zurich: Muslim Architecture Research Program (MARP), 1988

——. *Introduction to Islamic Architecture*. Architecture of the Islamic Cultural Sphere, 1a. Zurich: Muslim Architecture Research Program (MARP), 1986

——. *Islamic Arches*. Architecture of the Islamic Cultural Sphere, 4a. Zurich: Muslim Architecture Research Program (MARP), 1994

——. *Mosques*. Architecture of the Islamic Cultural Sphere, 2a. Zurich: Muslim Architecture Research Program (MARP), 1986

Prussin, Labelle. *Hatumere: Islamic Design in West Africa*. Berkeley: University of California Press/Aga Khan Program for Islamic Architecture, 1986

Raby, Julian and Teresa Fitzherbert, eds. *The Court of Il-Khans, 1290–1340*. Oxford Studies in Islamic Art, 12. Oxford: Oxford University Press for the Board of the Faculty of Oriental Studies, University of Oxford, 1996

Raby, Julian and Jeremy Johns, eds. *Bayt Al-Maqdis: Abd al-Malik's Jerusalem*. Oxford Studies in Islamic Art, 9/1. Oxford: Oxford University Press for the Board of Faculty of Oriental Studies, University of Oxford, 1992

al-Radi, Selma. *The Amiriya in Rada: The History and Restoration of a Sixteenth-Century Madrasa in the Yemen*. Ed. Robert Hillenbrand. Oxford Studies in Islamic Art, 13. Oxford: Oxford University Press for the Board of Faculty of Oriental Studies, University of Oxford, 1997

Rice, David Talbot. *Islamic Art*. Revised edn. London: Thames & Hudson, 1975

Richards, J. M., Ismail Serageldin and Darl Rastorfer. *Hassan Fathy*. Architects in the Third World. Singapore: Concept Media/Architectural Press, 1985

Robinson, B. W., ed., with a foreword by Basil Gray. *Islamic Art in the Keir Collection*. Keir Collection, 5. London: Faber & Faber, 1988

Robinson, B. W., ed., with an introduction by Ivan Stchoukine. *Islamic Painting and the Arts of the Book*. Keir Collection. London: Faber & Faber, 1976

Rogers, J. M. *Empire of the Sultans: Ottoman Art from the Khalili Collection*. Catalogue of exhibition organized by Art Services International, Alexandria, VA. London: Nour Foundation, 2002

————. *Islamic Art & Design, 1500–1700*. London: British Museum Publications for the Trustees of the British Museum, 1983

————. *Sinan*. London: I. B. Tauris, 2006

Rogers, J. M. and R. M. Ward. *Suleyman the Magnificent*. Secaucus, NJ: Wellfleet Press, 1988

Ruggles, D. Fairchild. *Gardens, Landscape, and Vision in the Palaces of Islamic Spain*. University Park, PA: Pennsylvania State University Press, 2000

Safadi, Yasin Hamid. *Islamic Calligraphy*. Contains 200 illustrations. London: Thames & Hudson, 1978

Safwat, Nabil F. *The Art of the Pen: Calligraphy of the 14th to the 20th Centuries*. The Nasser D. Khalili Collection of Islamic Art, 5. London: Nour Foundation/Azimuth Editions and Oxford University Press, 1996

el-Said, Issam. *Islamic Art and Architecture: The System of Geometric Design*. Ed. Tarek el-Bouri and Keith Critchlow. Reading, UK: Garnet, 1993

Sakr, Tarek Mohamed Raffat. *Early Twentieth-Century Islamic Architecture in Cairo*. Cairo: American University in Cairo Press, 1993

Salameh, Khader. *The Quran Manuscripts in the al-Haram al Sharif Islamic Museum, Jerusalem*. Reading, UK: Garnet/UNESCO, 2001

Scanlon, George T. and Ralph Pinder-Wilson. *Fustat Glass of the Early Islamic Period: Finds Excavated by the American Research Center in Egypt, 1964–1980*. London: Altajir World of Islam Trust, 2001

Schimmel, Annemarie. *Calligraphy and Islamic Culture*. New York: New York University Press, 1984

Serageldin, Ismail. *Space for Freedom: The Search for Architectural Excellence in Muslim Societies*. London: Butterworth Architecture for the Aga Khan Award for Architecture, 1989

Serageldin, Ismail, ed., with James Steele. *Architecture of the Contemporary Mosque*. London: Academy Editions, 1996

Serjeant, R. B. and Ronald Lewcock. *Sana, an Arabic Islamic City*. London: World of Islam Festival Trust, 1983

Shokoohy, Mehrdad. *Muslim Architecture of South India: The Sultante of Malabar and the Traditions of the Maritime Settlers on the Malabar and Coromandel Coasts (Tamil Nadu, Kerala and Goa)*. London: RoutledgeCurzon, 2003

Sims, Eleanor, with Boris Marshak and Ernst J. Grube. *Peerless Images: Persian Painting and Its Sources*. New Haven: Yale University Press, 2002

Sordo, Enrique. *Moorish Spain: Cordoba, Seville, Granada*. Trans. Ian Michael. London: Elek Books, 1963

Stanley, Tim, with Mariam Rosser-Owen and Stephen Vernoit. *Palace and Mosque: Islamic Art from the Middle East*. London: V&A Publications, 2004

Steele, James. *An Architecture for People: The Complete Works of Hassan Fathy*. Contains 213 illustrations, 100 in colour. London: Thames & Hudson, 1997

Steele, James, ed. *Architecture for a Changing World*. London: Academy Editions for the Aga Khan Award for Architecture, 1992

Stierlin, Henri. *Islam: Early Architecture from Baghdad to Cordoba*. Cologne: Taschen, 2002

————. *Islamic Art and Architecture*. London: Thames & Hudson, 2002

————. *Turkey: From the Selçuks to the Ottoman*. Cologne: Taschen, 2002

Stierlin, Henri and Anne Stierlin. *Splendours of an Islamic World: Mamluk Art in Cairo 1250–1517*. London: Tauris Parke Books, 1997

Tabbaa, Yasser. *The Transformation of Islamic Art during the Sunni Revival*. London: I. B. Tauris, 2002

Thompson, Jon and Sheila R. Canby, eds. *Hunt for Paradise: Court Arts of Safavid Iran, 1501–1576*. Milan: Skira Editore, 2003. Distributed in North and Latin America by Rizzoli International and elsewhere by Thames & Hudson

Tzareva, Elena. *Rugs and Carpets*. New York: Allen Lane, 1984

Unsal, Behcet. *Turkish Islamic Architecture in Seljuk and Ottoman Times*. London: Alec Tiranti, 1970

Vickers, Michael, ed. *Pots and Pans: A Colloquium on Precious Metals and Ceramics in the Muslim, Chinese and Greco-Roman Worlds, Oxford, 1985*. Oxford Studies in Islamic Art, 3. Oxford: Oxford University Press for the Board of Faculty of Oriental Studies, University of Oxford, 1986

Von Folsach, Kjeld. *Art from the World of Islam in the David Collection*. Trans. Martha Gaber Abrahamsen. Copenhagen: David Collection, 2001

Walls, Archie G. *Geometry and Architecture in Islamic Jerusalem: A Study of the Ashrafiyya*. London: Scorpion for the World of Islam Festival Trust, 1990

Ward, Rachel. *Islamic Metalwork*. London: British Museum Publications for the Trustees of the British Museum, 1993

Watson, Oliver. *Ceramics from Islamic Lands*. London: Thames & Hudson/al-Sabah Collection, 2004

Wenzel, Marian. *Ornament & Amulet: Rings of the Islamic Lands*. The Nasser D. Khalili Collection of Islamic Art, 16. London: Nour Foundation/Azimuth Editions and Oxford University Press, 1993

The World of Islam: The Arts of the Islamic World from the Early 18th to the End of the 20th Century. Catalogue by Jehan Rajab et al. Keszthely, Hungary: Helikon Castle Museum, 2002

Yatim, Othman Mohd. *Islamic Arts*. Kuala Lumpur: Dewan Bahasa dan Pustaka, Malaysian Ministry of Education, 1995

Yeomans, Richard. *The Art and Architecture of Islamic Cairo*. Reading, UK: Garnet, 2006

——. *The Story of Islamic Architecture*. Reading, UK: Garnet, 1999

Culture, literature and science

Culture and literature

Abdel-Malek, Kamal. *A Study of the Vernacular Poetry of Ahmad Fuad Nigm*. Studies in Arabic literature, 12. Leiden: E. J. Brill, 1990

Abu-Lughod, Lila. *Veiled Sentiments: Honor and Poetry in a Bedouin Society*. Updated 2nd edn. with a new preface. Berkeley: University of California Press, 1999

Ahmad, Aziz. *An Intellectual History of Islam in India*. Islamic Survey, 7. Edinburgh: Edinburgh University Press, 1969

——. *Studies in Islamic Culture in the Indian Environment*. Oxford: Clarendon Press, 1964

Allen, Roger. *The Arabic Literary Heritage: The Development of Its Genres and Criticism*. Cambridge: Cambridge University Press, 1998

——. *An Introduction to Arabic Literature*. Cambridge: Cambridge University Press, 2000

Allen, Roger, Hilary Kilpatrick and Ed de Moor, eds. *Love and Sexuality in Modern Arabic Literature*. London: Saqi Books, 1995

Alvi, S. M. Ziauddin. *Muslim Educational Thought in the Middle Ages*. New Delhi: Atlantic Publishers, 1988

Aminrazavi, Mehdi. *The Wine of Wisdom: The Life, Poetry and Philosophy of Omar Khayyam*. Oxford: Oneworld, 2005

Andrzejewski, B. W. *Islamic Literature of Somalia*. Fourteenth annual Hans Wolff Memorial Lecture. Bloomington: Indiana University Press, 1983

Arberry, A. J. *Classical Persian Literature*. London: Allen & Unwin, 1958

Asani, Ali A. *Ecstasy and Enlightenment: The Ismaili Devotional Literature of South Asia*. London: I. B. Tauris/Institute of Ismaili Studies, 2002

Asani, Ali A. and Kamal Abdel-Malek. *Celebrating Muhammad: Images of the Prophet in Popular Muslim Poetry*. Columbia, SC: University of South Carolina Press, 1995

Asfour, John Mikhail, trans. and ed. *When the Words Burn: An Anthology of Modern Arabic Poetry, 1945–1987*. Dunvegan, Canada: Cormorant Books, 1988

Ashtiany, J. et al., eds. *Abbasid Belles-Lettres*. Cambridge History of Arabic Literature. Cambridge: Cambridge University Press, 1990

Attar, Farid ud-Din. *The Conference of the Birds*. Trans. Afkham Darbandi and Dick Davis. Harmondsworth: Penguin, 1984

Badawi, M. M. *Early Arabic Drama*. Cambridge: Cambridge University Press, 1988

Badawi, M. M., ed. *Modern Arabic Literature*. Cambridge History of Arabic Literature. Cambridge: Cambridge University Press, 1992

Bakalla, M. H. *Arabic Culture through Its Language and Literature*. London: Kegan Paul International, 1984

Baloch, N. A. *Great Books of Islamic Civilization*. Islamabad: Pakistan Hijra Council, 1989

Barthold, V. V. *Cultural History of the Muslims*. Trans. Shahid Shuhrawardy. Delhi: Mittal Publications, 1988

Beeston, A. F. L. et al. *Arabic Literature to the end of the Umayyad Period*. Cambridge History of Arabic Literature. Cambridge: Cambridge University Press, 1983

Berkey, Jonathan. *The Transmission of Knowledge in Medieval Cairo: A Social History of Islamic Education*. Princeton, NJ: Princeton University Press, 1992

Bouhdiba, Abdelwahab, ed. *The Individual and Society in Islam*. Different aspects of Islamic Culture, 2. Paris: UNESCO, 1998

Boullata, Kamal, ed. *Women of the Fertile Crescent: Modern Poetry by Arab Women*. New edn. Trans. Kamal Boullata. Colorado Springs: Three Continents Press, 1994

Bowen, Donna Lee and Evelyn A. Early, eds. *Everyday Life in the Muslim Middle East*. 2nd edn. Indiana Series in Middle East Studies. Bloomington: Indiana University Press, 2002

Browne, Edward G. *A Literary History of Persia*. 4 vols. Cambridge: Cambridge University Press, 1964. Originally published 1902–1924

Cachia, Pierre. *An Overview of Modern Arabic Literature*. Edinburgh: Edinburgh University Press, 1990

——. *Popular Narrative Ballads of Modern Egypt*. Oxford: Clarendon Press, 1989

Cantarino, Vicente. *Arabic Poetics in the Golden Age: Selection of Texts Accompanied by a Preliminary Study*. Leiden: E. J. Brill, 1975

Cohen, Dalia and Ruth Katz. *Palestinian Arab Music: A Maqam Tradition in Practice*. Chicago: University of Chicago Press, 2006

Cole, Juan R. I., ed. *Comparing Muslim Societies: Knowledge and the State in a World Civilization*. Comparative Studies in Society and History Book Series. Ann Arbor: University of Michigan Press, 1992

Cook, Michael. *Studies in the Origins of Early Islamic Culture*. Variorum Collected Studies Series, CS784. Aldershot: Ashgate, 2004

Daun, Holger and Geoffrey Walford, eds. *Educational Strategies among Muslims in the Con-*

text of Globalization: Some National Case Studies. Muslim Minorities, 3. Leiden: E. J. Brill, 2004

Davis, Dick. *Epic Sedition: The Case of Ferdowsi's Shahnameh.* Fayetteville: University of Arkansas Press, 1992

Davis, Ruth F. *Maluf: Reflections on the Arab Andalusian Music of Tunisia.* Lanham, MD: Scarecrow Press, 2004

Dodge, Bayard. *Al-Azhar: A Millennium of Muslim Learning.* Washington, DC: Middle East Institute, 1961

——. *Muslim Education in Medieval Times.* Washington, DC: Middle East Institute, 1962

Dunn, Ross E. *The Adventures of Ibn Battuta: A Muslim Traveler of the 14th Century.* Revised edn. with a new preface. Berkeley: University of California Press, 2005

Eickelman, Dale F. *Knowledge and Power in Morocco: The Education of a Twentieth Century Notable.* Princeton, NJ: Princeton University Press, 1985

Eickelman, Dale F. and James Piscatori, eds. *Muslim Travellers: Pilgrimage, Migration, and the Religious Imagination.* London: Routledge, 1990

Erguner, Kudsi. *Journey of a Sufi Musician.* Trans. Courtenay Mayers. London: Saqi Books, 2005

Esmail, Aziz. *A Scent of Sandalwood: Indo-Ismaili Religious Lyrics (Ginan),* vol. 1. Selected and translated, with an introduction, interpretative essay and notes. Richmond: Curzon Press/Institute of Ismaili Studies, 2002

Faiz Ahmed Faiz. *Poems by Faiz.* Trans. with an introduction and notes by V. G. Kiernan. Delhi: Oxford University Press, 1971

Ferdowsi. *The Epic of the Kings: Shah-Nama, the National Epic of Persia by Ferdowsi.* Trans. Reuben Levy. London: Routledge & Kegan Paul/Royal Institute of Publication of Tehran, 1967

Foltz, Richard C. *Animals in Islamic Tradition and Muslim Cultures.* Oxford: Oneworld, 2006

Geertz, Clifford. *Islam Observed: Religious Development of Morocco and Indonesia.* Chicago: University of Chicago Press, 1968

Gellner, Ernest. *Muslim Society.* Cambridge: Cambridge University Press, 1981

Gibb, H. A. R. *Arabic Literature: An Introduction.* 2nd edn. Oxford: Clarendon Press, 1963

Gunther, Sebastian. *Ideas, Images and Methods of Portrayal: Insights into Classical Arabic Literature and Islam.* Leiden: E. J. Brill, 2005

Guppy, Shusha. *The Secret of Laughter: Magical Tales from Classical Persia.* London: I. B. Tauris, 2005

Guthrie, Shirley. *Arab Social Life in the Middle Ages: An Illustrated Study.* London: Saqi Books, 1995

Hafiz. *The Collected Lyrics of Hafiz of Shiraz.* Trans. Peter Avery. Cambridge: Archetype, 2007

——. *The Divan.* Translated for the first time out of the Persian into English prose, with critical and explanatory remarks, an introductory preface, a note on Sufism, and a life of the Author by H. Wilberforce Clarke. 2 vols. London: Octagon Press, 1974

——. *A Fine Selection of Hafiz's Poems.* Trans H. Nickbell, A. J. Arberry and H. W. Clarke. Comp. and ed. Farmarz Ghani. Tehran: Mirdashti Farhang Sara, 2000

——. *Teachings of Hafiz.* Trans. Gertrude Lowthian Bell with a preface by E. Denison Ross and an introduction by Idries Shah. London: Octagon Press, 1979

Harrow, Kenneth W., ed. *The Marabout and the Muse: New Approaches to Islam in African Literature.* London: James Currey, 1996

Hefner, Robert W. and Muhammad Qasim Zaman, eds. *Schooling Islam: The Culture and*

Politics of Modern Muslim Education. Princeton Studies in Muslim Politics. Princeton, NJ: Princeton University Press, 2007

Heinz, Halm. *The Fatimids and their Traditions of Learning*. Ismaili Heritage Series, 2. London: I. B. Tauris/Institute of Ismaili Studies, 1997

Hunsberger, Alice C. *Nasir Khusraw, the Ruby of Badakhshan: A Portrait of the Persian Poet, Traveller and Philosopher*. London: I. B. Tauris/Institute of Ismaili Studies, 2000

Iqbal, Sir Muhammad. *Poems from Iqbal: Renderings in English Verse with Comparative Urdu Text*. 3rd edn. Trans. V. G. Kiernan. Lahore: Iqbal Academy Pakistan, 2003

Janin, Hunt. *The Pursuit of Learning in the Islamic World, 610–2003*. Jefferson, NC: McFarland, 2005

Janin, Hunt, ed. *Modern Arabic Poetry: An Anthology*. New York: Columbia University Press, 1987

Jenkins, Jean and Poul Rovsing Olsen. *Music and Musical Instruments in the World of Islam*. London: World of Islam Festival Publishing Co., 1976

Kabir, Bashir bin Muhammad H. *A Guide to Islamic Names*. al-Mukarraham, Saudi Arabia: Safa Press, 1990

Kandiyoti, Denise and Ayse Saktanber, eds. *Fragments of Culture: The Everyday of Modern Turkey*. London: I. B. Tauris, 2002

Kassam, Kutub, ed. *Shimmering Light: An Anthology of Ismaili Poetry*. Trans. Faquir Muhammad Hunzai. London: I. B. Tauris/Institute of Ismaili Studies, 1996

Kassam, Tazim and François Mallison, eds. *Ginans: Text and Contexts. Essays on Ismaili Hymns from South Asia in Honour of Zawahir Moir*. New Delhi: S. K. Puri for Matrix Publishing, 2007

Katouzian, Homa. *Sadi: The Poet of Life, Love and Compassion*. Makers of the Muslim World. Oxford: Oneworld, 2006

Keshavarz, Fatemeh. *Reading Mystical Lyric: The Case of Jalal al-Din Rumi*. Studies in Comparative Religion. Columbia, SC: University of South Carolina Press, 1998

Khan, Mohammad Wasiullah, ed. *Education and Society in the Muslim World*. Jeddah: King Abdulaziz University, 1981

el-Kholy, Samha Amin. *The Function of Music in Islamic Culture in the Period up to 1100 A.D.* Cairo: General Egyptian Book Organization, 1984

Kilito, Abdelfattah. *The Author and His Doubles: Essays on Classical Arabic Culture*. Trans. Michael Cooperson with a foreword by Roger Allen. Syracuse, NY: Syracuse University Press, 2001

Knappert, Jan. *Islamic Legends: Histories of the Heroes, Saints and Prophets of Islam*. 2 vols. Religious Texts and Translation Series, NISABA, 15. Leiden: E. J. Brill, 1985

——. *A Survey of Swahili Islamic Epic Sagas*. Studies in Swahili Language and Literature, 1. Lewiston, NY: Edwin Mellen Press, 1999

Knappert, Jan, trans. and ed. *Swahili Islamic Poetry*. 3 vols. Leiden: E. J. Brill, 1971

Kraemer, J. *Humanism in the Renaissance of Islam: Cultural Revival during the Buyid Age*. 2nd edn. Studies in Islamic Culture and History, 7. Leiden: E. J. Brill, 1992

Kritzeck, James, ed. *Anthology of Islamic Literature: From the Rise of Islam to Modern Times*. Harmondsworth: Penguin, 1964

——. *Modern Islamic Literature: From 1800 to the Present*. New York: New American Library, 1970

Lawrence, Bruce B. *Notes from a Distant Flute: The Extant Literature of Pre-Mughal Indian Sufism*. Imperial Iranian Academy of Philosophy Publication, 27. Tehran: Imperial Iranian Academy of Philosophy, 1978

Levy, Reuben. *Persian Literature: An Introduction*. Westport, CT: Greenwood Press, 1974. First published by Oxford University Press, 1923

——. *The Social Structure of Islam: Being the 2nd edn of Sociology of Islam*. Cambridge: Cambridge University Press, 1969

Lewis, Bernard, ed. *The World of Islam: Faith, People, Culture*. Contains 490 illustrations, 160 in colour, 330 photographs, drawings, and maps. London: Thames & Hudson, 1976

Lewis, Franklin D. *Rumi: Past Present, East and West: The Life, Teaching and Poetry of Jalal al Din Rumi*. Oxford: Oneworld, 2000

Lopez-Baralt, Luce. *Islam in Spanish Literature: From the Middle Ages to the Present*. Leiden: E. J. Brill, 1992

Lyons, M. C. *The Arabian Epic: Heroic and Oral Story-Telling*. 3 vols. University of Cambridge Oriental Publications, 49. Cambridge: Cambridge University Press, 1995

Mackintosh-Smith, Tim. *The Hall of a Thousand Columns: Hindustan to Malabar with Ibn Battuttah*. London: John Murrray, 2005

Makdisi, George. *The Rise of the Colleges: Institutions of Learning in Islam and the West*. Edinburgh: Edinburgh University Press, 1981

——. *The Rise of Humanism in Classical Islam and the Christian West: with Special Reference to Scholasticism*. Edinburgh: Edinburgh University Press, 1990

Malti-Douglas, Fedwa. *Power, Marginality, and the Body in Medieval Islam*. Variorum Collected Studies Series, CS723. Aldershot: Ashgate, 2001

Marcus, Scott L. *Music in Egypt: Experiencing Music, Expressing Culture*. Oxford: Oxford University Press, 2007

Meisami, Julie Scott. *Medieval Persian Court Poetry*. Princeton, NJ: Princeton University Press, 1987

——. *Structure and Meaning in Medieval Arabic and Persian Court Poetry: Orient Pearls*. Culture and Civilization in the Middle East. London: RoutledgeCurzon, 2003

Menemencioglu, Nermin, ed. *The Penguin Book of Turkish Verse*. In collaboration with Fahir Iz. Penguin Poets. Harmondsworth: Penguin, 1978

Menocal, Maria Rosa, Raymond P. Scheindlin and Michael Sells, eds. *The Literature of Al-Andalus*. Cambridge History of Arabic Literature. Cambridge: Cambridge University Press, 2000

Mohd Nor Wan Daud, Wan. *The Concept of Knowledge in Islam and Its Implication for Education in a Developing Country*. London: Mansell, 1989

Nakosteen Mehdi. *History of Islamic Origins of Western Education, A.D. 800–1350, with an Introduction to Medieval Muslim Education*. Boulder: University of Colorado Press, 1964

Nasir-i-Khusraw. *Forty Poems from the Divan*. Trans. with introduction and notes by Peter Lamborn Wilson and Gholam Reza Aavani. Tehran: Imperial Iranian Academy of Philosophy, 1977

——. *Make a Shield from Wisdom: Selected Verses from Nasir-i-Khusraw's Divan*. Trans. and introduced by Annemarie Schimmel. London: Kegan Paul International/Institute of Ismaili Studies, 1993

Nasr, Seyyed Hossein, ed. *Ismaili Contributions to Islamic Culture*. Tehran: Imperial Iranian Academy of Philosophy, 1977

Nicholson, Reynold Alleyne. *A Literary History of the Arabs*. Cambridge: Cambridge University Press, 1969. First published by T. Fisher Unwin, 1907

Omar Khayyam. *The Quatrains of Omar Khayyam*. Persian Text with an English verse translation by E. H. Whinfield. London: Octagon Press for the Sufi Trust, 1980

Ouyang, Wen-chin. *Literary Criticism in Medieval Arabic-Islamic Culture: The Making of a Tradition.* Edinburgh: Edinburgh University Press, 1997

Owusu-Ansah, David. *Islamic Talismanic Tradition in Nineteenth Century Asante.* Lewiston, NY: Edwin Mellen Press, 1991

Pederson, J. *The Arabic Book.* Trans. Geoffrey French. Ed. and with an introduction by Robert Hillenbrand. Modern Classics in Near Eastern Studies. Princeton, NJ: Princeton University Press, 1984

Qureshi, Regula Burkhardt. *Sufi Music in India and Pakistan: Sound, Context and Meaning in Qawwali.* Cambridge: Cambridge University Press, 1986. Includes a CD of Qawwali music

Racy, A. J. *Making Music in the Arab World: The Culture and History of Tarab.* Cambridge: Cambridge University Press, 2003

Rosen, Lawrence. *The Culture of Islam: Changing Aspects of Contemporary Muslim Life.* Chicago: University of Chicago Press, 2002

Rosenthal, Franz. *Knowledge Triumphant: The Concept of Knowledge in Medieval Islam.* Leiden: E. J. Brill, 1970

Rumi, Jalal al-Din Maulana. *The Illustrated Rumi: A Treasury of Wisdom from the Poet of the Soul.* Trans. Philip Dunn, Manuela Dunn Mascetti and R. A. Nicholson; foreword by Huston Smith. San Francisco: HarperSanFrancisco, 2000

——. *The Mathnavi of Jalaluddin Rumi.* Edited from the oldest manuscripts available: with critical notes, translations and commentary by Reynold A. Nicholson. 6 vols. Cambridge: Trustees of E. J. W. Gibb Memorial, 1982. Distributed by Luzac & Co. Originally published 1926

——. *A Rumi Anthology: Rumi Poet and Mystic: Tales of Mystic Meaning.* Trans. Reynold A. Nicholson. Oxford: Oneworld, 2000

——. *Rumi: A Spiritual Treasury.* Comp. Juliet Mabey. Oxford: Oneworld, 2000

——. *Rumi's Divan of Shems of Tabriz: Selected Odes.* A new interpretation by James Cowan. Rockport, MA: Element Books, 1997. First published in the UK as *Where Two Oceans Meet* by Element Books, 1995

Rypka, Jan, in collaboration with Otaker Klima et al. *History of Iranian Literature.* Ed. Karl Jahn. Dordrecht: Reidel, 1968

Sadi. *The Gulistan or Rose Garden of Sadi.* Trans. Edward Rehatsek. London: Allen & Unwin, 1964

——. *Morals Pointed and Tales Adorned: The Bustan of Sadi.* Trans. G. M. Wickens. Leiden. E. J. Brill, 1974

Sadr, Hamid Reza. *Iranian Cinema: A Political History.* London: I. B. Tauris/Prince Claus Fund Library, 2006

Safavi, Seyed Ghahreman. *The Structure of Rumi's Mathnawi (A New Interpretation of Rumi's Mathnawi as a Book for Love and Peace, Book One).* London: London Academy for Iranian Studies, 2005

Said, Edward W. *Orientalism.* Repr. with a new preface. London: Penguin, 2003. Originally published by Routledge, 1978

Sakkut, Hamdi. *The Arabic Novel: Bibliography and Critical Introduction 1865–1995.* 6 vols. Trans. Roger Monroe. Cairo: American University in Cairo Press, 2000

Schimmel, Annemarie. *And Muhammad Is His Messenger: The Veneration of the Prophet in Islamic Piety.* Studies in Religion. Chapel Hill: University of North Carolina Press, 1985

——. *As through a Veil: Mystical Poetry in Islam.* New York: Columbia University Press, 1982

——. *Classical Urdu Literature from the Beginning to Iqbal.* Wiesbaden: Harrassowitz, 1975

———. *Islamic Literatures of India*. A History of Indian Literature. Wiesbaden: Harrassowitz, 1973

———. *Islamic Names*. Edinburgh: Edinburgh University Press, 1989

———. *The Triumphal Sun: A Study of the Works of Jalaloddin Rumi*. Persian Studies Series, 8. Albany: State University of New York Press, 1993. Previously published in London by East-West Publications, 1980

———. *A Two-Colored Brocade: Imagery of Persian Poetry*. Chapel Hill: University of North Carolina Press, 1992

Shafik, Viola. *Arab Cinema: History and Cultural Identity*. Cairo: American University in Cairo Press, 1998

Shannon, Jonathan Holt. *Among the Jasmine Trees: Music and Modernity in Contemporary Syria*. Middletown, CT: Wesleyan University Press, 2006

Shehadi, Fadlou. *Philosophies of Music in Medieval Islam*. Brill's Studies in Intellectual History, 67. Leiden: E. J. Brill, 1995

Shiloah, Amnon. *Music in the World of Islam: A Socio-cultural Study*. Aldershot: Scolar Press, 1995

Sibai, Mohamed Makki. *Mosque Libraries: An Historical Study*. London: Mansell, 1987

Sikand, Yoginder. *Bastions of the Believers: Madrasa and Islamic Education in India*. New Delhi: Penguin, 2005

Stanton, Charles Michael. *Higher Learning in Islam: The Classical Period, A.D. 700 to 1300*. Savage, MD: Rowman & Littlefield, 1990

Stetkevych, Suzanne Pinckney. *The Poetics of Islamic Legitimacy: Myth, Gender and Ceremony in the Classical Arabic Ode*. Bloomington: Indiana University Press, 2002

Sultan, Shah, and Great Mughal: The History and Culture of the Islamic World. Copenhagen: National Museum, 1996

Tapper, Richard, ed. *The New Iranian Cinema: Politics, Representation and Identity*. London: I. B. Tauris, 2002

Tibawi, A. L. *Islamic Education: Its Traditions and Modernization in the Arab National Systems*. London: Luzac & Co., 1972. Repr. 1979

Totah, Khalil Abdallah. *The Contribution of the Arabs to Education*. New York: Bureau of Publications, Teacher's College, Columbia University, 1926

Touma, Habib Hassan. *The Music of the Arabs*. New expanded edn. Trans. Laurie Schwarts. Gen. ed. Reinhard G. Pauly. Includes CD. Portland, OR: Amadeus Press, 1996

Von Grunebaum, G. E. *Islam: Essays in the Nature and Growth of Cultural Tradition*. 2nd edn. London: Routledge & Kegan Paul, 1961

———. *Medieval Islam: A Study in Cultural Orientation*. Chicago: University of Chicago Press, 1953

Von Grunebaum, G. E., with an introduction by C. E. Bosworth. *Muhammadan Festivals*. London: Curzon Press, 1951

Waugh, Earle H. *Memory, Music and Religion: Morocco's Mystical Chanters*. Studies in Comparative Religion. Columbia, SC: University of South Carolina Press, 2005

Willey, Peter. *Eagle's Nest: Ismaili Castles in Iran and Syria*. London: I. B. Tauris/Institute of Ismaili Studies, 2005

Wong, How Man and Adel A. Djani. *Islamic Frontiers of China: Silk Road Images*. London: Scorpion, 1990

Young, M. J. L., J. D. Latham and R. B. Serjeant. *Religion, Learning and Science in the Abbassid Period*. Cambridge History of Arabic Literature, 3. Cambridge: Cambridge University Press, 1990

Zia, Rukhsana, ed. *Globalization, Modernization and Education in Muslim Countries*. Education: Emerging Goals in the New Millennium. New York: Nova Science Publishers, 2006

Science

Acikgenc, Alparslan. *Islamic Science: Towards a Definition*. Kuala Lumpur: International Institute of Islamic Thoughts and Civilization, 1996

Bakar, Osman. *The History and Philosophy of Islamic Science*. Cambridge: Islamic Texts Society, 1999

al-Daffa, Ali A. and John J. Stroyls. *Studies in the Exact Sciences in Medieval Islam*. Dhahran, Saudi Arabia: University of Petroleum and Minerals/John Wiley and Sons, 1984

Hamarneh, Sami K. *Health Sciences in Early Islam: Collected Papers*. 2 vols. Ed. Munawar A. Anees. Blanco, TX: Noor Health Foundation/Zahra Publications, 1984

al-Hassan, Ahmad Y. and Donald R. Hill. *Islamic Technology: An Illustrated History*. Cambridge: Cambridge University Press; Paris: UNESCO, 1986

al-Hassan, Ahmad Y., M. Ahmed and A. Z. Iskander, eds. *Science and Technology in Islam*. 2 vols. Different Aspects of Islamic Culture, 4. Paris: UNESCO, 2001

Hill, Donald R. *Islamic Science and Engineering*. Islamic Surveys. Edinburgh: Edinburgh University Press, 1993

——. *Studies in Medieval Islamic Technology: From Philo to al-Jazari – from Alexandria to Diyar Bakr*. Ed. David E. King. Variorum Collected Studies Series, CS555. Aldershot: Ashgate, 1998

Hogendijk, Jan P. and Abdelhamid I. Sabra, eds. *The Enterprise of Science in Islam: New Perspectives*. Dibner Institute Studies in the History of Science and Technology. Cambridge, MA: MIT Press, 2003

Huff, Toby E. *The Rise of Early Modern Science: Islam, China and the West*. 2nd edn. Cambridge: Cambridge University Press, 2003

Ilyas, Mohammad. *Astronomy of Islamic Times for the Twenty-First Century*. London: Mansell, 1988

Iqbal, Muzaffar. *Islam and Science*. Ashgate Science and Religion Series. Aldershot: Ashgate, 2002

Islam, Philosophy, and Science: Four Public Lectures Organized by UNESCO, June 1980. Paris: UNESCO, 1981

Kamal, Hassan. *Encyclopaedia of Islamic Medicine, with a Greco-Roman Background*. Cairo: General Egyptian Book Organization, 1975

Khan, Muhammad Salim. *Islamic Medicine*. London: Routledge & Kegan Paul, 1986

King, David A. *Astronomy in the Service of Islam*. Variorum Collected Studies Series, CS416. Aldershot: Variorum, 1993

——. *In Synchrony with the Heavens: Studies in Astronomical Timekeeping and Instrumentation in Medieval Islamic Civilization: Studies I–IX*. Islamic Philosophy, Theology and Science, Texts and Studies, 55. Leiden: E. J. Brill, 2004

——. *Islamic Astronomical Instruments*. Variorum Collected Studies Series, CS253. London: Variorum Reprints, 1987

——. *Islamic Mathematical Astronomy*. Variorum Collected Studies Series, CS231. London: Variorum Reprints, 1986

——. *World Maps for Finding the Direction and Distance of Mecca: Innovation and Tradition in Islamic Science*. Islamic Philosophy, Theology and Science, Texts and Studies, 36. Leiden: E. J. Brill, 1999

Morewedge, Parviz. *The Metaphysica of Avicenna (Ibn Sina): A Critical Translation-*

Commentary and Analysis of the Fundamental Arguments in Avicenna's Metaphysica in the Danish Nama-i alai (The Book of Scientific Knowledge). Persian Heritage Series, 13. London: Routledge & Kegan Paul, 1973

Nasr, Seyyed Hossein. *Islamic Science: An Illustrated Study.* London: World of Islam Festival Publishing Co., 1976

Nasr, Seyyed Hossein, with a preface by Giorgio de Santillana. *Science and Civilization in Islam.* 2nd edn. Cambridge: Islamic Texts Society, 1987

Newman, Andrew J., ed. *Islamic Medical Wisdom: The Tibb-al-aimma.* Trans. Batool Ispahany. London: Muhammadi Trust, 1991

Pormann, Peter E. and Emile Savage-Smith. *Medieval Islamic Medicine.* New Edinburgh Islamic Surveys. Edinburgh: Edinburgh University Press, 2007

Qadir, C. A. *Philosophy and Science in the Islamic World.* London: Routledge, 1990. Originally published by Croom Helm, 1988

Rahman, Fazlur. *Health and Medicine in the Islamic Tradition: Change and Identity.* Health/Medicine and the Faith Traditions. New York: Crossroad, 1987

Rosenthal, Franz. *Science and Medicine in Islam: A Collection of Essays.* Variorum Collected Studies Series, CS330. Aldershot: Variorum, 1990

Sabra, A. I. *Optics, Astronomy and Logic: Studies in Arabic Science and Philosophy.* Variorum Collected Studies Series, CS444. Aldershot: Variorum, 1994

Sardar, Ziauddin. *Explorations in Islamic Science.* New York: Mansell, 1989

Sardar, Ziauddin, ed. *The Touch of Midas: Science, Values and Environment in Islam and the West.* Manchester: Manchester University Press, 1984

Sayili, Aydin. *The Observatory in Islam and Its Place in the General History of the Observatory.* Publications of the Turkish Historical Society, Series 7, 38. Ankara: Türk Tarih Kurumu Basimevi, 1960

Turner, Howard R. *Science in Medieval Islam: An Illustrated Introduction.* Austin: University of Texas Press, 1997

Ullmann, Manfred. *Islamic Medicine.* Trans. Jean Watt. Islamic Surveys, 11. Edinburgh: Edinburgh University Press, 1978

Watson, Andrew M. *Agricultural Innovation in the Early Islamic World: The Diffusion of Crops and Farming Techniques, 700–1100.* Cambridge Studies in Islamic Civilization. Cambridge: Cambridge University Press, 1983

Women and gender

Abadan-Unat, Nermin, ed. *Women in Turkish Society.* Social, Economic, and Political Studies of the Middle East. Leiden: E. J. Brill, 1981

Abbas, Shameem Burney, with a foreword by Elizabeth Warnock Fernea. *Female Voices in Sufi Ritual: Devotional Practices of Pakistan and India.* Austin: University of Texas Press, 2002

Abbott, Nabia. *Aishah, The Beloved of Mohammed.* London: Saqi Books, 1985. First published by the University of Chicago Press, 1942

Abdel Kader, Soha. *Egyptian Women in a Changing Society, 1899–1987.* Boulder: Lynne Rienner, 1987

Abu-Lughod, Lila., ed. *Remaking Women: Feminism and Modernity in the Middle East.* Princeton Studies in Culture/Power/History. Princeton, NJ: Princeton University Press, 1998

Acar, Faride and Ayse Gunes-Ayata, eds. *Gender and Identity Construction: Women of Central*

Asia, the Caucasus and Turkey. Social, Economic and Political Studies of the Middle East and Asia, 68. Leiden: E. J. Brill, 2000

Afkhami, Mahnaz, ed. *Faith and Freedom: Women's Human Rights in the Muslim World*. London: I. B. Tauris, 1995

Afkhami, Mahnaz and Erika Friedl, eds. *In the Eye of the Storm: Women in Post-Revolutionary Iran*. London: I. B. Tauris, 1994

——. *Muslim Women and the Politics of Participation: Implementing the Beijing Platform*. Gender, Culture, and Politics in the Middle East. Syracuse, NY: Syracuse University Press, 1997

Afsaruddin, Asma, ed., with a foreword by Mary-Jo Del Vecchio Good. *Hermeneutics and Honor: Negotiating Female 'Public' Space in Islamicate Societies*. Harvard Middle Eastern Monographs, 32. Cambridge, MA: Center for Middle Eastern Studies of Harvard University, 1999. Distributed by Harvard University Press

Afshar, Haleh. *Islam and Feminism: An Iranian Case Study*. Basingstoke: Macmillan, 1998

Aghaie, Kamran Scot, ed. *Women of Karbala: Ritual Performance and Symbolic Discourse in Modern Shii Islam*. Austin: University of Texas Press, 2005

Ahmed, Amineh. *Sorrow and Joy among Muslim Women: The Pukhtuns of Northern Pakistan*. University of Cambridge Oriental Publications, 63. Cambridge: Cambridge University Press, 2006

Ahmed, Leila. *Women and Gender in Islam: Historical Roots of a Modern Debate*. New Haven: Yale University Press, 1992

Ali, K. *Sexual Ethics and Islam: Feminist Reflections on the Quran, Hadith and Jurisprudence*. Oxford: Oneworld, 2006

Ali, Shaheen Sardar. *Gender and Human Rights in Islam and International Law: Equal before Allah, Unequal before Man?* The Hague: Kluwer Law International, 2000

Alidou, Ousseina D. *Engaging Modernity: Muslim Women and the Politics of Agency in Post-Colonial Nigeria*. Women in Africa and the Diaspora. Madison: University of Wisconsin Press, 2005

Almunajjed, Mona. *Women in Saudi Arabia Today*. London: Macmillan, 1997

Altorki, Soraya. *Women in Saudi Arabia: Ideology and Behavior Among the Elite*. New York: Columbia University Press, 1986

Anees, Munawar A. *Islam and Biological Futures: Ethics, Gender and Technology*. London: Mansell, 1989

Anjum, Mohini, ed. *Muslim Women in India*. London: Sangam Books, 1992

Arat, Yesim. *Rethinking Islam and Liberal Democracy: Islamist Women in Turkish Politics*. Albany: State University of New York Press, 2005

Asghar Ali, Azra. *The Emergence of Feminism among Indian Muslim Women, 1920–1947*. Oxford: Oxford University Press, 2000

Ask, Karin and Marit Tjomsland, eds. *Women and Islamization: Contemporary Dimensions of Discourse on Gender Relations*. Oxford: Berg, 1998

Aswad, Barbara C. and Barbara Bilge, eds. *Family and Gender among American Muslims: Issues Facing Middle Eastern Immigrants and Their Descendants*. Philadelphia: Temple University Press, 1996

Aveling, Harry. *Shanon Ahmad: Islam, Power and Gender*. Siri Pemikiran Bangi. Bangi: Penerbit Universiti Kebangsaan Malaysia, 2000

Awde, Nicholas, trans. and ed. *Women in Islam: An Anthology from the Quran and Hadiths*. London: Curzon Press, 2000

Badran, Margot. *Feminists, Islam and Nation: Gender and the Making of Modern Egypt.* Princeton, NJ: Princeton University Press, 1995

Badran, Margot and Miriam Cooke, eds. *Opening the Gates: An Anthology of Arab Feminist Writing.* 2nd edn. Bloomington: Indiana University Press, 2004

Barazangi, Nimat Hafez. *Woman's Identity and the Quran: A New Reading.* Gainesville: University Press of Florida, 2004

Barlas, Asma. *'Believing Women' in Islam: Unreading Patriarchal Interpretations of the Quran.* Austin: University of Texas Press, 2002

Baron, Beth. *The Women's Awakening in Egypt: Culture, Society, and the Press.* New Haven: Yale University Press, 1994

Beck, Lois and Guity Nashat, eds. *Women in Iran from 1800 to the Islamic Republic.* Urbana: University of Illinois Press, 2004

Beck, Lois and Nikkie Keddie, eds. *Women in the Muslim World.* Cambridge, MA: Harvard University Press, 1978

Bennett, Linda Rae. *Women, Islam and Modernity: Single Women, Sexuality and Reproductive Health in Contemporary Indonesia.* ASAA Women in Asia Series. London: RoutledgeCurzon, 2005

Bewley, Aisha. *Islam: The Empowering of Women.* London: Ta-Ha Publishers, 1999

——. *Muslim Women: A Biographical Dictionary.* London: Ta-Ha Publishers, 2004

Bodman, Herbert L., Jr, comp. *Women in the Muslim World: A Bibliography of Books and Articles Primarily in the English Language.* Chapel Hill: University of North Carolina Press, 1990

Bodman, Herbert L. and Nayereh Tohidi. *Women in Muslim Societies: Diversity within Unity.* Boulder: Lynne Rienner, 1998

Bouhdiba, Abdelwahab. *Sexuality in Islam.* Trans. Alan Sheridan. London: Saqi Books, 1998. Originally published in French by Presses Universitaires de France, 1975

Boullata, Kamal, ed. and trans. *Women of the Fertile Crescent: Modern Poetry by Arab Women.* New edn. Colorado Springs: Three Continents Press, 1994

Brooks, Geraldine. *Nine Parts of Desire: The Hidden World of Islamic Women.* London: Hamish Hamilton, 1995

Bullock, Katherine. *Muslim Women Activists in North America: Speaking for Ourselves.* Austin: University of Texas Press, 2005

——. *Rethinking Muslim Women and the Veil: Challenging Historical and Modern Stereotypes.* Herndon, VA: International Institute of Islamic Thought, 2002

Callaway, Barbara and Lucy Creevy. *The Heritage of Islam: Women, Religion and Politics in West Africa.* Boulder: Lynne Rienner, 1994

Charrad, Mounira M. *States and Women's Rights: The Making of Postcolonial Tunisia, Algeria, and Morocco.* Berkeley: University of California Press, 2001

Corcoran-Nantes, Yvonne. *Lost Voices: Central Asian Women Confronting Transition.* London: Zed Books, 2005

Cortese, Delia and Simonetta Calderini. *Women and the Fatimids in the World of Islam.* Edinburgh: Edinburgh University Press, 2006

Deeb, Lara. *An Enchanted Modern: Gender and Public Piety in Shii Lebanon.* Princeton Studies in Muslim Politics. Princeton, NJ: Princeton University Press, 2006

Dogramaci, Emel. *Women in Turkey and the New Millennium.* Ankara: Atatürk Research Center, 2000

Donmez-Colin, Gonul. *Women, Islam and Cinema.* London: Reaktion Books, 2004

Doumato, Eleanor Abdella. *Getting God's Ear: Women, Islam, and Healing in Saudi Arabia and the Gulf.* New York: Columbia University Press, 2000

Doumato, Eleanor Abdella, and Marsha Pripstein Posusney, eds. *Women and Globalization in the Arab Middle East: Gender, Economy and Society.* Boulder: Lynne Rienner, 2003

Engineer, Asghar Ali. *The Rights of Women in Islam.* London: C. Hurst & Co., 1992

Engineer, Asghar Ali, ed. *Islam, Women and Gender Justice.* New Delhi: Gyan Publishing House, 2001

Esposito, John L. *Women in Muslim Family Law.* 2nd edn. Contemporary Issues in the Middle East. Syracuse, NY: Syracuse University Press, 2001

Falah, Ghazi-Walid and Caroline Nagel, eds. *Geographies of Muslim Women: Gender, Religion and Space.* New York: Guilford Press, 2005

Fernea, Elizabeth W., ed. *Women and the Family in the Middle East: New Voices of Change.* Austin: University of Texas Press, 1985

Fernea, Elizabeth W. and Basima Q. Bezirgan, eds. *Middle Eastern Muslim Women Speak.* Austin: University of Texas Press, 1977

Flueckiger, Joyce Burkhalter. *In Amma's Healing Room: Gender and Vernacular Islam in South India.* Bloomington: Indiana University Press, 2006

Gocek, Fatma Muge and Shiva Balaghi, eds. *Reconstructing Gender in the Middle East: Tradition, Identity, and Power.* New York: Columbia University Press, 1995

Gole, Nilufer. *The Forbidden Modern: Civilization and Veiling.* Ann Arbor: University of Michigan Press, 1996

Goodwin, Jan. *Price of Honor: Muslim Women Lift the Veil of Silence on the Islamic World.* Harmondsworth: Plume, 1995. Originally published by Little, Brown, 1994

el-Guindi, Fadwa. *Veil: Modesty, Privacy and Resistance.* Oxford: Berg, 1999

Haddad, Yvonne Yazbeck and John L. Esposito, eds. *Islam, Gender and Social Change.* New York: Oxford University Press, 1998

Haddad, Yvonne Yazbeck, Jane I. Smith and Kathleen M. Moore. *Muslim Women in America: The Challenge of Islamic Identity Today.* New York: Oxford University Press, 2006

Haeri, Shahla. *Law of Desire: Temporary Marriage in Iran.* London: I. B. Tauris, 1989. Published in the USA by Syracuse University Press as *Law of Desire: Temporary Marriage in Shii Iran*

Hambly, Gavin R. G., ed. *Women in the Medieval Islamic World: Power, Patronage, and Piety.* New Middle Ages, 6. New York: St Martin's Press, 1998

Hasan, Zoya and Ritu Menon. *Unequal Citizens: A Study of Muslim Women in India.* New Delhi: Oxford University Press, 2004

Haysim, Shafiq. *Understanding Women in Islam: An Indonesian Perspective.* Jakarta: Solstice Publishing, 2006

Heyat, Farideh. *Azari Women in Transition: Women in Soviet and Post-Soviet Azarbaijan.* Central Asia Research Forum. London: RoutledgeCurzon, 2002

al-Hibri, Azizah, ed. *Women and Islam.* Oxford: Pergamon Press, 1982

Hirsi Ali, Ayaan. *The Caged Virgin: Emancipation Proclamation for Women and Islam.* New York: Free Press, 2006. Originally published in the Netherlands in 2004. Published in paperback by Pocket Books as *The Caged Virgin: A Muslim Woman's Cry for Reason,* 2007

Hopkins, Nicholas S. and Saad Eddin Ebrahim, eds. *Arab Society: Class, Gender, Power and Development.* 3rd edn. Cairo: American University in Cairo Press, 1997

Husain, Sarah, ed. *Voices of Resistance: Muslim Women on War, Faith, and Sexuality.* Emeryville, CA: Seal Press, 2006

Hussain, Freda, ed. *Muslim Women.* London: Croom Helm, 1984

Ilkkaracan, Pinar, ed. *Women and Sexuality in Muslim Societies.* Istanbul: Women for Women's Human Rights/Kadinin Insan Haklari Projesi, 2000

Iqbal, Safia. *Woman and Islamic Law.* 2nd revised edn. Delhi: Adam Publishers and Distributors, 1994

Ismail, Ellen and Maureen Makki. *Women of the Sudan.* Bandestorf: Verlag Dr. Ellen-Schmidt, 1990

Jaschok, Maria and Shui Jingjun. *The History of Women's Mosques in Chinese Islam: A Mosque of Their Own.* London: Curzon Press, 2000

Jawad, Haifa and Tansin Benn, eds. *Muslim Women in the United Kingdom and Beyond: Experiences and Images.* Women and Gender, the Middle East and the Islamic World, 2. Leiden: E. J. Brill, 2003

Joseph, Suad, ed., with a foreword by Deniz Kandiyoti. *Gender and Citizenship in the Middle East.* Syracuse, NY: Syracuse University Press, 2000

Kamalkhani, Zahra. *Women's Islam: Religious Practice among Women in Today's Iran.* London: Kegan Paul International, 1998

Kamguian, Azam. *Islam and Women's Rights.* Stockholm: Nasim Publications, 2002

Kandiyoti, Deniz, ed. *Gendering the Middle East: Emerging Perspectives.* London: I. B. Tauris, 1996

——. *Women, Islam and the State.* London: Macmillan, 1991

Keddie, Nikki R. and Beth Brown, eds. *Women in Middle Eastern History: Shifting Boundaries in Sex and Gender.* New Haven: Yale University Press, 1991

Khan, Shahnaz. *Muslim Women: Crafting a North American Identity.* Gainesville: University Press of Florida, 2000

Khanam, Samuiddin R. *Muslim Feminism and Feminist Movement.* Delhi: Global Vision Publishing House, 2002

Kimball, Michelle R. and Barbara R. von Schlegell. *Muslim Women Throughout the World: A Bibliography.* Boulder: Lynne Rienner, 1997

Kousha, Mahnaz. *Voices from Iran: The Changing Lives of Iranian Women.* Gender, Culture, and Politics in the Middle East. Syracuse, NY: Syracuse University Press, 2002

Kusha, Hamid R. *The Sacred Law of Islam: A Case Study of Women's Treatment in the Islamic Republic of Iran's Criminal Justice System.* Aldershot: Ashgate, 2002

Lobban, Richard A., Jr, ed., with a foreword by Elizabeth W. Fernea. *Middle Eastern Women and the Invisible Economy.* Gainesville: University Press of Florida, 1998

Mahmood, Saba. *Politics of Piety: Islamic Revival and the Feminist Subject.* Princeton, NJ: Princeton University Press, 2005

Malti-Douglas, Fedwa. *Medicines of the Soul: Female Bodies and Sacred Geographies in a Transnational Islam.* Berkeley: University of California Press, 2001

——. *Women's Word: Gender and Discourse in Arabo-Islamic Writing.* Princeton, NJ: Princeton University Press, 1991

Marin, Manuela and Randi Deguilhem, eds. *Writing the Feminine: Women in Arab Sources.* The Islamic Mediterranean. London: I. B. Tauris/European Science Foundation, Strasbourg, 2002

Meriwether, Margaret L. and Judith E. Tucker., eds. *Social History of Women and Gender in the Modern Middle East.* Social History of the Modern Middle East. Boulder: Westview Press, 1999

Mernissi, Fatima. *Beyond the Veil: Male–Female Dynamics in a Modern Muslim Society.* Revised edn. Bloomington: Indiana University Press, 1987; London: Saqi Books, 1987

——. *Forgotten Queens of Islam.* Trans. Mary Jo Lakeland. Cambridge: Polity Press, 1993

——. *The Veil and the Male Elite: A Feminist Interpretation of Women's Rights in Islam*. Trans. Mary Jo Lakeland. Reading, MA: Addison-Wesley, 1991

——. *Women and Islam: An Historical and Theological Enquiry*. Trans. Mary Jo Lakeland. Oxford: Blackwell, 1991

——. *Women's Rebellion and Islamic Memory*. London: Zed Books, 1996

Metcalfe, Barbara. *Perfecting Women: Maulana Ashraf 'Ali Thanawi's Bihishti Zawar. A Partial Translation with Commentary*. Berkeley: University of California Press, 1990

Milani, Farzaneh. *Veils and Words: The Emerging Voices of Iranian Women Writers*. London: I. B. Tauris, 1992

Minai, Naila. *Women in Islam: Tradition and Transition in the Middle East*. London: John Murray, 1981

Mir-Hosseini, Ziba. *Islam and Gender: The Religious Debate in Contemporary Iran*. London: I. B. Tauris, 2000

——. *Marriage on Trial: A Study of Islamic Family Law in Iran and Morocco*. Revised edn. London: I. B. Tauris, 2000

Moghadam, Valentine M. *Modernizing Women: Gender and Social Change in the Middle East*. 2nd edn. Women and Change in the Developing World. Boulder: Lynne Rienner, 2003

——. *Women, Work and Economic Reform in the Middle East and North Africa*. Boulder: Lynne Rienner, 1998

Moghadam, Valentine M., ed. *Gender and National Identity: Women and Politics in Muslim Societies*. London: Zed Books for United Nations University, World Institute for Development and Economic Research, 1994

Moghissi, Haideh. *Feminism and Islamic Fundamentalism: The Limits of Postmodern Analysis*. London: Zed Books, 1999

Mozammel, Haque. *Islam, Socialism and Women*. Dacca: Society for Pakistan Studies, 1970

al-Mughni, Haya. *Women in Kuwait: The Politics of Gender*. 2nd revised edn. London: Saqi Books, 2001

Mumtaz, Khawar and Farida Shaheed, eds. *Women of Pakistan: Two Steps Forward, One Step Back?* London: Zed Books, 1987

Murata, Sachiko. *The Tao of Islam: A Sourcebook on Gender Relationship in Islamic Thought*. Albany: State University of New York Press, 1992

Nashat, Guity, ed. *Women and Revolution in Iran*. Boulder: Westview Press, 1983

Nashat, Guity and Judith E. Tucker. *Women in the Middle East and North Africa: Restoring Women to History*. Restoring Women to History. Bloomington: Indiana University Press, 1999

Ng, Cecilia, Maznah Mohamad and Tan Beng Hui. *Feminism and the Women's Movement in Malaysia: An Unsung (R)evolution*. Routledge Malaysian Studies Series, 2. New York: Routledge, 2006

Nouraie-Simone, Fereshteh, ed. *On Shifting Ground: Muslim Women in the Global Era*. Women Writing the Middle East. New York: Feminist Press at the City University of New York, 2005

Poya, Maryam. *Women, Work, and Islamism: Ideology and Resistance in Iran*. London: Zed Books, 1999

Rafidi, Samira, comp. *The Status of Arab Woman: A Select Bibliography*. London: Mansell for the Institute of Women's Studies in the Arab World, Beirut University, Lebanon, 1980

Robinson, Kathryn and Sharon Bessell, eds. *Women in Indonesia: Gender Equity and Development*. Indonesian Assessment Series. Singapore: Institute of Southeast Asian Studies, 2002

Roded, Ruth. *Women in Islamic Biographical Collections: From Ibn Sa'd to Who's Who*. Boulder: Lynne Rienner, 1994

Roded, Ruth., ed. *Women in Islam and the Middle East: A Reader*. London: I. B. Tauris, 1999

Rouse, Carolyn Moxley. *Engaged Surrender: African-American Women and Islam*. Berkeley: University of California Press, 2004

Ruggles, D. Fairchild. *Women, Patronage and Self-Representation in Islamic Societies*. Albany: State University of New York Press, 2000

Ruud, Inger Marie, comp. *Women's Status in the Muslim World: A Bibliographical Survey*. Material for the Study of History of Religions, 6. Cologne: E. J. Brill, 1981

Sabbagh, Suha, ed. *Arab Women: Between Defiance and Restraint*. New York: Olive Branch Press, 1996

el-Sakkakini, Widad. *First among Sufis: The Life and Thought of Rabia al-Adawiyya, the Woman Saint of Basra*. London: Octagon Press, 1982

Saliba, Therese, Carolyn Allen and Judith A. Howard, eds. *Gender, Politics, and Islam*. Chicago: University of Chicago Press, 2002

Shahidian, Hammed. *Women in Iran: Gender Politics in the Islamic Republic*. Contributions in Women's Studies, 197. Westport, CT: Greenwood Press, 2002

Shaukat Ali, Zeenat. *The Empowerment of Women in Islam: With Special Reference to Marriage and Divorce*. Mumbai: Vakils, Feffer and Simons, 1987

Shehadeh, Lamia Rustum. *The Idea of Women under Fundamentalist Islam*. Gainesville: University Press of Florida, 2003

Shoshan, Boaz, ed. *Discourse on Gender/Gendered Discourse in the Middle East*. Westport, CT: Praeger, 2000

Shukri, Shirin J. A. *Social Changes and Women in the Middle East: State Policy, Education, Economics and Development*. Aldershot: Ashgate, 1999

Sikri, Rehana. *Women in Islamic Culture and Society: A Study of Family, Feminism and Franchise*. New Delhi: Kanisha Publishers & Distributors, 1999

Skaine, Rosemarie. *The Women of Afghanistan under the Taliban*. Jefferson, NC: McFarland, 2002

Smith, Jane I., ed. *Women in Contemporary Muslim Societies*. Lewisburg, PA: Bucknell University Press, 1980

Smith, Margaret. *Rabia the Mystic and Her Fellow Saints in Islam: Being the Life and Teaching of Rabia Al-Adawiyya Al-Qaysiyya of Basra Sufi Saint ca. A.H. 99–185, A.D. 717–801. Together with Some Account of the Place of Women in Islam*. Amsterdam: Philo Press by arrangement with Cambridge University Press, 1974. First published 1928

el-Solh, Camillia Fawzi and Judy Mabro, eds. *Muslim Women's Choices: Religious Belief and Social Reality*. Cross-Cultural Perspectives on Women, 12. Providence, RI: Berg, 1994

Sonbol, Amira el-Azhary. *Beyond the Exotic: Women's Histories in Islamic Societies*. Gender, Culture and Politics in the Middle East. Syracuse, NY: Syracuse University Press, 2005

Sonbol, Amira el-Azhary, ed. *Women, the Family and Divorce Laws in Islamic History*. Syracuse, NY: Syracuse University Press, 1996

Spellberg, D. A. *Politics, Gender and the Islamic Past: The Legacy of Aisha bint Abi Bakr*. New York: Columbia University Press, 1994

Stowasser, Barbara Freyer. *Women in the Quran, Traditions, and Interpretations*. New York: Oxford University Press, 1994

Strobel, Margaret. *Muslim Women in Mombasa, 1890–1975*. New Haven: Yale University Press, 1979

Tekeli, Şirin, ed. *Women in Modern Turkish Society: A Reader*. London: Zed Books, 1995

Torab, Azam. *Performing Islam: Gender and Ritual in Iran*. Woman and Gender, Middle East and the Islamic World, 4. Leiden: E. J. Brill, 2007

Tucker, Judith E., ed. *Arab Women: Old Boundaries, New Frontiers*. Indiana Series in Arab and Islamic Studies. Bloomington: Indiana University Press, 1993

Van Doorn-Harder, Pieternella. *Women Shaping Islam: Indonesian Women Reading the Quran*. Urbana: University of Illinois Press, 2006

Van Nieuwkerk, Karin, ed. *Women Embracing Islam: Gender and Conversion in the West*. Austin: University of Texas Press, 2006

Waddy, Charis. *Women in Muslim History*. London: Longman, 1980

Wadud, Amina. *Inside the Gender Jihad: Women's Reform in Islam*. Oxford: Oneworld, 2006

——. *Quran and Woman: Reading the Sacred Text from a Woman's Perspective*. 2nd edn. Oxford: Oxford University Press, 1999. Revised edn. of *Quran and Woman*, published in Kuala Lumpur, 1992

Walther, Wiebke, with an introduction by Guity Nashat. *Women in Islam: From Medieval to Modern Times*. Revised edn. Princeton, NJ: Markus Wiener, 1993

Webb, Gisela, ed. *Windows of Faith: Muslim Women Scholar-Activists in North America*. Syracuse: Syracuse University Press, 2000

Wilcox, Lynn. *Women and the Holy Quran: A Sufi Perspective*, vol. 1. Riverside, CA: M. T. O. Shahmaghsoudi, 1998

Yamani, Mai, ed. *Feminism and Islam: Legal and Literary Perspectives*. Reading, UK: Ithaca Press for Centre of Islamic and Middle Eastern Law, SOAS, University of London, 1996

Zayzafoon, Lamia Ben Youssef. *The Production of the Muslim Woman: Negotiating Text, History, and Ideology*. After the Empire. Lanham, MD: Lexington Books, 2005

Zuhur, Sherifa. *Revealing Reveiling: Islamist Gender Ideology in Contemporary Egypt*. SUNY series in Middle East Studies. Albany: State University of New York Press, 1992

Primary sources in translation

Ali Ibn Abi Talib (c. 661). *Nahjul Balagha: Peak of Eloquence: Sermons, Letters and Sayings of Imam Ali Ibn Abi Talib*. Trans. Sayed Ali Reza. 4th revised US edn. Elmhurst, NY: Tahrike Tarsile Quran, 1985

Arberry, Arthur John. *Aspects of Islamic Civilization as Depicted in the Original Texts*. London: Allen & Unwin, 1964

Attar, Farid ud-Din (c. 1230). *The Conference of the Birds*. Trans. Afkham Darbandi and Dick Davis. Harmondsworth: Penguin, 1984

——. *The Ilahi Nama or The Book of God*. Trans. John Andrew Boyle with a foreword by Annemarie Schimmel. Persian Heritage Series. Manchester: Manchester University Press, 1976

——. *Muslim Saints and Mystics: Episodes from the Tadhkirat al-Auliya ('Memorial to the Saints')*. Trans. A. J. Arberry. London: Routledge & Kegan Paul, 1966

Averroes (Ibn Rushd, 1126–1198). *Averroes' Tahafut al-Tahafut (The Incoherence of the Incoherence)*. Translated from the Arabic with an introduction and notes by Simon Van Den Bergh. 2 vols. UNESCO Collection of Great Works, Arabic Series. London: Luzac & Co. for the Trustees of E. J. W. Gibb Memorial, 1969

——. *The Distinguished Jurist's Primer. A Translation of Bidayat Al-Mujtahid*. 2 vols. Trans. Imran Ahsan Khan Nyazee. Great Books of Islamic Civilization. Reading, UK: Garnet, 1994–1996

———. *Faith and Reason in Islam: Averroes' Exposition of Religious Arguments*. Trans. Ibrahim Y. Najjar with an introduction by Majid Fakhry. Great Islamic Writings. Oxford: Oneworld, 2001

———. *Ibn Rushd's Metaphysics: A Translation with Introduction of Ibn Rushd's Commentary on Aristotle's Metaphysics, Book Lam*. Trans. Charles Genequand. Islamic Philosophy and Theology, Texts and Studies, 1. Leiden: E. J. Brill, 1984

Avicenna (Ibn Sina, 980–1037). *The Life of Ibn Sina: A Critical Edition and Annotated Translation*. Trans. William E. Gohlman. Studies in Islamic Philosophy and Science. Albany: State University of New York Press, 1974

———. *The Metaphysics of the Healing: A Parallel English-Arabic Text: al-Ilahiyat min al Shifa*. Trans, introduced and annotated by Michael E. Marmura. Islamic Translation Series. Provo, UT: Brigham Young University Press, 2005

———. *A Treatise on the Canon of Medicine of Avicenna: Incorporating a Translation of the First Book*. Trans. Oskar Cameron Gruner. London: Luzac & Co., 1930. Repr. Augustus M. Kelley, New York, 1970

al-Baladhuri, Ahmad B. Yahya (892). *The Origins of the Islamic State: Being a Translation from Arabic Accompanied with Annotations, Geographic and Historic Notes of the Kitab Futuh al-Buldan of al-Imam abu-l'abbas Ahmad ibn Jabir al-Baladhuri*, vol. 1, trans. Philip Khuri Hitti; vol. 2, trans. Francis Clark Murgotten. New York: AMS Press, 1968–1969. First published 1916–1924

al-Bukhari, Muhammad ibn Ismail (810–870). *Sahih al-Bukhari: The Translation of the Meanings of Sahih al-Bukhari*. 9 vols. 5th revised edn. Trans. Muhammad Muhsin Khan. New Delhi: Kitab Bhavan, 1984

Faith and Practice of Islam: Three Thirteenth Century Sufi Texts. Trans. and introduced by William C. Chittick. SUNY Series in Islam. Albany: State University of New York Press, 1992

Firdawsi Abu al-Qasim Ḥasan (Ferdowsi) (c. 1020). *The Epic of the Kings: Shah-Nama: The National Epic of Persia*. Trans. Reuben Levy. Revised by Amin Banani. London: Routledge & Kegan Paul, 1985.

———. *The Legend of Seyavash*. Trans. with an introduction and notes by Dick Davis. London: Penguin, 1992

al-Ghazali, Abu Hamid Muhammad (1058–1111). *Freedom and Fulfillment: An Annotated Translation of Al-Ghazali's al-Munqidh min al-Dalal and other relevant work of al-Ghazali*. Trans. Richard Joseph McCarthy. Library of Classical Literature, 4. Boston: Twayne, 1980

———. *Al-Ghazali on the Ninety-nine Beautiful Names of God*. Trans. David B. Burrell and Nazih Daher. Cambridge: Islamic Texts Society, 1992

———. *The Incoherence of the Philosophers: Tahafut al-falasifah*. A parallel English–Arabic text translated, introduced and annotated by Michael E. Marmura. Islamic Translation Series. Provo, UT: Brigham Young University Press, 1997

———. *The Jewels of the Quran: al-Ghazali's Theory. A Translation with an Introduction and Annotation of al-Ghazali's Kitab Jawahir al-Quran*. Trans. Muhammad Abul Quasem. London: Kegan Paul International, 1977

———. *Niche of Lights: Miskat al-Anwar*. A parallel English–Arabic text translated, introduced and annotated by David Buchman. Islamic Translation Series. Provo, UT: Brigham Young University Press, 1998

———. *On Faith in Divine Unity and Trust in Divine Providence*. Trans. David B. Burrell. Louisville, KY: Fons Vitae, 2001

al-Hariri Qasim Ibn Ali (1054–1122). *The Assemblies of al-Hariri*. Translated from the Arabic with introduction and notes, historical and grammatical, vol. 1, trans. Thomas Chenery; vol. 2, trans. F. Steingass. Oriental Translation Fund. New Series, 3. London: Williams Northgate, 1867–1898

Ibn al-Arabi, Muhammad Ibn Ali (Muhyi al-Din) (1165–1240). *The Bezels of Wisdom*. Trans. and introduction by R. W. J. Austin. Preface by Titus Burckhardt. Classics of Western Spirituality. London: SPCK, 1980

———. *Journey to the Lord of Power: A Sufi Manual on Retreat*. Trans. Rabia Terri Harris. London: Inner Traditions International, 1981

———. *The Seven Days of the Heart: Prayers for Days and Nights of the Week: Awrad al-Usbu (Wird)*. Trans. and presented in English by Pablo Beneito and Stephen Hirtenstein. Oxford: Anqa Publishing, 2000

———. *Sufis of Andalusia: The Ruh al-Quds and al-Durrat al-Fakhira of Ibn Arabi*. Trans. with introduction and notes by R. W. Austin and with a foreword by Martin Lings. London: Allen & Unwin, 1971

Ibn Battuta, Muhammad ibn Ali (1304–1377). *The Travels of Ibn Battuta, A.D. 1325–1354*. Trans. with revisions and notes by H. A. R. Gibb. 3 vols. Cambridge: Cambridge University Press/Hakluyt Society, 1971

Ibn al-Haytham, Abu Abd Allah Jafar Ibn Ahmad Ibn Muhammad Ibn al-Aswad. (c. 10th century). *The Advent of the Fatimids: A Contemporary Shii Witness: An Edition and English Translation of Ibn al-Haytham's Kitab al-Munaarat*. Trans. and ed. Wilferd Madelung and Paul E. Walker. Ismaili Text and Translation Series, 1. London: I. B. Tauris/Institute of Ismaili Studies, 2000

Ibn Ishaq, Muhammad (c. 768). *The Life of Muhammad: A Translation of (Ibn) Ishaq's Sirat Rasul Allah*. Trans. with an introduction and notes by Alfred Guillaume. London: Oxford University Press, 1955

———. *The Making of the Last Prophet: Kitab al-Mubtada*. First section of *Sirat Rasul Allah*. Reconstructed by Gordon Darnell Newby. Columbia, SC: University of South Carolina Press, 1989

Ibn Khaldun, Abd al-Rahman bin Muhammad (1332–1406). *The Muqaddimah: An Introduction to History*. 3 vols. 2nd edn. with corrections and augmented bibliography. Trans. F. Rosenthal. Bollingen Series, 43. Princeton, NJ: Princeton University Press, 1967

Ibn Khallikan (1211–1282). *Ibn Khallikan's Biographical Dictionary*. 4 vols. Trans. Ben Mac-Guckin de Slane. Beirut: Librairie du Liban, 1970

Ibn Rushd *See* Averroes

Ibn Sina *See* Avicenna

Jeffrey, Arthur. *A Reader on Islam: Passages from Standard Arabic Writings Illustrative of the Beliefs and Practices of Muslims*. The Hague: Mouton, 1962

Jirji Zaydan (1861–1914). *Umayyads and Abbasids: Being the Fourth Part of Jirji Zaydan's History of Islamic Civilization*. Trans. D. S. Margoliouth. E. J. W. Gibb Memorial Series. New Delhi: Kitab Bhavan, 1981. First published 1978

Juvayni, Ala-ad-din Ata Malik (1226–1283). *Genghis Khan, the History of the World Conqueror: Tarikh-I Jahangusha*. Trans. from the text of Mirza Muhammad Qazvini by J. A. Boyle. Manchester: Manchester University Press/UNESCO, 1997

Kalabadhi, Muhammad ibn Ibrahim (10th century) *The Doctrines of the Sufis: Kitab al Taarruf li-Madhhab ahl al-Tasawwuf*. Trans. A. J. Arberry. Cambridge: Cambridge University Press, 1977. Originally published 1935

Masudi (956?) *The Meadows of Gold: The Abbasids*. Trans. and ed. Paul Lunde and Caroline Stone. London: Kegan Paul International, 1989 al-Mawardi, Ali ibn Muhammad (974?–1058) *The Ordinances of Government: A Translation of Al-Ahkam al-Sultaniyya w'al-Wilayat al-Diniyya.* Trans. Wafaa H. Wahba. Reading, UK: Garnet/Center for Muslim Contribution to Civilization, 1996

Mawdudi, Sayyid Abul A'la. *Towards Understanding the Quran: English Version of Tafhim al-Quran.* 7 vols. Trans. Zafar Ishaq Ansari. Leicester: Islamic Foundation, 1988

al-Mufid, Muhammad ibn Muhammad (1022). *The Book of Guidance into the Lives of the Twelve Imams: Kitab Al Irshad.* Trans. K. A. Howard with a preface by Seyyed Hossein Nasr. London: Bolagha Books/Muhammadi Trust, 1981

Muslim ibn al-Hajjaj, al Qushayri (821–875). *Sahih Muslim: Being Traditions of the Sayings and Doings of the Prophet Muhammad as Narrated by His Companions and Compiled under the Title al-Jami us Sahih: Jami al-Sahih.* Trans. Abdul Hamid Siddiqi with explanatory notes and brief biographical sketches of major narrators. Lahore: Shaikh Muhammad Asharaf, 1976

Nasir-i-Khusraw (c. 1004–1088). *Knowledge and Liberation: A Treatise on Philosophical Theology.* New edition and English translation of *Gushayish wa Rahayish* by Faquir M. Hunzai, with an introduction and commentary by Parviz Morewedge. London: I. B. Tauris/ Institute of Ismaili Studies, 1998

Nawawi, Yahya Ibn Sharaf (1233–1277). *An-Nawawi's Forty Hadith.* 2nd edn. Trans. Ezzedin Ibrahim and Denys Johnson-Davis. Damascus: Holy Koran Publishing House, 1977

al-Numan ibn Muhammad al-Tamimi (974). *Pillars of Islam: Daaim al Islam of al-Qadi al Numan.* Trans. Asaf A. A. Fyzee. Completely revised and annotated by Ismail Kurban Husein Poonawala. 2 vols. New Delhi: Oxford University Press, 2002–2004

al-Qurtubi, Muhammad (1273). *Tafsir al-Qurtubi: al-Jami li Akham al-Quran.* Classical Commentary of the Holy Quran, vol. 1. Trans. Aisha Bewley. London: Dar Al Taqwa, 2003

al-Shafii, Muhammad ibn Idris (c. 767–820). *Islamic Jurisprudence: Shafii's Risala.* Trans. with an introduction, notes and appendices by Majid Khadduri. Baltimore: Johns Hopkins University Press, 1961

al-Shahrastani, Muhammad Abd al-Karim (1086–1153). *Struggling with the Philosopher: A refutation of Avicenna's Metaphysics.* A new Arabic edition and English translation of Muhammad bin Abd al-Karim bin Ahmad al-Shahrastani's *Kitab al-Musaraa.* Trans. Wilferd Madelung and Toby Meyer. Ismaili Text and Translation Series, 2. London: I. B. Tauris/Institute of Ismaili Studies, 2001

A Shiite Anthology. Ed. and trans. William C. Chittick. Albany: State University of New York Press, 1981

al-Tabari (838–923). *The History of al-Tabari. Annotated Translations: Tarikh al-Rusul w'al Muluk.* 39 vols. Various translators. SUNY series in Near Eastern Studies, History of al-Tabari, Bibliotheca Persica. Albany, NY: State University of New York Press, 1985

——. *From the Creation to the Flood.* Trans. and annotated by Franz Rosenthal. History of al-Tabari, 1. Albany: State University of New York Press, 1989

——. *Prophets and Patriarchs.* Trans. and annotated by William M. Brinner. History of al-Tabari, 2. Albany: State University of New York Press, 1987

——. *The Children of Israel.* Trans. and annotated by William M. Brinner. History of al-Tabari, 3. Albany: State University of New York Press, 1991

——. *The Ancient Kingdoms.* Trans. and annotated by Moshe Perlman. History of al-Tabari, 4. Albany: State University of New York Press, 1987

——. *The Sasanids, the Byzantines, the Lakhmids, and Yemen.* Trans. and annotated by C. E. Bosworth. History of al-Tabari, 5. Albany: State University of New York Press, 1999

——. *Muhammad at Mecca*. Trans. and annotated by W. Montgomery Watt and M. V. McDonald. History of al-Tabari, 6. Albany: State University of New York Press, 1988
——. *The Foundations of the Community*. Trans. and annotated by W. Montgomery Watt and M. V. McDonald. History of al-Tabari, 7. Albany: State University of New York Press, 1987
——. *The Victory of Islam*. Trans. and annotated by Michael Fishbein. History of al-Tabari, 8. Albany: State University of New York Press, 1997
——. *The Last Years of the Prophet*. Trans. and annotated by Ismail K. Poonawala. History of al-Tabari, 9. Albany: State University of New York Press, 1989
——. *The Conquest of Arabia*. Trans. and annotated by Fred M. Donner. History of al-Tabari, 10. Albany: State University of New York Press, 1993
——. *The Challenge to the Empires*. Trans. and annotated by Khalid Yahya Blankinship. History of al-Tabari, 11. Albany: State University of New York Press, 1993
——. *The Battle of al-Qadissiyyah and the Conquest of Syria and Palestine*. Trans. and annotated by Yohanan Friedmann. History of al-Tabari, 12. Albany: State University of New York Press, 1992
——. *The Conquest of Iraq, Southwestern Persia, and Egypt*. Trans. and annotated by Gautier H. A. Juynboll. History of al-Tabari, 13. Albany: State University of New York Press, 1989
——. *The Conquest of Iran*. Trans. and annotated by G. Rex Smith. History of al-Tabari, 14. Albany: State University of New York Press, 1994
——. *The Crisis of the Early Caliphate*. Trans. and annotated by R. Stephens Humphreys. History of al-Tabari, 15. Albany: State University of New York Press, 1990
——. *The Community Divided*. Trans. and annotated by Adrian Brockett. History of al-Tabari, 16. Albany: State University of New York Press, 1997
——. *The First Civil War*. Trans. and annotated by G. R. Hawting. History of al-Tabari, 17. Albany: State University of New York Press, 1996
——. *Between Civil Wars: Caliphate of Muawiya*. Trans. and annotated by Michael G. Morony. History of al-Tabari, 18. Albany: State University of New York Press, 1987
——. *The Caliphate of Yazid b. Muawiyah*. Trans. and annotated by I. K. A. Howard. History of al-Tabari, 19. Albany: State University of New York Press, 1990
——. *The Collapse of Sufyanid Authority and the Coming of the Marwanids*. Trans. and annotated by G. R. Hawting. History of al-Tabari, 20. Albany: State University of New York Press, 1989
——. *The Victory of the Marwanids*. Trans. and annotated by Michael Fishbein. History of al-Tabari, 21. Albany: State University of New York Press, 1990
——. *The Marwanid Restoration*. Trans. and annotated by Everett K. Rowson. History of al-Tabari, 22. Albany: State University of New York Press, 1989
——. *The Zenith of the Marwanid House*. Trans. and annotated by Martin Hinds. History of al-Tabari, 23. Albany: State University of New York Press, 1990
——. *The Empire in Transition*. Trans. and annotated by David Stephan Powers. History of al-Tabari, 24. Albany: State University of New York Press, 1989
——. *The End of Expansion*. Trans. and annotated by Khalid Yahya Blankinship. History of al-Tabari, 25. Albany: State University of New York Press, 1989
——. *The Waning of the Umayyad Caliphate*. Trans. and annotated by Carole Hillenbrand. History of al-Tabari, 26. Albany: State University of New York Press, 1989
——. *The Abbasid Revolution*. Trans. and annotated by John Alden Williams. History of al-Tabari, 27. Albany: State University of New York Press, 1985

——. *Abbasid Authority Affirmed.* Trans and annotated by Jane Dammen McAuliffe. History of al-Tabari, 28. Albany: State University of New York Press, 1995

——. *Al-Mansur and Al-Mahdi.* Trans. and annotated by Hugh Kennedy. History of al-Tabari, 29. Albany: State University of New York Press, 1990

——. *The Abbasid Caliphate in Equilibrium.* Trans. and annotated by C. E. Bosworth. History of al-Tabari, 30. Albany: State University of New York Press, 1989

——. *The War between Brothers.* Trans. and annotated by Michael Fishbein. History of al-Tabari, 31. Albany: State University of New York Press, 1992

——. *The Reunification of the Abbasid Caliphate.* Trans. and annotated by C. E. Bosworth. History of al-Tabari, 32. Albany: State University of New York Press, 1987

——. *Storm and Stress along the Northern Frontiers of the Abbasid Caliphate.* Trans. and annotated by C. E. Bosworth. History of al-Tabari, 33. Albany: State University of New York Press, 1991

——. *Incipient Decline.* Trans. and annotated by Joel L. Kramer. History of al-Tabari, 34. Albany: State University of New York Press, 1989

——. *The Crisis of the Abbasid Caliphate.* Trans. George Saliba. History of al-Tabari, 35. Albany: State University of New York Press, 1990

——. *The Revolt of the Zanj.* Trans. and annotated by David Waines. History of al-Tabari, 36. Albany: State University of New York Press, 1992

——. *The Abbasid Recovery.* Trans. and annotated by Philip Fields and Jacob Lassner. History of al-Tabari, 37. Albany: State University of New York Press, 1987

——. *The Return of the Caliphate to Baghdad.* Trans. and annotated by Franz Rosenthal. History of al-Tabari, 38. Albany: State University of New York Press, 1985

——. *Biographies of the Prophet's Companions and their Successors.* Trans. and annotated by Ella Landau-Tasseron. History of al-Tabari, 39. Albany: State University of New York Press, 1998

——. *The Commentary on the Quran: Being an Abridged Translation of Jami al-Bayan an Tawil ay al-Quran.* Ed. W. F. Madelung and A. Jones with an introduction and notes by J. Cooper. New York: Oxford University Press, 1987

——. *The Early Abbasi Empire,* vol. 1: *The Reign of Abu Jafar al-Mansur A.D. 754–775;* vol. 2: *The Son and Grandsons of the al-Mansur: The Reigns of al-Mahdi, al-Hadi and Harun al-Rashid.* Trans. John Alden Williams. Cambridge: Cambridge University Press, 1988/1989

Tusi, Nasir ad-Din (1201–1274). *Contemplation and Action: The Spiritual Autobiography of a Muslim Scholar.* New edition and English translation of *Sayr wa Suluk* by S. J. Badakhchani. London: I. B. Tauris/Institute of Ismaili Studies, 1999

——. *The Nasirean Ethics.* Trans. G. M. Wickens. London: Allen & Unwin, 1964

——. *Paradise of Submission: A Medieval Treatise of Ismaili Thought.* New Persian edition and English translation of Tusi's *Rawda-yi Taslim* by S. J. Badakhchani with an introduction by Hermann Landolt and philosophical commentary by Christian Jambert. Ismaili Text and Translations Series, 5. London: I. B. Tauris/Institute of Ismaili Studies, 2005

Walker, Paul E. *The Wellsprings of Wisdom: A Study of Abu Yaqub al-Sijistani's Kitab al-Yanabi: including a Complete English Translation with Commentary and Notes on the Arabic Texts.* Salt Lake City: University of Utah Press, 1994

Zayn al-Abidin Ali ibn al-Husayn (c. 658–712). *The Psalms of Islam: Al-Sahifat al-Kamilat al-Sajjadiyya.* Trans. with an introduction and annotation by W. C. Chittick. London: Muhammadi Trust of Great Britain and Northern Ireland, 1988

Periodicals

American Journal of Islamic Social Sciences. Silver Spring, MD: Association of Muslim Social Scientists and International Institute of Islamic Thought, 1985– . (Continues *American Journal of Islamic Studies,* 1984)

Arabica: Journal of Arabic and Islamic Studies. Leiden: E. J. Brill, 1954–

Bulletin of the School of Oriental and African Studies. London: School of Oriental and African Studies, 1940– . (Continues *Bulletin of the School of Oriental Studies,* 1917–1940)

Central Asian Survey: The Journal of the Society of Central Asian Studies. Abingdon: Routledge Journals, Taylor & Francis, 1982–

Comparative Islamic Studies. London: Equinox, 2005–

Der Islam. Berlin: De Gruyter, 1910–

Encounters: Journal of Inter-Cultural Perspectives. Leicester: Islamic Foundation, 1995–

Hamdard Islamicus: A Quarterly Journal of Studies and Research in Islam. Karachi: Hamdard Foundation, 1978–

Harvard Middle Eastern and Islamic Review. Cambridge, MA: Cambridge Center for Middle Eastern Studies, Harvard University, 1994–

ISIM Review (International Institute for the Study of Islam in the Modern World Review). Leiden: International Institute for the Study of Islam in the Modern World, 2004– . (Continues ISIM Newsletter, 1998–2004)

International Journal of Islamic and Arabic Studies. Bloomington: International Institute of Islamic and Arabic Studies, 1984–

International Journal of Middle East Studies. London: Cambridge University Press, 1970–

Islam and Muslim Christian Relations. Centre for the Study of Islam and Muslim–Christian Relations. Abingdon: Routledge Journals, Taylor & Francis, 1990–

Islamic Law & Society. Leiden: E. J. Brill, 1994–

Islamic Quarterly: A Review of Islamic Culture. London: Islamic Cultural Centre, 1954–

Islamic Review & Arab Affairs. Woking: Woking Muslim Mission and Literary Trust, 1967– . (Continues *Islamic Review,* 1913–1966)

Islamic Studies. Islamabad: Islamic Research Institute, 1962–

Islamica: The Journal of the Islamic Society of the London School of Economics. London: London School of Economics and Political Science, 1993–

Journal of the American Oriental Society. New Haven: American Oriental Society, 1849–

Journal of Arabic and Islamic Studies. Bergen: Middle Eastern Languages and Culture, University of Bergen, 1997–

Journal of the Economic and Social History of the Orient. Leiden, E. J. Brill, 1957–

Journal of Islamic Studies. Oxford: Oxford Centre of Islamic Studies, Oxford University Press, 1990–

Journal of Muslim Minority Affairs. Institute of Muslim Minority Affairs. Abingdon: Carfax, 1996–. (Continues *Journal: Institute of Muslim Minority Affairs,* 1979–1994)

Journal of Quranic Studies. London: Centre of Islamic Studies, SOAS, University of London, 1999–

Journal of South Asian and Middle Eastern Studies. Villanova, PA: Pakistan American Foundation, Villanova University, 1977–

The Middle East Journal. Washington, DC: Middle East Institute, 1947–

The Middle East Studies Association Bulletin. Tucson: Middle East Studies Association of North America, 1967–

The Muslim World. Hartford, CT: Duncan Black MacDonald Center at the Hartford Seminary Foundation, 1947– . (Continues _Moslem World_, 1911–1947)

Periodica Islamica: An International Contents Journal. Kuala Lumpur: Berita Publishing, 1991–

Russia and the Moslem World: Bulletin of Analytical Reference and Information. Moscow: Institute of Scientific Information of Social Sciences, Russian Academy of Science. Trans. of _Rossiia i Musul'manskiĭ Mir_ (subtitle varies: _A Monthly Review of Critical Articles and Interviews_), 1993–

Studia Islamica. Paris: G. P. Maisonneuve et Larose, 1953–

Studia Islamika: Indonesian Journal for Islamic Studies. Jakarta: State Institute for Islamic Studies, Syarif Hidayatullah, 1994–